Discovering
Prehistoric
England

James Dyer

A SHIRE BOOK

Front cover: *Long Meg and Her Daughters, Cumbria, from the south-west. (Neil Stephenson)*

Back cover: *Abbotsbury Castle hillfort, Dorset, from the west. (J. Dyer)*

The maps on pages 234–43 were prepared by Robert Dizon.

British Library Cataloguing in Publication Data: Prehistoric England. – 2nd ed. – (Discovering; 283) 1. Historic sites – England 2. England – Antiquities I. Dyer, James, 1934– 936.2 ISBN 0 7478 0507 5.

Published in 2001 by Shire Publications Ltd, Cromwell House, Church Street, Princes Risborough, Buckinghamshire HP27 9AA, UK. Website: www.shirebooks.co.uk Copyright © 1993 and 2001 by James Dyer. First published 1993. Second edition, with additional text and illustrations and in a larger format, 2001. Number 283 in the Discovering series. ISBN 0 7478 0507 5.

Printed in Great Britain by CIT Printing Services, Press Buildings, Merlins Bridge, Haverfordwest, Pembrokeshire SA61 1XF.

Contents

Preface

Much of the material contained in this guide originally appeared in a series of books published by Shire between 1969 and 1973 called *Discovering Regional Archaeology*. In 1983 the Roman entries were revised and republished in a single volume called *Discovering Roman Britain* by David E. Johnston. In 1993 the prehistoric entries were similarly updated and published as a single volume using the revised 1974 county boundaries.

In the original 1970s volumes the late Leslie Grinsell was responsible for sites in Cornwall, Devon, Somerset and Dorset; the late Edward Sammes for Hampshire, the Isle of Wight, Kent, Sussex, Surrey and Greater London; Barry M. Marsden for England north of and including Herefordshire, Worcestershire, Northamptonshire, and Warwickshire, but excluding Lincolnshire. The remaining southern and eastern counties and the introduction were contributed by James Dyer. In the present volume a new format has been adopted and a large number of additional sites have been included. In many cases the original entries have been extensively updated, extended or rewritten.

Since the last edition the government has once again reshuffled county boundaries. In the hope of avoiding further confusion we have retained the 1974 boundaries, with the following amendments: sites in Avon are restored to Gloucestershire or Somerset; Herefordshire and Worcestershire resort to their separate historical boundaries; West Midlands is included with Warwickshire; Lancashire includes Greater Manchester; Durham includes Tyne and Wear; North Yorkshire includes Cleveland; Humberside becomes the East Riding of Yorkshire. If in doubt, consult the maps on pages 234–43.

In updating this guide valuable help has been received from a number of museums and county archaeological units. Particular mention must also be made of David G. Bird, Jenny Bradbury, Aubrey Burl, Brian Dix, Peter Ellis, Lady Aileen Fox, Paul Gilman, Clive R. Hart, Gary Lock, Barry M. Marsden, Edward Martin, C. J. Pinder, Joshua Pollard, S. C. Stanford, Alison Taylor, Maisie Taylor, Blaise Vyner and John Wymer. Thanks are also expressed to the photographers who have allowed me to reproduce their work. Each picture is individually acknowledged.

National Grid references are used with the permission of the Controller of Her Majesty's Stationery Office.

Note: The inclusion of a site in this book does not necessarily indicate right of access. If uncertain, always seek permission.

James Dyer,
September 2000

1
Introduction

The great British archaeologist Sir Leonard Woolley (1880–1960), once described archaeology as the perfect fieldsport. This book is intended as a guide to that sport, which will take the readers into the open air, and often to the most attractive parts of England. It describes nearly seven hundred prehistoric sites in England which can be easily visited and should help enthusiasts to recognise similar monuments for themselves. The sites are spread throughout the country, with distinct concentrations on the chalk downlands of the south and the wildest moors and highlands of the west and north. In the east, where intensive agriculture has been practised, many monuments have been levelled and are now visible only from the air, but a few remain for the determined investigator to find.

It is important to realise that the monuments that we can see today are isolated survivals from a landscape that has changed dramatically since the site was originally occupied. It is difficult to imagine a hillfort or henge monument in a forested or moorland setting, devoid of recent roads and buildings, hedgerows and plantations; yet this we must try to do if we are to view the past in anything like a true perspective. Our informed imagination has to fill the gaps, and sometimes our attempts are abysmally inaccurate. Today archaeologists are concentrating more and more on the relationship between the monuments and their prehistoric environment.

This guide was originally planned to be read in conjunction with *Discovering Archaeology in England and Wales* by James Dyer (Shire, 1997). Since that book was first published in 1969 the Shire Archaeology series has appeared, with many titles describing in detail the types of monuments to be found in this book. The relevant titles are listed in the bibliography on page 244.

Most of the sites included in this book are easily accessible at all times. Whilst many of them are in public ownership or on common land, others are on private land, and it is only courteous to seek permission before visiting. Although this guide was prepared with the motorist in mind, it will be necessary to explore on foot if anything like a detailed examination of an area is to be achieved. High summer is not the time to search for hut circles on heather- and bracken-clad moorlands. Throughout the book instructions for finding a site are given when it is thought helpful. It is advisable to use either the 1:50,000 (2 cm = 1 km) Landranger or 1:25,000 (4 cm = 1 km) Pathfinder Ordnance Survey maps. The former is usually quite adequate and marks public footpaths and rights of way. National Grid references are given for each entry.

2
The field monuments

PALAEOLITHIC AND MESOLITHIC

Early man wandered over western Europe at a time when Britain was still joined to the continent. His progress in England was limited from time to time by the spread of ice sheets, which at their maximum reached as far south as the Thames valley. During warmer interglacial periods the climate was suitable for mixed oak forests to establish themselves over much of the more fertile parts of the country and allowed a rich fauna to spread northwards, and man did likewise. His presence is indicated by the finds of stone tools, weapons and working places, and by the occasional discovery of fossilised bones. Although many hundreds of stone tools have been found in Britain, very few have come from actual working or living areas, and their interest is mainly academic. The remains of wandering food-gatherers are usually found in the open countryside: beside ancient river courses or on patches of hilltop gravel. There is seldom anything for the visitor to see, although at Swanscombe in Kent such a site is protected, being the finding-place of human remains some 350,000 years old. These 'open' sites have little popular appeal. On the other hand caves and rock shelters stir the imagination out of all proportion to their original importance. Very few people lived in caves; it was the exception rather than the rule. However, by their very nature, caves have survived, though their appearance may have changed significantly since palaeolithic times. Originally the area around the entrance would have been occupied: the interior was too dark and damp. Incidentally, caves with paintings are unknown in Britain. Caves that were used in England include Kent's Cavern (Devon), Gough's Cave (Somerset), Creswell Crags (Derbyshire) and the Victoria Cave (North Yorkshire).

Between about 12,000 and 4000 BC the climate steadily became warmer and small bands of hunters, food-gatherers and fishermen spread across England. By 8000 BC a rise in sea level had led to the formation of the English Channel and the establishment of Britain as an island. The period known as the mesolithic represents the transition from a nomadic to a more settled way of life. Small, scattered settlements of a temporary nature seem to have existed, often on the lighter soils. One such site is described at Abinger (Surrey). There is nothing to be seen at England's most famous mesolithic camping site, Star Carr in North Yorkshire. Caves were occasionally occupied. The remains of tiny microlithic flint implements, once used as hunting equipment, are the most common objects found. Hafted stone axes were used in the first tentative attempts at forest clearance.

NEOLITHIC (c.4200 TO 2200 BC)

From about 4500 BC the aboriginal inhabitants of Britain had begun to practise simple agriculture. Domesticated animals and plants arrived from Europe, although exactly how is open to question. Specialised axe production made more extensive tree-felling possible. Clearings in the forest cover and beside streams were utilised for animal husbandry and crop-growing. Production of plain, round-bottomed pottery indicates a sedentary life, though evidence of domestic dwellings is seldom

Shire Publications Ltd

Cromwell House, Church Street, Princes Risborough, Buckinghamshire HP27 9AA, UK.
Telephone: 01844 344301. Fax: 01844 347080.
Website: www.shirebooks.co.uk   Email: shire@shirebooks.co.uk

1 × PREHISTORIC ENGLAND

To replace faulty copy,
please accept our apologies.

With compliments

found. Monuments constructed in the neolithic period include causewayed enclosures, earthen and chambered long barrows, cursuses and henge monuments, and flint mines. Stone circles appeared from about 3300 BC and reached their zenith in the bronze age (see page 9).

Causewayed enclosures

These are usually roughly concentric rings of one or more ditches, broken at frequent intervals by causeways of undug soil, with more or less continuous banks of earth on their inner sides. Obvious entrances are seldom found, and there is little evidence for any internal structures. Detritus seems to be concentrated in the inner ditches, the amount diminishing towards the outer ones. This material consists of broken pottery, stone axes and other tools, and animal and human bones, often apparently deliberately buried. The enclosures seem to have had multifarious uses including the short-term corralling of cattle (though they lack a water supply); centres for the exchange of goods; places for settlement (though the remains of permanent houses are seldom found); and places of safety – but a number of enclosures have been shown by excavation to have been attacked by arrowhead and fire. Ceremonial use is attested at Crickley Hill (Gloucestershire) and Hambledon Hill (Dorset): at the latter human skulls were deliberately set up in the ditches and other decaying human remains were exposed to the elements within the main enclosure before being swept into the ditches. Pits were dug containing deposits of pottery and axes of types exotic to the site. Windmill Hill (Wiltshire) is the most famous and easily visited of these sites. In the south-west of England is a group of related stone-walled enclosures without ditches, including Carn Brea in Cornwall.

Earthen long barrows

Earthen long barrows were usually rectangular or wedge-shaped burial mounds, found mostly in central southern England, East Anglia, Lincolnshire and the Yorkshire Wolds. The earth was quarried from side ditches and often piled up over a wooden or turf mortuary building which frequently (though not always) contained a number of human burials. The corpses were often exposed for some time before the decayed remains were removed to the mortuary chamber together with grave goods. When sufficient bones were accumulated the barrow mound was piled over the chamber, which was sometimes burnt down beforehand. Some Wiltshire and Yorkshire long barrows contained cremated interments. Once the earthen mound was constructed, the long barrows could not be re-entered. Sometimes the mortuary enclosures were left without a covering mound, and today they are revealed only by aerial photography. The position of one is marked on the plan of the Normanton Down barrow cemetery (page 193, no. 26). In Dorset there is a localised group of extremely long, narrow mounds known as bank-barrows, which are clearly related to both long barrows and cursus monuments (at Martin's Down and Maiden Castle).

Chambered long barrows and cairns

Barrows containing stone-built burial chambers and known as the Cotswold-Severn tombs are found in an area stretching from the Mendips to the Cotswolds, with outliers along the Berkshire Ridgeway and in north Wiltshire. A different group is to be found in the southern Pennines and another in northern Kent. Since the chambers in all these barrows were constructed of stone, which would not decay, they could be re-entered on numerous occasions for the interment of further burials or the performance of religious rituals, and indeed some (*e.g.* West Kennet) seem to have been in use for almost a thousand years. There are numerous variations on barrow plan: some with long entrance passages leading along the length of the barrow with pairs of chambers on either side; others with chambers accessible from the outer sides of the mound; and yet others with inaccessible chambers sealed into the barrow, often with a false entrance (portal) at the highest end. This may have been a door for spirits, or to fool tomb robbers. In a large number of cases the barrow mound has totally disappeared and only the stone chamber, or parts of it, remains, as at Trethevy in Cornwall or the Whispering Knights in Oxfordshire. Such remains are sometimes referred to as dolmens or quoits. Some chambered barrows are circular in plan, and examples may be seen in the Isles of Scilly and Derbyshire (Five Wells).

Cursuses

These were long, narrow ceremonial enclosures, defined by parallel ditches with high internal banks and squared-off ends. Cursuses can vary in length from almost 10 km and in width from 80 metres (Dorset Cursus) to tiny examples visible only on aerial photographs, as little as 100 metres long and 5 metres wide. Most cursuses have no visible entrances and are usually sited close to long barrows. They are not necessarily completely straight and can stretch for long distances over undulating land. At Thornborough (North Yorkshire) one lies buried beneath a later henge monument. The function of cursuses is quite obscure, but they may have been enclosures for the exclusive use of spirits of the dead or those who served them. Some certainly seem to be major features of the ritual landscape, and more concerned with death than life. Even when they ceased to be in current use, their sanctity continued to be respected, hence the concentration of bronze age cemeteries, for example, beside the Dorset Cursus on Cranborne Chase (Oakley Down).

Henge monuments

About 3200 BC the first henges appeared in Britain. It has been suggested that they may have replaced the causewayed enclosures. In essence they consist of a flat, circular, central area surrounded by a ditch and external bank, with one, two or occasionally more entrances. There are exceptions: in eastern and northern England they may have two ditches, as at the three Thornborough sites, or no ditch at all, as at Mayburgh (Cumbria). They vary considerably in size from less than 75 metres in diameter (The Bull Ring, Derbyshire) to 450 metres at Durrington Walls (Wiltshire). Most henges occur on low-lying land close to rivers. Since excavations show that they seldom contain domestic refuse, it is probable that they were sanctuaries or meeting places, with observers sitting on the banks, watching religious or secular ceremonies. Some, like Stonehenge and Woodhenge, contain rings of stone or wood, and the former remained in use well into the bronze age. A few extremely large henges are known, including Durrington Walls, Marden and Avebury in Wiltshire, and possibly Waulud's Bank in Bedfordshire.

Mining

Although often found on the surface, the best-quality flint, for axe- and arrowhead production, is found in seams in the chalk. During the neolithic period shafts were often dug for its extraction, and areas of mining can be seen at a number of places on the chalk hills of southern England, especially Cissbury hillfort and Harrow Hill, both in Sussex. In Norfolk it is possible to descend one of the extensive series of mines at Grimes Graves. The Sussex flint mines, dating from around 4200 to 3200 BC, are somewhat earlier than those in East Anglia (c.3000–2000 BC). Igneous rocks were used continuously for axe manufacture for about 1500 years, but the sites of the relevant 'factories', such as Great Langdale in Cumbria, are for the most part extremely difficult to access, and not described in this guide.

BRONZE AGE (c.2200 TO 800 BC)

The transition from the neolithic or new stone age to the ensuing bronze age was very gradual and did not occur at the same time all over England, nor can the various monuments described be firmly placed in one period or the other: there was considerable overlap. The climate during the early bronze age was warmer than today, and this allowed higher land such as Dartmoor and the moors of north-eastern England to be brought under cultivation. Numerous small farming settlements were constructed with associated walled paddocks and pastureland. The climate seems to have become wetter and cooler by 1000 BC. Blanket bog appeared on the western moorlands and many settlements on marginal land were deserted.

Early metalworking techniques began to spread after about 2500 BC, leading to greater efficiency in crafts and agriculture. Bronze was a luxury item that had little impact on the lives of the majority of the population, but for those with access to metals such as tin, copper and gold there was a chance to become part of a wealthy hierarchy. It was these people who probably constructed specialised ceremonial monuments such as stone circles, standing stones and elaborate grave mounds. The last involved a specialised burial rite: inhumation of crouched individuals in single oval graves under round barrows or cairns. These were frequently accompanied by metal weapons and jewellery, fine flintwork and a variety of pots, especially beautifully decorated beaker drinking vessels. The growth of population towards the end of the bronze age created competition for good-quality land and a certain amount of unrest, which eventually led to the construction of fortified settlements and new developments in the manufacture of sophisticated weaponry.

Stone circles and avenues

The origin of stone circles is closely linked with that of henges and is firmly rooted in the neolithic period, perhaps as early as 3300 BC. As would be expected, the circles are almost exclusively found in western England, where a supply of building stone was readily available, though glacial erratics were sometimes used further east. The earliest circles were usually true geometric circles, over 30 metres in diameter, and quite often with a single standing stone outside that might be used to record the rising or setting of the sun or moon, especially at midsummer and midwinter (Long Meg, Cumbria). By the early bronze age circles were much larger: at Stanton Drew in Somerset the Great Circle was 113 metres in diameter, with an associated avenue of stones leading to a nearby stream. Flattened and oval 'circles' began to appear, as did pairs and treble rings of stones, such as the Grey Wethers (Devon) and the Hurlers (Cornwall). Stones grouped into three-sided settings known as coves appeared at Stanton Drew, Avebury and Arbor Low (collapsed) and may have been depositories for bones or gifts. The last stone circles to be built were very small, only a few metres in diameter, and some were reduced to only four stones. Examples include Barbrook II (Derbyshire), the Nine Stones (Dorset) and Goatstones (Northumberland). It was not unknown for the stones to be decorated with cup-and-ring marks or spirals (Long Meg). Only at Stonehenge was the construction so sophisticated that the stones were individually shaped with lintels that may have reflected an earlier timber structure. The rising and setting of the sun and moon at the equinoxes were particularly important at this unique site. It is worth noting that denuded round cairns often had kerb stones which can easily be mistaken for stone circles, as can the foundations of hut circles.

Stone avenues and rows span the neolithic and bronze ages and may have been processional ways like the West Kennet Avenue between Avebury and the Sanctuary (Wiltshire) or smaller examples at Stanton Drew (Somerset). Single lines of stones such as occur on Dartmoor (Merrivale) may have marked spirit paths. Although it is often suggested, most are too low to have had astronomical significance.

Standing stones and carved stones

Single standing stones may have marked territory, burials, mineral deposits or the site of some special, long forgotten event. Some in the West Country were set up in living memory for cattle to scratch on! Two or more together may mark significant alignments (Devil's Arrows), perhaps astronomical in origin. In northern England they are often decorated with incised and pecked decorations, most commonly cup marks, but often quite elaborate spirals, concentric circles and abstract patterns. These occur even more commonly on many outcrops of living rock (*e.g.* Ilkley Moor). Their meaning is unknown, but the appearance of designs on burial cists and in chambered tombs (Wales, Scotland) suggests a religious or protective motive in some cases.

Round barrows and cairns

By far the most common monuments of the bronze age are the various round barrows. In their simplest form they consist of circular mounds of earth or stones piled over a single grave containing a crouched burial or cremation: the so-called bowl-barrows or cairns. Such mounds are found throughout England. Many graves contained splendid fine-pottery vessels called beakers, with jewellery, or weapons and archery equipment. In the south and east during the early bronze age specialised barrows of Wessex type were constructed in fancy shapes (Oakley Down, Dorset) to fulfil particular roles: for example, bell-barrows appear to have been built exclusively for males, disc-barrows for women. The size and quality of grave goods were perhaps sometimes proportional to the status and wealth of the person whose remains they contained. In the north ring and banked cairns were possibly a regional variant of the same theme. As the bronze age progressed cremation burials in cinerary urns tended to replace crouched burials, and from time to time secondary cremations were added to earlier barrows. By the end of the bronze age cremations were being buried in flat urnfields that leave few surface indications today.

Settlements

Bronze age house foundations are usually found standing only in the stone areas of the west and north, where they have survived on the moors of Cornwall and Devon, parts of Yorkshire, Cumbria and Northumberland. Marked as 'hut circles' on the Ordnance Survey maps, they may occur as isolated examples – perhaps a farmstead, or grouped together as a tiny hamlet. A few settlements with massive surrounding stone walls, called pounds, have survived on Dartmoor (Grimspound). They are often associated with bronze age field walls, now partially grassed over, called reaves. In central southern England a few substantial hilltop enclosures began to appear towards the close of the second millennium BC, initiating the first hillforts (Norton Fitzwarren, Mam Tor and Ram's Hill, Berkshire). Artificial islands, constructed of timber and brushwood, once existed in the waterlogged fenlands of Yorkshire, Lincolnshire, Somerset and East Anglia. At Flag Fen near Peterborough remains of one can be seen at an ongoing excavation.

IRON AGE (*c.*800 BC TO FIRST CENTURY AD)

By the iron age the climate of England was much as it is today. Agriculture continued to form the basis of life, with scattered farms and associated Celtic field systems. Iron was much in demand and mining took place in a few geologically suitable areas (*e.g.* around Hunsbury, Northamptonshire). The appearance of a few large hilltop enclosure earthworks towards the end of the bronze age suggests cattle-ranching (Nottingham Hill, Gloucestershire). From at least 800 BC smaller hilltop defences mark the beginning of fortifications, which developed by 400 BC into a variety of much larger hillforts with single or multiple defences of earth, stone or timber, often commanding large territories. These territories were sometimes separated from each other by linear dykes. In spite of their great numbers, few hillforts were permanently occupied. Although there was great regional diversity, most people lived in small unenclosed villages or farmsteads, surrounded by their fields, which were separated by hedges and trackways edged by drainage ditches. They used the hillforts only to shelter themselves and their stock when danger was imminent, either from neighbouring tribesfolk, or eventually from the Roman army. The iron age is usually taken to have ended in southern England with the arrival of the Romans in AD 43, and somewhat later in northern England, where many isolated areas never became truly Romanised.

Hillforts

Hillforts ranged in size from a fraction of a hectare to 290 hectares (Stanwick) and their defences varied from a simple wooden stockade (Staple Howe) to multiple lines of timber- and stone-faced ramparts and deep ditches (Maiden Castle). Sites were carefully chosen to follow the contours of a high hill (contour fort), to ring a significant raised area of lower ground (plateau fort), or cut off a steep-sided spur, cliff or promontory, wherever maximum defence could be obtained. The weakest part of each fort was its gate and no effort was spared to design elaborate entrances (Maiden Castle, Danebury). A few forts seem to have contained rows of four-post huts about 2 metres square which may have been granaries or storehouses. Others contained circular houses: refuges in times of stress perhaps. In only a few does excavation suggest that the occupation was anything like permanent: these may have been centres for trade or the exchange of goods, and the tribal capitals of their regions (Hod Hill).

Defences changed over time, simple wooden stockades giving way to more massive earth-filled box-ramparts, or drystone walls 5 to 10 metres thick. Eventually many forts resorted to glacis ramparts: a dump of loose rubble that slipped forward towards the ditch as assailants tried to scale them. Occasionally unfinished forts are found that tell us something about the method of their construction (Ladle Hill). Towards the end of the iron age large commercial centres called *oppida* make an appearance in the south of England (Colchester, Winchester), often associated with massive protective dykes.

Settlements

There are few visible iron age settlements in south-eastern England. Most have long been ploughed flat. In the West Country and north, circular hut foundations resemble their bronze age predecessors and frequently only excavation can confirm a date. In Cornwall small stone-walled settlements exist containing free-standing courtyard-houses, sometimes incorporating stables, barns and garden plots (Chysauster).

On the chalk downland of Wessex low banks and ditches mark the foundations of small farming settlements, often with the lynchet banks of rectangular Celtic fields close by. These sites are seldom easy to understand without a plan, but circular huts and animal pens can sometimes be recognised (Smacam Down, Grimstone Down). Similarly in the north of England, enclosures defined by tumbled, grass-covered stone walls and banks mark the iron age sheep farms of the moors and fells (Crosby Garrett). In Somerset the lake village of Glastonbury and the neighbouring lakeside trading settlement at Meare remind us that water could afford both protection and food (both fish and fowl). In due course similar sites will undoubtedly be found in other waterlogged areas. Huts of iron age type have been reconstructed at a number of open-air museums in England and these help to give visitors an idea of what living conditions were like two thousand years ago. Examples include Butser Ancient Farm (Hampshire), Avoncroft Museum (Worcestershire), Flag Fen (Cambridgeshire) and the Peat Moors Centre near Glastonbury (Somerset).

Burials

Few barrows of the iron age are visible in England since current burial practice tended to favour the scattering of cremated remains, or their interment in flat urnfields no longer visible on the surface. On the Wolds of east Yorkshire many cemeteries of small round barrows enclosed in square ditches once existed. Almost all of these have been ploughed away, though the last remnants of a once large cemetery can be found at Arras (East Riding of Yorkshire). A few rich burials suggesting wealthy warriors or ladies have been found from time to time in southern England: their possessions are now in some county museums (for example, Birdlip mirror grave at Gloucester). At Lexden (Colchester) there can still be seen a large burial mound that probably covered the remains of the Trinovantian prince Addedomaros. The rich contents of the grave are displayed in Colchester Museum.

ROMAN BRITAIN

After the arrival of the first Roman troops in Britain in AD 43 a whole series of new roads was laid out. Towns, forts, temples and villas were built, often alongside the existing iron age settlements. In the south many of the native people were sufficiently influenced by the Roman style of life to absorb some of its ideas and become 'Romanised' or Romano-Britons. In the north the influence was not so strong, and isolated native settlements continued with little change in lifestyle for many more centuries. For more information about the visible remains of Roman times the reader is referred to the companion Shire guide book *Discovering Roman Britain* by David E. Johnston.

3
Prehistoric sites in England

BEDFORDSHIRE
(Map on page 238)

1. Five Knolls, Dunstable   **Neolithic and Bronze Age**
                                                              TL: 007210

On the northern end of Dunstable Downs. Car park on top of Downs to S.

The finest group of burial mounds in the Chilterns consists of two bowl-barrows, three bell-barrows enclosed within one ditch and two pond-barrows.

The most northerly bowl-barrow was excavated by Mortimer Wheeler and Gerald Dunning in 1928–9. A central grave 1 metre deep contained a crouched female skeleton with a polished flint blade of late neolithic type at her shoulder (both now in Luton Museum). A secondary cremation burial in a collared urn was later added. During the Saxon period about thirty bodies were buried in rows with their hands tied behind their backs, the prey of some kind of massacre. Yet more bodies were added to the mound some centuries later, perhaps gallows victims.

The three joined bell-barrows have been dug into from time to time but have not been properly excavated. They may belong to the Wessex tradition *c.*2000 BC. There is no record that the southern bowl-barrow or the pond-barrows have been opened.

Burial of a neolithic woman from the most northerly of the Five Knolls barrows on Dunstable Downs, Bedfordshire. Now in Luton Museum. (G. C. Dunning)

13

2. Galley Hill, Streatley

Neolithic, Roman, Medieval
TL: 092270

Reached by a footpath from Turnpike Drive, Luton, at 084265.

Two small barrows on the summit of Galley Hill have both been excavated. The most southerly had been badly damaged by a Home Guard trench. It contained parts of a human burial and pieces of early iron age pottery.

The northerly barrow was kidney-shaped (like the Whiteleaf Barrow, Buckinghamshire) and had a long history. The truncated remains of two young men were found in a shallow grave together with early neolithic pottery. A central prehistoric burial was destroyed many years ago. In the fourth century AD the barrow had been used as a slaughter cemetery for the remains of a number of men and women. In the fifteenth century it was the site of a gallows (giving the hill its name) and at the foot of this gibbet a witchcraft deposit had been buried consisting of a horse's skull and a dice (both in Luton Museum).

3. Houghton Conquest long barrow

Neolithic
TL: 055405

On the hill, 400 metres SE of Bury Farm.

What appears to be a long barrow, 50 metres long, 10 metres wide and 1.5 metres high, runs from south-east to north-west down the slope of the hill. It has side ditches. It is possible that the site is a pillow mound (an artificial rabbit warren of medieval date). About 90 metres east is a circular mound, which seems to be a round barrow.

4. Maiden Bower, Houghton Regis

Neolithic, Iron Age
SP: 997224

Approached from Sewell along a footpath beside a chalk quarry.

An early iron age plateau fort consisting of a single rampart and filled-in ditch surrounding a roughly circular area of about 4.4 hectares. Excavation of the entrance in the south-east side suggests that this was funnel-shaped with a bridge over the top. There is some evidence to suggest that during the middle phase of the iron age the fort was subjected to fighting with slingstones and resultant slaughter. A recent geophysical survey suggests that a smaller ditched enclosure lies buried within the fort. Its date is unknown.

The iron age fort seems to overlie a neolithic causewayed enclosure. Traces of this were found in the nineteenth century when a row of disconnected pits filled with split animal and human bones was destroyed in quarrying. It is possible to see the flat-bottomed neolithic ditches, cut by the V-shaped iron age ditches, in the edge of the disused quarry.

5. Sandy hillforts

Mesolithic, Iron Age
TL: 180490

Although Sandy has a long archaeological history and was a small Roman crossroads town, there is little for the casual visitor to see. The remains of three iron age hillforts are all on private land. **Caesar's Camp**, above the railway station, is a contour camp, unfinished on its northern side. **Galley Hill**, on Sandy Warren (185478), is rectangular with an entrance at its north-east corner, and completely forested. **The Lodge** camp is a promontory fort (187477) within the grounds of the Royal Society for the Protection of Birds nature reserve at Sandy Lodge. This latter camp consists of a single line of rampart and ditch cutting off a south-facing hill spur. Mesolithic flints have been found all over the sand hills in this area.

6. Sharpenhoe Clappers hillfort

Iron Age
TL: 066302

National Trust property, approached from car park to SW on the Streatley to

Sharpenhoe road.

This small iron age promontory fort occupies a magnificent spur of the Chilterns, with wide views to the west, north and east. An incomplete rampart and wide flat ditch separate the fort from the main hill mass to the south. Excavation has shown that the rampart is early medieval in date and was probably a rabbit warren. Beneath it, traces of an iron age footing trench for a wooden palisade and external ditch were found. A beech wood completely fills the area of the fort. It must originally have relied on scarping of the natural hillslopes for protection, as there is little sign of defence round the crest of the spur.

7. Waulud's Bank, Luton

Neolithic
TL: 062247

In a public park, with car parking near Youth House, 061243.

Now badly denuded, this massive D-shaped bank, still 2.6 metres high in places, and external ditch, 6 metres wide, sweep round from the source of the Lea in the Sundon Road recreation ground uphill towards Youth House. The river forms the straight side of the enclosure. The site lies immediately beside the Icknield Way. Waulud's Bank was found on excavation to be of neolithic date and is considered to have been a settlement site, later used as a henge monument, similar to Marden in Wiltshire. The interior has not been excavated. It was occupied by people who hunted and fished, as well as reared cattle, beside the Lea marshes to the west. Grooved ware and many flint arrowheads have been found within the enclosure: these are now in Luton Museum.

BERKSHIRE

(Map on page 238)

1. Caesar's Camp, Easthampstead

Iron Age
SU: 863657

In public recreation area on S side of Ninemile Ride. Parking at Heritage Centre (873657).

In plan shaped like an oakleaf, this contour fort encloses 8 hectares. It is unexcavated and covered by trees. It is protected by a single rampart and ditch which hug the 120 metre contour line. There are entrances; in valleys on the east and west, and two others to north and south. That on the north lies between two long parallel banks.

2. Grimsbury Castle, Newbury

Iron Age
SU: 512723

In woodland 800 metres S of Hermitage. A minor road passes through the fort.

This hillfort, situated on sloping ground, is roughly triangular in shape and encloses about 3.2 hectares. It is defended by an inner bank and ditch, with a high outer bank. On the west, some 55 metres from the camp, is a second line of defence. There were three probable entrances; one on the west is slightly incurved with a possible hollow-way leading out of it (as well as a bank of earth some 120 metres long), whilst a third gap in the south-east may have led to springs. Excavations show the fort was occupied towards the end of the early iron age.

3. Grim's Ditch, Aldworth

Iron Age
SU: 546785 to 570792

One of the best preserved sections of bank and ditch lies east of Beche Farm. 800 metres further east it makes a right-angled turn north. It splits into two where the road from Hungerford Green crosses it. Both forks end after a further 800 metres.

Another section covered with trees lies to the south on Hart Ridge, in Broom Wood and Bowler's Copse (585775). Yet another stretch, about 800 metres in length, lies between the A417 near the Grotto (on the Thames) and Hurdle Shaw (593796). In this area the ditch climbs steeply from the Thames valley and takes the unusual form of having its ditch facing up the hillslope. Such a work was almost entirely intended as a boundary and not for defence. At all times the ditch is on the north side of the bank, and its greatest height from ditch bottom to crest of bank is about 1.8 metres.

4. Inkpen long barrow (Combe Gibbet)

Neolithic
SU: 365623

Beside a bridlepath on the ridge between Walbury Hill and Inkpen Hill.
   This long barrow is 60 metres long and 22 metres wide, flanked by ditches 4.5 metres wide and 0.9 metre deep. The mound still stands some 1.8 metres high. It is crowned by a restored wooden gibbet, the original having been erected in 1676 to hang George Brooham and Dorothy Newman for the murder of Brooham's wife and son.

5. Lambourn Seven Barrows and long barrow

Late Neolithic and Bronze Age
SU: 328828

Mainly situated to the E of the minor road from Lambourn to Kingston Lisle, 3.6 km N of Lambourn.
   Although this cemetery contains more than forty burial mounds of probable

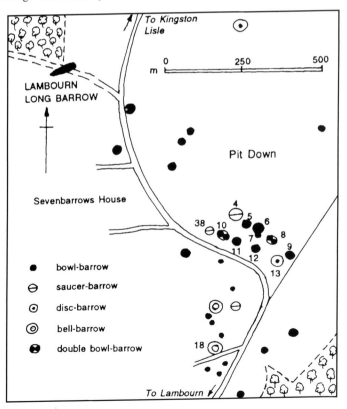

Lambourn Seven Barrows, Berkshire.

An aerial view of the Lambourn Seven Barrows, Berkshire, looking north.
(Cambridge University Collection)

bronze age date, only the group beside the road is accessible and will be described in detail. These barrows lie in two rows running north-west to south-east. The numbering given them by Mr Humphrey Case some years ago has been retained. Commencing at the north-west end of the row nearest the road, can be seen:

38. A small saucer-barrow, 14 metres in diameter, with a ditch 1 metre deep, and slight outer bank.

10. Two barrows enclosed by a single ditch. The mound of one is about 1.2 metres high, and the other 1.8 metres. A hollow on top of the north mound was made when it was opened by Martin Atkins about 1850. It contained the bones of an ox and a dog.

11. A bowl-barrow, about 3 metres high and 30 metres in diameter. There is no record of its contents although it has certainly been opened.

12. A bowl-barrow with a tree-planting earth ring around it. About 2.4 metres high and 21 metres in diameter.

13. A fine disc-barrow, 30 metres in diameter, it contains a central mound 18 metres in diameter and 0.3 metre high. Again, no record exists of its probable opening.

Second row, furthest from road, north-west end:

4. A large disc- or saucer-barrow, 36 metres in diameter, with a bank outside the ditch. No record of contents.

5. A bowl-barrow, 21 metres in diameter and 1.8 metres high. No records.

6 and 7. A large bowl-barrow, 25 metres in diameter and 1.8 metres high, with a tiny barrow on its south side.

8. Two barrows enclosed within a single ditch, their mounds overlapping, suggesting that one is earlier than the other. Both mounds are 1.8 metres high.

9. A bowl-barrow, 18 metres in diameter and 1.8 metres high. In a sarsen stone cist in this barrow a collared urn was found containing the cremated bones of a woman.

The best bell-barrow at Lambourn (no. 18) is beside a road, some 180 metres south of the group described above. It is partly covered by trees. The mound is 1.8

metres high and 18 metres wide and is separated from its ditch by a berm 3.6 metres wide. A cremation burial, together with a bronze awl and a jet pendant, were found in a sarsen stone cist that seems to have been added to the barrow some time after it was built.

A long barrow lies 400 metres north at the south end of Wescot Wood (323834). (Some Ordnance Survey maps show wrong position.) It can be approached along the cart-track which passes over it. It is 82 metres long and 21 metres wide at its east end, where it stands 1.2 metres high. Excavation showed that it contained a core of sarsen stones and a burial in a rough cist-like setting of sarsen stones, together with some perforated sea-shells.

6. Mortimer Common barrow cemetery

Bronze Age
SU: 643651

2.4 km S of Ufton Nervet on minor road to Stratfield Mortimer which runs over part of the mounds. Situated in a plantation.

There are at least five barrows in this group which lie in a straight line north-west to south-east. They consist from the north-west of a disc-barrow, overlaid by a small bell-barrow, then a second bell-barrow 42 metres in diameter and 1.8 metres high, and finally two small bowl-barrows. There is no record of what the barrows contained.

7. Walbury hillfort, Combe

Iron Age
SU: 374617

The minor road from Inkpen to Combe Hill passes beside the fort, and the Berkshire Ridgeway runs through it.

Walbury hillfort is situated on Combe Hill, the highest chalk hill in Britain, at 297 metres above sea level. Enclosing 33 hectares, it is the largest hillfort in Berkshire. It is trapezoidal in shape and is surrounded by a single bank and ditch, with faint traces of an outer counterscarp bank. There are two entrances, a small one in the south-east side and a more impressive one, slightly inturned, at the north-west corner. From this corner minor earthworks connected with hollow-ways run north-west down the hill, and in the same area two banks run across the hill spur. The larger west one, a cross-ridge dyke, seems to provide an extra line of defence, whilst the slighter bank, nearer the entrance, may have formed some kind of barbican outwork. It seems likely that circular depressions inside the camp may have been hut circles. The fort is unexcavated.

BUCKINGHAMSHIRE
(Map on page 238)

1. Boddington Camp, Halton

Iron Age
SP: 882080

A footpath climbs through the woods from the housing estate on the SE edge of Wendover.

This iron age hillfort has an area of some 6.2 hectares. The interior has been planted with trees by the Forestry Commission, but the single rampart and ditch are clearly visible on the north-west and south-east sides of the hill spur. The entrance seems to have been at the south-western tip. This simple contour fort guards the northern end of the Misbourne valley as Bulstrode Camp guards the southern end.

2. Bulstrode Camp, Gerrards Cross

Iron Age
SU: 994880

This oval-shaped earthwork is now a public open space. It is approached from the B416 through a residential area. Alleyways give access through the houses from Camp Road.

Enclosing 9 hectares, this is one of the largest Chiltern hillforts. It is surrounded by double ditches and ramparts, except where the outer ditch has been destroyed on the west and north-west. The entrance was probably where the rampart curves outwards on the north-eastern side. Excavation has proved that the gap on the south-west is not original. Trenches cut by Cyril Fox and L. C. G. Clarke in 1924 posed more questions than they answered and little is known of the site, which was presumably constructed to prevent entry into the Misbourne valley from the west. The fort lies nearly 1600 metres from the river valley.

3. Cholesbury Camp

Iron Age
SP: 930072

Situated in the centre of Cholesbury village, with the church inside the earthwork. A footpath leads off to the left from the church driveway along the rampart.

This fine oval plateau fort encloses 4 hectares within its circumference. The defences consist of two banks separated by a single ditch, although a second ditch and third bank appear on the southern side. On the west the inner and outer ditches are separated by a broad berm which terminates suddenly at a low cross-ditch, 92.5 metres north of the church drive. Excavation in 1932 showed that this cross-ditch was the earliest feature on the site and possibly belonged to some earlier agricultural complex. The fort dates from the middle and late phases of the iron age and produced early Belgic pottery.

4. The Cop Barrow, Bledlow

Bronze Age or Saxon
SP: 773011

Access by way of a minor road from Bledlow village to a point where it meets the Upper Icknield Way (777012). A track leads SW into the wood at this point. The barrow is off to the right after about 400 metres.

This small round barrow near the Bledlow Cross was excavated by J. F. Head in 1938. It had been constructed by scraping material from the surrounding area. The central burial had been robbed, but part of an axehead made from Cornish greenstone remained. Head considered the barrow to date from the bronze age, but in view of the lack of evidence it could just as easily be of Saxon origin.

If the visitor continues along the same track he will pass the Bledlow Cross, a cross cut into the chalk hillside, perhaps in medieval times; it has recently been scoured. Still further along the track and a few metres in Oxfordshire are two bowl-barrows enclosed within a single ditch (767006) on the summit of Chinnor Hill.

5. Danesborough hillfort, Wavendon

Iron Age
SP: 922348

Deep in Wavendon Wood. Can be reached from Aspley Heath (at 923347). It is advisable to follow the Ordnance Survey map using a compass.

This small contour fort encloses about 3.5 hectares. A single rampart and ditch with an outer counterscarp bank surround a roughly rectangular area, except on the north where the fort appears to be unfinished. There is an entrance at the south-east end. Extensive low banks and ditches once stretched from the fort for almost 1600 metres to the south-east (as far as the minor road passing south-east from Bow Brickhill to Bell's Copse). Unfortunately they have been destroyed by the golf course. They may have been connected with cattle-ranching or field boundaries. With destroyed forts at Heath and Reach and at Billington, Danesborough guarded the eastern side of the Ouzel valley.

6. Grim's Ditch, Chilterns

Iron Age
(See below)

Along the northern escarpment of the Chilterns are a number of sections of bank and ditch known as the Grim's Ditch: other sections are unnamed but almost certainly belong to the same system. Excavations near Berkhamsted have confirmed earlier fieldwork that suggested a middle iron age date for the ditch. The excavation revealed a bank 3 metres high and 6 metres wide, possibly crowned by a palisade, and fronted by a ditch 2.4 metres deep and 5 metres wide. Since the ditch runs for at least 40 km, and perhaps much further, it is unlikely that it was all constructed by the same workmen, or even at the same time. The earthwork is intermittent, with gaps possibly filled by dense forest land. Some sections are oddly sited on the side or lower slopes of hills, which suggests that it was non-defensive, and probably formed a boundary perhaps marking iron age expansion, possibly of the tribe of the Catuvellauni.

Grim's Ditch runs from Dunstable in Bedfordshire to Naphill near West Wycombe in Buckinghamshire, and possibly further south and west past High Wycombe to the Thames 5 km east of Marlow. The best sections to be visited in Buckinghamshire are those near Great Hampden, especially the stretch running north-east from Redland End (SP: 835023). South-east of Hampden House, two earlier burial mounds have been incorporated in the ditch (857020). A clear section of the earthwork can be seen in a small wood beside the road near Chambersgreen (900073). More can be traced for some distance on Pitstone Hill (949142 – not marked on Ordnance Survey maps).

7. Ivinghoe Beacon

Iron Age
SP: 960168

National Trust land with car park and picnic area 1 km S of Beacon Hill on the Ashridge road (at 964158).

Walking north from the car park notice small bowl-barrows on top of the two minor hills on your left. The highest part of the Beacon is also marked by a bowl-barrow.

The Beacon is ringed by a single line of rampart and ditch forming one of the earliest known hillforts in the country. The defence is strengthened on the weaker southern side by a second line of ditch facing the Icknield Way. (Notice that the Icknield Way ran on the south side of the hill, not the north as is marked on some Ordnance Survey maps.) There was originally an entrance at the eastern end of the fort. Excavations in 1963–5 showed that the fort had been defended by a timber-faced rampart and ditches 2.7 metres wide and deep. There were few traces of huts inside, but a bronze razor and pieces of sword suggest a very early date of construction, perhaps about 800 BC.

8. Lodge Hill, Saunderton

Bronze Age
SP: 789004

The road S from Bledlow slowly rises to Bledlow Ridge with Lodge Hill, Saunderton, on its E side. A public footpath runs up to Lodge Hill, from the W end of which a good view can be had of two barrows.

These were probably the two finest bell-barrows in the Chilterns. Although they have been ploughed out they still figure prominently as a feature of the landscape. Seen from Lodge Hill in June or July whilst the corn crop is still ripening, they stand out magnificently as crop-marks: some of the best to be seen, short of flying over the site.

9. Pitstone Hill and Grim's Ditch

Neolithic and Iron Age
SP: 949142

A minor road leaves the B488 from Ivinghoe for Aldbury. On the crest of the hill 1.6 km S of Ivinghoe is a car park on the E side of the road, with a public footpath up on to Pitstone Hill.

Pitstone Hill is covered with a series of fascinating earthworks, which include possible flint mines and a section of the Chiltern Grim's Ditch. The latter is an iron age boundary ditch which in this section (949143) forms part of an arc proceeding from Northchurch Farm on Berkhamsted Common to Dunstable. The dyke climbs up the western face of Pitstone Hill until it reaches the summit and then drops sharply down again to the edge of the chalk quarries. It then heads towards Steps Hill, south of Ivinghoe Beacon.

On the north-western spur of Pitstone Hill is a small group of what may be unexcavated flint mines probably of neolithic date. The tops of two shafts are visible and still about 3 metres deep, whilst on their lower edges can be seen the remains of waste dumps from the mines. The Upper Chalk which contains flint is rather restricted in its outcrops in this area. Immediately east of the mines traces of a causewayed ditch can be seen, which may also be neolithic in date.

10. Pulpit Hill, Great Kimble

Iron Age
SP: 832050

Approached by a minor unmetalled road from the S end of Great Kimble. Cars can be driven some distance along it in fine weather.

This little contour hillfort enclosing about 1.6 hectares is very overgrown. Shield-shaped in plan, its eastern side is defended by a double rampart and ditch. The north-eastern and south-western sides need only a single bank and ditch due to the natural steepness of the hill. The main entrance is in the middle of the eastern side. Numerous banks and ditches in the woods nearby may be connected with iron age agriculture or ranching. The fort commands excellent views in almost all directions.

11. West Wycombe Camp

Iron Age
SP: 827949

NW of the village of West Wycombe, whose church stands within its ramparts.

This little hillfort occupies a magnificent position on a steep-sided spur. It encloses 1.2 hectares, the whole of the churchyard. The rampart still rises 3.5 metres on the north-east side of the graveyard and is separated from an outer bank 2 metres high by a ditch 15 metres wide and 1.6 metres deep. The defences have been destroyed on the south-east to make way for the large eighteenth-century Dashwood mausoleum. The original entrance to the fort probably coincided with the north-west gate into the churchyard.

12. Whiteleaf Barrows, Princes Risborough

Neolithic
SP: 822040

Approached from the minor road from Monks Risborough to Great Hampden. A steep climb up the hillside, immediately above the Whiteleaf Cross.

On the false crest of the hill above the Whiteleaf Cross are the remains of a kidney-shaped barrow excavated between 1934 and 1939 by Sir Lindsay Scott. On the eastern side of the barrow was a forecourt, and the whole mound was surrounded by an almost circular ditch. Under the mound a wooden burial chamber some 2.4 metres by 1.7 metres had been constructed for the body of a middle-aged man, although most of the skeleton was found scattered on the forecourt outside the chamber. The remains of pieces of more than fifty neolithic pots and hundreds of flints had been scattered throughout the chalk mound of the barrow, suggesting that they had been lying on the ground surface when the material was scraped up for use in the building operation. Slightly to the east along the ridge is a second smaller mound with a cross-shaped depression in its centre. This may be a barrow, but it was possibly used as the site for a post-mill. A few metres further on at the eastern end of the ridge is a small scraped bowl-barrow.

CAMBRIDGESHIRE
(Map on page 238)

1. Flag Fen Prehistoric Fenland Centre, Peterborough — Bronze Age
TL: 227989

Situated in open fenland N of the Nene, less than 800 metres E of Peterborough's Eastern Industrial Area. Follow heritage signs off the ring road (A1139) or A47 (Eye bypass) or follow signs for Eastern Industry. Open daily 10–4 except between Christmas Eve and 2nd January; well-equipped Visitor Centre with museum and café; regular tours; for more information and prices telephone 01733 313414.

Flag Fen and Fengate form part of the same low-lying fen-edge landscape, immediately east of modern Peterborough. The Fengate fen margin was intensively and continuously occupied from earlier neolithic times until the Roman period, when regular flooding made life difficult. The site at Flag Fen was constructed in wet peaty fenland around 1000 BC. It consists of a large artificial timber platform and a massive, 800-metre-long alignment of posts, which may have served as a boundary. Within these posts and in the water to one side of them were placed hundreds, possibly thousands, of pieces of metalwork and other objects. Religion is now thought to have formed a major reason for the site's existence. Wood preservation is excellent, owing to waterlogging. Flag Fen today is drained (hence the excavation), but part of the site has been preserved by a large artificial lake. The site also includes a display hall and extensive reconstructions of fields, buildings and other aspects of bronze age life, including domestic animals.

2. Stonea Camp, Wimblington — Iron Age
TL: 448930

Signposted off B1093 along farm road through Stitches Farm. On site car parking.

This D-shaped earthwork rivals Holkham for the honour of being England's lowest-lying hillfort. It stands on a gravel island some 2 metres above sea level, surrounded by wet fenland. There is a single bank and ditch on the south-western fen side, and three lines of defence to the north. The ditches were probably water-filled. Excavations indicate that there were at least three periods of construction, and the excavators have suggested that Stonea Camp may have been the site of the battle between the Roman governor Ostorius and the Iceni in AD 47. Tacitus described the site as 'an earthwork with an approach too narrow for cavalry' through which the Romans broke and where the natives were 'imprisoned by their own barrier and overwhelmed'. Tacitus also says that the inhabitants built their defences of turf, and this material has been found in the upper layers of the Camp's U-shaped ditches. The excavators have found the skull of a four-year-old child, hacked by sword cuts, and a mutilated adult skeleton hastily thrown into a backfilled ditch. The earthworks, which were badly damaged by agriculture and quarrying, have been carefully restored by Cambridgeshire County Council, who have provided display boards and observation points.

3. Thornhaugh Henge — Neolithic
TF: 066008

Via footpath 800 metres N from Thornhaugh village, by Manor Farm.

This probable henge monument is situated on low ground in a classic position close to a stream. It consists of a low circular bank with internal and external ditches and traces of a further bank inside the inner ditch. The monument is 84 metres in diameter. The entrances to the north-northwest and south-southeast have been carefully squared off; there does not seem to be a break in the outer ditch. The site shows great similarity to the henges at Thornborough and Hutton Moor in Yorkshire.

It has been suggested that Thornhaugh is nothing more than a seventeenth- or eighteenth-century water garden or pleasance.

Part of the well-preserved timber platform on display at Flag Fen Prehistoric Fenland Centre, Cambridgeshire, dated to around 1000 BC. (Francis Pryor)

An aerial view looking south of the restored iron age site of Stonea Camp, Cambridgeshire. (Cambridgeshire County Council)

4. Wandlebury hillfort, Stapleford

Iron Age
TL: 493534

This fine iron age plateau fort lies 6.4 km SE of Cambridge on the N side of the A1307, on the hill above the Gog Magog golf course.

Two massive banks and ditches enclose a circular area of 6.5 hectares. The earthwork was badly mutilated in the eighteenth century when the site was extensively landscaped and the inner bank was flattened and its ditch filled in. At the same time the outer bank was breached in a number of places. There is tenth-century documentary evidence to show that the fort had only one entrance. This was located on the east, later destroyed by the landscaping.

Excavations in 1955–6 and 1995–6 showed that the hilltop was extensively occupied in the early iron age, before it was fortified in the third century BC by the rampart and outer ditch. The rampart at that time was 4 metres wide and was faced both inside and out with a timber revetment. The ditch outside had steep sides and a flat floor. When the rampart decayed it fell into disuse for some time. Later, perhaps in the first century BC, the silting ditch was recut, and the material from it dumped on the outside to form a counterscarp bank. The original rampart was replaced and all the defences strengthened by the construction of an inner V-shaped ditch and rampart. This new ditch was 5.2 metres deep and 11.5 metres wide. The rampart was given a strong timber outer facing. The inside of the camp was intensively occupied throughout its existence. One of many shallow storage pits contained the burial of an infant whose legs had been removed from its body before the flesh had time to decay. More skeletons have been found outside the fort; one group in a shallow grave seem to have been battle victims, at least one exhibiting sword cuts. The rebuilding of Wandlebury may represent the reaction of the Iceni of Norfolk to Belgic expansion in the Chilterns. On the other hand, similarities in its stages of construction with Ravensburgh (Hertfordshire) suggest that it might be the work of an unidentified tribal group occupying the eastern Chilterns and the Icknield Way.

CHESHIRE
(Map on page 240)

1. Castle Hill, Delamere

Iron Age
SJ: 553695

Immediately E of 'The Old Pale' via minor road leading N off A556 at Delamere.

A double bank and ditch enclose a flat-topped hill 4.5 hectares in extent. Excavations have revealed a four-stage development of the site, beginning with a simple wooden palisade defence, later replaced by a single bank and ditch surrounding the east part of the hill. This was entered via a sunken track on the east side, leading to the original entrance which was protected by two wooden guard huts. In the third stage the defences were extended to take in the remainder of the hill and a further entrance was added at the north-west end. Finally the site was strengthened by an outer ditch and bank and the entrances were improved by deep inturning. The fort was dismantled during the Roman occupation but heightened and reused in the tenth century.

2. Helsby hillfort

Iron Age
SJ: 492754

Steep climb E above Helsby town. National Trust.

On a sandstone bluff above Helsby is a semicircular promontory fort protected by steep cliffs on the north and west, and a bank 18 metres wide and 2.7 metres high on the south and east. The original entrance is beside the cliff at the south-west corner, where the entrance is inturned and forms a short passage about 3 metres wide.

3. Kelsborrow Castle, Kelsall

Iron Age
SJ: 532675

SE of Kelsall at Birchill, approached by numerous minor roads.

An oval promontory fort enclosing 3.6 hectares. A single bank up to 12 metres wide and a ditch 7.5 metres wide defend the north side and steep slopes make the site impregnable from the south-east and west. There is one original entrance on the east side.

4. Maiden Castle, Bickerton

Iron Age
SJ: 497529

Reached via track leading SE from Brown Knowl.

Steep slopes protect this diminutive 0.6 hectare promontory fort on the north-west, whilst a double bank separated by a single ditch defends the south-east. This is pierced by a single entrance with the inner bank inturned. Excavations have shown that the inner bank was originally 5.1 metres wide and 3.6 metres high and was strengthened by timbering and stone-facing. The outer bank was also stone-faced. The ditch was once flat-bottomed, 7.3 metres wide and 0.6 metre deep. The inner entrance was a sunken passage 15 metres long, narrowing from 4.8 metres to 2.4 metres wide. It was once cobbled and had a guard hut and wooden gate.

CORNWALL
(Map on page 234)

1. Advent triple barrow

Iron Age
SX: 137834

By Roughtor turning E off the A39 NE of Camelford (110839) and byroad from 125829.

This is one of only three known triple barrows in southern England, the others being near Amesbury (Wiltshire) and Dunstable (Bedfordshire). The Advent example comprises three mutilated circular mounds enclosed in an oval ditch (waterlogged in wet weather) with outer bank, the overall length being 60 metres. The mounds are *c*.1.5 metres high. The long axis is east–west.

2. Bodrifty, New Mill

Late Bronze Age and Iron Age
SW: 445354

Minor road from New Mill leads NW to Bodrifty Farm. Site lies to N on edge of moorland.

This site began life as an open village in the fourth century BC. In the second century BC a pound wall was constructed enclosing some 1.2 hectares. Eight huts were built inside, the largest being 14 metres in diameter. The pound was of no great strength and served mainly as an animal enclosure. Small fields, still visible, were cut into the hillside above the settlement. The village can be overgrown in summer.

3. Boleigh fogou, St Buryan

Iron Age
SW: 437252

Turn N from the B3315 at 437250 to Rosemerrin House, where permission should be sought as the site is in the garden.

This site was formerly within an earthwork now almost destroyed. Its entrance is at the south and leads to a gallery 11 metres long, with an L-shaped creep passage in the west side. Some have interpreted the uneven surface of the west door jamb as a carved figure. The fogou was probably built as a cellar or cold store.

4. Boscawen-un stone ring, St Buryan

Bronze Age
SW: 412273

Walk S across fields from the A30 at or near 410277, or from Boscawen-noon Farm.

This is among the best-preserved of the Cornish stone rings. Restored in 1862, it still contains nineteen stones and a stone in the centre. It is elliptical in shape with a greatest diameter of 24.4 metres. The stones stand 0.9 to 1.4 metres high, whilst that near the centre, which leans towards the north-east, is 2.4 metres tall. The name means 'Nine Maidens'. Medieval literature claimed the circle was one of the three great Druidic meeting places in Britain, but the ring is likely to date to the bronze age, about 1500 years before the Druids. The stones are in a walled enclosure and not easy to photograph.

5. Brane or Chapel Euny round barrow, Sancreed

Bronze Age
SW: 401282

Follow signposts for 'Carn Euny' as far as Brane. Very narrow road for cars. Permission should be obtained from Brane Farm.

The best-preserved of the west Cornish entrance-grave round barrows, of a type abundant in the Isles of Scilly, where over forty are known. It is about 6.1 metres in diameter and 2 metres high with an entrance at the south-east and has a fine retaining wall of stone slabs.

6. Carn Brea, Illogan

Neolithic and Iron Age
SW: 685407

By footpath from Church Town, or minor road N from Carnkie (686400).

This dominant hill has two summits, one capped with a castle on the east, and the stone Basset monument on the west. Round the castle is a massive stone wall enclosing 2 hectares which dates from the neolithic period around 3000 BC. Inside the wall are stone hut foundations which must be amongst the oldest in Britain. Quantities of neolithic pottery have been excavated, and more than seven hundred flint arrowheads suggest that the site was attacked. Two sets of ramparts between the two summits have often been described as iron age, but it seems just as likely that they are also neolithic. If so, they form the oldest known defended enclosure in Britain, an enormous 18 hectares in extent. The site was certainly used in the iron

The Chapel Euny barrow at Brane is one of the best-preserved of the west Cornish entrance graves. (J. Dyer)

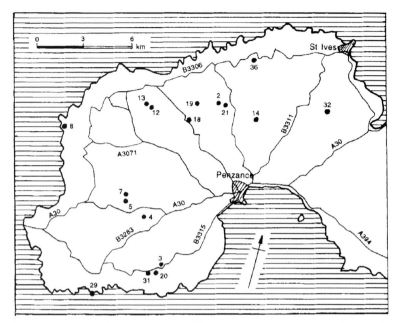

Prehistoric sites in the Penzance area. The numbers are those of sites described in this guide.

age, when a number of circular huts were built on the hilltop. Trade contacts with eastern Britain are suggested by the discovery of a hoard of iron age Kentish gold staters, discovered on the hill in the eighteenth century.

7. Carn Euny village and fogou, Sancreed   Iron Age and Romano-British
SW: 403288

Approach by a byroad N from Brane, which is reached from the A30 at Lower Drift. Car park at Brane Farm. Very narrow road.

The earliest settlement on this site comprised timber-built huts dating from the fourth century BC. These were replaced by four stone-built courtyard houses from the first century BC. The fogou, which is unusual in having a circular side chamber with corbelled roof, is probably of similar date. The underground passage is 20 metres long and was probably used for cold storage. An English Heritage guide pamphlet is available. A footpath east leads to **Caer Bran** (0.6 km), a small bivallate hillfort with a central roundhouse.

8. Carn Gluze (Ballowal), St Just   Bronze Age
SW: 355312

By lane from 364314 W of St Just, proceed for 800 metres to just beyond mine chimney. The barrow is signposted.

This highly complex round barrow, excavated by W. Copeland Borlase in 1878 and restored by the Department of the Environment, comprises two inner concentric ring-walls originally domed. In the innermost of these are three stone cists, two of which contained cremation urns. The whole is enclosed by a much larger cairn 22 metres by 20 metres, in the south-west sector of which is an entrance grave, probably the earliest feature on the site.

9. Castilly henge monument, Luxulyan — Neolithic and later
SX: 032627

Beside road between the A30(T) and the A391, SW of their junction at Lower Wood (038632).

In its present form this site comprises an oval enclosure about 48 metres by 30 metres, with ditch and outer bank largely covered with mixed scrub and brambles. The entrance at the north-northwest (lower) end is original; that at the south-southeast is believed to be thirteenth-century or later and connected with a complete remodelling of the site for use probably for Cornish medieval religious plays. It is also possible that the site may have been used during the Civil War. The interior is under grass and there is no difficulty of access.

10. Castle-an-Dinas, St Columb Major — Iron Age
SX: 946623

Approach from byroad N of the A30 up a lane W of Providence (946617).

This hillfort must not be confused with the smaller example of the same name at 485350 north of Penzance. The suffix *an-Dinas* means a stone-walled fort. This example, east of St Columb Major, is among the most massive hillforts in Cornwall and crowns a granite outcrop 210 metres high. It consists of three concentric and roughly circular ramparts, the first and third of which have deep ditches and an entrance on the south-west. The middle rampart is less bold and belongs to the earliest phase of occupation. It was abandoned and slighted. A number of hut circles can be traced in the centre and a ruined bronze age round barrow lies in the south quadrant. There is a spring feeding a pond on the north side. The site was damaged by wolfram (tungsten) mining during the Second World War.

11. Castle Dore, St Sampson — Iron Age and Early Christian
SW: 103548

Just E of the B3269 between Lostwithiel and Fowey.

A roughly circular hillfort with dependent enclosure (probably pastoral) to the east. Excavation in 1936–7 showed that it was in use from the fourth to first centuries BC by people using middle iron age pottery, glass bracelets and beads, among other articles. Defences and entrances at the east were remodelled around 50 BC. Circular hut foundations yielded cordoned late iron age pottery. The site was probably abandoned in the first century AD and reoccupied in the sixth century, to which period the foundations of a hall 27 metres by 12 metres have been attributed. Finds are in the Royal Cornwall Museum.

12. Chun Castle, Morvah — Iron Age and Dark Age
SW: 405339

SW from the road off the B3306 at Bosullow Common (417345), parking at Bosullo Lane End (409337); short walk up hill.

This small but fine hillfort is circular, with two concentric stone walls each 6 metres thick, having staggered entrances to the south-west, with parts of their gateways remaining. There are traces of circular iron age huts, but most of the interior foundations within the inner enclosure are of a reoccupation, perhaps as late as the fifth or sixth century AD. The well within this enclosure is undated. The occupants were probably connected with the tin trade. Methodists preached from 'pulpits' on the walls in the nineteenth century. Hectares of prehistoric fields surround Chun Castle and the adjoining Chun Quoit.

13. Chun Quoit, Morvah — Neolithic
SW: 402339

S from the B3306 or E from the B3318.

This is the best-preserved of the burial chambers in west Cornwall. It comprises a rectangular chamber about 1.8 metres by 1.6 metres with long axis north–south, limited by four upright slabs supporting a cover stone, the whole presenting the appearance of a gigantic mushroom. There are traces of a barrow, probably round, about 10 metres in diameter.

14. Chysauster, Madron
Iron Age and Romano-British
SW: 472350

2.3 km NW on minor road off B3311 at Badger's Cross (486332), well signposted. English Heritage; open daily, April to September 10–6; October 10–5. Admission charge. Guidebooks. Telephone: 07831 757934.

This is the classic example of an iron age and Romano-British village of court-yard houses, which includes eight arranged in pairs along a street, each with its own garden plot. The houses are roughly oval in plan, about 28 metres long, with walls still 3 metres high. Small rooms open off the central courtyard, providing living quarters, workshops and stabling. To the south-east is a ruined fogou, and there is a field system nearby. It is uncertain whether Castle-an-Dinas hillfort on the hill 1.2 km to the east (485350) was a defensive stronghold serving this village in times of unrest.

15. Duloe stone ring
Bronze Age
SX: 236583

Stands behind a farm near the centre of the village of Duloe.

This small ring of eight large quartz stones measures 12 metres by 11 metres. Leslie Grinsell suggested that it is quite possibly the retaining wall of a barrow. A ribbon-handled bronze age cremation urn was found by labourers in 1861, containing human bones 'that crumbled in the air'.

16. Four Barrows, Kenwyn
Bronze Age
SW: 762482

Beside the A30 between Carland and Redruth, 800 metres NW of the junction with A3075.

These are among the most prominent groups of round barrows in Cornwall, and have been shown and named as such on maps since the sixteenth century. One barrow (3 metres high) is north of the road; the others (2.4 to 4 metres high) are south of it. All four are arranged in an arc. One, called Burrow Belles or a variant of it, opened during the reign of William III (1689–1702), contained a megalithic burial chamber or large cist. These barrows are sited beside the great ridgeway through Cornwall, followed by many parish boundaries.

17. The Hurlers (Stone Circles), St Cleer
Bronze Age
SX: 258714

Approach from Liskeard from the B3254 by the road through St Cleer to the Cheesewring village.

A group of three stone circles in an approximate line between the Cheesewring village and the Cheesewring (a natural pile of rocks). Each is over 30 metres in diameter and at present they contain nine, seventeen and sixteen stones (from south to north). A recumbent stone is near the middle of the central circle. The southern circle has been damaged by a cart track, but the others are more complete. All the stones are of shaped granite and have been designed so that their tops are approximately level. There are two standing stones called the Pipers, about 120 metres south-west of the central circle.

18. Lanyon Quoit, Madron
Neolithic
SW: 430337

Situated immediately N of road between Madron and Morvah.

This is possibly the best-known and most readily accessible of the burial chambers in west Cornwall. The covering slab fell in 1815 and was re-erected in 1824, probably not quite accurately. The cover is supported by three upright slabs, but there were probably originally four, creating a rectangular burial chamber. This seems to lie at the north end of a long barrow some 25–27 metres by 12 metres.

19. Men-an-Tol, Madron

Neolithic
SW: 427349

Along path leading NE from road across Bosullow Common.

This alignment consists of three stones placed at present in a straight line. The central stone is pierced by a perfectly circular hole made by working from both sides. It is believed that at least one of the stones has been repositioned within the last two centuries. It has been suggested that the holed stone was the porthole entrance of a burial chamber but there is no proof of this: indeed there are other holed stones in Cornwall which almost certainly have other origins. Folklore connected with the site includes the passing of children through the hole as a cure for rickets and adults as a cure for the ague!

20. Merry Maidens stone circle, St Buryan

Bronze Age
SW: 433245

Just S of the B3315 and W of Lamorna valley.

This stone circle is known also as the Dawns Men (the Stone Dance) and the two stones 0.4 km to the north-east are called the Pipers, and one to the west the Fiddler, from the local tradition of nineteen maidens having been turned into stone for dancing on a Sunday to the accompaniment of the two pipers and the fiddler. The circle is in excellent condition and still comprises nineteen standing stones each between 0.9 and 1.2 metres high, the diameter of this perfect circle being 23.8 metres. It is in a grass field entered by footpath from the road at 432245. The Tregiffian entrance grave is on the edge of the road close by: it is kerbed, with a burial chamber (see no. 31, below). In the hedge at SW: 429244 is the Goon Rith standing stone.

Although children were once passed through the holed stone at Men-an-Tol as a cure for rickets, the site may originally have formed part of a neolithic burial chamber. (L. V. Grinsell)

The Merry Maidens stone circle near St Buryan consists of nineteen upright stones, each about a metre high. (J. Dyer)

21. Mulfra Quoit, Madron
Neolithic
SW: 452353

By footpath off road between Penzance and Porthmeor from 454356, about 450 metres up a hill.

This burial chamber consists of a cover slab resting on three upright slabs and sloping to the west, where there was probably originally a fourth upright slab. There are traces of a covering barrow, perhaps round, about 12 metres in diameter.

22. Nine Maidens, St Columb Major
Bronze Age
SX: 937676

From the A39 at 934676 there is a footpath leading straight to the site about 270 metres to E.

This is the most westerly stone row in England. Of nine original quartz stones, five are still more or less complete and standing; one is recumbent; stumps of two others are still visible; but the southern stone has been largely broken up although its stump may still be in place. A tenth stone between numbers 7 and 8 has been added in modern times. There does not appear (as with some of the stone rows on Dartmoor) to be any solar or lunar orientation, or to be any associated round barrow.

23. Pelynt round barrows
Bronze Age
SW: 200544

Turn from the B3359 at Pelynt on to road to S; the barrows are 800 metres S of the village.

A notable group of ten round barrows in a field called Five Barrow Field, which was arable when last visited. They range between 12 and 24 metres in diameter and between 0.15 and 1.2 metres in height. Some of them, opened in 1830 and 1845, contained cremations, one with an ogival bronze dagger, one with a greenstone macehead, and a third is believed to have contained the hilt of a late Mycenean short sword, now in the Royal Cornwall Museum. It is probably of the thirteenth or twelfth century BC.

24. Rillaton barrow, Linkinhorne
Bronze Age
SX: 260719

The site can be approached from the B3254 out of Liskeard through St Cleer, which enables Trethevy Quoit and the Hurlers stone circles to be visited as well. The barrow is about 800 metres walk from Cheesewring village.

A notable round barrow 36 metres in diameter and 2.4 metres high, with a large cavity in the top, situated just north of the Hurlers. On the east side of the mound is a stone-lined grave 2.2 metres long, 1.2 metres wide and 0.9 metre high, slightly above ground level. This grave was opened in 1818 and in it were found a human skeleton (perhaps extended) with a handled corrugated gold beaker of possibly Mycenean technique but south-western bell-beaker shape, remains of a pottery vessel which may or may not have contained the gold beaker, a bronze grooved ogival dagger, 'some pieces of ivory', and 'a few glass beads' which might have been faience. The gold beaker is closely paralleled by an earthenware handled food-vessel from Balmuick, Perthshire. The beaker was lost for many years, until Christopher Hawkes tracked it down to Buckingham Palace, where King George V was using it for storing his collar studs! Both the gold beaker and bronze dagger are in the British Museum.

25. Rocky Valley labyrinth carvings, Tintagel

Bronze Age or later?
SX: 073893

By footpath N from the B3263 at 072891 about 1.6 km E of Tintagel. The carvings are just E of a ruined mill.

These two small rock carvings on the cliff-like valley wall are of uncertain date. They are scheduled under the Ancient Monuments Acts as probably bronze age; but similar labyrinth designs are known to have been made at other periods including the middle ages and later, a circumstance which adds to their interest in this setting, which is among the most beautiful in south-western Britain.

26. Rough Tor area, St Breward

Neolithic to Iron Age
SX: 141815

Minor road signposted 'Rough Tor' E from Camelford at SX: 110839 to car park after 3.5 km. Part National Trust.

A number of roughly oval enclosures with hut circles around their perimeters lie at the south-west end of Rough Tor, midway between the stream and the hilltop. The enclosures, which were probably paddocks, are often linked to one another by stone 'walls' with lynchets and tracks amongst them. Stones have been cleared from fields in prehistoric times and piled in lines along their boundaries.

Between the two rock outcrops (and utilising them) on the summit of the Tor, a small walled enclosure was constructed. On the west two lines of stone walls can be traced with two entrances, but on the more precipitous eastern side little remains of any artificial defences, which could be as early as the neolithic. Round house platforms exist inside the enclosure. Evidence of the medieval Chapel of St Michael can be traced with difficulty inside a ruined bronze age cairn on the summit of Rough Tor.

27. The Rumps, Pentire Head, Polzeath

Iron Age
SW: 934810

Turn off the B3314 N of St Minver and continue W through Pentireglaze to Pentire Farm and then walk about 800 metres.

This magnificently situated cliff castle encloses just over 2.4 hectares and is bounded on its south side by three ramparts and ditches. The modern path passes through the original entrances, which were lined with timber and dry stone walls. A number of huts were found in the hollow behind Rumps Point, and at the back of the rampart. The site was excavated between 1963 and 1967 and produced fragments of cordoned urns of north-west French type common in the first centuries BC and AD, as well as pieces of wine amphorae of western Mediterranean types, implying the import of wine. The site is National Trust property and under grass.

28. Stripple Stones, Blisland   Neolithic or Bronze Age
SX: 144752

Take minor road from the A30 at 136737 and walk up path from 129748 passing the Trippet Stones and buildings on the left.

    On the slope of Hawk's Tor is an embanked enclosure with an internal ditch 68 metres in diameter. Inside it is an irregular circle of fifteen (formerly twenty-eight) granite blocks, only four of which are still standing. Almost at the centre is a single recumbent stone. The ditch, which excavation in 1905 showed to be very irregular, is broken by a single entrance on the west-southwest, facing towards the Trippet Stones. This is the only example of a circle-henge in the south-west peninsula.

29. Treen (Treryn) Dinas, Treen   Iron Age
SW: 397222

Approach by footpath from Treen 'to Treen cliff and Logan Rock'.

    This is among the finest of the Cornish cliff castles. With its surroundings, it is owned by the National Trust. The headland containing the logan rock is defended first of all by a bold rampart with ditch on the north and between this and the logan rock are two possible hut sites. Just north of the isthmus are two massive ramparts (probably originally three) with ditch on the north, and a little further north, on the edge of the National Trust boundary, is an even more massive rampart with ditch on the north.

The National Trust owns Treen Dinas, one of the finest of the Cornish iron age cliff castles. (L. V. Grinsell)

30. Tregeare Rounds, St Kew

Iron Age
SX: 033800

Between Port Isaac and St Teath. Approach from the B3314 by gate S of the road at 032800.

This is a fine and typical multiple-enclosure hillslope earthwork of a type characteristic of the south-west of England. The innermost enclosure is bounded by a bank with inner and outer ditch. On the south-east side there are two added enclosures each comprising a massive rampart with outer ditch. There is an entrance at the south-east through a kind of corridor linking the two added enclosures. The site has yielded middle iron age pottery. The land usage is normally pasture.

31. Tregiffian, St Buryan

Neolithic
SW: 431244

On the S side of the B3315 road from Newlyn to Land's End, 220 metres W of Merry Maidens.

This once circular barrow has been cut in half by the road. Its 17 metre diameter is defined by its stone kerb. Inside is a south-facing burial chamber 4.6 metres long, 2 metres wide and 1 metre high. Its walls are composed of stone uprights and coursed walling, and it is roofed with four capstones. The outer face of the eastern wallstone of the chamber was decorated with a number of deep cup marks. It has been removed to the Royal Cornwall Museum in Truro for safety, and a concrete replica now stands in its place. Excavations in the early 1970s uncovered two pits in the chamber floor, one of which held a collared urn containing a cremation burial, and the other pieces of an urn, showing that the tomb had been reused in the bronze age.

The burial chamber of Trethevy Quoit is the largest in Cornwall and stands some 2.7 metres high. (J. Dyer)

32. Trencrom, Ludgvan

Iron Age
SW: 517363

This National Trust property can be reached by footpaths from minor roads to N and S.

This granite hilltop is capped with a small oval hillfort of 0.4 hectare. The single drystone wall incorporates natural rock outcrops along with massive stone slabs to spectacular effect. Entrances on the east and west lead to an overgrown interior which contains at least a dozen stone hut foundations. Pottery from the site has been dated to the second century BC.

33. Trethevy Quoit, St Cleer

Neolithic
SX: 259688

Approach from Liskeard by the turning W off the B3254 through St Cleer. It is well signposted.

This is the largest and amongst the finest burial chambers in Cornwall. It is dominated by its massive sloping cover-slab, which is 3.7 metres long and stands about 2.7 metres high on its eastern side. This stone has a hole cut through its north-eastern corner. Seven large slabs form a high rectangular burial chamber 2 metres by 1.5 metres, which is divided into two parts. The inner area is almost completely sealed off, except for a small opening in the corner of the doorstone at the eastern end. This is just big enough for a body (alive or dead) to pass through. There is a forecourt in front of the entrance stone, created by two side stones jutting forward to the east. Although there is little trace of a surrounding mound today, W. C. Lukis recorded in the nineteenth century that it was oval in shape and measured 7 metres by 6 metres.

34. Trevelgue Head, Newquay

Iron Age to Dark Age
SX: 827630

By footpath W of the B3276, just N of St Columb Porth.

This cliff castle lies partly on the mainland, and partly on an island, linked by a footbridge. There are four ramparts to the east and two to the west of the bridge. Excavation in the 1930s uncovered the foundations of a number of huts, including one 14 metres in diameter, which had a ring of seven or eight post holes around a central hearth. Pottery ranged in date from the third century BC to the sixth century AD. A number of hut platforms and field banks can be traced on the island.

35. Trippet Stones, Blisland

Bronze Age
SX: 131750

Take byroad from A30 at 136737 and walk up path from 129748.

This impressive true stone circle is 33 metres in diameter and still contains twelve stones, eight standing and four fallen, out of an original twenty-eight. Most of the stones are roughly rectangular blocks, about 1.5 metres high. Near the centre is a modern boundary stone. As so often, Cornish folklore records that the stones were once maidens who were petrified for 'tripping lightly' on the Sabbath.

36. Zennor Quoit

Neolithic
SW: 469380

On hill S of the B3306, 1.6 km SE of Zennor; reached by a footpath from 467387.

This fine burial chamber is unusual in having a façade of two large slabs at the east end, a small antechamber, and to the west a chamber of four stones supporting a cover-slab. It was excavated in 1881 when the finds included neolithic pottery, some of which has been claimed to have affinities with pottery from Lough Crew in Ireland, and a perforated whetstone. There are traces of a mound which appears to have been circular and about 12 metres in diameter.

ISLES OF SCILLY

37. Bant's Carn and Halangy Down, St Mary's   Neolithic and Iron Age

Carn at SV: 911123

On Halangy Down, St Mary's; near N end of golf course. English Heritage.

This Scillonian chambered cairn or entrance grave is about 8 metres in diameter, and stands on a damaged low-walled platform, originally 12 metres in diameter. An unroofed passage 4.5 metres long and 1 metre wide leads through the platform to where a substantial jamb-stone marks the entrance to the burial chamber. This is 5 metres long, 1.5 metres wide and 1.5 metres high, and is roofed with four large capstones, the outermost weighing about 11 tonnes. When the tomb was excavated by George Bonsor in 1900 he found four piles of cremated human bones at the back of the chamber. In the passageway through the outer platform were pieces of neolithic and bronze age pottery, since lost.

Halangy Down (SU: 910124). Below the Carn are the remains of an iron age and Romano-British settlement, consisting of oval hut foundations, each about 7.5 metres in diameter with a single doorway, and a courtyard house, all built of granite blocks. Traces of small gardens and pathways can be made out. The settlement was modified many times and was probably in use for about 500 years, perhaps by the same extended family. There are contemporary field systems and round houses on the surrounding hillside.

Halangy Lower is a ruined entrance grave about 50 metres north of the settlement, by the lynchet at the bottom of the hill. Its burial chamber is 3 metres long and 0.5 metre wide, with two cover-slabs still in position. There is no record of its contents.

Bant's Carn entrance grave on St Mary's in the Isles of Scilly. (Paul Ashbee)

38. Cruther's Hill, St Martin's
Neolithic
SV: 929152

On the southernmost tip of the island, S of Higher Town.

There are barrows on top of each of the three hills running from north to south. The northern is about 6 metres in diameter, with a burial chamber 5.5 metres long penetrating it from the south-west. There are traces of kerb stones that may have retained the barrow mound.

The central hill is crowned by an entrance grave 8 metres in diameter, with a burial chamber on the east 4.6 metres long. Like many of the graves in the Isles of Scilly, it is narrow at its entrance, 0.9 metre, and widens at its inner end to 1.4 metres. There are two round barrows on the southern hill, one with an exposed burial chamber, the other ruined.

39. Giant's Castle, St Mary's
Iron Age
SV: 924101

Footpath from Old Town, 800 metres E along coastal path.

A small rocky promontory is cut off by four curving lines of stone ramparts and rock-cut ditches. The inner rampart incorporates natural outcrops, and all the ramparts have been severely robbed, perhaps for building Old Castle. Duck-stamped iron age pottery has reputedly been found here.

40. Innisidgen entrance graves, St Mary's
Neolithic
SV: 921127

The road over Helvear Down passes close by. English Heritage.

This is an entrance grave 8 metres in diameter with an entrance passage from the south-east in remarkably good condition. It has a surrounding platform as at Bant's Carn, and a burial chamber 4.5 metres long and 1.5 metres high covered by five granite roof slabs. Lower down the hill is the **Lower Innisidgen** entrance grave. It is 6 metres in diameter, with a trapezoidal burial chamber partially covered by two surviving roof slabs. The entrance faces south. Most of the surrounding kerb is missing.

41. Porth Hellick Down entrance grave, St Mary's
Neolithic
SV: 928108

Approached from road skirting E part of the island.

There are seven entrance graves on the Down. The largest and most impressive, the 'Great Tomb', has been heavily restored. It is 12 metres in diameter and 1.5 metres high. At its centre is a burial chamber 3 metres long and 1 metre high, walled with large upright stones, and covered by four massive capstones. It is entered at an angle along an unroofed passage 4.2 metres long. An outer kerb ring 17 metres in diameter was destroyed by the former Ministry of Works whilst restoring the site! When it was excavated by George Bonsor in 1899, most of the contents had already been removed. Pieces of late bronze age pottery suggest that the tomb may have been reused at that time.

A little over 100 metres south on the Down are other entrance graves and cairns, all in varying states of decay.

CUMBRIA
(Map on page 242)

1. Asby Common
Iron Age
NY: 673109

Take minor road SW of Great Asby. Follow footpath to SE at 668115 to Muddy Gill. The settlement is to the right of this path.

This triangular enclosure covers about 0.5 hectare. It is surrounded by a stone bank. Inside the inner face of the bank is a series of hut circles with a probable original entrance on the south.

2. Barnscar, Muncaster

Bronze Age and Iron Age
SD: 135958

A bridlepath leads E from A595(T) at 114952 along a steady climb to Birkby Fell.

This group of huts and cairns has not yet been scientifically excavated although nineteenth-century digs in some of the latter reportedly produced 'urns'. The cairns, some 360 in number, follow the ridge for 730 metres. They are 1.5 to 7.5 metres across and 0.3 to 0.6 metre high. On the west side of the cairn group are six ruined hut sites covering 0.3 hectare. Twelve cairns were dug in 1957 but proved sterile. The same year one circular hut site was cleared, revealing a central hearth.

3. Birkrigg Common, Urswick and Aldingham

Bronze Age and Iron Age
(see below)

Take minor road W from A5087 at 296737. Circle visible to N after 0.5 km.

1. Druid's Temple stone circle (SD: 292739). This double circle consists of two non-concentric rings of stones, the inner containing ten stones and a diameter of 9 metres, the outer fifteen stones and a diameter of 26 metres. None of the stones is above 0.6 metre high. Inside the inner circle were five cremations, one in an inverted collared urn.

2. At 282740 is a 'platform' cairn, 15 metres across and 0.3 metre high, with a level top. Large limestone blocks are visible around the edges. Ten cremations were found in the mound.

3. At 286742 are four diminutive barrows, one showing possible traces of a ditch. They have all been excavated without success.

4. At 285744 is a mound 12 metres across and nearly 0.9 metre high. A large angled stone at the centre suggests the capstone of a possible rifled cist.

5. A further mound at 289743 is 12 metres across and 0.6 metre high. It contained three skeletons and a bronze awl, and near the east side deposits of black earth covered by stone slabs, the whole of this area being surrounded by a circle of boulders and buried by the mound.

6. At 288746 is a mound 8 by 9 metres and 0.6 metre high. In the north-east area were seven cremations, three in cordoned urns.

7. North-east and south-west of the above barrow are two almost confluent enclosures. The north-east one is roughly oval and up to 90 metres across. It has an inturned entrance on the east, and the surrounding bank is 0.6 metre high and 3 to 4.5 metres wide. Inside the entrance three depressions probably represent hut sites. The south-west enclosure is oval and much larger than the first. It has an entrance at the north-west, but its bank is now very slight. These enclosures probably represent a fortified homestead and cattle pound of iron age date.

4. Blakeley Raise, Ennerdale

Bronze Age
NY: 060140

Beside the minor road 2 km S of Ennerdale Bridge.

This attractively sited ring of twelve stones was partially re-erected by Dr Quine in 1925. The circle is 17 metres in diameter and the stones are regularly spaced about 4 metres apart. The gap on the south may be an entrance, though it is reported that stones were removed in the past.

5. Broomrigg circles, Ainstable and Cumwhitton

Bronze Age
NY: 548468

Take minor road NE of Ainstable. The sites are to the S of the road in the dense Broomrigg Plantation. These are only for enthusiasts!

This group contains three stone circles and two smaller settings of boulders 3.6 metres across (tent weights according to the excavator). Inside one of the circles was a series of cremations, one in a collared urn.

6. Burwens, Crosby Ravensworth
Iron Age or Roman
NY: 622123

Take minor road S from Crosby Ravensworth and turn right along track to Crosby Lodge. The site is to the N of the track 180 metres NE of the Lodge.

A rectangular wall encloses a farmstead of about 0.4 hectare, containing a series of hut foundations. An entrance exists on the west side with a track leading south-east from it through the settlement. Several huts have courtyards, some detached, some built against the main enclosure wall. To the north and east are field systems covering 1.4 hectares.

7. Casterton circle
Bronze Age
SD: 640799

Take A683 N from Kirkby Lonsdale, and turn E on minor road at 622792. Track leads N off this at 641794. The circle is to the W of the track, N of a small plantation.

This circle has a diameter of 18 metres and stands on a flattened mound or platform. There are twenty uprights, none more than 0.6 metre high and suggesting perhaps the kerb of a destroyed cairn.

8. Castle How, Wythop
Iron Age
NY: 202308

Immediately S of the A66 on the minor road to Pheasant Inn.

Possessing fine views overlooking Bassenthwaite Lake, this hillfort encloses 0.6 hectare. On the north and south, steep hillsides afford sufficient protection. Below the outer bank the ground has been artificially steepened. At the east are two banks, ditches and counterscarp banks. The inner ditch is vertical-sided, flat-bottomed and 1.8 metres deep. An original entrance exists in this side. Some shaped rampart stones have been thought to suggest occupation of the site in Roman times, perhaps by natives building in the pre-Roman tradition.

9. Castlerigg circle, Keswick
Bronze Age
NY: 292236

Take signposted minor road E from Keswick. The circle is at the junction of this road with a minor road S. Small lay-by. National Trust; open at all times.

This fine circle of thirty-eight upright stones is pear-shaped in plan, with a diameter of 33 metres. Within the circle is a rectangular stone setting of ten uprights, touching its circumference at the east. A gap 3.3 metres across at the north may be an entrance. The equinoctial sun rises over Threlkeld Knott, a hill 3500 metres to the east, and is likely to be significant in the siting of the circle. It is believed to be one of the earliest European circles.

10. Castlesteads, Yanwath and Eamont Bridge
Iron Age
NY: 518252

Take minor road from Askham to Yanwath. Turn E to Lowclose at 514252. A footpath leads E to the site.

This diminutive defended site consists of an area 0.1 hectare in extent enclosed by three concentric banks and two ditches. The interior is divided into a group of small enclosures. The defences on the east have been destroyed. The site has affinities with Yanwath Wood to the north (see no. 51, below).

11. Crosby Garrett settlement
Iron Age and Roman
NY: 719064

Take metalled track leading NE from Newbiggin on A685. Follow to 719061 then cross disused railway. The settlement is a short distance N.

The settlement consists of three villages bounded by their field systems, and together covering 65 hectares. The main village, on the south-east slope of Begin

The northern sector of the Castlerigg stone circle near Keswick. Measuring 33 metres in diameter, the whole circle contains some thirty-eight stones. (J. Dyer)

Hill, consists of a series of hut enclosures and associated paddocks on the south and west sides. On the south side of the village is an oblong building with stone door-posts *in situ*. A second village lies 640 metres north-east with similar hut groups and paddocks, but only half the size of the first. 275 metres north-east of this is a third village, comparable in size with the second. The three villages and their field systems are all part of a composite whole, but as yet no excavations have been undertaken and nothing is known of the people occupying the sites.

12. Dunmallard hillfort, Dacre
Iron Age
NY: 468246

On a wooded hilltop at the NE end of Ullswater, NE of the junction of the A592 and B5320.

This oval hillfort enjoys fine views over Ullswater. It stands on a conical hill with steep sides and encloses about 0.4 hectare, defended by a bank, ditch and traces of a counterscarp bank. A probable entrance exists at the south-west.

13. Elva stone circle, Setmurthy
Bronze Age
NY: 176317

Take A66 E from Cockermouth and fork left on minor road. The circle is 0.5 km along the track from Elva Plain Farm (175314).

There are fifteen stones in this circle, the largest 1 metre high, forming a not very impressive ring 35 metres across. To the south-west was a single outlier. The original ring probably contained about thirty stones.

14. Eskdale Moor circles
Bronze Age
NY: 173025

A very steep footpath N from Boot with a gradient of 1 in 5.

Five stone circles can be seen in the area, all badly damaged and containing cairns. Approached from the south the Brat's Hill circle is about 30 metres across and consists of forty-one stones, mostly fallen. There is a single outlier to the north-west. Inside the circle are the remains of five small cairns, all kerbed, and each about 7.5 metres across. The cairns were dug in 1827; each contained a cremation in a cist. The two White Moss stone circles, both containing single cairns, and 15 metres across, can be seen 90 metres to the north-west.

A further 400 metres north on Low Longrigg are two paired circles, one with nine stones and 15 metres across, which contains a single cairn, and the other 22 metres in diameter, enclosing two cairns.

15. Ewe Close, Crosby Ravensworth

Iron Age and Roman
NY: 609134

Approach from Low Dalebanks Farm, taking path across stream, through gate ahead, and following field wall on right to hilltop. Site in field beyond.

This is a native settlement shown by excavation to have been occupied in the Roman period, but almost certainly of late iron age foundation. The site consists of grassed banks and hollows which are extremely confusing. The main settlement, with a large central hut (15 metres in diameter) and several smaller ones, is on the north-west. Numerous gardens and stock enclosures can be detected, and a large banked rectangular field lies on the upper slope to the south. A Roman road passes 18 metres to the west of the settlement.

16. Gamelands stone circle, Orton

Bronze Age
NY: 640082

Take minor road from Orton to Raisbeck. At 639079 a track leads N. The circle is on the right of this road.

This circle has a diameter of 42 metres. Originally about forty stones stood on a low bank, but now many have fallen, and none projects more than a metre above the ground. There may have been a central burial cist, destroyed about 1862.

17. Giant's Grave, Kirksanton

Bronze Age
SD: 137811

On the SW side of Kirksanton.

The monument is part of the Lacra complex (no. 31). It consists of two upright stones 3 metres and 2.4 metres high respectively. The larger stone bears a cup mark, 7.6 cm across and 3 cm deep.

18. Gretigate stone circles, Gosforth

Bronze Age
NY: 058036

Via bridlepath leading W from the village. The sites are N of the path 530 metres W of Gosforth.

The site contains three circles and nine small cairns. The south circle is 32 metres across. The north-west one is 22 metres across with a low central cairn. The third circle is immediately north of the second. It is 7.2 metres across and also encloses a small cairn. Excavation of the two latter cairns proved inconclusive.

19. Grey Croft circle, Seascale

Bronze Age
NY: 034024

Follow track from golf club house towards Seascale How, and walk round edge of golf course. Easily seen beyond barbed-wire barrier.

The present circle of ten standing stones, about 25 metres in diameter, was restored in 1949 when the stones buried in the nineteenth century were located and re-erected. Originally they numbered twelve. Their present heights above ground are 1.2 to 2 metres. A low oval mound at the centre produced burnt bone fragments and part of a jet ring. Beside one of the stones was found a partly ground stone axe of Langdale rock. There is a low outlying stone 20 metres to the north. The whole site is dominated by the adjoining Sellafield nuclear reprocessing plant.

20. Gunnerkeld circle, Rosgill

Bronze Age
NY: 568178

By track passing Gunnerkeld Farm from 572184.

Sometimes called Shap Central ring, it can be fleetingly seen from the southbound carriageway of the M6! It consists of two concentric ovals of recumbent stones which surround a low mound and burial cist. Only one stone remains upright in the inner ring, which is 16 metres in diameter. In the outer ring, which is 36 metres across, three stones are still standing.

21. Heathwaite Fell settlement, Kirkby Ireleth

Iron Age
SD: 251880

The enclosures and cairns are situated between two ungated roads, S of the fork at 248886.

This settlement consists of a complex of seven conjoined enclosures of irregular shape, and defined by drystone walls 0.9 to 2.2 metres thick. The sites had an entrance on the south. Numerous small cairns in the vicinity suggest clearance heaps.

22. Helm Hill, Natland and Stainton

Iron Age
SD: 531887

SE of Natland village, E of the A65(T).

This small, oval hillfort is defended by two banks and a medial ditch, best preserved on the north and south. To the east the ground slopes steeply and no protective works are visible.

23. Holborn Hill, Great Asby

Iron Age
NY: 682123

Via footpath S from the village.

This settlement consists of a stone bank enclosing a roughly oval area of about 135 metres diameter. Inside is a series of paddocks. The site has suffered damage, particularly on the north side.

24. Hollin Stump cairn, Great Asby

Bronze Age
NZ: 652117

Beside minor road from Great Asby to Bank Moor. The cairn is 200 metres to the S of the road.

This cairn is 21 metres across and 1.5 metres high. In the nineteenth century a crouched skeleton was found by Canon Greenwell in a stone cist. There are two more cairns at 647119. Both contained scattered human bones.

25. Holme Bank enclosure, Urswick

Iron Age
SD: 276734

W of the minor road from Scales to Ulverston.

This five-sided enclosure measures 18 by 49 metres and consists of an earth and stone bank, revetted on both sides by large upright slabs, up to 4.2 metres wide and 0.6 to 0.9 metre high, with an entrance on the east. A slight ditch is visible on the east and south-east. Inside are traces of two huts 4.5 to 7.5 metres in diameter, and a cross-bank, perhaps for livestock, on the north. 24 metres north-west of the enclosure is another hut site, with a bank and ditch round its north side.

26. Howarcles, Crosby Ravensworth

Iron Age
NZ: 627132

Immediately to the E of the minor road leading S from Crosby Ravensworth, 400 metres SE from Woodfoot House.

A series of oval and sub-rectangular huts and paddocks lies either side of the road and covers an area of about 0.6 hectare. A very large oval hut can be seen at the north-east.

27. Hugill
Iron Age
NZ: 437009

Take minor road NW from A591 at Ings. Turn N to High Borrans. The site lies to the E.

This 0.8 hectare settlement is surrounded by a modern wall, built on the foundations of the original enclosing bank. There are three entrances, on the west, at the western end of the east side and near the northern end of the east side. The eastern area of the settlement consists of a series of paddocks and terraces, the western area a group of circular hut-like enclosures.

28. Kemp Howe, Shap
Bronze Age
NY: 567133

Between the A6(T) and the railway line, which partly overlies it.

Lying about 1 km east of the river Lowther is the badly damaged Kemp Howe circle. Only six of its great Shap granite boulders survive, all fallen and about 2.5 metres long. They once formed a circle about 14 metres in diameter. The fragmentary remains of a stone avenue that once ran for at least 3 km north-west from the circle, passing the Skellaw Hill barrow (556155) and the massive Thunder Stone (552157), can still be seen. Avenue stones can be found near Shap village at 562147, 555153, 559150 (the Goggleby Stone) and 558152 (Asper's Field). The latter two stones carry minor rock carvings. The Goggleby Stone has a cup mark on its north vertical face with an artificial circular depression above it. There is a cup-and-ring mark on top of the Asper's Field stone.

29. King Arthur's Round Table, Eamont Bridge
Neolithic
NY: 523284

King Arthur's Round Table is above the river Lowther, in an angle formed by the A6 and B5320, 2 km SE of Penrith.

King Arthur's Round Table is a damaged henge monument about 90 metres in diameter with two original entrances, of which only that on the south-east survives. It has an external bank 1.5 metres high surrounding an internal quarry ditch. The site was badly disturbed in the nineteenth century when an attempt was made to turn it into a pleasure garden. A low mound on the central plateau may be fairly recent. In the seventeenth century two standing stones were recorded outside the north entrance. Excavations in 1937 and 1939 showed the ditch to have a flat floor, and dimensions of 9 metres across and 1.4 metres deep. In the central plateau was a cremation trench 2.4 metres long, 0.8 metre wide and 0.25 metre deep, containing cremated bones. It was covered by a stone structure, too damaged for interpretation and probably not ancient.

75 metres to the south was the site of the Little Round Table, probably another henge monument of comparable size, destroyed in the early nineteenth century.

30. Kirkby Moor, Kirkby Ireleth
Bronze Age
SD: 251827

Take minor road from Beck Side to Chapels. At 241831 a bridleway leads E across Kirkby Moor. The ring cairn lies a short distance S of this, the round cairn a short distance N.

This ring cairn has a diameter of 23 metres. The bank is 1.8 metres wide and 0.6 metre high, and the inner bank shows the remains of a revetment circle of large stones. There is an entrance on the south-east. 30 metres to the north-east are three pairs of stones, each about 0.6 metre high, probably representing part of an avenue.

At 251830 is a round cairn 24 metres across and 0.9 to 1.2 metres high. On the south-west, a stone cist (still visible) originally contained a cremation.

31. Lacra stone circles, Millom   Bronze Age
SD: 150814 (first circle)

Take A593 E from Whicham, then minor road to Po House, and track SSW uphill for 1.5 km.

There are the remnants of five circles and two possible stone avenues here. The first circle is 15 metres across and has six surviving stones, two placed close together facing east. The second circle is to the south and again has six stones, and a diameter of 14.5 metres. It once contained eleven uprights. A low central mound once had a kerbed ring of stones 4.2 metres across placed on it and contained a cremation. A third circle exists east-southeast of the second but only four stones remain, one 1.5 metres high. Originally it would have measured 18 metres across. Further east-southeast is a fourth circle and traces of two avenues. The avenues are irregular, confused by rock outcrops and almost impossible to find. The circle is about 18 metres across and has a ragged double line of stones running east-northeast from it. There is a large flat stone in the circle centre and a stone on the north side of the ring had collared-urn sherds by its base. 7.5 metres north-west of the fourth circle are traces of a further circle of six stones, 4.8 metres across, with a central stone. South-west of this are traces of a second avenue 15 metres wide and running west-southwest for 70 metres, although most of the stones on the north side are gone.

32. Leacet circle, Brougham   Bronze Age
NY: 563263

On S side of Leacet Plantation, N of minor road from Clifton Dykes to Cliburn.

This circle is 11 metres across and consists of seven stones, the retaining kerb of

One of the spirally carved stones at the ruined Little Meg stone cairn circle, near Glassonby in Cumbria. (S. W. Feather)

Long Meg (left) and Her Daughters: the largest stone circle in northern England. (Joshua Pollard)

a destroyed round cairn. A nineteenth-century excavation produced a cremation. Certain stones of the kerb had pottery vessels placed at their bases, including collared urns, a food vessel and a miniature cup.

33. Little Meg and Glassonby cairn circles
Bronze Age
NY: 577375 and 573393

Little Meg is forward (W) beside hedgerow, at right angles to the Little Salkeld to Gamblesby road. The Glassonby cairn circle is 2 km N of Little Meg and N of the road from Glassonby to Kirkoswald.

Little Meg is a circle of eleven stones, originally surrounding a cairn which covered a cist containing a cremation in an urn. Two of the stones are decorated by cup marks and spiral carvings.

Only twenty-nine kerb-stones survive in Glassonby cairn circle, forming an oval ring. Excavation in 1900 revealed an empty burial cist at the south-east side. Carved on the most southerly stone of a run of six on the east side is a very feint set of overlapping concentric circles and chevrons.

34. Long Meg and Her Daughters, Hunsonby
Bronze Age
NY: 571373

Take minor road from Little Salkeld to Gamblesby. A metalled track at 570365 leads N direct to the site.

This circle is an oval setting of fifty-one stones (twenty-seven still upright and each about 3 metres long) and perhaps originally numbering seventy. It measures 110 by 93 metres. Long Meg is an outlying block of red sandstone 18 metres south-west, 3.6 metres high, and bearing a cup-and-ring mark, spiral and concentric circles carved on its north-east face. It is believed to be earlier than the stone circle. Two entrance stones can be seen at the south-west between Long Meg and the circle (her daughters), and two enormous stones mark the east and west cardinal points. It seems that this circle was once enclosed within a bank, best preserved to the west. Aerial photography has revealed a large enclosure adjoining the circle on its northern side, and encircling the farm. It is not visible on the ground and its age is unknown. Smaller enclosures have been noted to the east and west.

35. Lowick ring cairn, Kirkby Ireleth
Bronze Age
SD: 279843

To the E of the minor road leading S from Wood Gate.

This ring cairn is 30 metres across and its bank is up to 2.7 metres wide. There was an inner ring of retaining stones, of which only five survive *in situ*. An entrance exists on the south-west.

36. Mayburgh henge, Eamont Bridge
Neolithic
NY: 519285

In an angle between the B5320 and the M6 motorway.

A slip road leads to this imposing tree-crowned henge monument. It consists of a bank, 110 metres in diameter, composed of grey, water-worn boulders from the nearby river Lowther. It is broken by a single entrance that faces east towards King Arthur's Round Table (no. 29), 300 metres away. The bank rises on either side of the entrance and (although unexcavated) seems in places to have been built as a series of connected cells (like the destroyed Hazleton North long barrow in Oxfordshire). The internal height of the bank varies from 2.5 to 5 metres, and it must be significant that when it is viewed from the north it appears to be quite horizontal. Of the four stones that stood in the centre, only one, 2.8 metres high, survives. The others were destroyed with gunpowder about 1720. It is possible that four other stones once flanked the entrance.

37. Mecklin Park cairn, Irton with Saunton
Bronze Age
NY: 126019

Take minor road E from Santon Bridge. At 122013 a footpath leads NE of Irton Pike. The cairn lies just N of the footpath E of a plantation.

This cairn is about 9 metres across and 0.9 metre high and its revetment kerb is still visible. Excavation produced no burials, but a single sherd of corded-beaker pottery was found.

38. Moor Divock, Askham Fell
Bronze Age
NY: 496216

Approached along unfenced road from Helton to 497214.

A broad path north-west across the moor passes several sites, with magnificent views towards the Ede valley and Ullswater.

The Cop Stone (496216) is a glacial erratic some 1.2 metres high, which seems to have a slight surrounding bank some 21 metres in diameter.

To the north-west is a barrow (494220) with eleven standing stones in a circle upon it. Excavation by Simpson and Greenwell in the nineteenth century found a central pit 0.6 metre deep, containing ashes and a broken pot. The barrow also contained a food vessel covered in herringbone decoration.

Close by are a number of low cairns and scattered erratic stones that may once have formed part of stone rows. Close to the bridleway is a small compact barrow or hut circle with stones lining the interior.

At 489224 is the White Raise barrow with the remains of a rectangular cist 1.2 metres by 0.5 metre, which originally contained a contracted skeleton. Close by is an oval barrow with a large stone at its west end.

The track to the west leads through marshy ground to the Cockpit (Waverton), which might be either a stone circle or a ring cairn. Two concentric rings of stone 1.2 metres apart enclose an area 28 metres in diameter. There are three small mounds around the perimeter.

South of the Cockpit is a large row of cairns called Three Pow Raise, three of which were excavated in the nineteenth century with unknown results.

39. Mungrisdale cairns, Caldbeck

Bronze Age
NY: 353337

On lower hillslopes of Carrock Fell W of unfenced minor road from Mosedale to High Row.

This group contains over two hundred small cairns, including examples of ring cairns. One example of each type has been examined. The round cairn covered a cremation in a pit, but nothing was found in the ring cairn.

40. Raiset Pike long cairn, Crosby Garrett

Neolithic
NY: 683073

About 800 metres W of minor road from Little Asby to Newbiggin.

This badly damaged long cairn is 55 metres long and 18 metres wide at its broader south-east end. Excavations by Greenwell in the nineteenth century suggest that the cairn contained a mortuary building covering a cremation trench set transversely to the axis of the mound. The remains of at least six cremated bodies were found, bounded at one end by a standing stone 1.8 metres high, buried in the mass of the mound. Further, secondary burials, many of them children, were also discovered in the body of the cairn.

41. Reecastle Crag, Borrowdale

Iron Age
NY: 275175

On the top of Reecastle Crags, 400 metres E of minor road running S from B5289 at 269203. National Trust.

This 0.1 hectare fort is oval in plan and is defended by steep slopes on the west. On this side are the remains of triple banks, with a single rampart on the east. An entrance may have existed at the south.

42. Shoulthwaite hillfort, Castlerigg

Iron Age
NY: 300188

Take minor road along W side of Thirlmere lake. A path leads W to the site at 307191 just N of the road junction.

This fort is roughly circular in plan and covers about 0.2 hectare. It has one main bank, reinforced on the east side by a second rampart.

43. Sizergh settlement, Levens

Iron Age
SD: 495868

Take minor road NE from Levens. The sites are to the N of the road on Sizergh Fell.

The site consists of an oval embankment enclosure covering 0.2 hectare, with secondary enclosures to the south. Interior hollows may indicate the sites of huts. On the hilltop is a small round cairn, 7.5 metres across, which contained a collared urn. To the east a further cairn, 9 metres across and 0.9 metre high, covered five skeletons.

44. Skelmore Heads, Urswick

Neolithic
SD: 262744

Just N of minor road from Dalton-in-Furness to Little Urswick, about 400 metres NW of the latter.

This almost destroyed burial chamber consists of two large boulders supporting a capstone. The uprights are strengthened by packing stones. Further stones nearby and to the east were probably once part of the chamber.

45. Skirsgill Hill, Askham Fell

Iron Age
NY: 499233

Bridleway from Askham.

Two settlements with field systems stretch over some 12 hectares. One settlement

(497231) is roughly oval in shape and is enclosed by a strong bank, with traces of a ditch on the south side. There is one certain circular hut inside, as well as other possible oval structures. Disturbed ground and field systems separate it from the second settlement to the north-east at 499233, which contains two or three circular huts in their own enclosures. A long walled entrance trackway can be traced on the eastern side. To the west of this second settlement there are traces of a medieval farmstead which may cause some confusion.

46. Studfold Gate stone circle, Dean

Bronze Age
NY: 040224

A short distance N of the minor road from Pica to Ullock, NE of the Greyhound inn.

This circle is now incomplete and has a modern wall cutting across, incorporating one stone. Eleven others survive, some only 20 or 30 cm high.

47. Swinside stone circle, Millom

Bronze Age
SD: 172883

Take minor road N from A595 at 180865 to Crag Hall at 181874. A path leads NW from there. Walk of 1.3 km.

Sometimes known as Sunkenkirke, this fine circle is 29 metres across and consists of fifty-five stones with two outlying portal stones at the south-east, 2.7 metres apart, suggesting an entrance. Excavation has shown that the site had been levelled before erecting the stones, which are bedded in a layer of small packed pebbles. The tallest stone in the circle (2.3 metres high) stands at the north cardinal point. A sight line from the centre of the circle through the southernmost portal stones appears to mark midsummer sunrise.

48. Threlkeld Knott, St John's in the Vale

Bronze Age and Iron Age
NY: 330241

Follow footpath leading SE from Threlkeld former railway station.

This settlement includes five or more sub-rectangular enclosures with four or five hut circles among them, covering an area of 120 by 90 square metres. An original entrance can be seen on the north-west. The excavation of the largest hut showed it to have walls 1.5 metres thick and an internal diameter of 6 metres, with a south-eastern entrance. To the north and north-east of the settlement are at least thirty small cairns, averaging 6 to 7.5 metres across. Traces of charcoal found in several suggest that they are burial structures.

Looking north across the beautiful Swinside stone circle near Millom. The portalled entrance is on the extreme right. (Aubrey Burl)

49. Towtop Kirk, Bampton
Iron Age
NY: 494179
Take minor road W from Bampton to 494182. A footpath leads S to the site.

The settlement is encircled by an oval enclosure wall surrounding an area of 50 by 38 metres. At its centre is the outline of a U-shaped hut, with a second enclosure to the east. An entrance to the enclosure is visible at the north-west where there are traces of a second hut, obscured by later features.

50. Urswick Stone Walls, Urswick
Iron Age or Romano-British
SD: 260741
To the S of minor road from Dalton-in-Furness to Little Urswick, 800 metres NW of the latter.

Of the two enclosures here, the western is roughly oval, the south-eastern one rectangular. The former covers 0.6 hectare and is surrounded by a stone wall 3 to 3.6 metres across and now only 0.3 metre high. There is a south-eastern entrance, obscured by a modern field wall which passes through it. Inside there are a number of rectangular cattle paddocks, with walls 1.5 metres thick and comprising large upright or horizontal stones. Five hut circles, 6 to 9 metres across, are visible at the centre of the enclosure, all with east-facing entrances.

The south-eastern enclosure has a bank 4.5 to 6 metres across and 0.3 to 0.6 metre high, with an entrance at the south-east corner. The enclosures represent a family settlement and animal pound. North-west and north-east of the sites is an associated cultivation terrace 150 metres long.

51. Yanwath Wood, Yanwath
Iron Age
NY: 519260
Take footpath leading N through wood, starting a short distance E of Castlesteads (no. 10). The settlement lies N of the wood and W of the path.

This settlement is D-shaped and is associated with a ditch and bank forming the straight side to the D and running north to south for 230 metres. The site covers about 0.4 hectare and is protected by two banks and a ditch. There is a north-western entrance. Several small enclosures are visible inside the defences.

DERBYSHIRE
(Map on page 240)
1. Arbor Low and Gib Hill, Middleton
Neolithic and Bronze Age
SK: 160636
Via minor road (Long Rake) E of A515 at Parsley Hay. English Heritage signposted. Entrance fee at farm.

A fine example of a late neolithic ceremonial site of henge monument type. A circular rubble bank 2.1 metres high and 76 metres in diameter encloses a rock-cut ditch 9 metres wide and 1.8 metres deep from which the material for the bank was quarried. On the north and south the central plateau delineated by the ditch is interrupted by two entrance causeways providing access to the central area. Around the edge of the plateau is a circle of forty-six large recumbent limestones, with a further group of similar stones at the centre forming a 'cove'. A skeleton was found east of this cove during excavations in 1901–2 but its relationship to the henge is questionable. East of the south entrance a large round cairn 2.1 metres high and 21 metres across stands on the bank of the monument and is constructed of material robbed from the bank. Excavation of the cairn by Bateman in 1845 revealed a cist of limestones on the old ground surface, containing a cremation scattered on the floor, two food-vessels, a bone pin and a flint strike-a-light. These finds are in Sheffield City Museum. The cairn was probably erected because of Arbor Low's religious significance.

320 metres south-west of the henge is Gib Hill, a huge round cairn still 4.5 metres high despite numerous assaults on it in the past. It has the suggestion of a surrounding quarry ditch. Old excavation reports and visual examination suggest that the round cairn is superimposed on a pear-shaped long cairn, but this effect may be due to spoil-dumping during earlier diggings. In 1848 Bateman discovered a limestone cist just below the centre surface, containing a food-vessel with a cremation. The cist was removed by Bateman and placed in his garden at Lomberdale House. It was returned to Gib Hill in 1938. Only the cist lid can be seen in the top of the cairn today.

Over many centuries Arbor Low was probably the focus of a ritual landscape containing at least eight early neolithic chambered tombs and hundreds of late neolithic and bronze age burial cairns.

2. Bateman's Tomb, Middleton-by-Youlgreave

Nineteenth Century
SK: 194633

Behind the former Congregational Chapel in Middleton-by-Youlgreave, accessible via footpath.

This interesting tomb of the nineteenth-century archaeological pioneer Thomas Bateman (1821–61) and his wife is well worth a visit as an antiquarian curiosity. Bateman lived at nearby Lomberdale House and personally excavated over two hundred burial mounds during his short lifetime; his collection can be seen in Sheffield City Museum. He chose interment in a limestone vault

Bee Low, Derbyshire, showing a crouched skeleton in a cist. (B. M. Marsden)

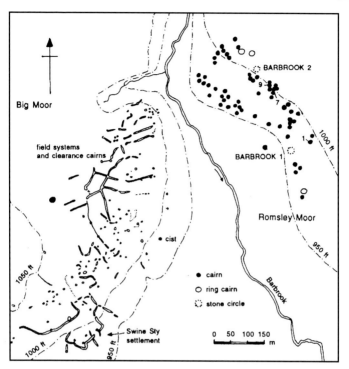

Big Moor and Ramsley Moor, Derbyshire. (After Butcher, Riley and Hart)

covered by this railed tomb surmounted by a stone representation of a bronze age collared urn.

3. Bee Low, Youlgreave
Neolithic to Bronze Age
SK: 192647

In plantation accessible via track leading N from Long Rake minor road from Bakewell to Parsley Hay.

This round cairn, 12 metres across and 1.5 metres high, is partly tree-covered and stands at the south-east corner of the plantation. Digs by Bateman in 1843 and 1851 and excavation by B. M. Marsden in 1966–8 showed that the mound had been utilised by successive Beaker communities for over three hundred years. The earliest interments were six skeletons buried collectively in a near-central cist with a corded beaker. The cist was covered by a large limestone slab. Five other burials were found, three with beakers, as well as a number of other skeletons disturbed by later burials. One skeleton in a cist on the east side was over 2.1 metres tall. Another, in a central cist, was disarticulated. The cairn also contained three cremations, one with a bronze knife-blade and one with an awl. The finds are in Sheffield City Museum.

4. Big Moor and Ramsley Moor, Baslow and Holmesfield
Bronze Age
SK: 277756

On the W side of the A621 between Baslow and Owler Bar, accessible NW from stile at 281752. Signposted footpaths.

This whole complex is an example of a 'fossilised landscape' of early and middle bronze age date, consisting of several settlement sites including the Swine Sty, with associated clearance cairns and field systems, and a burial and ritual area to the east, superimposed on an earlier system of field cairns. The eastern area contains over sixty cairns and three ring banks. The south circle, Barbrook 1, consists of thirteen upright stones on the inner edge of a rubble bank 12 metres in diameter. Barbrook 2, restored by the Peak Park, originally featured ten uprights set into the inner perimeter of a well-built circular drystone wall 13 metres across. There is a north-east entrance, and near the centre are a robbed cist with cup-marked lid, a stone cairn and a cremation pit. The first two are still visible, and the last covered an urned cremation with a flint knife and scraper. Six cup-marked stones were unearthed, including two in the cairn kerb and one covering the cist. A charcoal sample from the urn cremation gave a radiocarbon date of about 1800 BC. Three cairns in the cemetery were excavated in the 1960s; two of them, nos. 7 and 9 on the map, proved sterile, apart from a polished stone axe from a pre-barrow clearance found beneath one. The third cairn, no. 1, now restored, contained an urn cremation in a rectangular compartment on the east side of the main structure.

To the south-west is the Swine Sty bronze age settlement (272750), a series of stone-banked enclosures on sheltered ground below the escarpment edge, outlining an area of about 0.4 hectare at 274 metres OD. Stone foundations of a 6 metre diameter hut replacing an earlier timber structure were uncovered, and finds included urn-type pottery and evidence of a cannel coal working industry producing rings and bracelets from the local raw material. Radiocarbon tests suggest a date of approximately 1900 BC, and pollen analysis suggests that large areas of these gritstone uplands were being cleared at this period, for crop growing and animal pasturage. The field systems and foundations of possible associated buildings north of the Swine Sty have not yet been fully examined, but at 275753 is a fine, free-standing stone cist, with a displaced capstone and collapsed side slab.

5. Bull Ring, Dove Holes   Neolithic
SK: 078783

Behind the church on the main A6 road passing through the village. In a recreation ground.

A henge monument of Arbor Low type, although not nearly as imposing, and encroached on to the north and east by old quarry workings, this has been the subject of much modern vandalism. The circular surrounding bank stands to a height of 1.2 metres and is about 76 metres in diameter. The ditch was up to 12.2 metres wide and 1.8 metres deep. There are two causeway entrances at the north and south. In the eighteenth century a stone circle stood on the plateau and skeletons were disinterred there, but the stones have long since gone. As at Arbor Low a round cairn stands south-west of the monument. It is 2.1 metres high but no excavation records survive.

6. Creswell Crags, Whitwell   Palaeolithic and Mesolithic
Visitors' Centre: SK: 538743

The B6042 road E of Creswell passes through the ravine. Guided tours available at Visitors' Centre (telephone: 01909 720378).

Creswell Crags is a wide ravine traversed by a small stream. Its Magnesian Limestone rockfaces are riddled with two dozen caves and shelters. Many of these were seasonally occupied by hunting and fishing communities of late palaeolithic and mesolithic date, although certain finds suggest sparse habitation by Neanderthal man. The main caves and their entrances have been dug into many times from 1875 onwards, often indiscriminately. It is now accepted that the caves were occupied about 43,000 BC, then between 30,000 and 28,000 BC and later about 10,000 BC. Evidence of neolithic, bronze age, Roman and post-medieval occupation has also been found.

The Visitors' Centre explains the caves, and a trail can be followed. Unfortunately the caves cannot be entered, but they can be seen from their entrances. The main caves, from east to west along the north side of the B6042 are:

Mother Grundy's Parlour (536743). A horseshoe-shaped cave with a cramped passage leading off north-east. Numerous finds include flints and split bones. The cave was sporadically occupied until mesolithic times.

Robin Hood's Cave (534742). Dug out in the 1870s. It contains two main chambers. Many fine flint tools and a piece of bone engraved with a horse's head have come from this cave, as well as bones of many extinct species of animals including the woolly rhinoceros. By 10,000 BC the inhabitants were trapping arctic hares for subsistence.

The Pin Hole (533741). A narrow diminishing cave 15 metres long. It was occupied by Neanderthal man and served as a hyena den. Finds include a bone engraved with a human figure and the base of an ivory point, decorated with incised lines.

On the south side of the Crags (in Nottinghamshire) is **Church Hole** (534741), a straight cave about 60 metres long and occupied until Roman times.

7. Fivewells, Taddington

Neolithic
SK: 124711

N of minor road from Taddington to Chelmorton, via signposted track leading N from the entrance to Fivewells Farm.

Said to be the highest megalithic tomb in England, Fivewells stands about 425 metres above sea level, commanding extensive views somewhat spoiled by quarrying on Calton Hill to the immediate north-west.

The circular cairn, first disturbed in 1782, contains two large burial chambers built of limestone slabs, standing back to back and originally approached by separate passages from the east and west. The east chamber is comparatively well preserved apart from the loss of its roofing slabs, and its two fine portal stones still

The eastern burial chamber of the Fivewells passage grave contained twelve burials when excavated in the nineteenth century. (B. M. Marsden)

stand. The west chamber is less impressive; it is half buried and its portals have collapsed against each other. Thomas Bateman, digging in 1846, found the remains of twelve skeletons in the east chamber and in 1899 fragments of neolithic pottery and flints were found. This type of chambered tomb, belonging to the 'Peak' series, appears to have its origins in south-west England and is perhaps related to the Cotswold-Severn series.

8. Green Low, Aldwark

Neolithic
SK: 233580

Via minor road to Aldwark leading off A5012 at 217588. Track leads through Green Low Farm.

Another of the 'Peak' series of passage graves, Green Low is 18 metres in diameter. Excavations in 1963–4 showed that the entrance was revetted by a straight-fronted dry wall 10 metres long. The chamber and passage are the same width, the former delineated by large septal slabs. The site has been rifled perhaps as early as Roman times; the only contemporary burial found was a skeleton in the mound material east of the chamber, and neolithic pottery and flints were found in the area in front of the passage entrance.

9. Hartington Cairns

Bronze Age
(See below)

Three round cairns E of A515 Buxton to Ashbourne road.

These three large cairns occupy successive low hills alongside the A515 road, running north to south. To the visitor travelling south from Buxton they appear in the following order on the right-hand side of the road:

Parsley Hay (SK: 144631). A round cairn 18 metres across and 1.84 metres high. In 1848 Bateman found a rock-grave covered by stone slabs containing a skeleton 'in a sitting posture' with sherds from a beaker. On the covering slabs was a later burial, a crouched skeleton with a bronze round-heeled three-riveted dagger-blade and a granite battleaxe.

Lean Low (SK: 149622). A conspicuous mound 15 metres across and 1.2 metres high. Bateman, digging in 1843, found a crouched skeleton in a rock-grave, a skeleton on the south side, and a cremation with a food-vessel in a cist. The skull and long bones of a young person, together with a jet bead, were discovered by B. M. Marsden in 1972.

End Low (SK: 156605). A huge mound 21 metres across, 2.1 metres high, very prominent against the skyline. A large central hole shows where Bateman, after a series of attempts, finally located the primary burial in a rock-grave 1.8 metres below the old ground surface (i.e. 4 metres below the top of the mound!). In the grave was a crouched skeleton with a bronze round-heeled three-riveted dagger-blade and a flint knife.

The finds from all the cairns are in Sheffield City Museum.

10. Liffs Low, Hartington

Neolithic
SK: 153577

Immediately W of minor road off A515 to Biggin.

Although much of this mound has been destroyed, the site is interesting as a scarce example of a late neolithic single-grave burial under a round cairn. In 1843 Bateman found a crouched skeleton in an octagonal cist of limestones with an interesting array of grave goods including a small and unique pottery flask, two polished-edge flint axes, a polished-edge flint knife, a flint saw, two rhomboid flint arrowheads, a perforated macehead of deer's horn, two boar tusks and three pieces of red ochre. Some of these finds can be seen in Sheffield City Museum. Another dig in the 1930s produced a skeleton, beaker and polished stone pendant, which are now in Buxton Museum.

11. Mam Tor, Castleton

Bronze Age and Iron Age
SK: 128838

Minor road to Barber's Booth leads off A625 at 123832. Mam Tor track is E of this road where it passes through a narrow cutting below the ridge.

Impressively sited on a high ridge with sweeping views in most directions, Mam Tor is the largest hillfort in Derbyshire. Bracing in summer, it is bleak and inhospitable in the winter months! A bank, ditch and counterscarp bank enclose an area of 6.5 hectares in a roughly triangular platform. Excavations between 1965 and 1967 show that on the east side the bank was 5.5 metres wide and 3 metres high and rested on an artificial platform cut into the hillside. The bank was stone-faced at the front and rear. The ditch here was 2.4 metres wide and 2.4 metres deep. Small-scale excavations within the bank have produced pottery, house platforms, corn-storage pits, post holes, hearths and gulleys relating to the occupation of the site. There is an inturned entrance through the south side of the defences, forming a narrow passage 30 metres long. At the north end of the hillfort another inturned entrance can be seen, which incorporates a passage 15 metres long. Radiocarbon dates suggest that the fort was in use as early as the fourteenth century BC.

At the south-west end of the ridge are the remains of two bronze age round cairns, but no authenticated finds have been recorded from them. On the south-east side the shales making up the hill have slipped, removing part of the defences and giving the hill its local name of the 'Shivering Mountain'.

12. Minning Low, Ballidon

Neolithic and Bronze Age
SK: 209573

Minning Low picnic site is S of the A5012 at 195581. From there take the High Peak Trail SE. Minning Low Hill is a prominent eminence on the left of the trail.

The largest chambered round cairn in the Peak, Minning Low stands at 365 metres OD in a plantation of dying beeches, though the area has been fenced in and replanted. There are two cairns in the enclosure, a small bronze age example on the north-west containing a visible limestone cist, and a huge neolithic cairn, 36 metres across and still 3 metres high, despite long-term stone-robbing and exploration. Limited excavations by B. M. Marsden in 1973–4 showed that Chamber 1 at the centre, with a capstone and approached by a dry-walled passage, was the primary structure and was covered by a small cairn. Being unstable, this has been refilled with imported limestone and clay by English Heritage. Chamber 2, on the south, its roofed passage and burial vault still visible, was later in date, as was Chamber 3, a simple closed structure with no passage to the west. Chamber 4, on the south-west edge of the cairn, is another, part-destroyed chamber and passage. A retaining wall, located on the north-east, apparently surrounds the whole multiphase complex, which may originally have been oval in shape and may still hold at least one further tomb. Bateman cleared many of the chambers, though most of the finds were Romano-British in date, apart from neolithic and beaker sherds, and a bronze earclip discovered in Chamber 3. Like Five Wells, this megalithic monument has many affinities with the Cotswold-Severn barrows of south-west England and may well be an outlier of that group.

13. Nine Stone Close, Harthill Moor

Bronze Age
SK: 225626

E of minor road from Elton to Alport via footpath at 224626.

Four large upright stones still remain *in situ* forming part of a circle, with traces of a round cairn within, that may have been about 14 metres in diameter, if they originally numbered nine. One of the stones has weathered cup markings on its south face. A stone in the wall to the south was probably robbed from the circle, whose uprights stand to a height of over 2 metres. Both Bateman and later Canon

The four remaining uprights of the Nine Stone Close circle at Harthill, Derbyshire. (B. M. Marsden)

Greenwell dug in the centre of the circle, and the site was restored by the Heathcotes in 1936.

This monument is one of a series of bronze age ritual and burial monuments on the moor. There are also a fine series of enclosed settlements close by and a tiny iron age hillfort, **Harthill Castle Ring** (221628), with a single rampart, ditch and counterscarp bank enclosing 0.3 hectare.

14. Stanton Moor cairn cemetery
Bronze Age
SK: 247630 (centre)

Via minor road from Stanton-in-Peak to Birchover. Car park at 242628.

Stanton Moor is a sandstone plateau 60 hectares in extent with picturesque and extensive views particularly to the south and east. It was used extensively as a burial area in early bronze age times and 70 cairns and other contemporary sites can be identified. The main monuments are shown on the plan and should be seen as follows:

Doll Tor. A small circle consisting of six stones, two now fallen. Bateman dug within the circle in 1852, finding fragments of small bucket urns and miniature cups. Further excavations by the Heathcotes in 1931–4 revealed five cremations within the circle and around it, some with bucket urns. At the centre of a low cairn forming an east extension to the circle was a gravepit with a cremation and a segmented faience bead. Around the east side of this cairn were four cremations, three with small bucket urns and the fourth with a faience star bead.

T13. A rectangular cairn 12 metres by 6 metres and 1 metre high. It covered thirteen cremations, mostly young females. Seven were simply cremations, six were with collared urns. Four of these urns were inverted and a fifth contained a miniature cup and a clay stud.

T36. A small cairn 9 metres across and 0.6 metre high. A central pit contained a cremation and a small dolerite battleaxe.

T2. A large and conspicuous cairn 15 metres across and 1.5 metres high, crowned by two bushes. Over half the mound has been removed showing two concentric stone kerbs. At the centre can be seen the primary cist, originally containing a

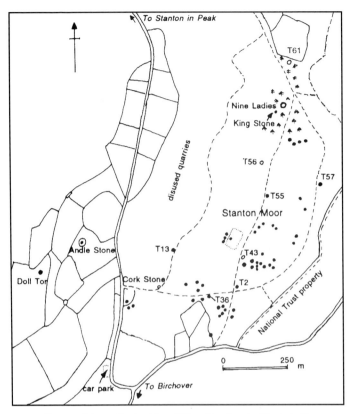

Stanton Moor, Derbyshire. (After Heathcote, Hart et al)

cremation with bronze and pottery fragments. On the capstones of the cist were food-vessel sherds. The mound contained twelve other cremations, eight with collared urns, one with a food-vessel and one with a miniature cup. Flint tools accompanied most of the burials.

T43. An embanked stone circle, perhaps a northern derivative of the Wessex disc-barrow. It consists of a rubble bank 18 metres across with an entrance on the south. No finds are recorded from the site.

T55. A massive stone cairn 15 metres in diameter and 1.5 metres high.

T56. Another embanked stone circle 24 metres across, with a south entrance. A segmented faience bead was found in the disturbed centre surface, giving rise to the suggestion that these circles were the stone country equivalents to Wessex-type disc-barrows.

T57. A large cairn 18 metres across and 1.5 metres high, with a sizeable hole in the top suggesting previous digging. Casual finds from this disturbed centre include the rim-sherd of a food-vessel, burnt bones and flints.

Nine Ladies. A circle of nine small stones 10.5 metres in diameter. A tenth stone was found lying flat in 1979. The stones are set in a low bank surrounding the remains of a central mound. A miniature cup in the Ashmolean Museum at Oxford supposedly came from this mound. 44 metres to the south-west of the circle is a single upright stone called the King Stone, broken by vandals.

T61. A ring cairn partly hidden in a small plantation. The site was dug by Major

Collared urn and cremation from cairn T13 on Stanton Moor, Derbyshire. (J. P. Heathcote)

Rooke in 1787 and J. C. Heathcote in 1938–46. A small cairn once stood at the centre and was found to cover three collared urns. Heathcote found five cremations, four with collared urns and two miniature cups, and one with a cordoned urn. A bronze awl accompanied one of the burials. In 1964 two collared urns with cremations were found in the bank of the circle.

Finds from the many excavated sites can be seen in the Sheffield City Museum.

The Nine Ladies stone circle on Stanton Moor, set within a slight circular bank. (K. Fadden)

15. Swarkestone Lows

Bronze Age
SK: 365295

E of the track to Lows Farm, N of the A514 at Swarkestone.

A cemetery consisting of four round barrows. Only the most westerly has escaped elimination by the plough. All except one, the second from the west, are surrounded by double ditches, shown in aerial photographs. The exception has a single ditch.

The west barrow is a fine example, standing 3.6 metres high and 30 metres across. East of this is a plough-damaged mound 1.2 metres high, identified as a bell-barrow during excavation in 1955. It had been built of stacked turves and covered a central cremation and two intrusive Anglo-Saxon burials, one with a cruciform brooch, an iron knife, belt buckle and five glass beads.

The next barrow to the east is also ploughed down and was excavated in 1956. Turf-built, it was apparently a small round barrow with a primary skeleton (decayed away) with a flint knife, in a boat-shaped wooden coffin. The mound was later enlarged into a bell-barrow containing three cremations in collared urns. On the pre-barrow surface were stake holes and pottery belonging to an earlier beaker occupation of the area. North-east of this mound is a fourth unexcavated barrow, now very much ploughed down and spread.

DEVON
(Map on page 234)

1. Berry Down, Berrynarbor

Bronze Age
SS: 569436 (rough centre)

Beside the A3123 W and SW of Berry Down Cross.

A group of about nine round barrows, ranging in diameter from 10 to 30 metres, and in height from 0.1 to 2 metres. One, opened in 1883, yielded a cremation beneath an inverted large ribbon-handled urn of Cornish Trevisker type, now in Exeter Museum.

2. Blackbury Castle, Southleigh

Iron Age
SX: 187924

Just S of road from Lovehayne Common to Hangman's Stone, and signposted at both points (171927 at the former, and 204909 on the A3052). Enter at NE end.

Blackbury Castle is a splendid univallate hillfort covering about 2.6 hectares, with massive flint-built rampart and deep outer ditch. On the south side is the original entrance, which is slightly out-turned and originally contained a timber gateway which was probably bridged. To this entrance was added a triangular outer defence or barbican which was never completed. The present gaps in the north, west and east are modern. The site, which is in the care of English Heritage and open at all times, is in a beech plantation clear of undergrowth.

3. Blackdown Rings, Loddiswell

Iron Age and Norman
SX: 720520

Beside minor road to Gara Bridge. Owned by the Arundell Charity, with public access and car park.

Also known as Loddiswell Rings, this large iron age fort of about 2 hectares is situated on a ridge running from Dartmoor towards the river Avon at Gara Bridge. It has a small Norman motte and bailey castle inserted into its north-west corner. Although it has not been excavated, its massive single rampart, about 1.7 metres high, and accompanying deep ditch seem to have been modified by the Normans, especially on the south side. The two opposing entrances have been enlarged for farm traffic. That on the east still retains one of its original iron age inturns. The Norman castle's history is unknown.

4. Black Hill, Manaton

Bronze Age
SX: 767793

W of road between Manaton and Haytor Vale.

A cairn 14 metres in diameter with a stone row of fifteen stones extending north down the slope from it. The north end of the row is marked by a larger stone at right angles to the axis of the row.

5. Bolt Tail promontory fort, Malborough

Iron Age
SX: 670397

Overlooking Bigbury Bay and accessible by the coastal path from the E, or from car park at Hope Cove. National Trust property.

This fine promontory fort encloses 4.9 hectares at the end of Bolt Tail. Across the narrow neck of the headland runs a rampart 274 metres long and 4.6 metres high in places. At its centre is an inturned entrance approached by a hollow-way and guarded by an arc-like outwork on the north. The hollow-way leads north-west to a second minor fort on lower ground. This seems to have been an annexe to the main fort, and guarded a freshwater supply.

6. Brisworthy stone circle, Sheepstor

Bronze Age
SX: 565655

Minor roads to Brisworthy Farm at 560652. 0.5 km walk to NE.

The Brisworthy circle stands on an east-facing slope, 300 metres north of the river Plym. Some twenty-four stones survive in this 25 metre diameter ring. Evenly spaced 1.8 metres apart, it may once have held forty-two stones. They were graded in height up the slope from the south, with the tallest, 1.1 metres high, at the north. Restored in 1909, this is one of the nicest Dartmoor circles. There is a small burial cairn 100 metres to the east.

On the south side of **Legis Tor**, 550 metres to the south-east, are four pounds (walled enclosures) butting on to each other and enclosing some 1.7 hectares (570653). The walls are 1 metre thick and are built with inner and outer facing blocks filled with rubble. Within the pounds are traces of at least eleven hut foundations, some with paved floors and steps at the entrance. These huts probably had conical roofs thatched with bracken and turves. The site, which has produced early Trevisker-style pottery, has been dated to the middle bronze age, between 1200 and 1000 BC. There are more hut circles on the moor close by.

7. Broad Down, Farway

Bronze Age
SY: 173940 (rough centre)

Beside and near the road between Seaton and Honiton, E of Roncombe Gate (168945).

A scattered group of about twenty-four round barrows. Two of the seven in a line north to south on Ball Hill (the four at the south were much reduced in 1948) had circles of stones around their circumference. The central of the seven barrows yielded a shale cup, and another was found in a round barrow between here and Roncombe Gate. The barrow north-east of Roncombe Corner yielded a pigmy cup. A barrow (destroyed in 1948) between this and the southernmost of the row of seven contained a primary cremation beneath an inverted urn, and a secondary cremation with a debased beaker near the edge of the mound. Surviving finds are in Exeter Museum.

8. Burridge Camp, Roborough

Iron Age and/or Saxon
SS: 569352

Accessible by the turning NE of Barnstaple, off the A39, towards Brightleycott (580354); there is a gate near the top of this hill, N of the road.

A damaged example of a roughly oval multiple-enclosure fort of 1.2 hectares. The special interest of this hillfort is that its circumference, about 375 metres, is almost identical with that of the Saxon *burh* of Pilton-with-Barnstaple, AD *c*.900. As there is an outwork to the east, just east of the gate, this site must be an iron age hillfort adapted for use as a *burh*.

9. Butterdon Hill, Harford   Bronze Age
SX: 657594 (rough centre)
To Harford Moor Gate (643596) and then a walk of about 1.5 km.

From a small round barrow about 10.5 metres in diameter, with retaining circle, there extends northwards for about 1900 metres a single stone row, the second longest on Dartmoor. It terminates at the re-erected Longstone (2.6 metres high). Butterdon Hill is crowned by several other cairns.

10. Cadbury Castle   Iron Age
SS: 914053
Track from S opposite entrance to Cadbury House, then beside wood for 400 metres.

Sited on a hilltop 252 metres above sea level, this oval hillfort of 1.6 hectares commands wide views in all directions. There is a steep scarp slope providing natural defence on the north-west. Elsewhere the single rampart is massive, at least 6 metres high, and broken by an original entrance at the south-east. The gap at the north-east is modern. The encircling ditch is mostly filled in. A ridge some 30 metres inside the southern defences may represent the line of an earlier rampart. In the centre of the earthwork is a deep hollow. Excavated in 1847, this appeared to be a funnel-shaped shaft, nearly 18 metres deep and 1 metre in diameter at the base. It contained a mixture of pottery, animal bones and ashes, twenty metal bracelets and four of shale, beads, a finger ring, and near the bottom an iron knife-blade. Since the shaft was not deep enough to reach water, it is assumed that it was dug for religious and votive purposes.

11. Chapman barrows, Challacombe   Bronze Age
SS: 695434 (rough centre)
Accessible from Two Gates (690434) at S end of lane from Parracombe.

A group of about eleven or more round barrows on the north part of Challacombe Common. They range from 10.5 to 30 metres in diameter and from 0.3 to 2.7 metres in height. That to the south-east, opened in 1905, contained in the centre burnt bones covered by a small cairn. This barrow was edged with a stone retaining wall which had become overspread by the mound. About 450 metres south-east of the easternmost barrow is the Long Stone (705431), the tallest standing stone on Exmoor, 2.7 metres high, and most likely bronze age.

12. Clovelly Dykes   Iron Age
SS: 311235
Just N of the A39(T) and W of the B3237 turning into Clovelly. Permission to visit should be sought at East Dyke Farm.

Sited at a junction of important ridgeways, this is a fine multiple-enclosure hillfort with five widely spaced ramparts having outer ditches on the west, and three elsewhere. The rampart ends are knobbed at the original entrances. As far as can be learned by non-excavational fieldwork, the two innermost enclosures, with slightly staggered entrances at the east, appear to be earlier than the others. It has been suggested that the added enclosures were for segregating herds of domestic animals for various purposes and possibly before shipment to the continent. The site is normally under grass.

13. Corringdon Ball, South Brent
Neolithic
SX: 670614

By car through South Brent to Aish, then follow lane and footpath W across moor for 2.5 km

This is the only known chambered long barrow on Dartmoor. It is 40 metres long, 20 metres wide and 2 metres high and is placed south-southeast/north-northwest, with its larger end at south-southeast, where there is a megalithic structure, probably of a burial chamber. It is under rough pasture. 0.5 km further west, a number of rows of tiny stones run uphill to a ruined cairn at 666612. Only a few of the stones are more than 30 cm high, so they must be viewed when the vegetation is at its lowest.

14. Cranbrook Castle, Moretonhampstead
Iron Age
SX: 739890

Byroad from the A382 at Easton (729888) and then by public footpath from 742889.

A small roughly circular hillfort on the north-east fringe of Dartmoor, overlooking the river Teign. It is essentially univallate with berm, ditch and counterscarp. The rampart is stone-built. The north side is either unfinished or largely levelled. There are original inturned entrances certainly at the east and probably at the west. The land usage is rough pasture.

15. Denbury, Torbryan
Iron Age
SX: 816685

On wooded crest of hill SW of Denbury village.

When visited (1996) this site was very overgrown, but plans were in hand for it to be cleared. It consists of an inner and outer enclosure. The inner has an inturned entrance on the west. The outer rampart diverges from the inner to form an outer stock enclosure. On the south and east both ramparts are on a major scale. It is difficult to judge the age of the outer entrance in its present overgrown state. The site is unexcavated.

16. Dumpdon Great Camp, Luppitt
Iron Age
ST: 176040

By turning off the A30(T) NE of Honiton. National Trust car park at 178041.

A fine hill-spur fort, at present under grass; the ramparts are covered with bracken. There is an inturned entrance just south of the north-east corner. The strongest defences are on the north side where there are two widely spaced ramparts and ditches; elsewhere there is one rampart with ditch and counterscarp.

17. Farway Hill and Gittisham Hill
Bronze Age
SY: 155958 (rough centre)

Between the inn at 146962 and Roncombe Gate (168945).

Two scattered groups of round barrows: about thirteen on Gittisham Hill and twenty on Farway Hill and its south-east extension. That at 148967 had a peristalith but this is no longer visible. The largest, at 152961 west of Ring in the Mire, is 42 metres in diameter and about 3.6 metres high and is ditched. South-east of a tree-clump circle on Farway Hill (161955) is a closely set group cut through by the road. At about 164949 is a good example 24 metres in diameter and 2.1 metres high, ditched, with a boundary stone on top.

18. Fernworthy stone circle, Lydford
Bronze Age
SX: 655841

4 km N of Postbridge. Approached from Fernworthy Reservoir car park at 660839. Follow forest track WNW for 0.5 km. (Avoid first track N on right.)

This circle is just inside the plantation. It is 18 metres in diameter, and composed of some twenty-seven blocks of local granite graded in size, the largest (1.2 metres high) on the south side. A damaged double row of stones leads to the south side. In 1897 the excavators found a scatter of charcoal over the centre of the circle, but nothing else. There are cairns, cists and stone rows in the forest close by.

19. Five Barrows, North Molton   Bronze Age
SS: 732368 (rough centre)

Approached by walking about 365 metres from the metalled part of the ridgeway forming the county boundary with Somerset.

A group of about nine round barrows, including a bell-barrow (mound enclosed by berm and ditch) of Wessex type. They range from 12 to 33 metres in diameter and from 0.45 to 3.3 metres in height. The bell-barrow is the only well-preserved example of this type on Exmoor. There are no known records of excavation of any barrows in this group.

20. Foales Arrishes, Widecombe   Bronze Age
SX: 737758

On hillside, about 350 metres SW of road at Hemsworthy Gate (742761). Beware of areas of marshy land.

This settlement site comprises a group of eight large hut circles each between 6 and 9 metres in diameter, set amongst parallel 'reaves' or ancient field walls. Banks were built between the walls to create small rectangular paddocks in which the houses were situated. All the houses were excavated in 1896 and can be clearly seen, with walls constructed of large stone slabs, and paved floors. Finds were few, but included bronze age pottery, flint and stone flakes and charcoal. The site derives its name from Foales, who was the keeper of a nearby inn, demolished about 1900, and Arrishes, a Devonshire dialect word meaning 'cornfields'.

21. Grey Wethers, Lydford   Bronze Age
SX: 638832

4 km N of Postbridge. Approached from Fernworthy Reservoir car park at 660839. Follow forest track WNW for 1.6 km. Turn left at end of forest; circles lie due S after 1.2 km.

The Grey Wethers are a pair of associated stone circles 9 metres apart, on a north–south alignment. 32 metres and 36 metres in diameter, they are composed of tall, local granite stones, each about 1.3 metres high. They were excavated in 1898 and restored in 1909 when deep spreads of charcoal were found over the interior of both. Two very low cairns can be seen immediately to their south. Wethers, incidentally, are castrated rams.

The paired stone circles known as the Grey Wethers near Lydford on Dartmoor. (Aubrey Burl)

The footings of a stone hut at Grimspound, excavated in 1894 and 1895. It would probably have had a conical roof thatched with turf or heather. (J. Dyer)

22. Grimspound, Manaton

Bronze Age
SX: 701809

Turn S off the B3212 between Postbridge and Moretonhampstead at Shapley Common (695830); the site is signposted E of the road where it makes an angle in a valley containing the Grimslake stream, which runs through the site.

This is the best-known and among the most accessible of the prehistoric settlements on Dartmoor. It lies in a valley between Hookney Tor and Hameldown Tor and contains some twenty-four circular huts, of which about sixteen were probably dwellings, the rest store huts. These huts vary in size between 2.5 metres and 4.5 metres diameter with walls at least 1 metre thick. They were insulated against the severe winters by having an inner and outer 'skin' of stone slabs, with smaller stones and turf packed between them. Two huts have porches, and all except the store huts had hearths. A massive stone 'pound' wall surrounds the settlement 3 metres wide and still 1 to 1.5 metres high. At least part of this wall was hollow, and consisted of an inner and outer face, both 1 metre thick, with a 1 metre wide passage between them. There were probably a number of entrances into this passage: one survives near the modern (downhill) west entrance. There is a strong stone-built paved entrance on the south side, 1.8 metres wide, and facing uphill to Hameldown. All the other entrance gaps are modern. Grimspound was partially excavated and 'restored' in 1894 and 1895.

23. Halwell Camps

Iron Age or Early Christian
NE SX: 784532
SW SX: 773517

Cut through by the A3122. Just E of the A381 and behind Stanborough Lodge guest house.

The north-east earthwork is about 360 metres in circuit. The part north of the road is under grass and has a well-preserved rampart and outer ditch.

The south-west earthwork is roughly circular and under grass. It has a well-preserved rampart and outer ditch.

One or other of these earthworks may have been the *burh* before it was moved to Totnes.

24. Hameldown, Widecombe   Bronze Age
SX: 706795 (rough centre)

Approach from the B3212 by road from Shapley Common southwards; can be combined with a visit to Grimspound (no. 22, above).

A group of round barrows following a ridgeway; among them are Broad Barrow, Single Barrow and Two Barrows. The largest is Broad Barrow, about 36 metres in diameter and 1.2 metres high. The northern of the Two Barrows was opened in 1877 and yielded, well south-east of centre, a cremation with a grooved bronze ogival dagger having an amber pommel decorated with gold pointillé pins arranged in a cruciform pattern. The finds were destroyed by enemy action in Plymouth in 1943. The barrow had a small cairn in the centre and a stone wall formed its circumference.

25. Hembury fort, Payhembury   Neolithic and Iron Age
ST: 113031

N of A373. Most easily approached from woods to N at 112035.

Between 1930 and 1935 Dorothy Liddell carried out a classic excavation on this beautiful hilltop and revealed the ramparts and ditch sections of a neolithic causewayed enclosure cut across the long axis of the hill. A timber gateway through the earthwork and post holes of a possible oval building were found. There were signs that this first enclosure had been destroyed by fire, and more than 120 arrowheads, many of them burnt, suggest that this was connected with early warfare. There are more neolithic features in the northern area of the later hillfort, as yet only partially excavated. None of these features is visible.

In the iron age a multivallate hillfort with closely set ramparts, and two inturned entrances on the west and north-east, was constructed. The ramparts are boldest to the north, the side most vulnerable to attack. The defences may have begun as a simple timber palisade. Excavations between 1980 and 1983 by Malcolm Todd show that a box-rampart was next constructed, later followed by a dumped structure dated to the end of the second or early first century BC. It was then abandoned until after the conquest when Roman troops built a series of wooden buildings, including workshops, in the northern half of the hillfort. The Romans probably occupied the site for about twenty years, before it was eventually deserted soon after AD 60.

Finds from the excavations are in the Royal Albert Memorial Museum, Exeter.

26. Huccaby Rings, Hexworthy   Iron Age
SX: 656744 and 659738

Just N of the road between Two Bridges and Ashburton.

Outer Huccaby Ring is a hillslope enclosure on the south-west slope of the moor overlooking the West Dart. Huccaby Ring is a smaller hillslope enclosure to the south-east. If these are not pounds connected with hut circles, they would appear to be hillslope stock enclosures of the type which often occurs in the south-western counties.

27. Kent's Cavern, Torquay   Palaeolithic
SX: 934641

In Ilsham Road, a turning off Babbacombe Road, and well-signposted. Free car park.

This show cave was inhabited during the palaeolithic period. The finds include lower and middle palaeolithic handaxes, early upper palaeolithic laurel-leaf blades of British Solutrean type, as well as later Creswellian implements of flint, with a few of antler and bone. A human mandible fragment has been radiocarbon-dated to about 30,000 years: the earliest known example of modern man in Britain. Abundant remains of Pleistocene animals have also been found. There are display cases of finds in the entrance to the cave, but the best material is in Torquay Museum (529 Babbacombe Road) and the Natural History Museum, South Kensington.

28. Kestor settlement, Chagford
Bronze Age and Iron Age
SX: 665867

From the A382 or the B3212 along byroads W of Chagford; the road to Batworthy passes through the site.

On the north, north-west and north-east slopes of the hill crowned by Kestor Rock is a group of about twenty-seven circular huts, mostly 6 to 11 metres in diameter, but a few are smaller; there is an associated layout of rectangular fields defined by lines of upright slabs, and there are two probably contemporary sunken roads each running north-northeast–south-southwest, one on each side of the road between Batworthy and Teigncombe. To the west of this road is Round Pound, 33 metres in diameter, entered from the west from the western of the two sunken roads, and containing a single hut 11 metres in diameter and the largest in the settlement. Excavation has shown this settlement to date from the iron age. (The four radial walls extending from the hut to the limits of the pound are probably medieval.)

29. Lakehead Hill, Lydford
Bronze Age
SX: 644775 to 644782

Leave car near Youth Hostel at Bellever, which can be approached from the B3212 at Postbridge.

On the unplanted hilltop are three stone cists. At 643774 is one in the centre of a cairn circle about 6.3 metres in diameter. At 643777, in the unplanted edge of the plantation, is a cist without any conspicuous associated structure. At 645776 is an impressive monument comprising a large stone cist with walls and cover-slab above ground level, in the centre of a cairn circle from which a stone row extends downhill

This stone cist and stone row at Lakehead Hill, Devon, was restored somewhat inaccurately in 1895. (L. V. Grinsell)

A double stone row at Merrivale on Dartmoor. (J. Dyer)

to the east. This is, however, a restoration of 1895 and probably inaccurate in at least three respects: the cist is too large, the stone row begins within the circle instead of on its circumference, and it forms a curve instead of a straight line. There is an enclosed settlement to the north at 644782.

30. Merrivale, Walkhampton

Bronze Age
SX: 553746 (rough centre)
Just S of the B3357 between Tavistock and Two Bridges.

This is the finest and most easily accessible group of stone monuments on Dartmoor. It includes two double stone rows placed west to east, of which the southern, which is 264 metres long, has a tiny round barrow surrounded by a circle of seven stones in the middle; and there is a single stone row extending south-west from a cairn. To the east of this row is a large stone cist, 2.1 metres long and 1 metre wide, with a cover slab split in two. It is slightly above ground level, and has been 'restored' larger than it was originally. About 180 metres to the south-west of this is a stone circle 20 metres in diameter and composed of eleven small stones. There is one of a pair of standing stones, 3.2 metres tall, to the south: its companion has fallen. Near the east end of the rows and running 380 metres to the south-east is part of the Great Western Reave, a major bronze age field boundary dating from 1700–1600 BC. There are groups of hut circles on both sides of the road.

31. Milber Down Camp, Haccombe

Iron Age
SX: 884699
Road from Newton Abbot via Watcombe to Torquay cuts through the site. Enter by public footpath at 885698.

This is a typical hillslope stock enclosure comprising four roughly concentric and fairly widely spaced ramparts with outer ditches, the outermost of which is destroyed on the north and north-east side. The south-west portion is well preserved. The outermost rampart is turned inwards in its north-west sector (the lower side) and continued inwards to meet the third rampart, forming a sunk entrance corridor between two parallel ramparts. It is believed that the entrances to the other enclosures were destroyed when the road was made and were also in the north-west sector. Excavation (1937–8) showed that the site was built in the first century BC and abandoned at or before the Roman conquest. Pottery included iron age decorated wares of Glastonbury type. Among the finds was a collection of bronze figurines including a bird, duck and stag, believed to be Celtic work but showing early Roman influence. These and the other finds are in Torquay Museum.

32. Scorhill stone circle, Gidleigh

Bronze Age
SX: 655874

From the A382 W through Gidleigh to car park at 661877, and then a walk of about 800 metres.

This is among the finest and most accessible of the free-standing stone circles on Dartmoor. It is 26 metres in diameter, and there are twenty-five stones standing and nine fallen; originally the circle may have contained between sixty-five and seventy stones. The tallest stone is about 2.4 metres high.

33. Setta Barrow, High Bray

Bronze Age
SS: 726381

Approach from road between Simonsbath and Challacombe by the metalled road from Mole's Chamber following the county boundary and ridgeway.

This fine round barrow with retaining circle of stones edging the circumference is the best example of a retaining circle in the Exmoor region. The barrow is 29 metres in diameter and 2 metres high. Its summit is marred by a large robbers' hollow. In turn this is crossed by a later field wall that marks the Devon–Somerset county boundary and the medieval bounds of Exmoor Forest. Traces of retaining stones can also be seen around two barrows that lie fairly close to the wall to the north and south of Setta Barrow. Also to the south-west is a setting of three standing stones with a fourth almost at right angles to the rest.

34. Shoulsbury Castle, Challacombe

Iron Age
SS: 706391

Approached by road between Five Cross Way and Mole's Chamber, S of the B3358 and S of Challacombe. The ground to the N and E of the site can be marshy at times.

Shoulsbury Castle is superbly sited on a ridge with wide views on a clear day to

The Scorhill stone circle is considered by many to be the finest on Dartmoor. Measuring 26 metres in diameter, it contains twenty-five standing stones. (L. V. Grinsell)

Tradition says that the Spinsters' Rock was set up by three spinsters one morning before breakfast. It is part of a neolithic burial chamber. (L. V. Grinsell)

Bodmin Moor and south Wales. This iron age hillfort is bivallate on its higher parts on the north and east sides, and univallate above the steep slopes to the south-west and south. Original entrances may be in the middle of the west side of the inner rampart, and near the south-east corner of the outer rampart. The outer enclosure covers about 2.4 hectares. Inside the north-east corner is a possible round barrow. The rectangular shape of Shoulsbury has led some observers to suggest that the Castle is of Roman workmanship, but the writer feels confident that it is of iron age origin.

35. Soussons Plantation, Manaton

Bronze Age
SX: 676785

By road from the B3212 just E of Postbridge. Site is in a plantation a few metres N of road.

There are twenty-two stones in this beautifully preserved retaining circle which once surrounded a round cairn some 8.5 metres in diameter. In the centre is a damaged stone burial cist, measuring 1.4 metres by 0.6 metre and excavated in 1903. The contents had been disturbed and the coverstone removed.

36. Spinsters' Rock, Drewsteignton

Neolithic
SX: 700908

Beside the A382 about 1.6 km S of Whiddon Down.

This monument comprises three upright slabs supporting a cover-slab. It collapsed in 1858 and was afterwards reconstructed not quite in its original form. It is most likely the chamber of a chambered tomb; but there is no evidence whether the covering mound was long or round. Its name derives from the local tradition that it was erected by three spinsters one morning before breakfast.

37. Three Barrows, Upton Pyne

Bronze Age
SX: 910990 (rough centre)

Turn E to Upton Pyne village and N off the A377.

A fine but scattered group of round barrows. The largest is north-east of Starved Oak Cross at 915991 and is about 39 metres in diameter and 1.8 metres high. The two examples in Long Plantation are also large. The central of the Three Barrows, south-east of Stevenstone Farm, was opened in 1869 and yielded a cremation with small grooved bronze dagger, bronze pin, necklace of lignite and fossil encrinite beads, and a pigmy cup. A barrow (now destroyed) just north-east of Starved Oak Cross, opened in 1967, yielded cremations and several urns including three with Cornish Trevisker connections. Finds from both excavations are in Exeter Museum.

38. Wind Hill promontory fort, Lynton and Lynmouth

Iron Age
SS: 740493

Steep footpath from A39 at 743496. Alternatively use Countisbury church car park 1 km E and walk along roadside. National Trust property.

A massive cross-ridge dyke runs from the sea on the north to the steep slopes above the East Lyn river on the south. Some 400 metres long, its rampart rises about 9 metres above the bottom of a ditch on its eastern side and, together with a counterscarp bank, it cuts off a promontory of some 60 hectares. The rampart is broken by a single original entrance which has slight inturns and shows traces of stonework. A low bank runs for a short length along the south side of the promontory but soon disappears. There is little doubt that this is one of the largest promontory forts in Britain. L. V. Grinsell suggested that it may have formed a late iron age invasion beach-head similar to Bindon Hill in Dorset (*q.v.*), but as yet there is no supporting evidence. It has also been identified with the site of *Arx Cynuit*, which in the ninth century AD was occupied by the Christian West Saxons, who defeated the Danes and killed their leader, Hubba, there in AD 878.

39. Woodbury Castle

Iron Age
SY: 032874

The B3180 runs through the fort. Car parking clearly marked.

A roughly pear-shaped hillfort of about 2 hectares surrounded by a massive rampart, ditch and counterscarp rampart on the east and south. The defences are triplicated on the west and north (west of the road). Dead ground to the north is cut off by a further rampart and ditch about 50 metres north of the main fort. There are traces of yet another apparently unfinished and earlier rampart along the western edge of the spur, with an entrance at the south. The main fort has entrances on the north and west at points where the road passes through. The gap on the south-east is relatively modern. Excavation has shown that there was a small palisaded enclosure, probably along the line of the inner rampart, between 600 and 500 BC. Some time later the present earthworks were constructed, with elaborate timber breastworks and a possible northern gate tower. Inside were rectangular four- and six-post structures which may have been granaries or small huts. The fortifications were again strengthened prior to 300 BC, by which time the fort probably ceased to function.

40. Wrangworthy Cross, East Putford

Bronze Age
SS: 384174 (centre)

From the A39(T) via byroads to S. The barrows are in fields beside the road.

A group of eight round barrows between 12 and 36 metres in diameter and up to 1.8 metres high, on pasture. Two of them, excavated in 1934, were shown to have contained interments beneath timber-built structures.

41. Yar Tor stone rows and round barrow

Bronze Age
SX: 682738

By turning off the B3357 for 800 metres to NW.

This site, just west of the road, comprises a triple stone row originally about 456 metres long, with at its north-west end a round barrow, and near its south-east end a round barrow with interior stone cist and double retaining circle. The stone rows have in the past been robbed, especially at each end, for road-making materials.

42. Yelland stone rows, Fremington

Bronze Age
SS: 491329

Approach the site from the B3233, leaving car at Lower Yelland Farm. Walk along path (usually muddy) S of old railway line, cross bridge, and walk along shingle bar. The site is difficult to find and should be visited at low tide.

A pair of parallel stone rows 34 metres long and 1.8 metres apart. The stones in each row average 2 to 2.3 metres apart. The axis of the rows is roughly east–west. As a pair of stone rows at river level it is unique and well worth the effort to find. It may owe its existence to influence from Dartmoor (where such stone rows are abundant) via the Torridge valley.

43. Yellowmead Down, Sheepstor

Bronze Age
SX: 575678

Track E from Sheepstor to Yellowmead. Site 400 metres on moor to E.

Four roughly concentric stone circles, the largest about 20 metres in diameter, the smallest 6 metres, once enclosed a burial cairn which is now almost flattened. On the south-west side of the circles is a vestigial stone row crossed by a disused leat, which carried water to a tinworks three or four centuries ago. The site was carefully restored in 1921 after excavation by the Reverend H. Breton and is well worth a visit.

DORSET
(Map on page 236)

1. Abbotsbury Castle

Iron Age
SY: 555866

N of the B3157 at 558862.

This is a small triangular hillfort enclosed by two ramparts and a single ditch, except at the south-eastern end where the defences have been increased. There is an original entrance on the eastern side, and another on the north-west. A number of hollows in the north-east corner of the fort are probably stone hut foundations. There is a round barrow inside the southern rampart 1.5 metres high. A small enclosure in the western corner of the fort resembles a Roman signal station, but excavation has failed to confirm this claim.

2. Badbury Rings, Shapwick

Iron Age and Roman
ST: 964030

The B3082 between Blandford and Wimborne passes just to S. Car park provided.

This is amongst the most massive and spectacular of all the great hillforts of Dorset. It has never been excavated but is likely to be of at least two periods of construction. Period 1 is likely to consist of the two inner ramparts and ditches, with a straight inturned entrance on the east, and another on the west that is protected by a rectangular barbican with a south-western entrance gap. Period 2 is represented by a slighter outer rampart and ditch some 15 to 30 metres outside the inner defences. It has original entrances on the east and south-west. It resembles the outer rampart at Danebury (Hampshire) and may have been a stock enclosure. An entrance gap on

The Abbotsbury Castle hillfort from the west. From its ramparts the site commands dramatic views along the Chesil Beach. (J. Dyer)

the west aligns with a similar gap in the barbican and may be evidence of Roman alterations. Badbury may well have been one of the *oppida* which fell to Vespasian's troops in AD 43–4.

The summit of Badbury Rings is a well-known landmark. The earthwork forms a meeting point of Roman roads including the Ackling Dyke, which is clearly visible, skirting the western side of the fort, on its way from *Sorviodunum* (Old Sarum) to *Durnovaria* (Dorchester). Three round barrows stand beside this road (near the car park). Once considered to be Roman, it is now generally accepted that they are bronze age bowl-barrows. Between them and the western entrance to the fort is a much flattened disc-barrow.

3. Bindon Hill, Lulworth
Iron Age
SY: 835803

Approached by footpath from West Lulworth. Partly Ministry of Defence land.

These earthworks, excavated by Sir Mortimer Wheeler in 1950, may have been an invasion beach-head of the early iron age, perhaps about 550 to 500 BC. They could equally well have provided protection for a trading post. The ditch is on the north, thereby enclosing about 160 hectares and protecting the natural harbour at Lulworth Cove. The single line of rampart and ditch runs for almost 2400 metres along the northern edge of Bindon Hill, with a western extension on the miniature golf course near the car park in Lulworth. There are clear indications that the earthwork was unfinished, and an unfinished bank which runs north to south above Lulworth Cove may have been an attempt to reduce the area enclosed.

4. Bokerley Dyke
Bronze Age to Late Roman
SU: 035200

The A354 between Blandford and Salisbury cuts through the site.

This is one of the great linear earthworks of Wessex. It ran across a neck of land about 6.4 km wide, with its ends tucked into woodland. Detailed study shows that, beside the main earthwork, there were numerous minor lines of dykes forming land divisions that can be dated as early as the middle bronze age. Bokerley Dyke itself seems to overlie a bronze age predecessor and remained in use throughout the iron age, forming a prehistoric land boundary. A Roman road later passed through this barrier. As we see it today, the main dyke was probably a frontier work of post-Roman date, separating the downland of north-east Dorset from that to the south-west. The complicated history of the dyke and its satellites is as yet only partially unravelled.

5. Buzbury Rings, Tarrant Keyneston

Iron Age
ST: 919060

The B3082 between Blandford and Wimborne cuts through the site.

This earthwork is unusual in being sited on a slight hillslope although not as noticeably so as the typical hillslope enclosures of south-western England. The earthworks are slight and essentially bivallate but with additions between the inner and outermost banks on the south and east sides. There are suggestions of about six hut circles inside the inner enclosure, and the outer enclosure was probably pastoral. An unusual feature is the ditch *inside* the outermost bank. The part of the site north of the road is on a golf course; that to the south is farmland and the banks appear never to have been ploughed.

6. Came Wood, Whitcombe, etc

Neolithic and Bronze Age
SY: 699855

From the A354 between Dorchester and Weymouth, take the turning along the Ridgeway from 671860 to E.

The round barrows south of Came Wood are generally under cultivation, but those in Came Wood include two bell-barrows and a pond-barrow. To the east of Came Wood is a linear group of special interest. At the western end is Culliford Tree barrow, formerly the meeting place of a hundred. Excavation in this barrow in 1858 revealed four interments, one of which had a necklace of amber beads, two of which had gold casings. Among the other barrows are pond-barrows and a bank-barrow with a round barrow at each end. The Came Wood barrows lie at the eastern end of the cemetery of neolithic and bronze age barrows that stretch along the South Dorset Ridgeway. Spread over a distance of 15 km is one of the densest concentrations of barrows in England. It has been suggested that they formed the boundary of territory centred around the major neolithic ritual monuments of Maiden Castle, Maumbury Rings, Mount Pleasant and the destroyed Flagstones and Greyhound Yard sites in Dorchester.

7. Cerne Giant, Cerne Abbas

Romano-British?
ST: 667016

On hill E of the A352. National Trust property.

Although the evidence is inadequate, this club-wielding hill-figure, which is 55 metres long and 51 metres wide, has often been referred to the period of the Emperor Commodus (AD 180–93), who posed as the incarnation of Hercules and assumed the title of Hercules Romanus. It has also been suggested that it might be a representation of the Celtic Jupiter and thus belong to the pre-Roman iron age, but this is open to debate. Since the giant does not appear in documentary evidence before the 1730s, it may even be as late as that. The only comparable hill-figure in southern England is the Wilmington Long Man in Sussex, which is probably Saxon.

8. Chalbury, Bincombe

Iron Age
SY: 695838

Minor road passes on W side.

A roughly triangular fort of about 4 hectares overlooking Weymouth Bay. It was protected by a single ditch and a rampart built of limestone slabs, the latter obtained from quarry ditches inside the fort. The single ditch was found to be 5.5 metres deep and 7 metres wide. There is an entrance on the south-east side. Seventy depressions in the interior have been shown to represent huts and storage pits. Some of the huts had walls of wood and daub; others were of stone construction with paved floors.

The large number of huts suggests that the fort was intensively occupied around 450 BC.

9. Combs Ditch, Winterborne Whitechurch

Iron Age or Post-Roman
ST: 851021 to 890000

The A354 between Dorchester and Blandford cuts across this earthwork at 857018.
This linear ditch has its rampart on the south-west and may therefore have been constructed as a defence against an attack expected from the north-east, and probably also as a boundary. Its certain course is about 6.5 km long. Nothing is known of its date, but it has been compared with the post-Roman Bokerley Dyke (no. 4), which is similarly sited.

10. Coney's Castle, Whitechurch Canonicorum

Iron Age
SY: 372975

Minor road passes through middle of fort.
A small promontory fort at the southern end of a ridge, bisected by the modern road. There is a main enclosure, with a smaller one to the south, separated from each other by a ditch with ramparts on either side. The west side is protected by a steep escarpment. Elsewhere there is a surrounding ditch with inner rampart and counterscarp bank. The northern defences are particularly impressive. Unfortunately the northern entrance has been completely destroyed by the road, which may also have removed one at the south. The relationship between Coney's Castle and Lambert's Castle on the hill to the north is interesting. Lambert's Castle may have been a stock enclosure serving as an outlier to Coney's Castle (see no. 27).

11. Deverel Barrow, Milborne St Andrew

Bronze Age
SY: 820990

Just W of the A354 between Milborne and Winterborne Whitechurch.
This round barrow is well known because the Deverel-Rimbury culture of the middle bronze age (formerly regarded as late bronze age) was named from this site and Rimbury (where there is nothing to be seen) north-east of Weymouth. The Deverel Barrow is covered with bushes and enclosed by a circular stone wall. On the site are large slabs inscribed WAM, the initials of W. A. Miles, who excavated the barrow in 1824 and found numerous cremation urns, nearly all of which are now in Bristol City Museum. There are also on the site the remains of an inscribed slab commemorating the excavation:

> THIS BARROW WAS OPENED IN THE YEAR 1824 AND THE VARIOUS URNS WHICH IT CONTAINED ARE DEPOSITED SOME IN WHATCOMBE HOUSE AND SOME IN THE MUSEUM IN BRISTOL. IT HAS BEEN INSPECTED BY SIR RICD. COLT HOARE, BART, FRS, WHO CONSIDERS IT TO BE MORE ANCIENT AND MORE CURIOUS THAN ANY BARROW EVER YET DISCOVERED IN THE ISLAND. E.M.P. 1829.

12. Dorset Cursus

Neolithic
ST: 970123 to 040191

The SW end is approached from the Thickthorn turning off the A354 at 966130. The NE end is immediately S of Bokerley Dyke and reached by footpath from Woodyates.
This great earthwork is 9.7 km long and consists of two parallel banks with outer ditches, the banks being about 82 metres apart. The south-western end is close to two long barrows on Thickthorn Down, and the north-eastern end is close to a bank-barrow, more ploughed-out long barrows and a mortuary enclosure. Yet other long barrows are incorporated within it, during its course. The Cursus was built in two sections, the earlier south-western section ending in a transverse curve at Bottlebush Down south-west of the B3081. Looking west along the Cursus from this terminal

Cropmarks of the two parallel ditches of the Dorset Cursus run diagonally from bottom left to middle right (arrowed). The Ackling Dyke Roman road runs from top to bottom centre. (J. E. Hancock)

point and looking towards the long barrow on Gussage Cow Down, it will be noticed that the sun sets directly behind the barrow at midwinter. The eastern section of the Cursus extends almost as far as Bokerley Dyke. The Dorset Cursus was perhaps the linear focus of a broad ceremonial landscape which stretched in time and space from specialised neolithic long barrows and henge monuments to large cemeteries of early bronze age round barrows, and for well over a thousand years excluded domestic settlements, which were located to the north and south.

The Cursus is seldom easy to see, though visibility is best in the winter after ploughing, when it appears as soil marks, or in the spring as crop marks. The best place to view these is from beside the B3081. A stretch of the southern bank runs along the fence west of SU: 018159. The south-western terminal is visible just north of the Thickthorn long barrows at ST: 969124, but the north-eastern end has been ploughed away. The top of Bokerley Dyke makes a good viewing platform for the adjoining long barrows (SU: 042193).

13. Dudsbury, West Parley
Iron Age
SZ: 077979

Footpath from Hampreston to Parley Cross road.

A semicircular fort of about 3.2 hectares, on an escarpment above the river Stour. It is protected by double banks and ditches on all except the south side. Most of the outer fortifications have been badly damaged. Only two entrances, those on the west and south-west, seem to be original. The latter gave access to the river and a water supply. Limited excavations have proved unhelpful.

14. Eggardon Camp, Askerswell

Iron Age
SY: 541948

Approach from the A35 through Askerswell to 545943, within a short walk of the site.

Among the finest hillforts in Wessex, enclosing some 14.5 hectares, this is bivallate with entrances at the north-west and south-east, the latter being slightly inturned. It contains the remains of two probably bronze age round barrows; and there are signs of some five hundred depressions which are believed to have been iron age granaries. Slingstones from the Chesil Beach have been found here. The polygonal enclosure within the hillfort is a tree-clump enclosure of probable nineteenth- century date.

15. Five Marys, Chaldon Herring

Bronze Age
SY: 790842

By footpath from the A352 at 787848 or 793849.

This is a linear group of seven or eight round barrows placed beside the ridgeway, including three bell-barrows and one pond-barrow. All have been dug into in the past, but none has been scientifically excavated. The name may be derived from Five Meers or boundary marks, under which name they are shown on a map dated 1765.

16. Grey Mare and Her Colts, Long Bredy

Neolithic
SY: 584871

The easiest approach is from the road between Abbotsbury and Black Down, along a track W from 590867.

A chambered long barrow about 24 metres long and 1.2 metres high, placed south-east to north-west. At the south-east is a burial chamber with possible crescentic forecourt, and there are traces of a peristalith. Excavation in the early nineteenth century revealed many human bones and pottery.

17. Grimstone Down, Stratton

Bronze Age and Iron Age
SY: 646956

Track from Grimstone to Sydling St Nicholas road at 637957.

There are many hectares of Celtic fields, with small enclosures and hollow-ways on top of the Down. Although there are no traces of houses, there was certainly a well-laid-out settlement here. At least two enclosures have clearly defined entrances. There are half a dozen round barrows on the Down. The best has been clandestinely opened in Grimstone Clumps. North of Jackman's Cross is an upstanding cross-ridge dyke at 649962.

18. Gussage Hill, Gussage St Michael

Iron Age?
ST: 990140

From the A354, take the footpath from either 980139 or 987146.

Although ploughed, this is among the most spectacular settlement sites on Cranborne Chase. It should preferably be visited in winter (when showing well as soil marks) or spring (when showing as cropmarks). The probably iron age or Romano-British layout is clearly to be distinguished from the passage across it of the Dorset Cursus, which incorporates between its two parallel banks a neolithic long barrow, while there is another to the south-east. The settlement includes two oval 'banjo enclosures' and a system of ditches.

19. Hambledon Hill, Child Okeford

Neolithic and Iron Age
ST: 845126

Approach by footpath from road between Child Okeford and Iwerne Courtney at 847133 where signposted, or by various alternative paths.

The earliest of the earthworks on this hill are two neolithic causewayed enclosures south-east of the iron age hillfort, and a fine long barrow 68 metres in length within the hillfort. The smaller causewayed enclosure stood on the Stepleton spur and may have been a settlement. Nothing now remains to be seen. From it a bank and ditch ran north-west towards 849122, where the main enclosure lay. Excavation has shown that this consisted of a single ring of causewayed ditches, which are very difficult to see. The excavator has suggested that corpses were exposed in the centre of this enclosure, before they were removed for burial in a small long barrow, now destroyed, which lay to the south.

The iron age hillfort is amongst the finest in Britain. It is multivallate but probably began as a univallate enclosure of about 3 hectares in the northern sector of the fort. Later this was extended south of the long barrow to cover a further 2.2 hectares. Finally it was enlarged once more to its present 12.5 hectares and the ramparts were doubled. There are entrances at the north, south-east and south-west. The last has a protective hornwork 100 metres long. The hollows of numerous hut platforms can be seen scooped out of the hillside. There is evidence to suggest that around 300 BC the inhabitants abandoned the restricted hilltop ridge and moved south to Hod Hill (no. 24).

20. Hampton stone circle, Portesham — Bronze Age
SY: 596865

By footpath for 800 metres SW of the road between Portesham and Black Down at 601868.

Excavation during 1964 has shown that this monument is a fairly recent reconstruction of a genuine stone circle which remains partly beneath it. The original circle was 6 metres in diameter. Today nine stones remain in two arcs on the north and south sides.

21. Hardy Monument round barrows — Bronze Age
SY: 613876

By road from either Portesham or Winterbourne St Martin.

South of the Hardy Monument is a bell-barrow which was excavated in 1955; the primary burial had been dissolved by the acid soil; there were four secondary urns (three with burnt bones) near the top. Between the Hardy Monument and the south-east end of Bronkham Hill are about another twenty-five barrows, in some instances so close together as almost to touch one another. They include four bell-barrows. These are all part of the South Dorset Ridgeway barrow cemetery.

22. Hell Stone long barrow, Portesham — Neolithic
SY: 606867

The best approach is on foot from Portesham, the site being about 1 km to NE.

This is the burial chamber of a long barrow of which the mound was levelled long ago. The burial chamber now visible is an incorrect mid-nineteenth-century restoration by Martin Tupper (1810–89).

23. Hengistbury Head, Bournemouth — Bronze Age and Iron Age
SZ: 164910

On the S side of Christchurch Harbour 3.2 km SE of Christchurch. Approach from W via Southbourne.

The site had a long period of occupation starting with an upper palaeolithic working floor and later mesolithic hunter-gatherers lived there. These remains are not visible, but there are thirteen bronze age round barrows, eleven of which are sited on the headland and two at the north-west near the iron age earthwork. Finds from this period include a large collared urn, amber beads, an amber pendant, jewellery covered with sheet gold and an incense cup.

In the iron age two banks and ditches, possibly of seventh century BC date, cut off the promontory to make a fortified settlement area. The earthworks are more readily visible at the north end. After the fort was established it became an important port, with trade eventually from Gaul and the Mediterranean. By the first half of the first century BC Italian wine, coloured glass, figs and Breton pottery were being imported in large quantities. In return grain, metal ores, salt and cattle were shipped to Brittany. The site continued in use until the Roman period, after which it appears to have been largely neglected. The area may also have had a mint producing cast bronze staters, but this suggestion remains controversial. The finds are housed in the Red House Museum, Christchurch.

24. Hod Hill, Stourpaine

Iron Age and Roman
ST: 857106

Turn off the A350 near Stepleton House and park in wood near 853133, and then climb up to NW corner of the fort.

This magnificent site of 20 hectares has been comprehensively excavated and the general sequence of events is clear. A late bronze age palisade enclosure was followed by a timber-revetted rampart and ditch; this ditch was later re-cut and the resulting material used to form the outer rampart. At this time the north-eastern entrance was made by breaching the earlier rampart and filling part of its ditch to form a causeway. The only other prehistoric gate is that at the south-west leading to the river. The outermost ditch and counterscarp were made last of all, together with a timber box-rampart, topped by a parapet and sentry walk. These last were heavily reinforced with flints. The final rampart rose 11 metres above the bottom of the ditch. This defence is associated with an influx of people into Hod Hill from nearby Hambledon Hill about 300 BC. Many round huts about 6 metres in diameter were crammed into the fort. The site has been heavily ploughed, but a few hut circles can be seen in the south-east corner, together with the hollows made by many storage pits. These huts were subjected to a fierce attack by the Romans in AD 43–4. At that time the hillfort was captured and a Roman garrison fort was built within its north-western portion. Excavation of this fort has revealed foundations of the headquarters building, the commandant's house, barrack blocks for infantry and cavalry, and a latrine with ten compartments. The Romans constructed the entrances at the north-west corner and in the middle of the eastern side of the iron age fort. Most of the finds from the excavations are in the British Museum.

25. Kingston Russell stone circle

Bronze Age
SY: 577878

Approach from Abbotsbury to NE at 590867; a 1.6 km walk via Grey Mare and her Colts (no. 16).

A stone circle about 24 metres in diameter. All the stones are now fallen. It is on arable land and summer visits should be avoided. It is under English Heritage guardianship and well signposted.

26. Knowlton circles, Woodlands

Neolithic and Bronze Age
SU: 025100

The B3078 from Wimborne Minster to Cranborne passes through the South Circle. Limited parking beside Church Henge.

This is a complex of neolithic and bronze age ceremonial and mortuary sites spread along a terrace of the river Allen. It once consisted of three henge monuments, various enclosures and more than forty round barrows. Today most of the sites have been ploughed flat and are visible only from the air. The most accessible site is **Church Henge** (024103), an oval earthwork some 106 metres by 94 metres with a bank outside the ditch, and containing near its centre the ruins of a twelfth-century (and later) church, abandoned in the eighteenth century. The ditch is made

The Knowlton circles in 1995, with Church Henge in the centre. Cropmarks in a crop of peas reveal the circular ditches of barrows, including the Great Barrow (left) and the 'Old Churchyard' near the road (centre right). The South Circle is just visible to the left of the farm buildings. (Martin Green)

up of a number of sections, joined together like a string of sausages. There are three possible entrances, but only excavation will determine which is original. The bank may have served as a grandstand from which to observe ceremonies.

Due east of Church Henge is the overgrown and very large **Great Barrow**, some 6.4 metres high, which stands at the centre of two ploughed-out concentric ditches, the outer of which is 120 metres in diameter. It may have been a combined burial and ceremonial site. North-west of Church Henge traces of two ploughed-out earthworks can just be seen. North Circle is a D-shaped enclosure with internal ditch, suggesting that it was a henge. South-west of it, near the road to Brockington Farm, is a rounded-square site known erroneously as the 'Old Churchyard'.

200 metres south of Church Henge, cut by the B3078 road and enclosing Knowlton Farm (025100), is the **South Circle**, a large henge 227 metres in diameter. It has been almost entirely destroyed by agriculture, though its once massive bank and internal ditch can still be observed in the field south of the road. An arc of the bank standing 1.2 metres high is best preserved on the north-west side of the farm. There may once have been an entrance on the south side of the henge, just east of the road.

Of the many Knowlton bronze age round barrows, a few are still visible west of the Winterborne road, some 500 metres south of the South Circle. A much larger group of ploughed-out barrows lay to the north-east around 029106.

27. Lambert's Castle, Marshwood
Iron Age
SY: 372991

National Trust car park off B3165.

Situated on heathland with wide views, this is a small fort with a single bank and ditch around it. There is an entrance on the south side; that on the north is probably recent. The interior has been ploughed at some time, and there are slight banks and hollows of recent date. Lambert's Castle is not strongly defended and was probably a stock enclosure, perhaps connected with Coney's Castle to the south (no. 10).

Maiden Castle is the most spectacular of all the southern hillforts. The line of the causewayed enclosure runs across the centre of the site. (J. E. Hancock)

28. Maiden Castle, Winterborne St Martin — Neolithic, Iron Age, Roman
SY: 669884

By Maiden Castle Way, SW of Dorchester. Short walk from car park.

The earliest occupation of the hill on which Maiden Castle stands is represented by a neolithic causewayed enclosure dated to about 4000 BC, which rings the eastern hill summit within the circuit of the later iron age fort. A rather indistinct bank-barrow 546 metres long overlies the causewayed enclosure and is about five hundred years later in date. The burials of two young children found at its eastern end may be associated with it.

The iron age hillfort began about 600 BC as a 6 hectare enclosure, surrounded by a single dumped-turf rampart and ditch, with a single entrance to the west and a double entrance to the east. It covered almost the same site as the neolithic enclosure. About 450 BC the fort was extended westwards to enclose 18 hectares with a single rampart and ditch. There then followed a long period of almost continual rampart construction, when the defences were dramatically enlarged on all sides, with complex entrances on both the east and west. This construction was probably completed by the end of the third century BC. It is possible that around AD 25 the hillfort was taken over by the Durotriges, who in AD 43–4 were wiped out by Vespasian's Second Augustan Legion. A number of burials, more than a quarter with war wounds, were found in an established late iron age cemetery in the eastern entrance. These were interpreted by the excavator, Mortimer Wheeler, as the victims of Vespasian's attack. One of the dead had a Roman spearhead lodged in his backbone. Recent excavations have done little to alter this interpretation.

Within the eastern part of the hillfort a Roman temple was built after AD 367 and continued in use until the end of the Roman occupation. Finds from the excavations of 1934–7 and 1985–6 are well displayed in the Dorset County Museum, Dorchester.

29. Martin's Down, Long Bredy
Neolithic and Bronze Age
SY: 571911

SE of the angle of the Long Bredy turning with the A35.

A classic group of earthworks lies at the western end of the South Dorset Ridgeway, including a bank-barrow 198 metres long and 1.8 metres high, a long barrow 33 metres long and 1.8 metres high, several bronze age round barrows, and a probably later cross-ridge dyke. The site is now arable and summer visits are best avoided.

30. Maumbury Rings, Dorchester
Neolithic and Roman
SY: 690899

On SE side of Weymouth Road, before leaving Dorchester.

This striking earthwork was originally a neolithic ceremonial site or henge with a bank outside a ditch and an entrance to the north-east, and with an overall diameter of about 85 metres. The ditch was composed of a series of closely spaced funnel-shaped shafts, averaging 10 metres deep. During the Roman period this was converted into an amphitheatre about 100 metres in diameter with the entrance still at the north-east, but there was also at the south-western end an enclosure probably used by the performers. The earthwork was reused during the Civil War as an artillery fort.

31. Nine Barrows, Corfe Castle
Neolithic and Bronze Age
SY: 995816

By footpath from the B3351 at 987823 to the Ridgeway.

Strung along the Ridgeway, this is a fine linear group of round barrows and (near the eastern end) a long barrow 35 metres in length and 2 metres high. The second round barrow from the west has a ditch with four causeways, suggesting a survival of a neolithic tradition (compare Wor Barrow, no. 46) if the 'causeways' are not later blockings in the ditch. The best round barrow, east of the centre of the group, is about 32 metres in diameter and 3 metres high, and ditched. One of these barrows was opened before 1826 and contained burnt bones.

32. Nine Stones, Winterborne Abbas
Bronze Age
SY: 610904

In trees immediately S of the A35 and W of Winterborne Abbas. Small lay-by opposite, near barn.

A small but impressive stone ellipse some 7.5 metres by 9.1 metres. Of the nine stones still standing, two enormous blocks flank a tiny slab on the north side. In English Heritage guardianship and signposted.

33. Oakley Down, Wimborne St Giles
Bronze Age
SU: 018173

This group is enclosed by the triangle formed by the A354, the Ackling Dyke Roman road and the B3081 from Handley Hill to Cranborne. It is best to park at 016163 and reach the group via the Ackling Dyke.

This is the finest group of round barrows on Cranborne Chase. It is particularly remarkable for six magnificent disc-barrows including two (one an oval 'twin') cut by the Roman Ackling Dyke. Colt Hoare observed: 'it will be perceived that the Roman engineers were so devoted to the straight line that they deemed it not a crime to rob a British tumulus of a part of its circumvallation.' The group also contains two (perhaps originally three) bell-barrows and twenty of the usual bowl form. Almost all these barrows were opened in the early nineteenth century by Cunnington and Colt Hoare, and the finds, which included flint arrowheads, urns, bronze daggers and beads of amber and faience, are in Devizes Museum. The worst season for visiting this group is midsummer, when the impressiveness of the disc-barrows is

A bronze age necropolis: the Oakley Down barrows, with the Roman road, the Ackling Dyke, cutting a disc-barrow in the foreground. (Cambridge University Collection)

minimised by the long grass and the absence of shadows.

34. Pilsdon Pen — Iron Age
ST: 413013

From the B3164 at Lob Gate (414009) where there is a car park; it is a short walk uphill to the site.

This is a notable multivallate hillfort of about 3.2 hectares, with original entrances at the north and south-west. During the 1960s excavations revealed iron age hut sites, one of which contained a crucible with beads of gold adhering to its inner surface, attesting the practice of goldworking on this bleak hilltop. The head of a Roman ballista bolt was also found. Much of the excavation concentrated on the footings of a large rectangular structure, which, together with several oblong mounds resembling pillow mounds, turned out to be an elaborate artificial warren for breeding and trapping rabbits, of relatively recent date.

35. Pimperne long barrow — Neolithic
ST: 917105

Approach by short footpath marked 'Bridleway to Tarrant Gunville' at Collingwood Corner, on the A354 NE of Pimperne.

This well-known long barrow is 105 metres long, 30 metres wide, and 2.4 metres high and is placed south-east to north-west. An unusual feature is a well-defined berm (or platform) between the mound and the side ditches, which do not go round the ends. This berm is particularly well seen on the eastern side. This barrow was probably the meeting-place of Longbarrow Hundred, which was doubtless named from it.

36. Poor Lot, Kingston Russell — Bronze Age
SY: 589907

Just S of the A35 between Kingston Russell and Winterborne Abbas. Gateway to group near house at SE, 590907.

Among the finest groups of round barrows in Wessex, this includes barrows of bowl, bell and pond types, and 'Dorset type' variants of the disc-barrow (usually smaller than the normal disc-barrow, and with a ditch on either or both sides of the circumferential bank). Just east of the main group and north of the road is a twin bell-barrow at 591906, covered with trees and bushes. The largest barrow in the group is a ditched bowl-barrow 36 metres in diameter and 4 metres high, on the boundary between the parishes of Kingston Russell and Winterborne Abbas. Note also the disc-barrow and three conjoined bowl-barrows in the field north-east of the road. There are no known records of excavation of any of these barrows.

37. Poundbury, Dorchester

Iron Age
SY: 683912

From Poundbury Road, NW of Dorchester.

A trapezoidal-shaped hillfort of 5.5 hectares situated above the river Frome. It was protected by a V-shaped ditch 8.8 metres wide and 4.2 metres deep with a chalk bank 2.7 metres high which was continuously faced by a vertical timber palisade dating from the fourth century BC. This bank had been rebuilt at least once. In the mid first century BC the rampart was remodelled with a loose glacis slope of chalk rubble taken from internal quarry ditches. Limestone blocks formed a parapet on top, and a second rampart and ditch were constructed outside the fort. The original entrance seems to have been on the eastern side. An extensive Roman cemetery has been located outside this gate. Aerial photographs show indications of a dozen circular huts in the south-east corner of the hillfort. A Roman aqueduct runs along the outer north side of the fort. It once brought water from a dammed stream in Steppes Bottom near Frampton to Dorchester (*Durnovaria*), a distance of about 15 km.

38. Povington Heath, Tyneham

Bronze Age
SY: 880841

Beside the B3070 between Lulworth and Wareham.

The Five Barrows (876840) are in line from north to south. The three northern-most are bell-barrows; to the south are three bowl-barrows, and a bump in the road suggests that yet another is beneath it, making seven in all. East of the road, at 880841, are twin bowl-barrows enclosed by an oval ditch. No excavation records are known for any of these barrows.

39. Rawlsbury Camp, Stoke Wake

Iron Age
ST: 767057

A metalled road between Sherborne and Blandford passes the site.

This hillfort, on the western spur of Bulbarrow Hill, is remarkable for its magnificent situation overlooking the Blackmoor Vale. The earthwork is essentially bivallate and has an entrance at the east which is out-turned. The fort, which is pear-shaped, encloses 1.6 hectares.

40. Rempstone stone circle

Bronze Age
SY: 993823

Beside the B3351 between Corfe and Studland.

This stone circle is about 24 metres in diameter and in a dense wood beside the road. Of eight stones still visible, five are standing and three are recumbent. Remains of a stone avenue were identified in August 1957 about 800 metres west of and aligned with this circle. It is, however, very doubtful whether it was connected with it.

41. Shapwick, Sturminster Marshall

Bronze Age
ST: 934016

Across fields from the A350 between Spettisbury and Sturminster Marshall.

A well-formed barrow, about 25 metres in diameter and 1.8 metres high, famous as the subject of a poetic dialogue with notes, entitled *The Barrow Diggers: A*

Dialogue in Imitation of the Grave Diggers in Hamlet, by Charles Woolls (1838). The barrow was opened that year, when a probable primary cremation with an amber bead was found in a cist beneath a central cairn.

42. Smacam Down, Cerne Abbas
Iron Age and Roman?
SY: 657994

By path W from the A352 at 663998.

A well-preserved settlement with associated field system which is preserved (most unusually) also in the adjoining valley. An enclosure contains a hut circle and to the west are a cross-dyke and long barrow.

43. Thickthorn long barrows, Gussage St Michael
Neolithic
ST: 971123

From the A354 take the Ringwood turning at 966130, and the long barrows are just N of this road. Gate at 972122.

Both of these long barrows have the U-shaped ditch characteristic of several of the long barrows on Cranborne Chase; in both these instances the U has its opening at the south-east. The eastern barrow was excavated in 1933. The mound had been built in a series of bays, separated by stake fences, as at the destroyed South Street long barrow, near Avebury. No primary deposit was present but there were secondary crouched interments with beakers. Two chalk phalli were found in the primary silting of the ditch and are now (with the other finds) in the Dorset County Museum, Dorchester. The barrows lie at the south-western end of the Dorset Cursus (no. 12) and must be linked to the ceremonial that took place there.

44. Upwey Ridgeway, Weymouth
Bronze Age
SY: 663866

Just E of the B3159 between Winterborne St Martin and Upwey.

A group of round barrows, some very large. The most remarkable is a very large round barrow with berm, ditch and outer bank, the overall diameter being 78 metres: either a bell-barrow or a disc-barrow with exceptionally large central mound 2.1 metres high. This is part of the extensive South Dorset Ridgeway barrow necropolis (see Came Wood, no. 6).

45. Valley of Stones, Littlebredy
Various
SY: 597877

By footpath W of the road from Portesham to the Hardy Monument.

This valley is of interest in that it probably provided the stones for the various megalithic monuments in the vicinity. In addition, the valley and surrounding slopes are covered with an exceptionally fine rectilinear field system, which on the east side is covered with bluebells in late spring.

46. Wor Barrow, Sixpenny Handley
Neolithic
SU: 012173

Just W of the A354 and N of Handley Hill.

This oval long barrow was the scene of a classic excavation by Pitt-Rivers in 1893–4. The mound was 45 metres long and 22 metres wide and was originally about 4 metres high, and it lay south-east to north-west. It was totally excavated by Pitt-Rivers, who found towards the south-east end six skeletons inside a rectangular mound revetted by wooden uprights, with an entrance at the south-east. It was surrounded by a small ditch. Three of the burials were articulated, the others were bundles of bones. Later the mound was enlarged to form the final barrow, with a new surrounding ditch, which was irregular and had four causeways. Its primary filling at the south-east contained the burials of a boy and a crouched adult male with a flint leaf arrowhead in the ribs. Pitt-Rivers removed the mound and cleared out the surrounding ditch. Although this has now partly resilted, it remains the only permanently exposed long barrow ditch in southern England. Pitt-Rivers used the site as an amphitheatre in which his private band could give musical concerts. Wor Barrow is one of the many funerary monuments that focus on the ceremonial landscape of the Dorset Cursus (*q.v.*).

47. Wyke Down henge, Gussage St Michael   Neolithic
SU: 006152

A short walk off minor road from A354 to Monkton Up Wimborne, to this restored henge.

Two small henge monuments were discovered by aerial photography and excavated in 1983–4 by the local landowner, farmer-archaeologist Martin Green. The largest of them has been restored. Measuring 20 metres in diameter, it consisted of a ring of twenty-six closely spaced oval pits, which were separated from each other by narrow baulks of chalk. A gap 3 metres wide formed an entrance which faced due south. The pits were between 1.5 and 2 metres deep and about 2 metres across. The chalk extracted had been formed into a low bank on the outside of the circle. A radiocarbon date showed that deer antler, animal bone, pieces of worked flint and lumps of carved chalk had been deposited on the pit floors about 2600 BC. The pits were left to silt up for a short time before hollows were dug into the top of their fillings and small deposits of human bones and grooved ware pottery were inserted. There are clear similarities between this site and Maumbury Rings (no. 30), near Dorchester, and the Aubrey Holes at Stonehenge. The site was reused in the early bronze age when a central pit, 0.5 metre deep, was added. The henge seems to have been aligned on a low hill to the south where the Dorset Cursus would have been particularly prominent.

The second (unrestored) Wyke Down henge lay about 40 metres north-west of the first. Only 12 metres in diameter, it was also made up of adjoining pits. In one was the unusual combination of an almost complete grooved ware vessel and pieces of Peterborough pottery (ritual and domestic wares are not usually found together). Close by were some circular neolithic buildings that may have had a ceremonial purpose. They had unique plastered walls and seem to have served no domestic function.

The Wyke Down sites make little sense in isolation. They must be seen against the wider background of a multitude of neolithic and bronze age earthworks, mostly destroyed by ploughing, that were once densely ranged across this part of Cranborne Chase.

DURHAM
(Map on page 243)

1. Batter Law, Cold Hesledon   Bronze Age
NZ: 406460

Take minor road W from Hawthorn. At 406453 a footpath leads N. The mound is to the E of this on the highest immediate point of land.

This mutilated and ploughed-down barrow is about 18 metres across and 1.5 metres high. In 1911 a crouched male skeleton, protected by large stone slabs, was found in a grave with a flint knife.

2. Copt Hill, Houghton le Spring   Neolithic
NZ: 353492

W of the golf course S of the B1404 and E of the railway.

This large cairn is tree-planted and measures about 18 metres across and 2.4 metres high. Excavations in 1877 showed that the rotted corpses of a number of persons had been placed on the old ground surface, possibly after storage elsewhere. Blocks of wood and limestone had then been placed over them and the whole mass thoroughly incinerated. The mound had then been erected. In the early bronze age eight further burials had been deposited. Four were inhumations, one with a food-vessel. The others were cremations, one in a collared urn.

3. Hasting Hill barrow, Offerton
Bronze Age
NZ: 353544
Take minor road from East Herrington to the A183. The barrow is a short distance to the right of the road alongside a track at 352544.
The mound is 12 metres across and 0.9 metre high. The primary burial was a crouched skeleton in a cist west of the centre, with a rusticated beaker, bone pin and flint tools. There were two further inhumations in well-built cists (all reconstructed in Sunderland Museum); of the nine further burials in the mound, six were crema-tions, four in cists, two in collared urns. Pottery, including a food-vessel, and flints were found scattered in the mound.

4. Low Hills, Shotton
Bronze Age
NZ: 413415
Just W of the A19, S of Low Hills House.
An oval mound, roughly 19 metres by 14 metres, stands 1.8 metres high. A rough cist south of centre contained a cremation and flint knife. Below this a more carefully built cist was found sunk into the old ground surface. It was empty but may have held a completely decayed inhumation.

5. Maiden Castle, Durham
Iron Age
NZ: 283417
On the SE edge of Durham, accessible via footpaths leading N from the A177.
This promontory fort is roughly rectangular. Steep slopes protect it on all sides but the west. Slight traces of a bank are visible on the north, east and south. On the west a single bank crosses the promontory: it is 5.5 metres wide, 2.1 metres high, with an outer ditch still 1.2 metres deep and the remnants of a slight inner bank at the southern end. A break in the ditch at the northern end of the bank may signify an original entrance here.

ESSEX
(Map on page 238)
1. Ambresbury Banks, Epping Forest
Iron Age
TL: 438004
In the Forest, on the E side of Epping Road (B1393) 3 km S of Epping, and opposite the minor Crown Hill road to Upshire.
This plateau fort is rectangular in plan and encloses about 4.5 hectares. It is defended by a bank and ditch, with traces of an outer (counterscarp) bank in places. The main bank varies between 1.2 metres and 2.1 metres in height, and excavation has shown that the V-shaped ditch was 6.6 metres wide and 3 metres deep. The only original entrance is in the middle of the west side. The inturned entrance in the south-east is of medieval construction. A stream rises inside the fort, providing a water supply.

2. Colchester (*Camulodunum*)
Iron Age and Roman
TL: 995253 (centre)
Camulodunum was probably the capital of Addedomaros, ruler of the iron age tribe of the Trinovantes. Shortly after 5 BC the capital was captured by the Catuvellauni under their leader, Tasciovanus, who minted coins marked *CAMV* there. However, by about AD 10 Cunobelin, son of Tasciovanus, had acquired the Trinovantian throne and ruled the whole of south-eastern England from

Camulodunum until his death about AD 42.

The iron age capital was a large fortified promontory enclosing some 31 sq km, and bounded on the north, south and east by the Roman River and the river Colne. The western defences were supplied by a number of lines of dykes spanning the 5 km between the rivers. Some of the main dykes were probably built in the following order.

The earliest, known as **Heath Farm Dyke**, may have been built when Addedomaros moved to *Camulodunum* about 25 BC. It is bow-shaped in plan and protects the area around Gosbeck's Farm (at 964218 for example) south of the B1022 and north-west of Oliver's Farm, where the royal residence probably stood. Now largely destroyed, the dyke is visible in places between Oliver's Thicks Wood and Chest Wood, where it crosses the Roman River. Soon afterwards the **Lexden Dyke** was thrown up. It can be traced in places between 978270 and 974246. Part of it in Bluebottle Grove is owned by English Heritage and is accessible from Parson's Hill. It can be visited at any time. Beyond the river Colne to the north the earthwork is known as **Moat Farm Dyke** and is fenced but can be fleetingly seen in section from trains in the railway cutting!

The **Sheepen Dyke** protects the area of Sheepen Farm, which was probably the main industrial area of Cunobelin's settlement after AD 5. This lay south of the junction of Sheepen Road with the A12(T) bypass and north-east of Kingswode Hoe School in Sussex Road (around 987255).

The excavator, Christopher Hawkes, suggested that the **Triple Dyke** may have been built by the Roman army as a temporary encampment for the invasion force in AD 43. It was possibly an adaptation by the Romans of an earlier dyke. It ran from Lexden Straight Road (where the best section is in the care of English Heritage at 965246) to the river Colne.

Some of the other dykes are likely to date from after the Roman conquest, or even after Boudicca: perhaps about AD 60. One such is **Gryme's Dyke**, from the river Colne at 956267 to Layer de la Haye at 965200.

Most of the dykes are now hidden amongst the sprawl of modern Colchester, and it is essential to use the Ordnance Survey Explorer map sheet 184 when trying to trace them.

The iron age capital surrendered to the Roman Emperor Claudius in AD 43. Six years later it was created a *colonia* by the governor, Ostorius Scapula, and named *Colonia Claudia* (*Victricensis* was added, probably after the revolt of Boudicca). Here recently retired legionaries were settled, each with a dwelling and small plot of land. At this time the town probably became the religious centre of the province, and a great temple dedicated to Claudius was constructed, built on a huge masonry base measuring 32 metres by 24 metres and 3.5 metres high, with a further 4 metres below ground. The ruins of the upper parts of the temple were destroyed by the Normans. The vaults below it still exist under Colchester Castle and are shown on conducted tours. The castle itself now contains the fine Colchester and Essex Museum (999253).

In AD 60 *Camulodunum* was destroyed by Queen Boudicca (Boadicea) of the Iceni, in retaliation for atrocities committed by Roman officials against her people and family.

3. Colchester: Lexden Tumulus
Iron Age
TL: 975247

In the gardens of 36 and 30 Fitzwalter Road, near its junction with St Clare Road.

This burial mound dated to 15–10 BC may have contained the body of Addedomaros or one of his relations. Excavations in 1924 produced the burnt remains of splendid bronzes, a garment (possibly a shirt) made largely of gold threads, some decorative silver ears of wheat, chain mail, bindings for a chest, at least seventeen wine jars, and a coin of Augustus struck in 17 BC and mounted as a portrait medallion. There is evidence to suggest that there were other important graves close by: perhaps the area formed a royal burial ground of the local iron age tribe, the Trinovantes. All the finds from the Lexden Tumulus are in the Colchester and Essex Museum.

4. Danbury hillfort

Iron Age
TL: 779052

S of the A414 around St John's church.

As at West Wycombe and Cholesbury (Buckinghamshire) a church has been constructed within this plateau fort. Now very much destroyed, especially on the north side, it seems to have been a small oval fort defended by a single bank and ditch.

5. Loughton Camp, Epping Forest

Iron Age
TQ: 418975

In Epping Forest, 800 metres E of the A104 at Broom Hill and 800 metres N of Earl's Path.

This hillfort is roughly oval in shape. It encloses about 2.6 hectares and occupies the end of a spur with extensive views to the south. A stream rising in marshy ground in the south-east corner is an unusual feature. The steep hillslope on the west and south-west adds to the strength of a single bank and V-shaped ditch. The latter is 2.7 metres deep on the north (2.1 metres on the south). The original entrance has not been identified. Excavations were carried out in 1882 by General Pitt-Rivers.

6. Pitchbury Ramparts, Great Horkesley

Iron Age
TL: 966290

5 km NW of Colchester. Approached along edge of wood from minor road between Horkesley Heath and Westwood Park.

Only the northern third of this once strong hillfort survives inside the wood. It was partially bivallate, consisting of two banks on the north and east, the inner of dump construction and 3 metres high, with a wide ditch between them. The outer bank was not constructed on the south-west. A gap through both banks on the north-west may have been an original entrance. Excavations in 1973 found no sign of significant structures within the fort, which may have been only a temporary refuge. A date in the first century BC is postulated.

7. Ring Hill, Littlebury

Iron Age
TL: 515382

Lying on the E end of the chalk ridge between the B1383 and the railway, due W of Audley End.

This oval hillfort, enclosing 6.7 hectares, is completely overgrown with trees. It once overlooked the river Cam. It has a wide ditch separating an inner rampart from an outer counterscarp bank. A pathway made above the ditch in the nineteenth century has destroyed most of this rampart. The position of the original entrance is unknown.

8. Wallbury Camp, Great Hallingbury

Iron Age
TL: 493178

3 km S of Bishops Stortford, beside a minor road leading from the A1184 across the river Stort to Little Hallingbury.

Two banks and ditches which enclose 12.5 hectares surround a pear-shaped hillfort. In places the inner rampart is still 2.1 metres high. On the west, above the steep slope down to the river Stort, the earthworks seem to be incomplete, probably because the natural defence was sufficient on its own. Gaps in the north-east and west sides are possibly entrances, but only that on the east, 100 metres north of the modern entrance drive, is likely to be original.

GLOUCESTERSHIRE
(Map on page 236)

1. Avening burial chambers   **Neolithic**
ST: 879983

In the village of Avening, at the foot of a steep bank below minor road off B4014 and E of stream.

Three burial chambers were moved to this site in 1806 after the excavation of a long barrow in which they were contained, which lay to the south-east of the neighbouring hamlet of Nags Head.

The chambers are all rectangular in plan and from west to east measure respectively: I, 0.9 metre wide and 1.5 metres long; II, 0.9 metre wide and 1.7 metres long; and III, 2 metres wide and 1.8 metres long. Chambers II and III are roofed with single capstones and are approached by short passages. Chamber I has neither a capstone nor a passage. The great interest in the group lies in the fact that chamber III has a porthole entrance, and chamber II possibly has part of one. Porthole entrances consist of artificially cut holes large enough to allow the passage of a human body. The nearby Rodmarton long barrow (no. 37) also had portholes (no longer visible) and such features, although rare, are found elsewhere in Britain and western Europe.

2. Bagendon   **Iron Age**
SP: 018064

Off the A435, 800 metres E of the modern village of Bagendon.

This area of about 80 hectares, defended on three sides by earthworks, and on the fourth by forest, may possibly have been the *oppidum* or tribal headquarters of the Belgic people known as the Dobunni. Coin moulds and many coins suggest that the Dobunni had their mint at Bagendon around AD 20–30. Italian red pottery and bronze and iron brooches made by continental craftsmen indicate that the *oppidum* was flourishing at this time. Excavations have suggested that the site was occupied about AD 15–60.

The main dykes run for 550 metres beside Welsh Way near Perrot's Brook and for 1200 metres along the west side of Cutham Lane. A second line of ditches lies 75 metres east of this latter site. When the earthwork beside Cutham Lane was excavated the ditch was shown to be 3.2 metres wide and 1.8 metres deep. About 1600 metres north of the main system runs the earthwork called **Scrubditch** (010077). Although its ditch faces south and therefore seems to oppose the Bagendon earthworks, it is generally interpreted as part of their system.

3. Beckbury Camp, Hailes Abbey   **Iron Age**
SP: 064299

On the summit of a hill 800 metres E of Hailes Abbey. Can be approached by tracks through Hailes Wood from Hailes to Farmcote minor road.

This is a small rectangular promontory fort enclosing about 1.8 hectares. Its north and west sides are defended by steeply falling ground. A single upstanding rampart and silted ditch bound the east and south sides. Although there may have been entrances around the rampart ends at the north-east and south-west corners, the real access seems to have been by a hollow-way at the north-west undefended corner. A length of fire-reddened drystone outer facing wall is exposed at the north end of the east rampart.

There are fine views from this little fort, particularly to the south-west, where the opposite valley slopes show considerable disturbance, perhaps connected with a deserted medieval village.

The false entrance to the Belas Knap long barrow before it was vandalised. The lower courses of drystone walling are original. (J. Dyer)

4. Belas Knap long barrow, Charlton Abbots
Neolithic
SP: 021254

Signposted footpath leaves minor road from Winchcombe to Charlton Abbots at 022261. Small lay-by for one or two cars. Steep climb and walk of 800 metres, but well worth the effort for the view. English Heritage; open at any time.

This beautiful long barrow is 52 metres long, 18 metres wide (maximum) and 4 metres high and is orientated north to south. It was probably originally higher to cover the south chamber. The most striking feature of this long barrow is the false entrance at the north end, between convex horns edged with drystone walling of exceptional quality. It should be noted that the upper sections of this walling have been restored. There are a pair of burial chambers halfway along the barrow, a third chamber on the south-east side, and a long cist in the south end. All of these chambers were originally completely enclosed within the barrow, but since restoration they have been made accessible. The barrow was excavated in 1863–5 and 1928–31. The remains of about thirty people were found in the burial chambers, and the skull of a man and the bones of five children were found in the rubble blocking behind the false entrance stone. The name Belas Knap is medieval in origin and means a beacon mound.

A small ploughed-out round barrow can be seen as a low mound in the ploughed field due west of the long barrow.

5. Blaise Castle, Bristol
Iron Age
ST: 559784

On the Blaise Castle estate, SW of Folk Museum.

This oval hillfort of about 2.4 hectares commands a wide view of the Severn estuary. Steep sides on the south and south-east made only a slight defence necessary, but along the north and west there are two banks and ditches. Except for the highest point, the site is largely wooded, but access is eased by the footpaths laid out at the beginning of the nineteenth century. The original entrances are unknown at present, but excavation may reveal them. It has produced iron age pottery, jewellery and storage pits.

6. Bloody Acre Camp, Cromhall
Iron Age
ST: 689915

Wooded. In Tortworth Park (HM Prison) beside minor road 800 metres N of Cromhall.

This is probably the best of a small group of hillforts between the Cotswolds and the Severn. It is basically a promontory fort with steep sides overlooking a small stream 30 metres below. The promontory is cut off on the west side by banks and ditches which isolate some 4 hectares. On the south-west these earthworks consist of three large banks with silted ditches between them. Only two of the banks survive at the north end of the defences, at which point the inner bank turns east, perhaps forming part of an uncertain inturned entrance.

7. Brackenbury Ditches, North Nibley
Iron Age
ST: 747949

Wooded site beside B4060. Can be approached by turning off minor road NW of Bournstream.

A promontory fort of about 2.4 hectares sited on a west-facing spur of the Cotswolds. A bank and ditch follow the contour of the steep hillside; whilst two banks and ditches mark the north-east side, these are widely spaced in the south-western manner. What appears to be the original entrance is approached by a hollow-way in the south side. A number of pits in the vicinity are probably of natural origin.

8. Bury Hill Camp, Winterbourne Down
Iron Age and Roman
ST: 652791

Approached from minor road at Moorend.

Two banks are separated by a single ditch from the defences of this pear-shaped hillfort of about 2 hectares. Quarrying for Pennant stone has removed the west part of the earthwork. There are three possible entrances, but later Roman occupation has obscured the iron age structure to some extent. A Roman well was found south of the north-west entrance.

The U-shaped ditch was 6 metres wide and 1.5 metres deep and provided a quarry for rubble to build the ramparts, which still stand 2.7 metres high in places and have a drystone retaining wall. Excavation in 1926 showed that most of the interior features are Romano-British, including a long mound near the centre, on the west side, which covers a house.

9. Cleeve Hill, Southam
Iron Age
SO: 985255

Lay-by on B4632 5 km NE of Cheltenham at 985269. Long uphill walk across Cleeve Hill Common (magnificent views). Alternative route along minor road from same point on B4632 to Nutterswood. Very steep climb up to fort.

This small 0.8 hectare promontory fort is isolated by two semicircular ramparts, each with external ditches. A berm separates the inner ditch from the outer rampart. No entrance exists, and we may assume that access was originally gained around the ends of the ramparts, now quarried or eroded away. A golf green has destroyed part of the outer rampart and ditch on the north side, and visitors should keep a wary eye open for golfers who bombard the fort with golf balls. Hut circles can be seen inside the enclosure.

About 530 metres north of the fort is a linear earthwork running east to west just south of the trigonometrical station on the highest point of the hill. It has a ditch on its south (fort-facing) side.

Also on the hill, not far from the B4632 road, is an earthwork known as the Ring. This is a circular banked and ditched enclosure about 30 metres in diameter that has been utilised to contain a disused golf green. It is almost certainly of ancient construction.

10. Clifton Down Camp, Bristol — Iron Age
ST: 566733

North of the Clifton Suspension Bridge. Observatory stands inside the fort.

This is one of three forts defending promontories and facing one another across the Avon Gorge. The other two are Burwalls (largely destroyed) and Stokeleigh. All are less than 400 metres from each other. They are also similar in construction and may be contemporary, but the steep cliffs of the Avon Gorge and the river 75 metres below make access between the forts difficult, although a ford is known to have existed across the river, a few metres below the suspension bridge, until at least the mid nineteenth century.

The multivallate ramparts of Clifton Down Camp enclose some 1.2 hectares and form an arc, which is broken by a probable entrance on the east side. There may have been a further entrance close to the edge of the cliff on the north-west. The ramparts have been disturbed by quarrying and are obscured by bushes, but paths follow the lines of the ditches. On the south-west side of the interior is a bank and a rectangular earthwork which has not been excavated and is regarded by most authorities as being of later workmanship.

11. Cow Common barrow cemetery, Swell — Neolithic and Bronze Age
SP: 132263

4 km W of Lower Swell, N of minor road from Swell Hill Farm to Chalk Hill. Footpath NE leaves corner of wood to cross Cow Common.

Within a distance of 360 metres lies a cemetery of ten round barrows and one long barrow. The long barrow is of the false-entrance type and is 45 metres long and 1.5 metres high. Two stone chambers contained ten adult burials and one infant, as well as neolithic pottery and pieces of pottery spoons.

The round barrows vary in size and height from 9 to 18 metres in diameter and 0.3 to 1.2 metres high. Amongst five in an overlapping row at the west end of the Common, one contained a crouched male burial in a stone cist, with two later cremated burials in urns (one with a bronze razor) added to the barrow at a later bronze age date. Another contained a beehive-shaped chamber similar to one found at Bibury, and the other three all contained cremations. Nothing is known of the contents of the remaining barrows that lie west, south-west and east of the long barrow.

12. Crickley Hill, Coberley — Neolithic to Iron Age
SO: 928161

Signposted to country park, part owned by National Trust, on A417, 8 km from Gloucester. Open all year round. Car park and toilets.

This promontory fort has a long and complicated history, partly unravelled by many years of excavation. The main defence is an iron age rampart some 2.7 metres high at its east end, with an external ditch 2.4 metres deep. This was once topped by a timber-laced palisade. Two superimposed entrances were found, the earlier dating from the seventh century BC. This was associated with several rows of rectangular buildings inside the fort. The occupation was ended by fire. The fort was rebuilt with round houses and four-post granaries, but that was also burnt down, in the fifth century BC. The positions of some of the iron age houses have been marked out on the ground.

Some 180 metres inside the iron age rampart is a second, slighter rampart. This marks the position of a neolithic causewayed enclosure with two concentric circuits of ditches, dating from perhaps 3000 BC. After a period of abandonment it was replaced by a new, single-ring enclosure that seems to have been built for defence and eventually fell after a fierce assault involving arrows and burning, perhaps as late as 2600 BC.

Towards the end of the neolithic occupation a small shrine seems to have been set up at the western end of the hill, separated by fences and gates from the rest of the complex. This area was later covered by a long mound of rubble and a small circle of stones less than 50 cm high with a central slab for burning. Offerings seem to have been made at the long mound from neolithic times until at least the Roman period. The ritual involved remains unknown.

Display panels give the latest interpretation.

13. Gatcombe Lodge barrow, Minchinhampton Neolithic
ST: 884997

On the S side of the minor road from Minchinhampton to Avening, in the trees at the N end of Gatcombe Park. Restricted access.

This long barrow has a false entrance at its north-east end between drystone horns. The barrow measures 55 metres by 21 metres and is orientated north-east to south-west. There is an accessible burial chamber on the north side of the barrow not far from the east end. It contained a single skeleton when it was discovered in 1871. The chamber is constructed of five upright stones with a capstone, and some fine drystone walling. Two more stones form an entrance. Near the south-west end is a large slab of stone which may be the coverstone to another chamber.

Some 270 metres north of the long barrow stands **The Long Stone** (884999). This upright triangular slab of oolite stands 2.3 metres high and may be part of a burial chamber destroyed in the nineteenth century. Holes in the stone appear to be natural. A smaller stone block is built into a wall 11 metres away.

14. Haresfield Beacon and Ring Hill Iron Age
SO: 823090

Minor road from Haresfield to Whiteshill passes through the earthwork. National Trust property.

Haresfield Beacon and Ring Hill were initially enclosed within a single rampart and ditch forming a fort of some 6.5 hectares. There seems to have been an oblique entrance on the south side of Ring Hill. Later the earthworks were doubled in area by adding an extension east to enclose Haresfield Hill. A notable feature of the site is the wide view it commands of the Severn valley.

15. Hetty Peggler's Tump, Uley long barrow Neolithic
SO: 789000

Signposted from the B4066. Open at any reasonable time. Electric torch or candle required.

This long barrow measures 36 metres by 25 metres and lies east to west on a high ridge at the edge of the Cotswolds overlooking the vales of Berkeley and Severn. The burial chamber lies at the east end beyond a deep forecourt. It belongs to the type of stone-built chamber known as a 'transepted gallery grave', which means that it consists of a passage 6.6 metres long with two chambers on either side, rather like the transepts of a church. (The two on the right or north have been sealed off in modern times.) There is also a chamber at the end of the passage. The walls and roof are composed of large slabs of stone filled in with areas of drystone work. Excavations in 1821 revealed fifteen skeletons, and eight or nine others were found in 1854.

The name derives from Hester Peggler who was the owner, or owner's wife, in the seventeenth century.

The entrance to Hetty Peggler's Tump. This barrow is unusual in having its covering mound still intact. (J. Dyer)

16. Horton Camp
Iron Age
ST: 765845

Accessible from minor roads 400 metres S of Horton village.

This rectangular promontory fort of 2 hectares crowns a steep-sided hill. Its defences consist of a single bank and ditch, which are best preserved under fir trees on the north-east side, although the ditch is largely silted up. The site has been too much damaged to reveal its original entrance. Its position less than 1600 metres north of Sodbury Camp may be significant, since both lie on the same ridge looking west across the upper Frome valley. The camp is normally under grass.

17. King's Weston Hill, Bristol
Iron Age
ST: 557782

Minor road or footpath from B4057.

This small fort lies 400 metres south-west of Blaise Castle hillfort, at the north-east end of a narrow hill ridge. A single bank and ditch cut across the hill spur 275 metres west of the camp. Between this bank and the main fort is a small, roughly circular, banked and ditched enclosure, about 55 metres in diameter. Excavation in 1956 has shown it to be contemporary with the main fort. The ditch of the latter was cut into solid rock and was 1.8 metres deep and 4.5 metres wide, with a flat floor and vertical sides. Philip Rahtz, the excavator, was of the opinion that the owners of the fort might have been driven out by slingstones from the neighbouring Blaise Castle hillfort.

18. Lamborough Banks chambered long barrow, Bibury
Neolithic
SP: 107094

Approached on minor road from N off Salt Way. Situated in Lamborough Banks covert.

Orientated north-west to south-east, this badly damaged and overgrown long barrow is 85 metres long and 30 metres wide at its broadest end. It is surrounded by a double drystone wall, each facing outwards, with rubble between them. Early excavations showed that at the south end the walls curve slightly inwards to a false entrance stone. A stone chamber (consisting of four wall slabs at each side and one at each end) was found in the narrow (north-west) end of the barrow in 1854. It contained a single burial.

19. Leckhampton Hill
Iron Age
SO: 948184

Approached from S by minor road to Hartley Farm off B4070. Car park at 951178 and 800 metres walk (signposted 'Devil's Chimney') to fort.

This is a semicircular promontory fort, enclosing about 3.2 hectares. It is surrounded by a single rampart about 1.8 metres high, with an external rock-cut ditch. The rampart was drystone-faced and showed considerable signs of burning on the east side when examined. The entrance is also on the east, 60 metres north of the point where the modern road enters, and excavations in 1969–70 have clarified earlier reports (1925) of semicircular stone guard chambers which have been shown to lie on either side of the entrance passage. The steep cliff-like north and west sides are the results of modern quarrying, but the fort would almost certainly have relied on very steep natural slopes for defence on these sides.

Just outside the fort, and north of the point where the road enters, is what appears to be a round barrow enclosed by a square bank and ditch. It is very overgrown and its form is difficult to see. Limited excavation failed to reveal a burial. It may have been the site of a Celtic shrine.

20. Leighterton long barrow, Boxwell
Neolithic
ST: 819913

W of Leighterton village, on road to Boxwell. Covered with trees and enclosed within modern stone wall.

One of the largest chambered long barrows in the Cotswolds, it lies east to west and is about 51 metres long and 6 metres high. Three arched burial chambers containing skeletons were excavated in 1703, but they are no longer visible. John Aubrey referred to a stone standing 'at the great end' of the barrow, but this, too, has vanished. It is probable that this was a false-entrance grave, like Belas Knap.

21. Lodge Park long barrow, Farmington
Neolithic
SP: 142125

In Lodge Park, 3 km SE of Northleach.

This chambered long barrow is 45 metres long, 23 metres wide and 2.4 metres high. Two upright stones and the coverstone of the entrance can be seen at the wider south-east end. The whole mound is orientated south-east to north-west.

22. Lydney hillfort, temple, etc
Iron Age, Roman, etc
SO: 616027

Situated in Lydney Park. This is a private deer park and permission to visit must be sought in writing from the agent at Lydney Park Estate Office. Access from the A48(T) at 623021 and through farm.

A steep-sided promontory fort, enclosing some 2 hectares, was constructed during the first century BC, by erecting two banks with external ditches across the north-east end of the spur. There were two probable entrances: one at the south tip of the spur had inturned flanks, and a second lay at the south limit of the earthworks on the east side. The gap in the north rampart is of recent origin. The rampart was composed of rubble with an outer kerb of large stones; it supported a roughly paved rampart walk some 1.5 metres wide. It seems likely that the inner bank on the east side is a later, but pre-Roman, addition to the defences.

The inhabitants seem to have spent uninterrupted lives till well into the fourth century AD, living in rectangular timber huts and making deep, rounded pots of a type common in the Bristol Channel area, known, somewhat unfortunately, as 'flower pots'. They produced metalwork, including brooches, and mined iron on the site. Two iron mines have now been found and one is visible, its entrance marked by a trap-door, some 36 metres along the east side of the plateau, north of the Adam and Eve statues. It extends 15 metres underground and reaches a depth of 4.5 metres. It cuts through the iron age rampart, which was later rebuilt over the gallery. The mine was being worked not later than the third century AD. Original pick-marks can still be seen on the ferruginous walls of the mine. (Prospective visitors are warned to take protective clothing and torches.) The second mine lies under the Roman bath suite on the west side of the site.

Towards the end of the third century AD the prehistoric rampart was given a minor rebuild. Shortly after AD 364 a large temple with a guest house and bath suite was erected in the south half of the hillfort. The temple, which measures 24 metres by 18 metres, was dedicated to the native British cult of Nodens (Nodons), who was concerned with healing, the sun and water. His concern for healing clearly attracted many visitors who came to Lydney for cures, and consequently a guest house and bath suite were built to serve their needs.

The bath suite lies to the north of the temple. To the south lay a long, narrow building, divided into compartments which may have been cubicles for patients taking some form of health cure, or lock-up shops where tourists could purchase votive offerings and souvenirs.

The final building in the group, an extensive guest house, is no longer visible but clearly provided accommodation for visitors to the temple.

Objects excavated from the iron age and Roman sites by Dr and Mrs R. E. M. Wheeler in 1928–9 are in the private museum in Lydney Park House.

23. Minchinhampton Common earthworks   Neolithic and Medieval

Scattered over 240 hectares of Minchinhampton Common, in care of National Trust. Beware of careless golfers!

Of all Cotswold earthworks few are more tantalising than the maze of banks, ditches and mounds that are spread over Minchinhampton Common, and few have provoked such a variety of interpretations. The most prominent is a linear earthwork 2.4 kilometres long, known as **The Bulwarks**, which runs from SO: 857004 to 869012 and faces south-east. In 1925 the pioneer field archaeologist O. G. S. Crawford identified this as of medieval date. Somewhat inconclusive excavations in 1937 by Elsie Clifford led her to believe that they were constructed in the late iron age, a view she repeated in print in 1961, and which gained general acceptance for the next thirty years. Other linear earthworks include a length of rampart and south-east facing ditch 180 metres west of the reservoir, and a lesser curving stretch of bank and ditch running north and east of the Golf Club House towards the Bulwarks. North of this is another slight earthwork sometimes called **Amberley Camp**. It is now almost certain that all these linear features are of early medieval origin, lying on peripheral land. At that time most of the Common was heavily wooded, and the earthworks are wood banks which separated the woodland from the arable fields of Minchinhampton and Amberley. Also on the Common and originally within the woods are forty or more curious rectangular mounds known as pillow mounds. Averaging 15 metres long, 3 metres wide and 0.6 metres high, they were artificially constructed rabbit warrens probably built in the seventeenth century. A typical example can be easily found at the west end of the cattle trough that lies midway between the reservoir and the Golf Club House.

A much disturbed neolithic long barrow called **Whitfield's Tump** lies on the Common to the east of Littleworth (SO: 854017). Measuring about 23 metres long and 10.5 metres wide, it gets its name from the tradition that the Methodist George Whitfield (1714–70) stood on it to preach in 1743. There is an equally disturbed round barrow immediately to the east.

24. Nan Tow's Tump, Didmarton

Bronze Age
ST: 803893

On the E side of the A46, some 16 km S of Stroud, covered with trees.

One of the largest round barrows in the Cotswolds, it stands some 2.7 metres high and is about 30 metres in diameter. Nan Tow was supposed to have been a local witch who was buried upright in the barrow!

25. Notgrove long barrow

Neolithic
SP: 095212

Beside the A436, just E of the railway bridge. English Heritage signpost.

This chambered long barrow was excavated in 1881 and again in 1934-5. After lying open for forty years, it has now been grassed over. It was originally about 48 metres long and 24 metres wide. It contained the remains of a gallery grave with an antechamber and two pairs of side chambers. Excavation in the chambers produced the remains of at least six adult individuals, as well as three children and a newborn baby. Many animal bones, including a young calf, were also present.

Behind the west end of the gallery was a circular domed structure 7 metres in diameter, which had been built before the rest of the tomb. It contained a stone burial cist that held the crouched skeleton of a man aged fifty or sixty. On top of the domed structure were the bones of a young woman aged seventeen to nineteen.

A forecourt between horns of double drystone walling at the east end of the gallery grave revealed signs of fires, the bones of animals and the skeletons of two young people. These seem to indicate an elaborate burial ritual. The whole tomb displayed evidence that it had been robbed on a number of occasions since iron age and Roman times. The finds from the excavations are in Cheltenham Museum.

26. Nottingham Hill, Gotherington

Iron Age
SO: 984284

Minor road NW from B4632 800 metres NE of Cleeve Hill. A farm road runs through the fort. Muddy in bad weather.

This north-facing spur, 280 metres above sea level, juts out from the Cotswold ridge into the Vale of Gloucester. Although Oxenton Hill rises in front of it, its greater height allows it to look across to the hillforts on the outlying Bredon Hill 9.5 km and 11 km away.

The flat top of Nottingham Hill is surrounded by a remarkably unimpressive bank and ditch, which is doubled on the south-east side. These double banks and ditches on the south-east are very strong and are set closely to each other. The inner bank is still 3 metres high, the other 2.1 metres high above the outer ditch. This is the main feature on the site, and it may be seen to serve the function of a cross-dyke isolating the 48 hectare promontory spur on the north-west. Large hilltop enclosures such as this, perhaps containing a few huts and four-post buildings, were probably used for the seasonal round-up of livestock in the early iron age. There may have been an entrance at the north corner overlooking Prescott House, or more probably at the south-east corner, now quarried away.

27. Nympsfield long barrow, Frocester

Neolithic
SO: 794013

On W side of B4066, in Coaley Peak picnic area.

This chambered long barrow, which lies east to west, is 27 metres long and 18 metres wide. It was excavated in 1862 and re-excavated in 1937 and 1974 because of its 'deplorable condition'. It has since been left open to the sky. The barrow

The Nympsfield long barrow is preserved in the Coaley Peak picnic area beside the B4066 near Frocester. (J. Dyer)

contains a cross-shaped stone-lined gallery with one pair of side chambers and an end chamber. The mound of the barrow is enclosed by a drystone wall. At the horned east end this wall is doubled, and at the narrower west end it is concave. Post holes and ashes of fires were found in this west area. In the horned forecourt of the barrow were another area of burning and a small pit. Elaborate funeral rituals were probably carried out in each area. Between twenty and thirty burials, many with dental problems, came from the barrow during the excavations, as well as neolithic pottery and a leaf-shaped arrowhead. The finds from the excavations are in Stroud Museum.

28. Painswick Beacon

Iron Age
SO: 869121

Parking on minor road linking A46 with B4073 at N end of golf course.

This multivallate hillfort is sited on a prominent spur of the Cotswolds overlooking Gloucester. Much of the interior of the site has been badly damaged by quarrying and the laying-out of a golf course. Closely set double ramparts and ditches with a counterscarp bank exist on the west, south and east sides and enclose a triangular area of about 2.8 hectares. Traces of these ramparts without ditches can be seen along the steep north scarp. The main entrance is near the south-east end, where the inner rampart has long, sharply inturned ends. A second possible entrance could have existed in the north-west corner where an inturning of the surviving rampart meets a deep hollow-way. Owing to the quarrying no interior features can be identified with certainty, except for a large funnel-shaped hollow 2.7 metres deep, of unknown date and purpose in the centre of the camp. It may have been a Celtic ritual shaft.

29. Pole's Wood South, Swell

Neolithic
SP: 167264

Farm track W from minor road linking Upper and Lower Swell.

This damaged and irregular chambered long barrow measures 54 metres long, 21 metres wide and 3 metres high. Its higher end seems to have been horned with a forecourt, but there is no record of either an entrance or a false portal. A burial chamber, still visible, near the north side of the narrower west end, was entered by an approach passage, 1.8 metres long. Excavation in this chamber in 1874 produced the remains of at least nine individuals, together with animal bones and neolithic pot sherds, whilst three other skeletons lay in the entrance passage.

Three Saxon burials had been placed near the surface of the barrow many centuries later. They included a man with an iron spearhead and knife, and a woman with two saucer brooches and an amber bead.

Other barrows in the vicinity include **Pole's Wood East long barrow** (172265), 460 metres north-east, which had a horned forecourt and an enclosed burial chamber containing nineteen skeletons and neolithic pottery when excavated in 1875–6. The barrow still stands 1.5 metres high, 36 metres long and 12 metres wide, but the chamber is no longer visible.

The **Lower Swell long barrow** (170258) is 45 metres long, 15 metres wide and 3 metres high. It stands in a spinney surrounded by a ploughed field. The standing stone known as the **Hoar Stone** (170248) may once have been part of another burial chamber. **The Tump** (166259), 800 metres west of Lower Swell, is a round barrow now planted with trees and surrounded by a drystone wall. It is about 18 metres in diameter and 1.5 metres high. There are many more round barrows in this vicinity.

30. Randwick long barrow

Neolithic
SO: 825069

Situated in Standish Wood (National Trust) on the summit of the hill NW of Randwick church.

This ruined chambered long barrow is still about 54 metres long, 24 metres wide and 3 metres high. When dug in 1883, the horned entrance led directly to a single burial chamber which contained a mass of human bones, some 'very old British' pottery and three flint flakes. There were also Roman remains which suggested that the barrow might have been robbed at that time. The remains of several crouched skeletons were found outside the south-west end of the barrow. Mr G. B. Witts, the digger, considered that these were slaves buried with their chief.

31. Salmonsbury Camp, Bourton

Iron Age
SP: 175208

Between Bourton-on-the-Water and the river Dickler.

An unimpressive lowland camp, square in shape, which encloses some 23 hectares, this was originally protected on at least two sides by marshes. The defences consist of an inner loose gravel bank, now only 0.7 metre high and 18 metres wide, separated from an outer bank by a V-shaped ditch 10 metres wide and 3.6 metres deep. A filled-in outer ditch was 5.7 metres wide and 2.7 metres deep. There was probably a stone wall on top of the inner rampart, but evidence of ploughing of the site in Roman times suggests that the wall was thrown into the ditch during that time.

Excavation in 1931 revealed the foundations of a wooden hut 6.6 metres in diameter, which consisted of a ring of eighteen post holes and three central holes for supporting a roof. An entrance 2.4 metres wide faced south.

A hoard of 147 iron currency bars was found on the north-west side of the camp in 1860, which, with the pottery from the site, suggest a date for occupation in the first century BC. Pits of the third century BC beneath the rampart indicate that the site was inhabited a century before fortification took place.

32. Sodbury Camp, Chipping Sodbury

Iron Age
ST: 760826

Access by farm road from A46 on E or from Portway Lane from Chipping Sodbury. The site is normally under grass.

This is one of the finest multivallate hillforts on the edge of the Cotswolds escarpment. Rectangular in shape, it encloses about 4.5 hectares. On the north, east and south are widely spaced double ramparts 30 metres apart. The inner rampart of glacis construction stands 1.5 metres above the interior of the camp, and 4 metres above the exterior. This bank curves round the north-west corner and runs halfway along the west side. The silted ditch outside the inner rampart is 8 metres wide and 2.2 metres deep. The main entrance is midway along the east side, where the rampart ends are slightly overlapped. The core of the rampart, composed of fire-reddened limestone, is clearly visible at this point.

There are indications that the outer rampart is unfinished, since it is irregular in height, although in places reaching 3.6 metres high. A wide berm separates it from an equally irregular outer ditch which fades out on the north side. This rampart and ditch are broken in two places along the east side. Although the south break, opposite the entrance in the inner rampart, is the most logical for access to the camp, there is a possibility that the north break may also have been an entrance gap. The rampart at this point is out-turned, and there appears to have been a guard-chamber on the north side.

33. Soldier's Grave, Nympsfield

Bronze Age
SO: 794015

On W side of B4066, in wood 200 metres N of Nympsfield long barrow, on edge of Coaley Peak picnic area.

This unusual round barrow, which is 17 metres in diameter, was found on excavation to contain a rock-cut boat-shaped grave, lined with drystone walling. It measured 3.3 metres long, 1.3 metres wide and 1 metre deep. It contained the scattered remains of at least twenty-eight people, and pieces of early bronze age pottery. This seems to represent a mixture of neolithic ideas of collective burial and bronze age round barrow burial, and the grave is probably of transitional date. The burial chamber is not visible, and the barrow is in a poor state.

34. Tinglestone barrow, Avening

Neolithic
ST: 882990

W of the minor road from Avening church to Hampton Fields, and at SE corner of Gatcombe Park.

This barrow gets its name from the oolite standing stone 1.8 metres high at its north end. Unusual in that the barrow, which is 21 metres long, lies north to south, it is planted with beech trees and no chambers have been found. There is a local folk tradition that the Tinglestone runs round the field when it hears the clock strike twelve!

35. Uley Bury hillfort, Uley

Iron Age
ST: 785990

Access from B4066 at West Hill, or by footpaths from Uley or Crawley.

One of the finest promontory hillforts in the Cotswolds. At all points except the north corner the ground falls steeply 100 metres to the valley below. A rampart and a silted ditch enclose some 13 hectares. Lower down the hillside is a slighter ditch about 2 metres wide with a low rampart on the outer side. The main entrance at the north corner is defended by a mound and three ditches cutting across the narrow ridge which connects the promontory with the main Cotswold massif. Other entrances occur at the south and east corners where hollow-ways approach up the hillside. The latter entrance passage, lined with turf and timber, has been dated to the early iron age. The rampart on either side of the south entrance terminates in a conspicuous mound. An uninscribed Dobunic gold stater and two currency bars are amongst finds from the fort now in Gloucester City Museum. The interior of the camp is normally arable.

36. West Tump, Brimpsfield

Neolithic
SP: 912133

In Buckle Wood W of B4070.

This long barrow is 45 metres long and 20 metres wide. It is contained within drystone walls and has a visible false entrance at the east end. When opened in 1880 a single chamber 4.5 metres long and 0.9 metre wide was found at the end of a passage 2.1 metres long, leading in from the south side. It contained some twenty disordered burials, together with one at the back of the chamber which was raised on five stones. This was the skeleton of a young woman, with the remains of a baby nearby. Four more skeletons were found lying in the forecourt near the false entrance.

37. Windmill Tump, Rodmarton

Neolithic
ST: 932978

Tree-covered, in the middle of a ploughed field, S of the minor road between Rodmarton and Cherington.

Like the majority of Cotswold long barrows, Windmill Tump lies east to west. It is about 60 metres long and 21 metres wide and is contained within a modern wall. There is a fine false entrance at the east end. On either side of the barrow are rectangular burial chambers approached by passages and three steps down. The south chamber contained fragments of several skeletons and prehistoric pottery. The north chamber held ten adult skeletons and three children beneath a 9 ton capstone. Both had porthole entrances (see Avening, no. 1) with their original blocking. At present the chambers are inaccessible.

38. Windrush Camp

Iron Age
SP: 181123

S of A40 between Northleach and Burford. Approached by farm road.

A roughly circular plateau fort enclosing about 2.6 hectares, sited on level ground above the Windrush valley. Of the single bank and ditch, only the bank is now visible, the ditch having silted up and long been ploughed over. The entrance was probably on the west side.

GREATER LONDON
(Map on page 238)

1. Caesar's Camp, Wimbledon

Iron Age
TQ: 224711

This earthwork lies at the S end of Wimbledon Common, 1 km W of the junction of the A219 and B281. A footpath goes right through the centre of the camp, which is part of the golf club, but good views of the ditches can be seen from the path. There is a plaque erected in 1968, giving a short history of the site.

This circular plateau fort covers an area of about 5 hectares and consists of a single ditch with rampart and an entrance on the western side. The eastern entrance gap does not appear to be original. The surrounding ditch is about 9 metres wide and at least 3.6 metres deep. Excavations in 1937 were conducted in connection with a trench for a water main which crossed the site from east to west and revealed a small pit containing iron age pottery which suggests a third-century BC date. This dig also showed that the single rampart had been revetted and had a timber palisade.

2. Grim's Ditch, Harrow and Stanmore

Iron Age or Dark Age
TQ: 134923

Visible remains run, with interruptions, from 114904 to 174937, a distance of about 8 km. An impressive section is to be seen from Old Redding (road) at its junction with Oxhey Lane. For permission to walk the ditch apply to the Secretary, Grim's Dyke Golf Course, Oxhey Lane, Hatch End, Harrow.

Grim's Ditch is a linear earthwork very possibly of Belgic or post-Roman date. It consists of a V-shaped ditch with a substantial rampart on the north side. Visible remains which begin at Pinner Green continue as far as Harrow Weald Common, reappear on the western side of Pear Wood and end on the eastern edge of the wood about 180 metres west of Roman Watling Street. In parts it is 91 metres wide with a 3 metres high rampart.

Excavations were conducted at Pinner Green in 1953 and in Pear Wood in 1955, when a little iron age pottery was found in the infill of the ditch. In 1968 excavations in the field south of the hospital showed that the ditch did end on the eastern end of Pear Wood. Work by Stephen Castle even suggests a post-Roman date, although it is usually assumed that Grim's Ditch was a boundary ditch of the Belgic tribe of the Catuvellauni, whose capital was at Prae Wood, St Albans.

3. Hampstead Heath barrow

Bronze Age?
TQ: 273865

The bush-covered mound stands halfway between Hampstead and Highgate ponds. It is best approached from Millfield Lane, going between the second and third ponds by the path towards the Vale of Health.

Formerly known as Boadicea's Grave, this mound was excavated by Sir Charles H. Read FSA in 1894. It consists of a circular mound about 40 metres in diameter and 3 metres high, surrounded by a ditch varying from 4.8 to 6 metres wide. A trench was cut through the centre of the mound but no trace of a burial was found. Likewise no grave goods were present. Read concluded, however, that it was very probably a burial mound of the bronze age and that the burial, which was possibly by inhumation, had completely decomposed owing to the acidity of the soil.

William Stukeley's drawing of the round barrow on Hampstead Heath in 1725. (Museum of London)

Though it cannot be said with certainty that this is a bronze age burial of barrow type, confirmation of its antiquity is supported by a drawing of 1725 by William Stukeley.

4. Keston, Caesar's Camp hillfort   Iron Age
TQ: 422639

This earthwork is sited 5.6 km S of Bromley, and 1 km S of Keston Mark crossroads on the E side of A233. On 410 bus route. Cars can be parked on common opposite.

The impressive remains of a three-banked fort can be seen through the hedge. For permission to view apply to Holwood House. Excavation has shown that the bank was revetted with flints in the area of the west gate. Finds include a bronze terret, loom weights, a whetstone and iron age pottery. On Keston Common there is a second and less impressive earthwork (418642). The banks stand only 1 metre high; it may have been a cattle pound for the fort.

HAMPSHIRE AND ISLE OF WIGHT
(Map on page 236)

1. Afton Down, Freshwater, Isle of Wight   Neolithic and Bronze Age
SZ: 352857

At W end of Afton Down, 1.6 km SE of Freshwater. Tracks lead on to downs from Afton, N of A3055. In the care of the National Trust, always open.

Two dozen barrows were recorded here in the nineteenth century when they were dug by the Reverend J. Skinner. Starting from the west, there is a bowl-barrow, then further along north of the track a neolithic long barrow 35 metres long, but only about 0.9 metre high at its east end. It appears to be of the earthen type without chambers and could be the same age as the trackway alongside across the downs. The remainder consist of sixteen bowls, four bells and two discs, one of which is now a tee-green! Some finds are in the Carisbrooke Castle Museum. The more energetically inclined may care to walk this 5 km track to Shalcombe via Compton and Brook Downs, passing the Five Barrows on Brook Down (no. 9).

2. Beacon Hill, Kingsclere   Iron Age
SU: 458573

Hampshire County Park beside the A34. Car park and picnic area at foot of hill.

This magnificent hillfort encloses about 4 hectares and is surrounded by a single rampart, ditch and counterscarp bank. There is an inturned entrance 12 metres long on the south-east, and a possible blocked entrance in the middle of the western rampart. Inside the fort are about sixty hut circles and platforms, and some sixty storage pit hollows. These features are difficult to see when the grass is long. Two short lengths of bank and ditch on the highest part of the hill may represent an earlier enclosure, possibly of neolithic date. Traces of prehistoric field systems can be seen down the valley to the south. A railed enclosure in the western corner of the fort contains the grave of Lord Carnarvon, who dug on the hill with Leonard Woolley in 1912 and later financed the Tutankhamun excavations.

3. Buckland Rings, Lymington   Iron Age
SZ: 315968

Sited E of road leading from Lymington to Sway; 1.6 km from Lymington.

A fine triple-banked encampment in a downland situation only 27 metres above sea level, standing on a spur of gravel and enclosing 2.8 hectares. The outer bank lies under the road on the west side and on the south-east it is nearly ploughed out. The innermost bank stands 2.4 metres high whilst the middle one is lower but unusually wide. The entrance is inturned on the east side and excavation has shown that it had a pair of stout gateposts and that the ramparts were timber-faced. The camp has no natural water supply but there is a stream within easy reach. The fort was built in the first century BC and was demolished in about AD 44–5, possibly by the Romans. The finds are in Winchester Museum.

4. Bury Hill, Upper Clatford

Iron Age
SU: 345435

On N side of minor road 1 km SW from Upper Clatford.

This 9 hectare hillfort occupies a commanding position, rising steeply out of the surrounding area. It had two phases of occupation. The original builders in the sixth century BC threw up a timber-faced rampart 7.5 metres wide at its base and about 2.5 metres high. Outside, the ditch was 3.3 metres deep and the entrance was at the south-east side. Following a long period of abandonment, the southern half of the fort was reoccupied about 100 BC and protected by a massive new ditch with an inner and outer rampart enclosing 4.8 hectares. It then became circular instead of oval in shape. The 9 metres wide entrance through the now double ditch area ends unusually without any inturning fortifications. Finds of large quantities of horse bones, together with chariot and harness fittings, suggest that Bury Hill was at this time occupied by wealthy pony breeders, who produced high quality equestrian equipment, perhaps including chariots. Final abandonment came soon after the Roman conquest.

5. Butser Ancient Farm, Chalton

SU: 723162

Signposted E off A3 from Petersfield on road to Chalton. Admission charge. Open Easter to 31st October, daily 10 to 5. (Group visits arranged throughout year.) Telephone/fax: 023 9259 8838. Website: www.butser.org.uk

The Butser Archaeological Farm moved to its present site (from Little Butser Hill) in 1990. It is a unique open-air laboratory that researches into the agricultural economy of the iron age. Reconstructions of three iron age round houses dominate the site. The largest, 15 metres in diameter, is based on excavations at Longbridge Deverill Cowdown, Wiltshire. Beside them can be seen experimental pottery kilns and charcoal clamps, storage pits and haystacks. There is a field area devoted to research into prehistoric cereal types and legumes, and paddocks containing sheep of a prehistoric type dating back to about 9000 BC. Numerous experiments are being undertaken at the farm and visitors (especially school parties) are encouraged to ask questions. This is a living museum of prehistoric times.

6. Butser Hill cross-dykes, Petersfield

Iron Age
SU: 712201

In Queen Elizabeth Country Park, signposted to W of A3. Expensive car park within site.

The summit of Butser Hill has been isolated from its extension to the south-west by the construction of three banked ditches across the narrow neck of the hill. The most southerly of these has now almost vanished. (The modern road into the car parking area passes through these earthworks, which are overgrown with bushes.) There are other earthworks on the north-east and southern spurs of the hill. On the east slopes of the hill, stretching nearly down to the Portsmouth Road, are the remains of Celtic fields with their rectangular outlines. To the north of the area lie bronze age barrows, which have been dug into in the past.

Little Butser Hill (719206) was the original site of the experimental prehistoric farm conceived in 1968 but now sited at Bascomb Copse, Chalton (no. 5).

7. Danebury hillfort, Nether Wallop

Iron Age
SU: 323377

This prominent tree-clad fort lies between the A343 and the A30, 5 km NW of Stockbridge. Signposted from both roads, more easily approached from the A343. The site is a recreational area in the care of the Hampshire County Council (telephone: 01962 846034). Toilets, car parking. Coaches should park at foot of hill.

A splendidly sited fort of 5 hectares planted with beech trees. It has been extensively excavated and a signposted walk has been laid out around the site.

The earliest organised occupation of the hill took place in the first half of the first millennium BC, when a series of ritual pits was dug, some on the eastern side containing large posts, and burials were made. In the mid sixth century BC a defensive timber-laced rampart and ditch were constructed around the hilltop, broken by two gates on opposite sides of the fort. The gates were remodelled a number of times, and that on the west was blocked by *c.*350–300 BC. A road divided the interior, with granaries and storage pits to the north and huts to the south. By the late fourth century BC the defences had been trebled and the east entrance remodelled with elaborate hornworks, providing a sling platform, command post and narrow, easily defended entrance tunnel. It is assumed that the enemy were neighbouring tribesfolk. The fort continued to be divided by a road, and occupation became denser with circular houses built against the back of the rampart and four- and six-post granaries for storage. About 100 BC burning of the east gate seems to have occurred simultaneously with the destruction of houses and the massacre of some two dozen men, women and children. The fort was largely abandoned around that time, though it may have been partially retained as a corral for animals.

Finds from Danebury are extensively exhibited in the fascinating Museum of the Iron Age at Church Close, Andover (telephone: 01264 366283), which should not be missed!

8. Duck's Nest, Grans and Knap barrows, Rockbourne

Neolithic
SU: 105204; 090198

Duck's Nest, on S side of downland track S of Rockbourne Down and 3 km NW of Rockbourne.

Duck's Nest, an overgrown long barrow, is said to be the highest in the county, being 4.5 metres high. It is 40 metres long and 20 metres wide with traces of side ditches, and orientated north to south.

Grans and Knap barrows are found together 1.2 km along the track in the opposite direction, on Toyd Down, and 2 km east of Martin (090198). Here are two long barrows 180 metres apart, Knap Barrow being near the track and Grans Barrow 180 metres away. Knap Barrow, partly under cultivation, is the larger, 100 metres long, and Grans Barrow 58 metres. The side ditches which possibly exist are not readily visible. Both are orientated roughly south-west to north-west and probably date between 3400 and 2200 BC.

9. Five Barrows, Brook Down, Isle of Wight

Bronze Age
SZ: 390852

Situated on the N side of the track on Brook Down, 1.6 km N of Brook village and 1 km S of Shalcombe. In the care of the National Trust; always open.

This cemetery is possibly the best on the island and consists of eight barrows in a rough east to west alignment. At the east end of the group is a disc-barrow 35 metres in diameter. Next there are six bowl-barrows, the tallest of which is 1.8 metres and has a causeway running across its ditch at the north-east side. The most westerly one is of bell type and stands 2.4 metres high. They have been dug into, but there are no records of the results.

The unfinished hillfort on Ladle Hill. The dumps of soil can be clearly seen inside the enclosure. To the right is a fine disc-barrow. (Cambridge University Collection)

10. Ladle Hill, Sydmonton
Iron Age
SU: 478568

Most easily approached from E at 492566 following bridleway and field paths past ruined bell- and saucer-barrows.

This 2.8 hectare hillfort is important because it was never completed. Careful observation will make out a circular marking-out ditch some 3 metres wide and 0.5 metre deep with entrance gaps on the south-west and east. In places the ditch has been deepened, creating irregular sections from 15 to 80 metres in length and 2 metres deep. The topsoil and chalk rubble removed were dumped well inside the fort for later use. The lower, harder chalk was placed close to the ditch ready to build the rampart. At this point the construction suddenly ceased: whatever emergency had created the need for a fort had passed, and the unfinished earthwork was left frozen for eternity.

Due north of the fort is a fine disc-barrow 52 metres in diameter. There is a much smaller example inside the earthwork.

11. Old Winchester Hill, Meonstoke
Iron Age
SU: 641206

3.6 km S of West Meon, via side roads; a good starting point is the Nature Reserve at 647213; car park.

This is an iron age fort covering 5.6 hectares and having a good command of the surrounding countryside. The main rampart stands 2 metres high and there is a counterscarp bank. Inturned entrances are at the east and west ends with additional outworks at the eastern entrance; probably built second to first century BC. At the east end and within the camp are bronze age round barrows of 1800–1400 BC.

Aerial view of the hillfort on Old Winchester Hill. A number of bronze age barrows can be seen inside and outside the fort. (J. E. Hancock)

12. Petersfield Heath barrow group

Bronze Age
SU: 755225

1.2 km SE of Petersfield on the golf course N of B2146 and E of Heath pond.

There is a large scatter of barrows amongst the trees in this area, of which at least fifteen are bowl-barrows. The most northerly of the group is cut by the road, is tree-covered and stands 2.4 metres high. There are also four saucer-barrows, a disc-barrow and a bell-barrow. There are no excavation reports, but they have probably been robbed. Probable date 1800–1400 BC.

13. Popham Beacon round barrows, Micheldever

Bronze Age
SU: 525439

The barrows lie 1.2 km NW of Micheldever Station on the N side of the A30, and close to the W side of the minor road leading to Ashe and Deane.

Here are five fine bronze age barrows, in line running north-east–south-west, forming a small Wessex-type cemetery. They are capped with trees and with the surrounding land under plough the differences in shape tend to be concealed. There are two bell-barrows and two bowl-barrows, with an older saucer type partly obscured by bowl- and bell-barrows. The bowl-barrow to the north is 27 metres in diameter and stands 1.8 metres high; its surrounding ditch is visible. After a gap of 13 metres the main group of barrows starts. These are larger in size, averaging 44 metres in diameter, but the surrounding ditches are not clear. Possible dating 1800–1400 BC.

14. St Catherine's Hill, Winchester

Iron Age
SU: 484276

Footpath from car park on southbound carriageway of Winchester bypass (A33).

A single rampart and ditch enclose 9 hectares of fine chalk downland above the river Itchen. Only on the north-east are the defences broken by a sharply inturned entrance 12 metres wide that was excavated between 1925 and 1928. The excavations showed four phases of occupation which included an undefended settlement about 500 BC, followed by the building of a dumped chalk rampart and V-shaped ditch a century later, and ending with burning in the middle of the first century BC, when the fort may have been sacked by neighbouring tribesfolk.

Under the trees on the top of the hill are traces of the twelfth-century chapel of St Catherine, whilst to the east lies the turf-cut Labyrinth or Mizmaze reputedly made by boys from Winchester School in the eighteenth century.

15. Seven Barrows, Burghclere
Bronze Age
SU: 462533

Sited mostly on W side of A34(T) 7 km N of Whitchurch. There are two barrows E of the road and one at the far side of the disused railway embankment.

The cemetery tends to be laid out in a line in a manner similar to that used for burial groups in the Stonehenge area. All the barrows have been reduced in height by cultivation and they now stand about 3 metres above the surrounding ground. Diameters vary from 8.5 to 48 metres. They probably date from between 1800 and 1400 BC.

16. Winchester
Iron Age
SU: 475297

After its sacking about 50 BC the hillfort on St Catherine's Hill was abandoned in favour of a new site beneath modern Winchester. A Belgic coin mould was found close to the Cathedral, and this lends support to the belief that the new settlement was the oppidum of *Venta Belgarum*. There is little to be seen today except for parts of an iron age earthwork called Oram's Arbour between Clifton Road and Clifton Terrace. This was a rectangular enclosure of at least 18 hectares, with an inturned entrance on the west. It lies just outside the first Roman defences of AD *c.*70.

HEREFORDSHIRE
(Map on page 236)

1. Aconbury Hill, Kingsthorne
Iron Age
SU: 504331

Via minor road leading N from Kingsthorne.

A wooded contour fort, rectangular in shape, with a bank, ditch and counterscarp bank enclosing 7 hectares, steeply sloping on the north and west. The site is hidden in heavy undergrowth. There are entrances on the south-west and south-east, the latter inturned and probably original.

2. Arthur's Stone, Dorstone
Neolithic
SO: 318431

1.6 km N of Dorstone, alongside minor road connecting B4348 and B4352. English Heritage signposted.

This long cairn is surrounded by a wooden fence. The much denuded mound is about 26 metres long and contains a burial chamber at the south end. This consists of a massive 25 ton capstone supported by nine uprights. There are the remains of an approach passage which leads into an antechamber north of the main burial chamber.

3. Brandon Camp, Adforton
Iron Age and Roman
SO: 401724

East of the A4110 and north of Brandon Villa.

This simple triangular-shaped fort of some 3.2 hectares lies at the western end of

Arthur's Stone, Dorstone, consists of a neolithic burial chamber and vestiges of its approach passage on the left. (J. Dyer)

a flat-topped hill. The northern side is protected by a steep natural scarp with little sign of a man-made defence. On the south and east a rampart still stands some 3 metres high. Nowhere are ditches visible, but parch-marks in 1984 showed that there were inner and outer ones along the south and east sides, with a main gate halfway along the east side. A single ditch was probably present at the break of scarp along the northern edge. Gaps in the ramparts at the north-east corner and on the south side may also be original entrances. Aerial photographs have revealed a bronze age ring ditch, and several Roman structures, inside the camp. Excavations by Professor S. S. Frere proved that the hillfort was reused by the Romans, probably as 'a temporary campaign base created to support an attack on the central part of the Welsh front'.

4. Capler Camp, Fownhope

Iron Age
SO: 593329

The minor road from Ladyridge to Fownhope passes the site to the W. A track leads from this road at 591324.

A double bank and ditch enclose a partly wooded area triangular in shape and 4 hectares in extent. The site commands the river Wye. The well-protected entrance is on the east side.

5. Coxall Knoll, Buckton and Coxall

Iron Age
SO: 366734

Approached through wood alongside B4367 road at 368730.

This wooded hillfort consists of three separate constructions, an oval fort on the west part of the hill and two additional enclosures on the east. The total area is about 5.6 hectares. The main earthwork has a triple bank and ditch on the north, a double bank and ditch on the east, and a single bank and ditch on the south where the slope is precipitous. The well-defined original entrance is on the west side.

The two additional enclosures are both protected by banks, ditches and counterscarp banks. Both are in a damaged condition. One contains a quarry ditch within the main bank from which extra material was excavated for the earthworks.

6. Credenhill Camp

Iron Age
SO: 451445

Via track leading N from Credenhill off A480 at 455440.

Before this hillfort was tree-planted it commanded a view of the later Roman

109

town of *Magna* (Kenchester). The south-west corner has been quarried away. A prominent bank, ditch and counterscarp bank surround a rectangular area 20 hectares in extent. There are two entrances, one at the south-east corner and one on the east, both inturned, perhaps with guard-chambers. Limited excavations showed that a number of square huts with raised floors had stood in rows inside the camp.

7. Croft Ambrey   Iron Age
SO: 444668

Via Cock Gate on B4362. Sharp left inside Croft Castle Park towards castle, then right over cattle grid. Park at end of tarmac road on left and walk 1.2 km uphill. National Trust.

A triangular hillfort enclosing 8 hectares, protected by a steep escarpment on the north and three lines of defence on the south and west. The inner defence is marked by a quarry ditch surrounding some 2.4 hectares of intensively occupied land. This area was later extended to enclose 3.2 hectares by the addition of a massive dumped rampart with two other ditches and banks. The whole area has produced rows of rectangular timbered buildings and was occupied for four or five centuries before the Roman conquest, at which time the site was abandoned. A further 5 hectares was enclosed by two low banks and ditches, forming an annexe on the south side. It was probably a corral for animals. It contains some low north–south banks, which may have been artificial rabbit warrens, and a circular mound identified as a Romano-British sanctuary to which the inhabitants returned for worship even after the fort had been abandoned.

The main south-west entrance was inturned and S. C. Stanford's remarkable excavations have revealed at least fifteen periods of construction. At the north-west corner a postern gate appears to have existed.

8. Dinedor Camp   Iron Age
SO: 524364

A metalled road at 521366 leads direct to the north rampart.

This hillfort is an elongated oval in shape and encloses 4 hectares defended by a single bank and ditch. Much of the bank is flattened except on the north-east. Superficial excavation indicates that the fort was densely occupied. One entrance is visible on the east side.

9. Herefordshire Beacon, Colwall   Iron Age
SO: 760399

Via footpath leading S of A449 800 metres SW of Little Malvern opposite British Camp Hotel.

A massive hillfort occupying a ridge on the Malvern Hills. The original earthwork is at the centre of the site where a single bank and ditch (with a counterscarp bank on the north-east) enclose 3.2 hectares with entrances on the north-east and south-west. A medieval castle ringwork now obliterates part of these defences. The whole area was later surrounded by a bank, ditch and counterscarp bank enclosing 13 hectares. Material for the inner bank was obtained from large quarry scoops just behind the rampart and probably providing shelter for huts. On the west side these later defences merge with the earlier ones but on the east they outlie them, doubling the bank area. Four entrances were provided at the north-east, east, west and south-east sides.

10. Ivington Camp, Leominster Out   Iron Age
SO: 484547

Off minor road from Park Gate to Gattertop, via metalled road to Camp Farm at 478547. It is possible to drive into fort and park by farm.

This large triangular-shaped hillfort occupies the flat top of the hill. Two ditches

Aerial view of the Herefordshire Beacon. There is a medieval castle motte at the highest point of the hill. (Cambridge University Collection)

with inner banks surround some 8 hectares. On the north, west and south sides the ground falls away sharply. On the east the earthworks are stronger since they protect the fort promontory. The entrance at the south corner is strongly inturned to protect a steep covered way flanked by two banks on its east side. There is a curious cross-shaped earthwork between these banks which may have formed a base for some kind of watch-tower. A second entrance in the east corner is of the 'inturn out-turn' type. It was protected by further external earthworks, now destroyed, but which can just be seen in the ploughing to the east.

An earlier earthwork of about 3.2 hectares can be seen in the north-west corner of the camp. It has a single bank and ditch and its entrance was probably under the present farm buildings. A gap on the east appears to be modern.

11. King Arthur's Cave, Whitchurch   Palaeolithic and Mesolithic
SO: 546156

From minor road on S side of Great Doward, take footpath past quarry at 548157. Follow English Heritage signpost. Torch required.

Two chambers in this cave were originally occupied during the late palaeolithic and mesolithic periods. Reached by short passages from a wide entrance and penetrating some 16 metres into the hillside overlooking the river Wye, they were first dug in 1871 by the Reverend W. S. Symonds, who found the remains of many animals now extinct or foreign to Britain, including mammoth, woolly rhinoceros, lion, cave and brown bear, as well as many flint tools. The earliest inhabitants lived around a much used hearth inside the cave, but the later ones moved to the mouth and ledge outside. Finds from the cave can be seen in the Gloucester, Cheltenham and Bristol University Spelaeological Society museums.

12. Midsummer Hill, Hollybush
Iron Age
SO: 761375

Via track immediately N of Hollybush village. National Trust.

An irregularly shaped contour fort comprising a bank, ditch and counterscarp bank enclosing about 12 hectares. The main bank was stone-faced. There are two original entrances at the north and south-west, with inturned banks and at one time guard-chambers. Both had been renewed many times. Hollows in the enclosed areas particularly near the south-west gate represent the foundations of circular and rectangular buildings. Pottery from the camp suggests occupation began about 400 BC. On the north-west and the south a medieval earthwork known as the Red Earl's Dyke joins the fort.

At the north end of Hollybush Hill (760377) is a long barrow or pillow mound with side ditches still visible. It is 45 metres long, 8 metres wide and about 1 metre high. North of this mound are three round barrows, none really prominent. The largest is 12 metres in diameter, 0.6 metre high and has the remains of a surrounding ditch.

13. Pyon Wood, Aymestrey
Iron Age
SO: 424664

Via track leading W off A4110 to Ballsgate Common.

This tree-covered hillfort has a triangular plan. A ditch, bank and counterscarp bank enclose 3.6 hectares on the top of a steep sloping hill. The original entrance is on the south-east where a hollow-way approaches the inturned bank.

14. Risbury Camp, Humber
Iron Age
SO: 542553

E of minor road from Stoke Prior to Risbury.

A low-lying plateau fort, resting in the angle formed by two streams and protected by marshes. A rectangular area almost 3.6 hectares in extent is defended by massive earthworks. On the north, south and east sides there are wide-spaced triple banks and ditches and on the west a double bank and ditch of massive proportions. The inner bank and probably the outer ones were drywalled, and a modern cut through the east side shows that they were constructed of dumped clay. The only original entrance is on the west side; it is approached through lateral banks and is only slightly inturned. Outside this entrance are several cross-banks resembling those at Old Oswestry (Shropshire, no. 9).

15. Sutton Walls, Sutton
Iron Age
SO: 525464

Via track leading N from Sutton St Michael. Interior used as dump for toxic waste!

A steep-sided hill is defended by a single massive ditch and bank enclosing 12 hectares. The site is a flattened oval in plan and there are original entrances at the east and west. Much of the interior has been destroyed by quarrying but excavations have shown that the earthworks were constructed at the end of the second century BC, the bank material coming from the ditch (originally 4.5 metres deep) and from workings inside the bank. The bank and ditch were enlarged at least once and faced in timber and stone. The modern quarrying has destroyed many huts and storage pits, traces of which can still be seen in the quarry edges. The fort was attacked by Roman forces sometime shortly after AD 43. They threw the skeletons of twenty-four defenders into the ditch at the west entrance. Some had been decapitated.

The site continued in use during Romano-British times, at least till the third century AD. A large pre-Roman iron anvil from the site is in Hereford City Museum.

16. Wapley Camp, Staunton-on-Arrow

Iron Age
SO: 345625

By Forestry Commission gated roadway from 359621 or 353618.

Although the hillside is forested, the interior of this triangular camp is open, but rather overgrown. It commanded the valley of the river Lugg and its tributary, some 180 metres below its steep north scarp, where it needs no additional defences. On its south side were four strong lines of banks and ditches, and on the east five lines, the outer two widely spaced. There is a strong oblique entrance on the south side, 114 metres long, which turns markedly left as it reaches the end of the deeply inturned ramparts. There may have been a simple entrance in the north-east corner.

Inside the camp are four low pillow mounds and a well or ritual shaft (to the west of the entrance).

HERTFORDSHIRE
(Map on page 238)

1. Arbury Banks, Ashwell

Iron Age
TL: 262387

Best approached along a hedgerow from the Newnham to Ashwell road at 257388.

An oval plateau fort, enclosing 5 hectares and defended by a single bank and ditch with an outer counterscarp bank. Excavation has shown the ditch to be V-shaped, 6 metres wide and 4.5 metres deep. The defences have been levelled on the north and east sides. Aerial photographs show that the fort contained a large hut with smaller buildings and intensive agricultural occupation around it. This is borne out by the early excavations, which produced bones of long-horned ox, deer, goat, horse and pig, but no sheep. A few finds are in Ashwell Village Museum.

2. The Aubreys, Redbourn

Iron Age
TL: 095113

800 metres SW of Redbourn church in angle between (and W of) M1 and B487. Perhaps best seen from the minor road running from Holtsmere End under M1 to Redbourn. Excellent fleeting semi-aerial view from M1 (northbound).

An unusually sited and not very impressive plateau fort of about 7 hectares, lying in a side valley off the Ver valley and a kilometre back from the Watling Street. It has a double bank and ditch on all sides except the west and it has been suggested that the site is unfinished. There seem to have been two entrances, one facing west and one north-west. Unpublished excavations by Mortimer Wheeler failed to produce dating material, but there is no reason to consider it as a contender for the site of the capital of the Catuvellaunian tribe attacked by Caesar, more usually placed at Ravensburgh or Wheathampstead. It lacks the position of great natural strength which Caesar ascribed to it. The lack of iron age pottery and its proximity to a plentiful supply of water and grazing land combine to suggest that it was a seasonal stock enclosure and was not permanently occupied.

3. Beech Bottom Dyke and Devil's Ditch, St Albans

Iron Age
Centres at TL: 155093 and 123084

Best seen in the trees NE of the Ancient Briton restaurant beside the A1081 at 150088.

The western end of Beech Bottom Dyke now begins along the northern edge of Townsend School playing field in Batchwood Road, from where it runs east under the A1081 and beneath trees to the railway. Here it is 9 metres deep and 27 metres wide. Beyond the railway it runs into the B651 Sandridge road. This road may follow the line of the dyke as it ran towards Wheathampstead, though there is no proof that it ever joined up with the Devil's Dyke (no. 6). It is probable that the dyke spanned the open ground between the Ver and Lea valleys.

Westwards it may have joined up with the Devil's Ditch, near Mayne Farm on the Gorhambury Estate (124085), close to the drive to Gorhambury House (ask at the farm for permission to visit the dyke). This ditch is still 15 metres wide though its depth is not known. It seems to have run from the Ver into wooded land on the west, perhaps making a northern boundary to land directly connected with the later Catuvellaunian capital at Prae Wood.

4. Ravensburgh Castle, Hexton

Iron Age
TL: 099295

Advance permission required from Hexton Manor Estate Office for visits in winter and early spring.

This is the finest contour hillfort in the Chilterns and encloses 9 hectares. It is completely wooded and very difficult to locate. It is also largely on strictly private land used for pheasant rearing. However, sufficient of its general character can be seen from the Barton Hills which adjoin it and run up to its ramparts on the west.

The fort is rectangular in plan with very deep steep-sided dry valleys on three sides. It is surrounded by a single bank and ditch, which is doubled on the west side. Excavation has shown the ditch to be 3.6 metres deep and 6 metres wide whilst the rampart on the east still reaches a height of 5.5 metres. This rampart was held in position by stout timbers in front and behind, tied together with cross-bars. The fort had two entrances, a main one on the north-west facing the Barton Hills, and another in the south-east giving access to a spring in the valley bottom. Excavation has suggested that the fort was occupied around 400 BC, and again about 50 BC. The latter occupation may have been against Caesar, since the site fits very accurately the description he gives of Cassivellaunus' tribal capital.

Therfield Heath near Royston. Medieval ridge and furrow ploughing surrounds a neolithic long barrow and group of round barrows. The Icknield Way runs in the background. (Ashmolean Museum)

5. Therfield Heath, Royston

Neolithic and Bronze Age
Long barrow: TL: 342402

Lying on the S side of the Icknield Way.

The barrows on Therfield Heath form one of the finest and most accessible groups in eastern England. Unfortunately a golf course has been laid out around the barrows and one has to watch out for golfers who consider that they have priority. There are ten round barrows on this part of the Heath and one small but good long barrow. 800 metres further west on Pen Hills are two more round barrows (11 and 13), an iron age boundary dyke called the Mile Ditches, which can often be seen as

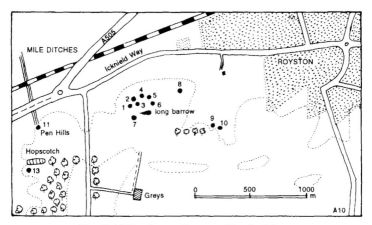

Therfield Heath near Royston, Hertfordshire.

three dark lines in the grass running downhill to cross the dual carriageway and continue north for 2 km to springs near Bassingbourn, and a mysterious earthwork, called the Hopscotch, linked with local folklore.

The long barrow was opened by Edmund Nunn in 1855 and excavated by C. W. Phillips in 1935. It is relatively small by Wessex standards, being 31 metres long, 17 metres wide and 1.8 metres high. A heap of human bones was found near the lower west end (though more burials may still await discovery). Over this had been built a substantial stack of turf. A ditch had been dug all round the stack and chalk from it piled over the barrow. There is no record of any internal timbering, or of any grave goods. A later Saxon burial with a spear was found near the eastern end.

Of the round barrows, a group of six known as 'The Five Hills' lies immediately north of the long barrow. Most of them were opened by Nunn in the mid nineteenth century. One of them (4) contained the disarticulated remains of nine corpses; others held cremations. All probably belong to the transitional years of the late neolithic and early bronze age. Closer to Royston overlooking the cricket pavilion is a barrow (8) called 'Earl's Hill' with an iron seat on its summit. Two more barrows (9 and 10) lie on the slopes of the dry valley south of the cricket pitch. Some finds from the barrows are in the Museum of Archaeology and Anthropology in Cambridge.

6. Wheathampstead, Devil's Dyke

Iron Age
TL: 186133

1 km E of Wheathampstead centre are two dykes. One on the W beside a minor road (Dyke Lane) is known as Devil's Dyke. The other on E as The Slad.

Sir Mortimer Wheeler suggested that the two dykes formed one earthwork enclosing about 35 hectares. Excavation has shown the massive Devil's Dyke to be 12 metres deep and at one point 40 metres wide at the top. On its eastern side is a bank 2.7 metres high, with another 1.8 metres high on the western edge. No excavation has taken place at The Slad and many people doubt its artificial nature. It has been suggested that these earthworks formed the tribal headquarters of Cassivellaunus, which were attacked by Caesar in 54 BC. In his war memoirs, *The Gallic Wars*, Caesar wrote that the stronghold, which was protected by forests and marshes, had been filled with a large number of men and cattle and was a place of great natural strength and excellently fortified. Wheathampstead, overlooking the marshy valley of the river Lea, would fulfil these requirements, though Ravensburgh Castle (no. 4) is much more likely.

KENT
(Map on page 238)

1. Addington and Chestnuts long barrows   **Neolithic**
TQ: 653592 and 652592

These form a small group across and just N of a minor road running W from Addington village, between the M20 and A20, and N of Addington church. Signposted.

Addington barrow, just west of the entrance to Addington Park stables, was first documented by Josiah Colebrooke in 1745. It is rectangular in plan and situated on the lower greensand. The road cuts through the barrow, the stones being much scattered. Petrie recorded twenty-four stones in 1880. Its general orientation is north-east to south-west and the remains of a burial chamber are at the north-east end. Across the road are the remnants of an orthostatic revetment of vertical stones marking the sides of the barrow. It was dug into by a local parson in 1845, producing coarse pottery. No material survives, but neolithic-type pottery sherds were found by Bennett at the beginning of the twentieth century. The site is very overgrown.

Chestnuts barrow is reached from the above site by continuing across the road to 'Rose Alba', a house on the north side. Permission must be sought for viewing this barrow. This partially restored burial chamber was first recorded by John Harris in

The Chestnuts long barrow in Kent showing the entrance façade. (J. Dyer)

the eighteenth century and later Josiah Colebrooke designated it as a temple of the ancient Britons. By 1957 it was in a ruinous state, when on the initiative of the landowner, Mr R. Boyle, it was excavated by Dr John Alexander. Based on the evidence of this dig, some of the fallen stones were restored to their original upright positions. First evidence of occupation is from the mesolithic period, remains of flint-knapping being found on the old ground surface beneath the barrow. In the neolithic period a megalithic chamber, about 3.6 metres by 2.2 metres, was constructed. It had a façade of four upright stones, and most of this can be seen today. The remains of at least nine cremation burials were found. If there were any inhumations they have been lost owing to the acid nature of the soil. The surrounding barrow mound was probably D-shaped or trapezoidal, being about 20 metres long by 15 metres wide. Three barbed and tanged arrowheads and a small pendant of baked clay were amongst the grave goods. Early neolithic pottery sherds, late rusticated ware and early bronze age pottery were found. In all the barrow had a long period of use and, as with many sites, the Romans were attracted to it. A small Romano-British hut was built on the north side of the barrow. It is the only one of the Medway barrows which has been carefully excavated. The finds are in Maidstone Museum.

2. Bigbury Camp hillfort, Harbledown

Iron Age
TR: 116576

3.2 km W of Canterbury on minor road SW from Harbledown, midway between the A2(T) and A28.

A late iron age, univallate hillfort of irregular shape and about 10 hectares in extent, Bigbury Camp is mostly covered with chestnut woods. It has an inner bank with a ditch 4.8 metres wide outside it, and beyond there is a small counterscarp bank. The main bank and ditch run along the 60 metres contour line of the hill. At the north-west end an extra area of about 3.2 hectares has been added; this could have been a cattle pound. Original entrances have been located at the east and west ends. At the east end, where there is a modern road, the entrance is defended by a staggered earthwork, with two ditches and a bank. Gravel-digging in various areas in the nineteenth century has produced a collection of iron agricultural tools and kitchen utensils, including one firedog. A less cheerful find was a slave chain with lock, connected with the trade in slaves between Britain and Gaul before the Romans came. Harness fittings, snaffle bits, linch-pins with bronze mounts and a portion of an iron tyre suggest a well-to-do farming community. Pottery from the site was of the earlier iron age, and for the later period fine wheel-turned Belgic pots of the Aylesford-Swarling culture. The fort was possibly occupied for a long period before the conquest by Caesar and is probably the native *oppidum* stormed in 54 BC by the Seventh Legion. A branch of the North Downs trackway, the Pilgrims' Way, runs through the fort in an east–west direction. The finds may be seen in Maidstone and Canterbury museums.

3. Coldrum long barrow, Trottiscliffe

Neolithic
TQ: 654607

Between the Pilgrims' Way and the Folkestone Road (A20), 4.4 km NE of Wrotham, the site is 1.6 km E of Trottiscliffe village. Signposted. Car park at 650607; walk of 400 metres. National Trust; always open.

Here are the remains of a stone-chambered long barrow 27 metres by 16.5 metres and orientated east to west. It has a rectangular burial chamber at its east end, the uprights of which are still standing. The burial mound itself has nearly disappeared, but despite this its condition is possibly the most complete of the Medway group of megaliths. Twenty-four of the stones forming the retaining revetment wall lie on the terrace on which the barrow stands. The seventeen along the east end have fallen on the slope. The barrow was dug by J. M. 'Saxon' Kemble in 1856, and in 1910 the

Coldrum long barrow is surrounded by a revetment wall of large stones (foreground). The unroofed burial chamber is in the background. (J. Dyer)

excavation by F. J. Bennett found the remains of twenty-two persons of both sexes within the burial chamber. This chamber is 4 metres by 1.5 metres and it had a stone pavement. Many of the bones appeared to have been deliberately broken, and some had rheumatic conditions.

The barrow is preserved as a memorial to Benjamin Harrison, the Kentish prehistorian responsible for discovering the controversial eoliths attributed to the palaeolithic period.

4. Julliberrie's Grave, Chilham

Neolithic
TQ: 077532

400 metres S of Chilham station on the lower slopes of Julliberrie Downs above the river Stour.

This is an unchambered, earthen long barrow. It is orientated north-east to south-west. Unfortunately chalk quarrying has removed the north end, which would most probably have contained the burials. As it stands today, it is 44 metres by 15 metres at its widest, with a maximum height of 2 metres still standing. Previously dug into by various antiquaries in the eighteenth and nineteenth centuries, parts of the barrow were excavated in 1936–7. This excavation revealed the presence of a ditch surrounding the barrow which had silted up. No revetment wall or other type of stonework was found. Within the filling of the ditch four Roman burials were uncovered. These were located at the south-east end and have been dated to about AD 50. The core of the barrow was composed of turf taken from the ditch area. Within this core was found a fine thin-butted polished flint axe similar to ones found in Scandinavia, Germany and Holland. Towards the north-west end of the west side of the barrow was a ritual pit. This had been dug into the chalk and contained flint cores, flakes and scrapers. Similar flints were also found in parts of the ditch filling. No burials have been located.

5. Kit's Coty House and Countless Stones, Aylesford   Neolithic
TQ: 745608 and 744604

Just W of A229. Badly signposted. Park near Lower Bell public house and walk from 744606 or 746610. Lower Kit's Coty House is in the opposite direction down the road on the left-hand side. Monuments in the care of English Heritage; open at all times.

Kit's Coty House: the visible remains are those of a chambered long barrow, mostly destroyed by ploughing and partially vandalised. It is almost certainly another one of the Medway group. It is orientated east to west with the striking remains of a burial chamber, or dummy entrance, at the east end. It consists of two large sarsen uprights, one 2.4 metres tall, with a cross-slab, arranged in 'H' plan. This structure is capped by a large stone about 4 metres by 2.7 metres. In its original form it would all have been covered with earth to make a rectangular mound and would have contained burials. A drawing published by William Stukeley in 1772 shows the mound very much reduced in height, with a single stone known as the General's Tombstone at the west end. This was removed about 1867.

Countless Stones (Lower Kit's Coty): this is about 450 metres south of Kit's Coty and is surrounded by railings with trees growing from it. It is a confused jumble of some twenty sarsen stones. Judging from a reconstruction by Stukeley, it was possibly a long barrow of similar form to Coldrum (no. 3). In the surrounding area there are several single standing stones, possibly the remains of other barrows. An example is the Upper White Horse Stone at 753603. The footings of a rare neolithic long house, measuring 18 metres by 8 metres, were excavated close to the stone in 1999, whilst clearing land for the Channel Tunnel Rail Link.

6. Oldbury hillfort, Ightham   Iron Age
TQ: 582562

1.6 km SW of Ightham village on A25. Turn right just before the Crown Point public house and park in car park (signposted). This gives access to the W side of the fort. Mainly in care of the National Trust and always open.

A large hillfort of 50 hectares, in a position commanding a natural corridor from the Weald into the north of Kent. There are gateways at the north and south ends (the latter near Seven Wents junction). There is little need for fortification on the east side, which is very precipitous. Within the camp area there is a natural spring for water supply. Excavations were carried out here by J. B. Ward Perkins in 1938 and F. H. Thompson in 1983–4. No evidence of a major settlement was found and Thompson has suggested that the fort 'was rapidly constructed on a massive scale, never occupied in a permanent fashion, and abandoned by about 50 BC'. Piles of slingstones were found in the interior and many individual stones were found down the outside of the banks. There was evidence of burning, which suggests that the defenders fell beneath the onslaught of the attackers, possibly the advancing troops of Caesar. Two Belgic pedestal cremation urns were found in the rampart. The finds are in Maidstone Museum.

7. Oldbury rock shelters, Ightham   Palaeolithic
TQ: 585562

The site is at Ightham on the E side of Oldbury hillfort and 36 metres S of the NE corner of the fort; N of the A25. Go up lane by Cob Tree public house. There is very limited room for parking at the top of this lane and it is best to park at the bottom and walk up. The shelters are in woods on the right-hand side after the last house. In the care of the National Trust; always open.

The remains exist here of rock shelters of the middle palaeolithic period. Considerable weathering and quarrying of the rock have taken place since palaeolithic times, but the basic form of a rock shelter, due to the weathering of soft sandstone overlain by harder greensand rock, can be seen. The site was excavated in the nineteenth century and more recently by D. M. Collins. The main artefacts are of the Mousterian period with characteristic hand-axes. The finds are in the British Museum, London, and Maidstone Museum.

8. Ringwould barrows, Dover
Bronze Age
TR: 365471

On Free Down, 1.6 km S of Ringwould by footpath from A258, or a similar distance SW from Kingsdown by downland track. Barrows are just S of this track.

This site consists of two bowl-barrows which were excavated in 1872. For its period this was a very careful excavation. No burials were found in the barrow to the east, perhaps a cenotaph. The other mound, 22 metres in diameter, contained four primary cremations, each in inverted cinerary urns. They were individually cut into the chalk and covered with soil and flints. Three incense-type cups were found with two of the burials and also four faience beads. The grave goods are in Maidstone Museum.

9. Squerryes Park hillfort, Westerham
Iron Age
TQ: 442522

1.6 km S of Westerham and 400 metres E of road running S to Kent Hatch and Crockham Hill. Fort is at N end of Crockham Hill Common. The easiest approach is by walking up the drive just N of junction with B269, marked 'No motors except to Hunters Lodge'. S bank of fort is just N of gate across green track and continuing on E side.

A late iron age fort triangular in shape and covering 4.4 hectares. It possibly dates from the first century BC. On its east and west sides it follows the line of the promontory and there is only a single rampart. To separate it from the level land to the south there are double ramparts, much hidden in rhododendrons and bracken. The original entrance is at the south-east corner and has extra defensive ditches. Excavation has produced late iron age material. Finds are in the British Museum. They include a strange flint money box and Belgic coins.

10. Swanscombe: Barnfield Pit
Palaeolithic
TQ: 598746

800 metres SW of Swanscombe station at Milton Street. A rough track opposite the Rising Sun public house is marked by a notice board. This gives restricted access to the site, which is in the care of the Nature Conservancy Council.

The gravel quarries in this area have been particularly rich in hand-axes of the Acheulean period and tools of the Clactonian tradition. This area is on the 30 metres terrace of the Thames and in it in 1935, 7.2 metres below the surface, Mr A. T. Marston found an occiput and, nine months later, the left parietal of the skull of 'Swanscombe Man'. John Wymer and his team, digging on the same site in 1955, were fortunate to find the right parietal of the same skull. These fossil remains, possibly of a young adult, have been dated to approximately 350,000 years ago. Acheulean hand-axes, many thousands of flakes and the remains of at least twenty-six mammal species all suggest a living area, although it is possible that the material has been deposited by river action.

Excavations on this site under the direction of Dr J. d'A. Waechter were conducted in 1968–72 and revealed an old shoreline of the river and an activity area. Interesting finds of animal bones and footprints together with flint flakes, some of which have been found to fit together, have been made.

The Swanscombe skull is in the Natural History Museum, London. Selections of implements from this area can be seen in most of the major museums in Britain. Three concrete obelisks and an inscribed plaque now mark the find spots of the oldest human remains yet found in Britain.

LANCASHIRE
(Map on page 240)

1. Bleasdale circle　　　　　　　　　　　　　　**Bronze Age**
SD: 577460

Follow track N from Bleasdale for 400 metres. A path leads E of the vicarage here to the site, which is enclosed in a small plantation.

This interesting 'palisade' barrow consisted of a turf mound 11 metres across and 0.9 metre high, surrounded by a circle of eleven oak posts (now shown by concrete pillars), the whole ringed by a ditch lined with birch poles with an entrance at the east, where two parallel rows of three posts led to an outer circle. This comprised a palisade of closely spaced small posts set between larger ones 4 to 5 metres apart, with an entrance to the south-east, marked by two large posts. The inner mound was not centrally sited in relation to the palisade but almost touched it to the east. In the central mound was a grave containing two collared urns, one holding a miniature cup, and both filled with charcoal and cremated bone.

2. Buckton Castle, Mossley　　　　　　　　　　　**Iron Age**
SD: 989076

On the summit of the W edge of Buckton Moor, reached via track leading N from Carrbrook, off the B6175.

A well-protected, though diminutive, hillfort, oval in plan. The defences consist of a bank, ditch and counterscarp bank. The main rampart consists of earth and rubble and was probably drywalled. In places it is still 1.5 metres high. A possible entrance exists at the north-west.

3. Castercliffe Camp, Nelson　　　　　　　　　　**Iron Age**
SD: 885384

Take the Colne to Haggate minor road to the fork 1 km E of Nelson. The hillfort is immediately W of the fork.

This damaged hillfort is oval in plan and encloses 0.8 hectare. It has three ramparts and seems to have been of at least two periods of construction. The central rampart was of box type with timber revetting, fronted by a rock-cut ditch 3.6 metres deep and probable counterscarp bank. These fortifications seem to have been abandoned before completion. The inner rampart was damaged in the nineteenth century, but sufficient remains to suggest that it was stone-faced with timber lacing but no associated ditch. Many of the stones of this inner rampart are burnt and the excavations showed that it is heavily vitrified, the stone having melted into a solid mass, perhaps as the result of an attack. There is a radiocarbon date of 510 BC. It is uncertain which of the ramparts is the earlier.

4. Chapel Town (Cheetham Close), Turton　　　　　**Bronze Age**
SD: 717158

Take minor road from Toppings to Dimple. At 712159 a track leads to Turton Heights. The sites are to the SE of the track at the summit.

This circle has been damaged, but six stones survive. Originally it was about 15 metres across. 13.5 metres south-west of the circle is a single standing stone. 18 metres south-west is a ring cairn 22 metres across with a bank 1.2 metres wide, carefully revetted on both faces with upright slabs.

5. Fairy Holes, Bowland with Leagram　　　　　　**Bronze Age**
SD: 651467

Take footpath N of minor road through Fair Oak Farm to New Lound Hill. The cave is to the left of the path on the S slope of the hill.

This south-facing cave is 20 metres long, 1.8 metres wide and 3 metres high.

There is a high platform in front of the cave mouth which provided occupation debris of bronze age date, including sherds of a collared urn.

6. Mosley Height, Cliviger
Bronze Age
SD: 881302

100 metres N of The Long Causeway, 1.2 km due E of Walk Mill.

An embanked stone circle, 13 metres in diameter, consisting of eighteen large boulders, three of non-local millstone grit. They are irregularly spaced with a gap at the west. When excavated in 1950, the interior was found to be coarsely paved. Beneath this were a central cist containing two Pennine urns and cremated bones, and three other cists with urns and cremation fragments.

7. Pikestones, Anglezarke
Neolithic
SD: 627172

Take minor road along E side of Anglezarke reservoir to the Manor House at 621172. The cairn lies E of this.

The Pikestones consist of a trapezoidal cairn 45 metres long and 18 metres wide, set on a low ridge commanding an extensive view. At the broader north end is a part-collapsed setting of five large gritstone slabs originally delineating a rectangular chamber 4.5 metres long and 0.9 metre wide, perhaps originally divided into two compartments. Behind the chamber was a circular drywalled structure. Traces of a double drystone revetment are visible at the north end. The cairn is perhaps most closely associated with the Derbyshire group of chambered tombs, although a link with southern Scotland has been postulated.

8. Portfield Camp, Whalley
Iron Age
SD: 747355

In the triangle formed by the A671 and the minor roads leading S and W from Portfield.

This hillfort is on a slight promontory facing south. The defences, a double bank and ditch, are visible only on the north-west. Excavation has revealed two phases of construction. The earliest defences consisted of a single bank, revetted with stone, 6 metres behind the present inner ditch. The bank was subsequently levelled and replaced by a double bank and ditch. The inner bank was stone-faced and clay-cored. It was separated from its ditch by a 6 metre berm.

9. Warton Crag hillfort
Iron Age
SD: 492727

S of the bridlepath leading across Warton Crag from minor road at 499731 or 481732.

This promontory fort occupies the southern end of Warton Crag. Three lines of widely spaced banks protect a roughly rectangular area 6 hectares in extent. The east and west sides of the Crag are precipitous. A south-eastern gap in the inner bank may represent an original entrance to the inner area, which covers 2.8 hectares. The middle and outer ramparts are hard to trace owing to dense undergrowth.

10. Whitelow, Bury
Bronze Age
SD: 805163

Take bridlepath leading E of A56(T) at 801160 to old quarry road. The cairn stands alongside this road.

This much damaged cairn occupies a picturesque viewpoint. It was 8 metres across, but robbing has left only a small central cairn and the arc of a possible kerb on the north as prominent features. Excavation in 1960–2 produced seven cremations, five in the south-eastern area and two in the central cairn. Three were with inverted collared urns, one containing a miniature cup, and the fourth was with a cordoned urn. A fifth cremation was with a burnt flint knife and a sixth had a clay stud or lip plug. The primary burial had a deliberately broken bronze awl.

LEICESTERSHIRE
(Map on page 238)

1. The Bulwarks, Breedon-on-the-Hill
Iron Age
SK: 406233

Access up steep hill signposted 'Church' from Breedon village.

Most of the south and east sides of this 9.2 hectare hillfort have been destroyed by quarrying, although the single bank and external ditch pass round the west side of the churchyard. A number of excavations have taken place in recent years showing that the fort had two periods of construction. In the first it was surrounded by a wall of limestone reinforced with wooden posts at front and back. Later, when the timbers had decayed, a drystone wall held a bank of turf in place. The ditch was cut into the solid limestone of the hill and was 1.5 metres deep and 6 metres wide.

Due west of the church is a very disfigured inturned entrance with part of the churchyard wall on top of it. Excavations indicate that this was probably the main entrance into the fort and that the walls on either side were of drystone construction. It has been much altered by the medieval roadway up to the church, which approached between the bank and the ditch on this side. The fort seems to have been occupied from the third century BC until the beginning of the Roman occupation.

2. Burrough-on-the-Hill
Iron Age
SK: 761119

Approached by a bridleway from the Burrough to Somerby road at 767114.

This large, roughly rectangular hillfort encloses some 4.8 hectares. A massive rampart and ditch surround three sides of a steep spur, whilst an even more

The excavation of the southern side of the entrance passage to the hillfort at Burrough-on-the-Hill, Leicestershire. The iron age road surface is in the foreground. (J. Dyer)

123

formidable rampart cuts across the spur to complete the fourth side. The latter side is breached by a very long inturned entrance, which has been shown by excavation to have been enlarged, perhaps by the local iron age tribe, the Corieltauvi, and to have been guarded by stone sentry chambers. The ramparts were faced with drystone walling. Inside the camp were many storage pits, which were filled with pottery and animal bones. The pottery ranges in date from the second century BC well into the Roman period, suggesting that the fort was occupied for a long period of time. Bones of pig, sheep, cow and horse indicate considerable animal husbandry, whilst finds of rotary querns (hand grinding-stones) show that much grain was also being produced. Excavations have so far failed to identify any huts with certainty. The interior of the fort was used as a fairground in medieval times, and in 1873 the Grand National was run there.

LINCOLNSHIRE
(Map on page 238)

1. Ash Hill long barrow, Binbrook   Neolithic
TF: 209962

2 km due N of Binbrook. A cart-track leads right up to barrow from a minor road on the S side of Swinhope Park. It is behind an industrial building.

Once considered the best-preserved of the Lincolnshire long barrows, it is now overgrown and once had a wartime air-raid shelter at its north end. It is 42 metres long and 17 metres wide at its broader north end, which stands about 2 metres high. Its side ditches are filled in, though the western has been shown by excavation to be 2.5 metres deep. The barrow itself is unexcavated, but fragments of a Mortlake bowl have been found in a pit near the north end. Burials of Viking age were also found at the north-west corner of the barrow in 1983.

2. Ash Holt long barrow, Cuxwold   Neolithic
TA: 190012

Overgrown with trees and bushes, on the side of a small wood, and close to the road from Swallow to Thorganby.

This long barrow has been damaged on its southern end by a pit dug into it. It is one of the smallest in Lincolnshire, measuring only 24 metres in length by 11.5 metres at its widest end. Its side ditches are no longer visible.

The Bully Hills barrows at Tathwell, Lincolnshire, outlined against the skyline. (J. Dyer)

3. Bully Hills, Tathwell
Bronze Age
TF: 330827

An excellent view of this barrow cemetery as it straddles the skyline can be had from 326829 on the Tathwell to Haugham road.

Seven bowl-barrows stand in a spectacular line, one slightly apart from the rest. Their heights vary from 1.5 metres to 3 metres and their diameters between 15 metres and 24 metres. It is not known what the mounds contain.

4. Burgh on Bain long barrow
Neolithic
TA: 213849

On the top of the greensand hill 90 metres to the E of High Street, an ancient ridgeway, 400 metres S of Burgh Top Farm.

This barrow is oval in shape and measures 27 metres long by 14 metres wide and 2 metres high. It is covered by a clump of beech trees and has been damaged by burrowing animals. It is the smallest long barrow in Lincolnshire, and its oval shape resembles a shorter type of barrow found in Yorkshire.

5. Butterbumps barrow cemetery, Willoughby
Bronze Age
TF: 493724

From the minor road between Willoughby and Cumberworth, a farm drive to Butterbumps Farm passes the ploughed-down remains on their E side.

The twelve round barrows in this cemetery are now all less than 1 metre high and are best seen when the ground has been freshly ploughed. They seem to have lain in two rows. One contained a cremation in a pit, covered by wooden planks. Nearby were a whetstone and an ogival dagger in a wooden sheath. There is a radiocarbon date of 1750 BC.

6. Careby Camp
Iron Age
TF: 040157

Within Careby Wood and best approached from a cart-track past Monks Woods on its S side.

This small oval fort is very overgrown and difficult to find. It has two rings of fortifications which enclose an area measuring about 250 metres by 220 metres. The inner bank is about 0.9 metres high, the outer seldom more than 0.3 metre. An unusual feature is the wide space between the two ramparts, a distance of more than 36 metres. Whilst the site was probably built in the iron age, the possibility of an earlier or later date should not be ruled out. It is advisable to visit this fort in winter.

7. Deadmen's Graves long barrows, Claxby
Neolithic
TF: 444720

A minor road off the A1028 running between Ulceby and Claxby.

Two long barrows on the skyline can be clearly seen from the road near the farmhouse at 443716. They lie above a narrow, steep-sided valley with lynchets on its southern side. The western barrow is 48 metres long, 16 metres wide at its eastern end and 1.8 metres high. The south-eastern barrow is 53 metres long, 18 metres wide and 1.8 metres high. Both lie east to west and neither has any sign of side ditches showing.

8. Fordington barrows, Ulceby
Bronze Age?
TF: 417714

Two round barrows visible from the road.

These are surrounded by the banks and ditches of a deserted medieval village, with a disused churchyard site close by. Probably of bronze age date, they could be the bases for circular medieval structures such as windmills or dovecotes.

9. Hoe Hill long barrow, Binbrook

Neolithic
TF: 215953

Park on B1203 opposite Hoe Hill Farm, and walk down hedgerow opposite. Covered with beech trees.

This well-preserved long barrow lies in a small wood visible from the road. It measures 50 metres long and 17 metres wide at its eastern end and must be 3 metres high. The mound has suffered some damage near its centre but has not been excavated. The northern ditch was found to be 2.2 metres deep when examined in 1984.

10. Honington Camp

Iron Age
SK: 954424

Approached by cart-track from A153 due E of Honington village. As the earthwork is low in profile it is not easily seen from a distance.

Roughly rectangular, this hillfort lies on a limestone plateau above the river Witham. It is extremely small, enclosing about 0.4 hectare, but is strongly defended by double banks and ditches with a third outer bank. The gap on the eastern side is probably the original entrance. Although the hill is low and broad, the camp commands a wide area in all directions and seems to be of iron age construction. Roman coins were recorded from the site in the seventeenth century, and Camden wrote that 'bits of weapons and bridles' were found there in 1691.

11. Revesby Barrows

Bronze Age or Roman
TF: 303616

Two large round barrows beside the A155, 400 metres E of Revesby village.

Both barrows are about 2.4 metres high and 20 metres in diameter. They are surrounded by well-marked ditches. One is reported to have contained a pit cut into the clay containing burnt bones. They could be of bronze age or Roman date, more probably the latter.

12. Round Hills fort, Ingoldsby

Iron Age
SK: 992308

Beside a minor road from Ingoldsby to Boothby Pagnell.

A short cart-track leads into this camp. A low bush-covered bank about 1 metre high with an external ditch encloses what appears to be a circular iron age plateau fort covering about 0.8 hectare. It is one of a series of small forts on the limestone uplands of south Lincolnshire and does not appear to have been excavated.

13. Spellows Hills, Langton by Spilsby

Neolithic
TF: 402723

This long barrow can be clearly seen from the A16(T) road; there is no footpath access.

Measuring 55 metres long, 12 metres wide and 1.8 metres high at its southern end, this barrow has been much damaged and now appears to be a line of three round barrows. Although there is no record of its opening, many human bones are reputed to have been found scattered around this barrow in the past. This is probably why it is also known as 'Hills of the Slain'.

14. Tathwell long barrow

Neolithic
TF: 294822

Visible from the A153, but not accessible unless fields under stubble.

This extremely overgrown barrow can be easily spotted because of a single large tree which grows upon it. Although much disturbed by rabbits, the barrow still measures 32 metres in length, is 16 metres wide at its south-eastern end and stands some 1.8 metres high.

NORFOLK
(Map on page 238)

1. Arminghall henge monument, Bixley
Neolithic
TG: 240060

Beside the minor road from Trowse Newton to Caistor St Edmund.

This site is included because of its great importance, although there is practically nothing to see on the ground, except a slight circular depression surrounded by a low bank, close to the electricity pylon. Discovered in 1929 by aerial photography, it belongs to the group of later neolithic temple sites called henge monuments. Two concentric ditches, the inner one 36 metres in diameter, were separated by a bank. Inside was a horseshoe-shaped arrangement of eight massive oak posts, each about 1 metre in diameter and 7 tons in weight. One has been radiocarbon-dated to 2490 BC. An entrance facing south-west passed through the inner ditch (and probably the outer one which lies under the garden hedge) and would have faced midwinter sunrise.

2. Bircham Common barrows, Great Bircham
Bronze Age
TF: 775316

This line of barrows runs roughly N to S and crosses the road from Great Bircham to Houghton Hall Park.

The barrows are widely spaced and very overgrown, but are important because of their connections with the Wessex culture. Whilst those to the south of the road (two bowls and one bell-barrow) can be seen but not reached without crossing ploughed land, the bell-barrow north of the road can be visited by following a cart-track beside a wood. The mound of this bell-barrow is about 1.8 metres high and 27 metres in diameter. It is surrounded by a ditch and external bank.

Of the inaccessible barrows south of the road, the bell-barrow is 45 metres in diameter and 2.4 metres high. It contained a flint cairn under which a cremation had been buried in an inverted collared urn with looped handles, together with a bronze awl and a number of beads or buttons covered with sheet gold and decorated with incised lines. Unfortunately these finds have since been lost.

3. Broome Heath long barrow, Ditchingham
Neolithic
TM: 344913

Best approached from the minor road from Ditchingham village to Broome, which passes on the NW side of Broome Heath.

A footpath from the northern end of the row of houses leads east across the Heath passing the last remnants of a large barrow group. On its right an overgrown round barrow stands about 1 metre high. Further east is the long barrow, lying east to west, about 1.5 metres high and about 24 metres long. It appears to be slightly higher at its eastern end and is damaged on its southern side. It has not been excavated, although it has produced Windmill Hill pottery. Another round barrow lies immediately west of the long barrow, and half of another can be seen passing under the fences of nearby houses. An adjoining enclosure, excavated in 1970, has produced hearths, pits and early neolithic pottery.

4. Grimes Graves flint mines, Weeting
Neolithic
TL: 817898

Well signposted. Approached by car along metalled trackway beside a cottage. English Heritage guardianship. Open daily April to September, 10–6, and October, 10–5; November to March 10 to dusk on Wednesday to Sunday only; closed 1–2 daily. Last admission 30 minutes before closing. Closed 24th to 26th December and 1st January. Entrance charge. Telephone enquiries: 01842 810656.

The neolithic flint mines at Grimes Graves form what is possibly the most exciting archaeological monument in eastern England. Extracting flint from the

Looking into the gallery of one of the neolithic flint mines at Grimes Graves, Norfolk. (British Museum)

chalk is one of the oldest manufacturing industries practised in Britain: flint-knapping is a dying craft but it survives in Brandon 5 km from the mines.

There are more than 470 flint mines at Grimes Graves, ranging over an area of 6.5 hectares, whilst a further 7 hectares contains shallower workings, some of an 'opencast' nature, and others involving simple pits without galleries leading from them. Three shafts in the 'deep mine' area have been cleared and one can be visited. The mines were of two types. Where the flint was fairly close to the surface, simple bell-shaped pits were dug. Where the flint was deeper, up to 12 metres, shafts were sunk with galleries radiating out from them. It is probable that only one shaft was worked at a time, the debris from it being thrown into a neighbouring disused mine. For tools, red deer antlers seem to have been used as picks, levers and rakes. The flint nodules and waste material were hauled to the surface in baskets. There the nodules were roughed out on the spot into the shape of the desired implements. One shaft might produce 50 tonnes of flint.

One of the excavated shafts failed to provide good-quality flint, perhaps owing to geological faulting. Before abandoning it, the miners had set up a fertility shrine. A pile of flints was covered with antlers, and on a ledge overlooking it a chalk figurine of a pregnant woman was placed. (The authenticity of this figure is now considered suspect.) In the entrance to an adjacent gallery, a phallus and balls of chalk were set up. A chalk lamp stood nearby. Corrected radiocarbon dates indicate that the mines were in use between 3000 and 1900 BC.

The shaft open to the public has a concrete protective roof and is entered down an iron ladder some 9 metres long. A selection of objects from the mines is kept in the centre on the site. The best objects are in the British Museum and local museums.

On the south-east side of the mined area is a mound called Grimshoe. It is nothing more than dumped material from one of the mines. It is fairly certain that this was the meeting place for the medieval hundred court.

5. Harpley Common barrow cemetery
Bronze Age
TF: 755287 to 766279

This fine row of round barrows curves SE from the B1153, E of Anmer towards Harpley.

Although these barrows are overgrown they are very upstanding, some 3 metres high. These monuments were once densely distributed over Norfolk, and one can only regret that so many have been destroyed, especially during the Second World War.

6. Holkham Camp
Iron Age
TF: 875443

Restricted parking space opposite entrance to church in Holkham Park on A149. A private track leads down to the camp: 1.2 km.

This roughly oval fort was built at the south end of a sand spit and encloses 2.2 hectares. Access was from the north. A bank and ditch protect all except the west side: there is an extra external bank on the south and south-east. A steep scarp and water afford natural protection on the west. There is an entrance facing south, which could be original. Two dewponds are likely to be post-medieval in date.

7. Little Cressingham barrow cemetery
Bronze Age
TL: 861986

This group of barrows lies S of the Bodney to Little Cressingham road, and N of Seven Acre Plantation. They are accessible from the track leading S to Bodney Lodge.

The round barrow (grid reference above) at the north-west corner of the plantation is probably the largest in Norfolk, being about 4.5 metres high and 60 metres in diameter. A second barrow nearer the road to the north-east has been ploughed but is still well over 30 metres in diameter and 0.9 to 1.2 metres high.

The most important round barrow so far excavated in Norfolk once lay 400 metres east of the Seven Acre group, in the field on the western side of Hard Clump Plantation (867992). Unfortunately it has been destroyed by the plough. This was the Little Cressingham barrow. It contained the crouched skeleton of a man, buried with a grooved bronze dagger that had a wooden hilt, a flat bronze dagger and an elaborate amber necklace. Sewn to clothing on his chest was an engraved rectangular gold plate and other sheet-gold mountings. This burial shows that the Wessex culture had extended to Norfolk by about 1700 BC.

8. Salthouse Heath, Cley and Salthouse
Bronze Age
TG: 077423

Scattered over the Heath (see Ordnance Survey sheet 143). Difficult to find and best visited in winter when the bracken and gorse are low.

Norfolk's largest barrow cemetery. Three Halfpenny Hill is a spectacular banked bowl-barrow with flat top, almost 27 metres in diameter at the above grid point. South of it is Three Farthing Hill, an overgrown bowl-barrow. On the north side of the Salthouse Heath to Weybourne road is Gallows Hill, another fine banked bowl-barrow about 27 metres in diameter. There are more bowl-barrows in the wood at 068421, and slightly further north in the triangle of heath at 067425 where about thirty small mounds sometimes called mini-barrows have been found. Some contained bucket urns. They are extremely difficult to find, as is the elusive disc-barrow on the northern edge of the heath at 075429.

9. Seven Hills barrow cemetery, Thetford
Bronze Age
TL: 904814

These bronze age barrows lie on the ridge SE of Thetford and are approached from the A1088 along the Great Snarehill Belt trackway.

This area was badly damaged by the military during the two world wars. Now only six of the Seven Hills barrows survive, consisting of two bowl-barrows and a bell-barrow in a western group, and three bowl-barrows further east. The barrows are unexcavated but damage shows that they are constructed of sand, capped with chalk dug from the surrounding ditches.

Large bowl-barrows can also be seen west of the A1088 on Elder Hill and Tutt Hill.

10. South Creake hillfort

Iron Age
TF: 848352

On the summit of Bloodgate Hill, 1 km SW of South Creake.

This site is only for the most enthusiastic student of hillforts. In a ploughed field can be seen traces of a univallate camp, circular in shape, enclosing about 3.5 hectares. Deliberately levelled in the nineteenth century, the site can best be seen from the north-east and the farm road to the west. Aerial photography suggests an entrance on the eastern side. The extreme circularity of the fort elicits comparison with the bivallate fort at Warham St Mary (no. 12).

11. Thetford Castle

Iron Age
TL: 875828

On the eastern side of Thetford.

The double banks and ditches surrounding the bailey of one of the largest Norman mottes in England were first built as an iron age hillfort. Its original extent is uncertain, but it probably used the river Thet to mark its southern boundary. The Icknield Way probably forded the river at this point.

12. Warham Camp, Warham St Mary

Iron Age
TF: 944409

A grass bridletrack leads to the camp, off the minor road running S from Warham All Saints to Wighton.

This is the most magnificent hillfort in Norfolk. Although its site is not very high by Wessex standards, its symmetrical defences are upstanding and very impressive.

The river Stiffkey runs along the western side of the camp, with marshland beyond. Two banks and ditches laid out on an almost circular plan surround an area of 1.4 hectares. Late-eighteenth-century landscape gardening resulted in the river being diverted and the outer bank and ditch adjoining it demolished. All the banks still stand 2.5 metres high with deep outer ditches. The inner ditch has been shown by excavation to be flat-bottomed. The entrance was probably on the south-west. None of the breaks in the rampart has been shown to be original. Excavation in 1959 showed that the site was probably constructed by the Iceni in the second century BC and occupied until the early first century AD. In the field immediately north-east was an unfinished rectangular fort of the same date.

The excavations produced nothing to substantiate the claim that the main camp was constructed by the Danes, an assumption based on the remarkably regular shape of the defences, which is a feature of tenth-century Danish camps of 'Trelleborg' type in Denmark.

13. Weasenham Plantation, Weasenham All Saints

Bronze Age
TF: 853198

1 km S of Weasenham All Saints, mainly to the E of the A1065, beside the minor road to Tittleshall.

This once fine group of barrows has suffered badly as a result of wartime ploughing and afforestation. In the middle of a ploughed field at 853198 is a fine bell-barrow, 2.1 metres high and 42 metres in diameter, with an outer bank. It is clearly visible from the road, but very overgrown with nettles and not accessible.

Warham Camp, Norfolk, is one of the few upstanding hillforts in eastern England. It is remarkable for its almost perfect circular plan. (Cambridge University Collection)

Further east along the minor road on Litcham Heath is a good bowl-barrow, 1.8 metres high, just inside a wood (opposite a stile on the south side of the road). In the ploughed field at this point the outlines of two more bowl-barrows can just be made out. A fine disc-barrow further east has been totally destroyed.

In the Weasenham Plantation west of the A1065 are a saucer-barrow and bell-barrow (marked 'tumuli' on the Ordnance Survey map), both of which are very overgrown but measure about 45 metres in diameter. There are another saucer-barrow and a bowl-barrow in the same wood closer to the main road; both are difficult to find.

14. West Rudham long barrows, West Rudham and Harpley   Neolithic
TF: 810253

These two long barrows lie N and S of a minor road from Harpley to Weasenham All Saints.

The northern barrow, excavated by A. H. A. Hogg in 1938, lies 500 metres from the road and is approached up the side of the wood. It is clearly visible and marked by concrete corner posts. Its main axis runs north–south and it is 57 metres long. It is about 15 metres wide and is surrounded by a ditch shown on excavation to be 3.5 metres wide and 1.2 metres deep. The ditch of a small horseshoe-shaped forecourt containing a small 'libation' pit joins the barrow at its southern end and is also covered by the barrow mound, which was composed largely of sand. At the southern end of the main barrow structure was a platform on which a body had been cremated.

Adjoining the road on the south side at 809252 is a second long barrow, oval in shape, and also marked by concrete posts. It has been badly reduced by ploughing. In 1938 it measured 45 metres by 27 metres and was surrounded by a ditch 4.5 metres wide. Although unexcavated, it has produced pieces of Windmill Hill style pottery.

NORTHAMPTONSHIRE
(Map on page 238)

1. Arbury Camp, Chipping Warden
Iron Age
SP: 494486

Alongside the A361, on the W of the road SW of Chipping Warden.

This small circular hillfort, some 180 metres in diameter, is surrounded by a single bank and ditch and has an entrance on the south-east. It looks down on to the upper Cherwell valley and may have guarded a through-route between the Nene and Avon valleys.

2. Borough Hill, Daventry
Iron Age
SP: 588626

E of Daventry town centre. From the A45 follow signs to Southbrook. An access road leads from Admiral's Way to the hillfort, where there is a free car park and picnic area.

This hillfort is of two periods. The smaller, stronger iron age fort encloses 5 hectares at the north-west end of the hill. It is triangular in shape and has a massive bank, ditch and counterscarp bank. On the south it has an additional outer ditch. The south side is broken by an overlapping entrance. It overlies an enclosure of some 54 hectares which stretches to the south of the main fort (formerly occupied by a BBC radio station). Parts of this earlier enclosure can be seen on the west, beside the golf course. Occupation dates from the late bronze age.

3. Hunsbury, Northampton
Iron Age
SP: 737584

Hunsbury Hill Country Park, laid out around the hillfort, is signposted from the A45 S of Northampton. Admission and car parking free; there is also an ironstone railway museum.

Known locally as 'Danes Camp', a roughly circular bank and ditch enclose some 1.6 hectares broken by an original entrance on the south-west. Other gaps seem to be modern. In the nineteenth century most of the interior was lowered some 2.4 metres by ironstone digging. This makes the bank appear higher than it really was. During the quarrying more than three hundred storage pits, some stone-lined, were uncovered. These contained many tools and weapons as well as mostly late iron age pottery. Excavations in 1952 and 1988 suggest that Hunsbury began life as an ironworking site. This was fortified, perhaps in the fourth century BC, by the erection of a box-rampart and timber revetment with a V-shaped ditch outside it. After burning, part of this was rebuilt in the first century BC by people making Glastonbury-type pottery with curvilinear decoration. An outer line of defence, now destroyed, 73 metres to the north of the fort may have been constructed at this time. The fort was abandoned soon after the Roman conquest. Amongst the finds from the site were more than 150 corn-grinding querns, chiefly of Derbyshire millstone grit, and a fine bronze sword scabbard decorated with an incised and cast curvilinear design (now in Northampton Central Museum). A neolithic causewayed enclosure was excavated at Briar Hill, 1 km to the north of Hunsbury. Nothing is now visible.

4. The Larches, Stowe Nine Churches
Iron Age
SP: 633567

On north side of the road to Church Stowe.

Triple banks and ditches run for about 270 metres. They are undated and may be part of prehistoric cross-ridge dykes. On the other hand there are medieval earthworks to the west and they may be connected.

Excavation of the entrance to Rainsborough Camp, Northamptonshire. The semicircular guard-chambers are clearly visible in this aerial view. (Michael Avery)

5. Rainsborough Camp, Newbottle

Iron Age
SP: 526348

Approached by track W from Camp Farm on road from Charlton to Croughton.

Rainsborough is a roughly oval hillfort enclosing 2.5 hectares. It has a double bank and ditches, although the outer ditch is now filled in and the bank much ploughed down. However, it is still 1.5 metres high in the hedge on the south side. The inner bank stands some 3 metres high and the ditch is still 1.5 metres deep in places. The only certain original entrance is in the centre of the west side. Excavations between 1961 and 1965 showed this to be strong and complex, with stone-built semicircular guardrooms on either side of an 18 metre long entrance passage, a massive gate 3.6 metres wide and a probable bridge carrying a sentry walk over the top.

The excavators were able to show a number of periods of occupation. Sometime in the fifth or sixth centuries BC the hill was in use, but it was not till the end of the fifth century that the double bank and ditch were constructed. The inner bank was of elaborate design, built in three tiers with drystone inner and outer faces like a wedding cake. The outer face was probably covered with turves and crowned with a wooden stockade and parapet wall. The inner ditch was 2.5 to 4.5 metres deep and nearly 6 metres wide. The outer bank was a dump of turf and limestone rubble with an irregular outer ditch 1.8 to 4.5 metres deep. Early in the fourth century BC the gateway seems to have been deliberately burnt and was disused for many years. The charred skull of a middle-aged man was found in the debris. Then in the second century BC it was refortified with dump-constructed banks and U-shaped ditches. A further period of disuse followed, with Romano-British occupation in the late first and late fourth centuries AD.

In 1772 the site was landscape-gardened; the banks were raised and drywalling built along the summit of the inner bank (often mistaken for iron age walling), and the ditch was deepened and beech trees (cut down in 1950) planted.

NORTHUMBERLAND
(Map on page 243)

1. Bellshiel Law, Rochester
Neolithic
NT: 813014

Take minor road through Redesdale army camp off A68(T). The site lies to the E of the road, its E end marked by a plantation.

This long cairn is 112 metres long and is orientated east to west. It is 18 metres wide at the east, 9 metres wide at the west and 1.2 metres high. 21 metres from the eastern end on the north side of the cairn is a large stone, perhaps once part of a burial chamber. Excavations showed that the mound had a carefully built kerb retaining a mound of boulders and smaller stones. At the east end the corners of the mound project slightly, suggesting a pair of horns, as found at the east end of some southern British long cairns.

Just within the mound at the eastern end was a grave which may have held the main burial. 90 metres south-east of the cairn is a group of round cairns.

2. Clinch Castle, Fawdon and Clinch
Iron Age
NU: 032147

Take minor road W off A697 through Branton to Forden. The site is S of the latter, with a plantation to its NE.

This contour fort is roughly oval in plan and encloses 0.3 hectare. On the south and west there are two banks, on the north-east three. There are two entrances, one facing south where the banks are tripled for a short length; the other is on the north-east. Both run diagonally through the defences.

3. Coupland henge, Ewart
Neolithic
NT: 940330

Immediately W of the A697, S of Milfield.

Although plough-damaged, this site has a diameter of 100 metres, with an outer bank and inner ditch, with entrances to the north and south. Like many henges, it lies on low ground close to water.

4. Dod Law, Doddington
Bronze Age and Iron Age
NU: 004317

On hill SE of Doddington, via footpath uphill from village, or by semi-metalled track from the golf club house to the Shepherd's House.

There were originally about six defensive sites on this stretch of sandstone moorland, and a series of bronze age rock carvings. **Dod Law West** is a tiny hillfort, with an annexe on the north-west. The outer rampart of the oval fort consists of an earthwork bank that had a timber revetment on the inner side, constructed about 500 BC. This was later revetted in stone and a palisade was set up on top of the bank. During the second century BC the inner rampart, built entirely of stone, was constructed and remained in use until about AD 100. The main enclosure has entrances on the south-east and north-west. The annexe, which remains undated, has possible entrances on the west and north-east. At least eight hut circles have been detected inside the fort, and others outside the annexe on the north-east. They are undated, and some may belong to the Roman period.

Middle Dod Law and **Dod Law East** (006317) lie a short distance to the east and are slight banked and ditched enclosures of about 0.6 hectares each. They may have been stock enclosures.

The moor contains some very fine rock carvings. The best are on the northern edge of Dod Law West annexe and are decorated with a number of motifs, including concentric rings, heart and rectilinear shapes, grooves and cups. There are more carvings near the annexe hut circles. On the eastern side of Dod Law East is a stone with cup marks.

5. Duddo stone circle

Bronze Age
NT: 931437

Take minor road W from Duddo and follow trackway leading N at 933426. This leads to within a short distance of the circle.

This circle, about 10 metres in diameter, and standing on an isolated knoll above the river Tweed, consists of five large blocks of weathered local sandstone. The stones are 1.5 to 2 metres high, and it is fairly certain that their number was once greater.

6. Five Barrows and Five Kings, Holystone

Bronze Age
(see below)

S of Holystone village, via footpath from village.

The Five Barrows (NT: 953020) consist of a cemetery of nine cairns, varying from 0.3 to 1.2 metres high and 3.6 to 18 metres across. Past excavations have produced both inhumations and cremations, together with food-vessels, urns, bone pins and flint tools.

The Five Kings (955015) on Dues Hill are an alignment of four standing stones 18 metres long. Their heights range from 1.5 to 2.5 metres. One stone is recumbent.

7. Fordwood Camp, Ford

Iron Age
NT: 972365

Take minor road from Milfield through Kimmerston and turn N at 961356. Turn E at Fordwood House. The fort is to the S of the house overlooking a ravine.

This oval hillfort, covering 1 hectare, is protected by a steep hillslope on the south, and elsewhere by one main bank with traces of additional defences at the north-east (two inner banks) and south-west (one outer bank). In places the main bank is 1.2 metres high and 5.5 metres across.

8. Goatstones Circle, Simonburn

Bronze Age
NY: 829748

Take minor road NW from Simonburn. The circle is S of the gated track, SW of Ravensheugh Crags.

This small circle consists of four equidistant stones 4.9 metres apart. One at the east has a flat top with thirteen cup markings. The stones appear to surround a flattened mound.

9. Great Hetha Camp, Hethpool

Iron Age
NT: 885274

Take minor road from Westnewton to Hethpool. S of the latter the road becomes a bridlepath. Hethpool stone circle (no. 11) is to the W of the path. The fort is on Great Hetha Hill to the SW of the circle.

Steep slopes protect this 0.5 hectare hillfort on all sides except the south-west. It is enclosed by two massive stone ramparts, the inner one probably once carrying a wall. At the north-east the outer rampart curves out to enclose a small oval site with a hut of much later date at its eastern end. A staggered entrance to the fort exists at the north-west where the inner bank is slightly inturned. The small enclosure contains an entrance at its north-east, but there is no entrance from this annexe to the main earthwork.

10. Harehaugh Camp, Holystone

Iron Age
NY: 969998

Immediately S of minor road from Swindon to Holystone.

A bank running north–south through the centre of this oval hillfort above Coquetdale suggests that the site began life as a single circuit of bank and ditch with an entrance at the north-west. It was later enlarged and strengthened by adding two further ramparts and ditches across the spur on the west, and two ramparts and ditches (with an inturned entrance at their centre) 90 metres further to the east, thus increasing the area of the fort to 1.3 hectares. Steep scarps provide the main defences to the north and south. An entrance at the south-west corner approached by a hollow-way is likely to be fairly recent.

11. Hethpool stone circle
Bronze Age
NT: 892278

See directions for Great Hetha Camp (no. 9).

The circle is a rather ragged setting of eight stones, up to 2 metres high, with a maximum diameter of 60 metres. Three other stones exist to the north-east of the circle, perhaps once part of it. The most southerly of these is ring-marked.

12. Lordenshaw hillfort, cairns and carved stones, Hesleyhurst
Bronze Age and Iron Age
NZ: 055993

Take minor road leading N off B6342 at 060977. At 053988 a footpath leads NE to the fort.

This small fort encloses 0.4 hectare with oval earthworks, including a main inner bank 1.5 metres high with two surrounding ditches, then an outer bank with a ditch and counterscarp bank. There are entrances at the east and west, each a narrow walled passageway through the defences. To the south-west are further outwork defences. A series of circular hut sites can be seen inside the fort, some built into the inner bank on the south-west.

275 metres south-west of the centre of the earthwork are two groups of cup-marked stones. The larger group is on a large rock west of the deer-park wall, the others 40 metres north-west. Another group exists on the rocks east of the fort.

On the north-eastern slope of the hill at 056993 is a group of six cairns, one 6.5 metres across and 0.3 metre high. It has a central cist 1 metre by 0.6 metres with its capstone alongside. Two cairns to the south-west show traces of retaining kerbs.

13. Old Bewick hillfort, Bewick
Bronze Age and Iron Age
NU: 075216

E of Old Bewick via bridlepath from village.

The hillfort is on the south side of a spur. On the south are precipitous slopes. To the north are massive banks. The fort consists of two pairs of banks and ditches arranged spectacle-fashion. They are surrounded by a small continuous semicircular bank and ditch; 60 metres to the north a small bank runs along the northern edge of the fort. The western inner enclosure has entrances at the north-west and south-east. The eastern enclosure has one at the south-east. The banks have been proved by excavation to consist of a clay core faced and covered with rubble from the ditches. The western enclosure has hut circles, the eastern one paddock walls.

A short distance south-east of the fort a group of three isolated rocks bears cup-and-ring marks. A good example is the one at 078216. A further rock from this site is in Alnwick Castle museum. 1 km north-east near Blawearie is a restored ring-cairn 12 metres in diameter, containing five exposed burial cists (at 082223).

14. Roughting Linn, Doddington
Bronze Age
NT: 984367

Immediately W of the Wooler to Bewick road. English Heritage signposted.

The Roughting Linn carved sandstone rock is the largest in northern England. Measuring some 18 metres by 12 metres, it is incised with a variety of cup-and-ring marks, concentric rings and grooved flower-like designs. The visibility of patterns will vary according to time of day and lighting conditions. When the rock

The profusely ornamented cup-and-ring rock at Roughting Linn, Doddington, Northumberland. (S. W. Feather)

is wet after rain is often the best. Although the rock is hidden from the road by bushes, it is easily accessible.

15. Roughting Linn hillfort, Doddington
Iron Age
NT: 984367

Immediately W of minor road connecting the A697 and B6525.
   The promontory fort here encloses a roughly rectangular area of 0.7 hectare. On the east are three banks, with part of a fourth at the south-east, and evidence of a fifth inner bank here. Outside the fourth bank is a ditch. At the north-east is an entrance. On its south side the fourth rampart is inturned to define a passageway.

16. Swinburn Castle standing stone, Chollerton
Bronze Age
NY: 937746

In the grounds, SW of the castle.
   This fine monolith is 3.6 metres high and deeply weather-grooved down the sides. Its faces bear some possible cup markings.

17. Tosson Burgh, Great Tosson
Iron Age
NU: 023005

A short distance W of Great Tosson village.
   This oval promontory fort commands the river Coquet. It encloses 0.4 hectare with steep hillslopes on the north and south-west. Around the northern part the defences are formed by scarping the natural slopes. Along the south and east there are a strong bank and ditch, the former 2.7 metres high in places. The entrance is on the south, approached by a hollow-way. Here the gaps through the earthworks are staggered.

18. Weetwood Manor, Chatton

Bronze Age
(see below)

On Weetwood Moor, W of the B6348, N of plantation running NE to SW.

The area contains a series of cup-and-ring marked stones and a single recon-structed cairn 6 metres across and 1 metre high at NU: 021281, also with a decorated stone.

At 022282 is a rock with six carvings, consisting of cups ringed by up to six concentric circles. At 023282 is a rockface 18 metres long covered with markings. A further rock at 010280 contains thirteen well-cut cup-and-ring decorations.

19. West Hill Camp, Kirknewton

Iron Age
NT: 909295

On hill, SW of Kirknewton village.

Two oval banks enclose an area of only 0.3 hectare with an entrance on the east. The banks are of earth and stones. There are traces of seven interior huts with diameters of 4.5 to 6 metres.

At the north-east a small D-shaped enclosure interrupts the outer bank. It has an entrance in its straight side at the north-east. It contains a small group of huts, each about 6 metres across.

20. Wooler hillfort

Iron Age
NT: 984277

SW of Wooler, via bridlepath at 985277.

This promontory fort, 1.8 hectares in extent, is divided by triple banks running east to west. The north-western half of the fort has a single stone bank along the south-west, and a broad outer bank at the north, with a slight scarped bank between them. An entrance exists here. On the southern side of this half is an inturned entrance leading through triple banks to the south-eastern part of the fort. Here are two banks and a ditch with a south-eastern entrance, and a series of interior dividing walls.

21. Yeavering Bell, Old Yeavering

Iron Age
NT: 928293

From B6351 to farm at Old Yeavering, from which follow track SW for about 800 metres, then strike E across stream and commence long, steep climb to summit.

This is the largest hillfort in Northumberland, enclosing some 5.2 hectares. It overlooks the Anglo-Saxon royal township of *Ad Gefrin* (see below). The remains of a great single stone wall 4 metres wide encloses the hilltop, with small annexes to east and west. Inside are traces of about 130 hut platforms. It has been suggested that the stone wall was slighted by the Romans. Limited excavations in the nineteenth century and in 1958 produced a little Roman material, but insufficient to justify any conclusions about the extent of occupation. The shallow ditch encircling the eastern summit was dug out in the nineteenth century and produced burnt wood, which might indicate a palisade trench. It is uncertain if the power of the hillfort was transferred to the Anglo-Saxon township below.

The site identified as *Ad Gefrin* (mentioned in Bede's *Ecclesiastical History*) lies north of the B6351 at 926305. A stone monument beside the road commemorates the palace site of King Edwin, to which the Christian missionary Paulinus came in AD 627. Excavation in 1953–7 revealed a complex history beginning with a late neolithic cremation cemetery, Celtic fields and a late iron age enclosure. During the last quarter of the sixth century the first major buildings of the royal township were constructed and lasted during the reigns of Aethelfrith, Edwin, Oswald and Oswy, before the site was abandoned around AD 670.

NOTTINGHAMSHIRE
(Map on page 238)

1. Oldox Camp, Oxton　　　　　　　　　　　　　**Iron Age**
SK: 635532

Via trackway leading N from Oxton to Robin Hood Hill.

This diminutive hillfort is protected by a triple bank and ditch on the east side and by a bank, ditch and counterscarp bank on the west, enclosing less than a hectare. It is in fine condition. There are entrances on the north-west and east, the latter reached by a sunken approach road.

Outside the north-west entrance is a large mound 27 metres across and 6 metres high, called Robin Hood's Pot. It is most probably a round barrow, and a Roman coin hoard and an Anglian burial have been dug up from the site.

OXFORDSHIRE
(Map on page 236)

1. Alfred's Castle, Ashbury　　　　　　　　　　**Iron Age**
SU: 277822

National Trust. Car park at Ashdown House (estate closed Fridays). Can be approached by bridleway round S side of Ashdown Park from the B4000. Site lies on NE edge of park.

Strong earthworks surround this hexagonal-shaped plateau fort of 1.2 hectares. It is univallate, with a rampart rising to 3 metres above the ditch bottom. There are three possible entrances, but only that on the north-west has been shown to be original. The north-eastern is untested. That to the south-east was probably made in Romano-British times and is likely to be associated with a substantial stone building that stood in the centre of the site. The building faced south-east, so this entrance would have led directly to it. Immediately outside this south-east entrance, what appears to be an outwork has been shown to be naturally high bedrock.

The rampart on the south-east was constructed of courses of large sarsen blocks, in rows some 1.5 metres wide, backed by a bank of compacted chalk on the inside. At the north-west the rampart also had front and rear sarsen faces, but the compacted chalk bank had been added later on the outside, and the inner face revetted with large posts, clearly indicating two building phases.

Excavation of the interior revealed the footings of a double stake-wall round house and a large number of slightly beehive-shaped storage pits (*i.e.* wider at base than top). Many contained carbonised seeds, pottery, metalwork, loom weights and bones – some human. An early iron age date is postulated for the fort. The large number of loom weights and spindle whorls found has led the excavators to suggest that the fort's economy could have been based on sheep husbandry and wool processing. Aerial photographs show a large ploughed-out elongated oval enclosure stretching some 320 metres north from Alfred's Castle, which seems to have been built in the early iron age, perhaps as a stock enclosure. It may be contemporary with the main earthwork. Traces of prehistoric field systems have also been traced north of the castle and into the adjoining woods (see also no. 12, Knighton Bushes).

At the end of the first century AD a substantial Roman villa was erected within the fort. More than a dozen infant burials have been found amongst the foundations.

No Anglo-Saxon finds have been made at the site and, in spite of its eighteenth-century name, there is no direct evidence to connect it to King Alfred.

Natural deposits of sarsen stone can be seen in the fields between the B4000 and the front of Ashdown House.

2. Blewburton Hill, Blewbury

Iron Age
SU: 547862

Approached off W end of bridle road between Blewbury and Aston Tirrold.

This oval hillfort enclosing 4 hectares was excavated by A. E. P. and F. J. Collins between 1947 and 1953, and again in 1967. The first settlement seems to have consisted of a few huts enclosed by a palisade, erected about 550 BC and enclosing an area about half the size of the later fort. In the fourth century BC the hill was surrounded by a bank held in place by posts on its inner and outer faces, made of material quarried from an external ditch. A gate on the west side was 11 metres wide and may have had an overhead footway. It was given added strength by the presence of a defensive ditch at the back of the entrance, later filled in.

For some time, the fort fell into decay, but around 100 BC it was refortified; the ditch was re-cut and the material thus obtained was dumped on top of the existing bank. The entrance was narrowed to 7.5 metres and faced with drystone walling. An unusual feature was the presence of horse burials within the entrance area. The end of the occupation of the fort is dated to around 50 BC. The excavators thought that this might have been brought about by Belgic expansion. 'The evident signs of violence, with corpses of animals strewn about the street and covered by the crashed-in ramparts with their retaining walls, plus abundant traces of charcoal perhaps from burnt gateway timbers, could fit such an explanation.'

During the Anglo-Saxon period a cemetery was dug inside the fort. There is nothing to see of this today.

3. Chastleton Camp, Chastleton

Iron Age
SP: 259283

Off the A436, beside the road signposted to Chastleton House. Gated footpath from road NW of camp.

This circular fort encloses 1.4 hectares. It is unusual in that its defences are faced with large blocks of stone and probably have a rubble core, and yet there is no sign of a ditch from which the material was quarried. Excavation showed that the wall was 6 metres wide at the base and still stands 3.6 metres high in places today. There was little sign of any permanent occupation although very early iron age pottery was found. There were two entrances, one at the east, the other north-west. The camp may have served as a cattle enclosure; modern cattle are rapidly destroying it.

4. Cherbury Camp, Kingston Bagpuize

Late Iron Age
SU: 374963

1.6 km N of Charney Bassett by cart-track, or S from A420 passing Lovell's Court Farm.

Oval in shape, this fort has three ramparts separated by ditches, and enclosing 3.6 hectares. Excavation in 1939 showed that the ditches were broad and fairly shallow, the inner rampart faced with drystone walling both inside and out, and the other ramparts of dump construction. Leading to the one original entrance on the east side was a metalled roadway with traffic ruts 1.5 metres apart. The gate had been on the outer side of the entrance passage, which had also been lined with drystone walling.

The most unusual thing about this site is its position on low ground. It has been shown that in prehistoric times it formed a narrow-necked peninsula surrounded by marshes on all sides except the north-east (where the entrance causeway ran), thus making it an ideally protected fortress. Late iron age pottery from the site is now in the Ashmolean Museum, Oxford.

5. Churn Farm, Blewbury

Bronze Age
SU: 515837

On the S side of Churn Hill, E of Churn Farm. Approached by metalled track SW from the A417 at Blewbury (527856).

East of Churn Farm are three barrows in a row, measuring respectively 27 metres, 38 metres and 24 metres in diameter and all 1 metre high. A cremation was found in one of the barrows in 1848. 800 metres south-east of the farm (520833) are two bell-barrows, each about 2.4 metres high; one is 27 metres in diameter, the other 23 metres in diameter. These have been dug into on a number of occasions. The larger produced a riveted bronze dagger and a cremation. The line of the Grim's Ditch passes 140 metres south of the barrows. It is not visible. Two other barrows worth looking for in this area are **Churn Knob** (522847) and **Fox Barrow** (506831).

6. Devil's Quoits, Stanton Harcourt

Neolithic
SP: 411048

On a promontory in the largest man-made lake in Oxfordshire.

This henge monument was partially destroyed to make way for a wartime airfield and by later gravel-digging. It has since been reconstructed and somewhat vandal-ised. It consisted of an elliptical ditch with an outer bank and entrances on the east and west. It measured 76 metres in diameter. Inside was a ring of at least twenty-four conglomerate stones and an irregular post-setting. The site was excavated before the interior was destroyed by gravel extraction. The original stones that survived have been re-erected, together with replicas of the remainder. The ditch, which contained hearths, bones and flints, has been preserved. The original site was used between 3000 and 1800 BC.

7. Dyke Hills, Dorchester-on-Thames

Iron Age and Roman
SU: 574937

A footpath leads from the S end of Dorchester, N of the river bridge.

Dyke Hills is the name given to the earthwork isolating a low-lying promontory fort situated between an angle of the Thames and the Thame. Some 46 hectares are enclosed by two large banks and ditches running east to west across the north end of the peninsula. The other sides are protected by the two rivers. There are a number of gaps in the ramparts, but all seem to be modern, and the position of an original entrance is unknown, but it may well have been on the east side, where it could be aligned with a road leaving the Roman town of Dorchester. Aerial photographs show that the enclosed area contains many pits, circles and rectangular enclosures of a settlement site. It is possible that the fort represented a local iron age town, which was later replaced by the small Roman township of Dorchester-on-Thames.

Nothing remains of **The Big Rings** and other neolithic ceremonial monuments, excavated at Dorchester between 1946 and 1950, which were all discovered by aerial photography and have now been totally destroyed by gravel-quarrying (573954).

8. Grim's Ditch, East and West Hendred to Blewbury

Iron Age
SU: 435850 to 542833

This earthwork lies N of the Ridgeway and can be reached by various field tracks N from the Ridgeway. It is best identified by using the Ordnance Survey map.

This earthwork may have been continuous, but it is now broken into a number of sections, largely as a result of agriculture. Its antiquity is demonstrated by the fact that a number of parish boundaries run along it. Its date is uncertain, but current opinion tends to place such earthworks in the iron age, often rather as boundaries than defensive works. The greatest height of the earthwork from the crest of the bank to the bottom of the ditch is about 2 metres.

9. Grim's Ditch, North Oxfordshire

Iron Age
(See below)

At least five lengths of Grim's Ditch occur in the triangle between Charlbury, Kiddington and Woodstock. These ditch sections all seem to have been constructed across stretches of open country, in between areas of woodland. They were possibly dug during the first century AD by Belgic iron age people moving west from Hertfordshire. They seem to have isolated an area between the rivers Evenlode on the west and Glyme on the east, with the dykes facing north. The best sections to view are at:

1. *Blenheim Great Park* (SP: 427183). Approach on foot through Ditchley Gate off B4437. 800 metres south the dyke crosses the drive. A gap in the dyke seems to have been used by the Romans as a crossing place for the Akeman Street.

2. *Glympton Farm* (SP: 423197). Approach along cart-track off A34. The dyke runs roughly parallel to the main road.

3. *Out Wood and Berrings Wood* (SP: 413208). Footpath through Berrings Wood from A34 (at 419209). Both butt-ends of this section of the dyke can be clearly seen.

4. *Home Farm* (SP: 402215). Visible beside minor road from Over Kiddington to Charlbury, through Ditchley Park.

5. *Model Farm* (SP: 383209). Approach from minor road (4 above) to Model Farm and follow path east beside dyke. The east butt-end of this section can be clearly seen.

Callow Hill (SP: 383209). Here two additional lines of ditch can be seen faintly crossing a low east-facing spur. Both cross the B4437. Presumably this ground was very open and considered particularly vulnerable. A small Romano-British settlement has been excavated north of the road and west of the ditches. Traces of a rectangular platform for a building can still be seen.

The dyke on excavation proved to have a bank which was 6 metres broad and about 1.8 metres high, with a V-shaped ditch of similar width and 2 metres deep in front of it.

10. Hoar Stone, Enstone   Neolithic
SP: 378236

In a small walled enclosure at the N end of Enstone plantation, at junction of B4022 with the Enstone to Ditchley road.

This is the ruined remnant of a chambered long barrow. Three rough stones, the largest 2.7 metres high, form a roofless U-shaped chamber, with an opening facing east. Three fallen stones lie in front of the chamber and must once have formed part of it. The mound of the long barrow, still standing 1 metre high in 1824, has now completely disappeared, and a reservoir has been constructed immediately behind the monument to the west.

11. Hoar Stone, Steeple Barton   Neolithic
SP: 458241

In a wood midway along the bridle road from Barton Abbey to the Rousham Gap to Wootton road.

A long barrow, 15 metres in length, with a pile of broken sandstones at its east end, is probably the remains of a chambered long barrow described in the nineteenth century.

12. Knighton Bushes, Compton Beauchamp
Iron Age and Romano-British
Centre at SU: 300830

Approached by minor road from Upper Lambourn, then cart-track.

On the hillside to the west of Knighton Bushes are the remains of about 800 hectares of 'Celtic fields', together with at least three Romano-British settlements and a cross-dyke. These cover a wide area, stretching almost as far north as the Ridgeway, and to Ashdown Park on the west. Little is to be seen of the settlements. One is sub-rectangular in shape and encloses about 0.4 hectare. It lies due west of Knighton Bushes Plantation at 298831. A second rectangular settlement lies between Woolstone Down and Uffington Down. It is on the north edge of the fields (302853) but is separated from them by a massive cross-ridge dyke. The third settlement is roughly polygonal in shape and encloses about 0.8 hectare. It lies east of the small wood at Compton Bottom (286843) and trial excavation produced Romano-British occupation material.

Ancient tracks through the Celtic fields lead from the settlements and join south of the Knighton Bushes Plantation site.

13. Lyneham Camp   Iron Age
SP: 299214

Beside the A361. Gate on to main road in trees just N of minor road junction.

A roughly circular camp enclosing 1.8 hectares. It is surrounded by a single well-marked bank and ditch, which have been destroyed by a quarry and the A361 road on the south-east. The bank still stands 1.8 metres high in places and is faced with drystone walling. The ditch, which can be clearly seen in the wood to the west, is U-shaped and has been proved by excavation to be 5.4 metres wide and 2.1 metres deep. There is a gap in the rampart facing north which may have been an original entrance. Like Chastleton Camp (no. 3), 10 km north-west, Lyneham may have been used as a cattle enclosure.

14. Lyneham long barrow   Neolithic
SP: 297211

On W side of A361, 400 metres S of Lyneham Camp.

A single upright stone 1.8 metres high and 1.5 metres broad stands at the north-east end of this long barrow and may once have formed part of a false entrance. The mound, which is now 47 metres long, has been considerably reduced by ploughing, as can be seen from the scatter of stones in the field around. The remains of two apparently unconnected burial chambers were found in excavation in 1894, and skulls and animal and human bones were found scattered throughout the mound. Two Saxon graves were also uncovered at that time. Numerous holes in the top suggest various other diggings. The site is overgrown with bushes, and traces of an old field wall run across the east end of the barrow.

15. Madmarston hillfort   Iron Age
SP: 386389

Bridle road NW of Tadmarton from Lower Lea Farm towards Farmington Farm.

This fort of 2.1 hectares is rectangular in shape and is surrounded by two banks with a ditch between them, and an additional bank and ditch on the south and west sides. All the earthworks have suffered badly from ploughing. An entrance lay in the centre of the south side. Excavation has shown that the site was first occupied in the middle of the iron age, when coarse hand-made pottery and metalwork was produced, and a cattle-raising economy was practised. A dozen sword-shaped iron currency bars were found in a pit cut into the back of the rampart. After a period of desertion the site was re-occupied late in Romano-British times (fourth century AD), when it was again a centre of agricultural activity.

There was also a Romano-British settlement, some 270 metres south-east of the fort, close to Swalcliffe Lea Farm.

16. Rollright Stones, Little Rollright   Neolithic and Bronze Age
SP: 296308

On ridge road W of A34(T), 800 metres N of Little Rollright church. Privately owned, but accessible at any reasonable time.

The Rollright Stones, together with the Whispering Knights chambered barrow 400 metres east, form the most celebrated group of prehistoric antiquities in north Oxfordshire.

The gnarled stones of the Rollright circle in Oxfordshire. According to legend they are the petrified remains of a king's army and cannot be counted. (J. Dyer)

The King's Men. This consists of a perfect circle of about seventy stones (originally nearer eighty), touching each other, and with a diameter of 33 metres. They stand on or in a broad, low bank, and there appears to be an entrance on the south-east marked by two external portal stones. Viewed from the centre, the northern portal stones are aligned on the major midsummer moonrise. No attempt has been made to shape the stones, which present a gnarled and weathered appearance, though they may originally have been graded in size and weight with the highest at the north-west. The site is unexcavated but was restored in 1882. It is likely to date from the late neolithic or early bronze age. There is a legend that the stones are countless.

The King Stone. Situated 76 metres east of the circle on the north (Warwickshire) side of the road. This standing stone is 2.4 metres high and 1.5 metres wide and is very weathered; the notch in the side is fairly modern. Carbon 14 assays have produced an average date of 1792 BC, which is considerably later than the stone circle and suggests that it was probably a marker stone connected with a small early bronze age cairn, now destroyed.

The Whispering Knights (299308). Although 400 metres east of the King's Men (a track leads to them from the road, beside a hedgerow), these stones are part of the Rollright tradition. They once formed the burial chamber of an early or middle neolithic portal dolmen. Four stones still stand upright, creating a chamber about 2 metres square, whilst a fifth stone, probably the coverstone, leans at an angle. The stones vary in height between 1.5 and 2.5 metres. In 1764 Stukeley claimed that the stones stood on a round barrow and excavation lends some support to the idea.

The Rollright Stones are the subject of much folklore. The most famous legend tells how a king was riding across Oxfordshire, with his knights and men, when he was challenged by a witch, who cried:

Seven long strides thou shalt take,
And if Long Compton thou can see,
King of England thou shalt be.

Whilst the king's knights whispered together about what they heard, and the men stood by in a circle, the king strode forward seven paces; but instead of seeing Long Compton in the valley below his view was blocked by rising ground. Then with a cackle the witch exclaimed:

As Long Compton thou canst not see,
King of England thou shalt not be,
Rise up stick, and stand still stone,
For King of England thou shalt be none.
Thou and thy men hoar stones shall be,
And I myself an elder tree.

17. Segsbury Camp or Letcombe Castle, Letcombe Regis Iron Age
SU: 385845

1.2 km W of A338 along Ridgeway. Road passes through centre of camp. Interior heavily ploughed until mid 1993.

This large D-shaped hillfort has an area of 10.5 hectares. It is defended by a single bank and ditch, with a counterscarp bank on the south side. Thomas Hearne, writing in 1725, recorded that 'within the Bank that lies on the Inside of this Camp . . . they dig vast red Stones, being a red Flint, some of which a Cart will hardly draw. They have dug up a great many Loads of them, and with many of them they build.' Excavations in 1996 and 1997 show that the history of the ramparts was quite complicated. In their simplest terms they can be provisionally divided into three phases:

1. Initially a wooden stockade backed by a chalk bank, and retained at the rear by a turf wall. The revetment was enlarged from time to time.
2. Rotten posts were replaced and realigned to create a box-rampart containing some crude drystone walling and a chalk revetment at the rear.
3. Finally a massive dump rampart was created, revetted by a sarsen wall at the rear.

Outside the rampart was a V-shaped ditch 8 metres wide and 4 metres deep with a narrow flat bottom. There were indications from the ditch filling that parts of the rampart might have been destroyed during the Romano-British period.

Inside the fort excavations in a limited area revealed the footing trenches of two round houses, one about 12 metres in diameter, and a concentration of about forty storage pits. Pottery indicated continuous occupation from the early iron age through to the late middle iron age.

The original entrance is on the east, flanked by out-turned rampart ends. Whether either of the two gaps where the modern track passes through the camp is ancient is uncertain. That at the south-west could possibly belong to the Romano-British period.

In 1871 excavations in the southern rampart by a Dr Phené revealed a small stone cist containing human bones, flint scrapers, perhaps the *umbo* of a shield and fragments of pottery. This sounds like a Saxon burial but might possibly be an iron age dedicatory deposit.

18. Sinodun Camp, Little Wittenham Iron Age
SU: 570924

The road from Sotwell to Little Wittenham climbs up the side of the Sinodun Hills, and a cart-track leads to Castle Hill.

This fort is magnificently sited on the eastern summit of this steep-sided hill, with wide views in all directions, especially along the Thames valley. Heart-shaped, it encloses about 4 hectares and consists of a deep quarry ditch, the material from which has been thrown downhill to make an outer rampart. There is little trace of an inner bank, although this may well have been buried by a build-up of plough soil behind it. The western entrance is a simple gap. Finds of iron age pottery have been made within the camp and outside the entrance. It overlooks the large promontory fort of Dyke Hills (46 hectares) which lies on the Dorchester side of the Thames, nearly 1.6 km to the north (no. 7).

The **Brightwell Barrow** is clearly visible to the east of Castle Hill. It produced iron age pottery.

19. Slatepits Copse, Wychwood
Neolithic
SP: 329165

In a clearing in Wychwood Forest, 400 metres E of the Leafield to Charlbury road.
This chambered long barrow is 30 metres long, 14 metres wide and 1.8
metres high. It lies east to west with a much-ruined burial chamber composed
of three upright stones at the east end. It is recorded that three skulls were
found in the chamber in the middle of the nineteenth century.

20. Uffington Castle
Iron Age
SU: 299864

*Approached by car along a one-way road, signposted 'White Horse', from the
B4507 near Dragon Hill. There is a car park 800 metres to the W. Parking for
disabled on crest of hill.*
A single bank and ditch surround about 3.2 hectares of land. They are broken
by an entrance facing west. At this point the bank curves outwards along either
side of the entrance causeway and seems to join up with a small outer
counterscarp bank. A second entrance on the eastern side was probably blocked
during the fourth century BC. The fort originally had a V-shaped ditch and
box-rampart with rows of posts at the front and back, and a sloping bank
behind it. Later a much deeper V-shaped ditch produced material for a dump-
rampart on top of the box-rampart. This was probably surmounted by a sarsen
parapet wall, which was later slighted and tumbled into the ditch. Excavations
in the interior have produced isolated postholes, none of which can be identified as
a specific feature. Numerous pits contained sherds of iron age pottery, loom
weights, scraps of bronze and iron and many animal bones in their lower fill, with
Romano-British material at the top.
Although the hillfort was constructed in the early iron age (eighth to seventh
centuries BC), it seems to have been most actively occupied during the Roman
period. Breaches in the middle of the rampart on the north side of the fort and east

*Uffington Castle, looking north-west. The White Horse is out of view in the shadow
to the right, whilst the Ridgeway crosses the front of the picture. (Cambridge
University Collection)*

of the angle in the southern rampart were made during the early fourth century AD. By that time it seems likely that the fort was re-occupied and possibly contained a shrine, whilst the surrounding hilltop may have acquired a ritual significance.

Between Uffington Castle and the White Horse are two oblong mounds. One, opened in 1857 by E. Martin Atkins, contained forty-six Romano-British skeletons, most of which lay east and west. The second mound, difficult to find, contained about eight burials, three of them decapitated, and associated with early Saxon objects.

The Ridgeway runs along the south side of Uffington Castle. In fine weather it is well worth walking the 2 km west to Wayland's Smithy (no. 22), but in winter it can be extremely muddy.

21. Uffington White Horse   Iron Age
SU: 302866

Best viewed from a distance of 3 or 4 km, to the N, from the Longcot to Fernham road for example (277909). The horse is approached by car along a signposted one-way road system off the B4507 near Dragon Hill. An 800 metre walk NE from the car park leads to the horse, with Uffington Castle on your right.

This curious 'bird-headed' horse, measuring 110 metres from tip of tail to ear, has been carved through the turf into the chalk bedrock. It had long been thought that this happened in the late iron age, shortly before the birth of Christ, as the design of the horse is very similar to that found on Celtic coins of the period. However, excavations in 1994 produced a surprise. By using a new method of dating called optically stimulated luminescence, three dates were obtained which show that the horse dates from between 1400 and 600 BC and is not of late iron age date. It is, perhaps, surprising that the horse has survived for so long. Every few years in the past it had to be cleaned, and many villagers took part in these scourings, which were celebrated with festivals which did not die out until the beginning of the twentieth century. Today English Heritage is responsible for the upkeep of the figure and discourages walking on it.

The scouring festivities, or 'pastimes' as they came to be called, lasted two days and, apart from the actual job of cleaning the horse, involved all the fun of the fair with booths and stalls, races and wrestling, and games and dances of all sorts, usually held inside Uffington Castle earthwork above the horse. Cheeses were raced down the steep hillside into the dry valley known as The Manger below.

The reason for cutting the horse is obscure. It may well represent an emblem or totem connected with the builders of Uffington Castle, one of a number of forts and settlements along this part of the Ridgeway that began to flourish in the late bronze age and early iron age. It is possible that instead of the design being influenced by horses depicted on Celtic coins or the Marlborough Bucket, as was once thought, it might instead have been the source which influenced them!

There are numerous legends connected with the White Horse. It was, for example, considered lucky to wish when standing on the eye of the horse! The flat-topped hill immediately below the horse is known as Dragon Hill. It was here that tradition says St George slew the dragon. The bare patch of chalk on the hill is where the dragon's blood spilled on the ground and poisoned the turf. No grass has grown there since.

The Blowing Stone is a block of natural sarsen stone which stands in the front garden of a cottage (originally the Blowingstone Inn) at the foot of Blowingstone Hill (324871) 2 km away. There is a hole in the stone some 46 cm long, and when it is blown in the correct way a loud siren-like note is produced which can be heard for 3 or 4 km on a suitable day. There is good reason for thinking that the stone originally stood on White Horse Hill and was removed to its present position about 1750. In spite of a tradition that King Alfred blew through the stone to summon his Saxon warriors, the stone appears to be quite natural and to have no real archaeological significance. Both the Blowing Stone and the White Horse are mentioned by Thomas Hughes in his book *Tom Brown's School Days* (1857). Hughes spent his childhood in the village of Uffington.

22. Wayland's Smithy, Ashbury   Neolithic
SU: 281854

1.2 km NE of the B4000 road, walking along the Ridgeway; alternatively 1.6 km walking W from the Uffington Castle car park.

Beautifully situated in a clump of beech trees, this long barrow has been proved by excavations in 1962–3 to be of two periods of construction. In Period I a rectangular wooden mortuary chamber had been constructed, with a sarsen stone floor. In this the bodies of some fourteen people had been laid. Whilst some of the bones were articulated, others were quite separate, suggesting that some of the bodies were stored elsewhere after death for varying lengths of time before being placed in the chamber. When the mortuary building was considered full, sarsen boulders were placed around it, and then chalk from two flanking ditches was piled on top to form an oval barrow, the whole being retained by a kerb of boulders. All this was covered over in Period II and is not visible today.

The Period II barrow consisted of a trapezoidal mound of chalk 54 metres long and tapering in width from 15 metres to 6 metres. The material for this mound had been quarried from ditches on either side (now filled up) which had been some 1.8 metres deep and 4.5 metres wide. The chalk was held in place by a continuous kerb of large sarsen stones, which ran over the silted-up ditch of Period I. At the south end of the new barrow stood six large sarsen slabs, averaging 3 metres high, and flanking the entrance to a stone burial chamber. This chamber is cruciform in plan and consists of a passage 6.6 metres long

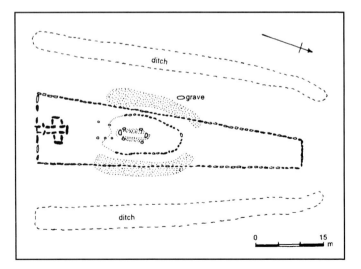

Wayland's Smithy, Oxfordshire. (After R. J. C. Atkinson)

with one stone chamber at either side. The passage was some 1.8 metres high, and the roof of each chamber 1.3 metres high. Gaps between the stones had been filled in with drystone walling. Earlier excavations in 1919 showed that the remains of at least eight people including a child had come from this barrow. Radiocarbon dates suggest that barrows I and II were constructed around 3700 BC and 3400 BC.

After the barrow was excavated it was reconstructed, not without criticism, by the former Ministry of Public Building and Works.

The legend of Wayland Smith has been told by a number of writers, including Sir Walter Scott in *Kenilworth* and Thomas Hughes in *Tom Brown's School Days*. Writing to her father in 1758, the daughter of William Stukeley, the antiquary, wrote:

'…the remains of a round temple of the Druids called Wayland Smith. Here the country people have a notion of an invisible smith living there; and if a traveller's horse happens to lose a shoe, leave him there, and a penny, and your horse shall be well shooed.'

The coins, it seems, had to be left on the roofstone of the right-hand burial chamber, known traditionally as the Cave. The site was referred to as 'Welandes smidde' in a charter dated AD 855.

SHROPSHIRE
(Map on page 240)

1. Bury Ditches, Lydbury North
Iron Age
SO: 327837

5 km S of Bishop's Castle, turn S off B4385 along minor road through Lower Down; stop at 334840 and reach fort by a climb through woods.

This small but strongly fortified hillfort encloses 3 hectares. The fort appears to be of two phases although not proved by excavation. In the first period the hill seems to have been surrounded by two banks with an intermediate ditch. Later the weaker north-west side was strengthened by two further banks and ditches, and yet a fifth at the north-east adjoining the entrance.

The entrances are very elaborate. The main bank of the larger one on the north-east is strongly inturned, suggesting the presence of guard-chambers, and the outer banks are staggered. The south banks of the south-east one are both inturned, whilst the north banks are out-turned, providing an 'inturn out-turn' entrance.

2. Caer Caradoc, Church Stretton
Iron Age
SO: 477953

Best approached by car from the E via Willstone, along minor road to 481950. Steep 400 metre walk uphill to height of 459 metres OD.

One of the most spectacularly sited hillforts in Britain, on a narrow craggy ridge commanding extensive views in all directions, and at its most dramatic in a thunderstorm! An artificial terraceway leads up the east face to the only entrance at the south-east end. This is inturned and quite wide with traces of a possible guard-chamber on the south side. The main bank, of stone, encloses 2.6 hectares and surrounds the ridge almost continuously whilst an outer line of defence, consisting of a bank of stone quarried from inside the fort, lies about 27 metres outside, wherever a weak slope requires it.

It is hard to imagine habitation in such a wild and desolate spot, yet there is every indication that it was permanently settled by the tribe known to history as the Cornovii.

3. Caer Caradoc, Clun

Iron Age
SO: 310758

Footpath off minor road between Five Turnings and Pentre, just E of Wax Hall at 303762.

Another finely sited hillfort with extensive views, especially over the valley of the river Redlake to the north. 2.3 hectares in area, the site is defended by two banks and an intermediate ditch. On the north side two extra ditches and a bank were added. Much of the material was scooped from quarry holes visible inside the camp. There are inturned entrances at the east and west. The latter has extra banks and ditches for protection.

4. Caynham Camp

Iron Age
SO: 545737

Via track leading E through farmyard from Poughnill.

A well-preserved earthwork consisting of 3.2 hectares enclosed by rectangular ramparts. On the east, west and south sides are a bank, ditch and counterscarp bank with an inturned entrance at the east. On the north, where the slope is steep, a flattened bank is visible. On the west a large bank crosses the camp interior from north to south, forming an annexe. A similar bank exists outside the defences on the west, again running north–south, both perhaps serving as extra vantage points.

Excavations by Peter Gelling identified four phases of occupation. At first the fort was surrounded by a bank of drystone and timber and a rock-cut ditch 3 metres deep. This was later replaced by dumped ramparts, which were twice rebuilt. Traces of buildings and many grain storage pits containing carbonised wheat were also located.

5. Hoarstone circle, Chirbury

Bronze Age
SO: 324999

W of minor road off A488 at 327995.

A stone circle half hidden in marshy undergrowth. It is 20 metres in diameter and consists of thirty-seven uprights with a single stone at the centre. Many stones are obscured and the tallest is only about 0.75 metre high. Two small mounds on the north-west of the circle may be barrows.

6. Mitchell's Fold, Chirbury

Bronze Age
SO: 304983

Via track leading N off minor road from the A488 at 302977.

This stone circle offers extensive views, particularly to the west. Originally more, there are now sixteen visible uprights with a diameter of 23 metres. A number of the stones are now mere stumps; but the highest stands 1.85 metres tall. 70 metres south-west is a cairn with a flat stone on its top known as the Altar Stone.

7. Nordy Bank, Clee

Iron Age
SO: 576847

S of minor road from Upper Heath to Cockshutford. Park car at 573849 and take footpath up hillside.

A small hillfort set on a steep-sided spur of Brown Clee Hill, enclosing 1.6 hectares. It is protected by a single bank and ditch and a probable counterscarp bank; traces of additional defences can be seen on the west side at the foot of the slope. The only probable original entrance is an inturned one on the north-west.

Numerous tracks leading to old quarries make the identification of earthworks difficult. There are further forts on the twin summits of Brown Clee Hill. **Abdon Burf** encloses 6 hectares within a stone bank at 540 metres OD. Clee Burf, at 488 metres, is much smaller.

8. Oldfield barrows, Bromfield

Bronze Age
SO: 495776

S and W of B4365 from Culmington to Ludlow.

A barrow cemetery consisting of five large round barrows, four of them in a line in the north-east corner of the racecourse and a fifth east of 'The Butts'. The latter, dug in 1884, contained a cremation with a bronze knife-blade. Of the linear group, the three northerly mounds contained cremations whilst the south one covered a primary cremation in a cist and a cremation in a collared urn just below the barrow surface.

9. Old Oswestry, Selattyn

Iron Age
SO: 296310

Immediately to the E of minor road from Oswestry to Weston Rhyn.

Called by Sir Cyril Fox 'the outstanding work of early iron age type on the Marches of Wales', this is is an impressive and well-preserved hillfort, and its complicated defences suggest a four-phase development. At first a group of unde- fended circular wooden huts was built. Next a double bank and ditch enclosed an area of almost 5.2 hectares. It had two entrances on the east and west, both with the inner banks inturned. Inside were circular stone huts. The defences were later rebuilt and a third bank added, except on the south-east where the steep slope made it unnecessary. A third stage of construction involved the redesign of the west entrance, where series of hollows separated by ridges were constructed and de- fended by outworks. Excavation has failed to prove the purpose of these hollows. The 90 metres long sunken entranceway was flanked by a bank. Finally two further banks and ditches were thrown around the whole site and the east entrance was also provided with a flanking bank. The hill was occupied intermittently from the sixth century BC until the Roman period.

The magnificent hillfort of Old Oswestry in the Welsh Marches. The west entrance with its unusual flanking hollows is in the background. (Cambridge University Collection)

10. The Roveries, Lydham

Iron Age
SO: 325925

Via private road off A489 at 325919; approached through woods from below.

A single bank surrounds the oval top of the hill, enclosing 2.4 hectares. The bank has an outer face of drywalling and no ditch. There is an inturned entrance on the north-east with stone-built guard-chambers and evidence for a bridge over the gate, and a second narrower entrance at the south-west.

400 metres from the north-east gate, on high ground, was a small promontory fort protecting about 0.4 hectare. This has now been destroyed by forestry clearance. This tiny fort was constructed at a point where the view from the main fort was blocked, and it would have prevented surprise attack on the latter from higher ground on the north-west.

11. Titterstone Clee Camp, Bitterley

Iron Age
SO: 592779

Via A4117 to 580758, where a track signposted 'Dhustone' should be followed to a disused quarry at 592776. A steep climb uphill leads to triangulation point shown on map.

This hillfort is remarkable for its size as it encloses 28 hectares. The defences consist of an earth and rubble bank without a ditch and in some places hard to find. It is broken by entrances at the north and south-east, near the east quarry. The latter is inturned and was originally timber-lined. A wooden gate hung at the inner end and may have had a bridge over it. Later the entrance was rebuilt in stone, and elaborate trapezoidal guard-chambers were added.

The fort has suffered badly at the hands of stone quarriers in the past. There is a radar installation inside the camp today, but this does not prevent visitors from seeing the site.

12. The Wrekin, Wellington Rural

Iron Age
SJ: 630083

Via a series of tracks off the minor road leading N and W from Little Wenlock.

A prominent hillfort on a hogsback ridge high above the surrounding Shrewsbury Plain, with the lower slopes wooded, the site was probably the tribal capital of the Cornovii before their resettlement at *Viroconium*. The defences consist of an Inner Camp area of 2.8 hectares with an Outer Camp mainly to the east and west enclosing a further 1.4 hectares. The Inner Camp is protected by a single bank and a slight counterscarp bank, with the hillsides below artificially steepened. The outworks on the east and west are less imposing than the inner ones. The north-east outwork is defended by double banks of dump construction and has an inturned entrance with guard recesses. It was later given a timber revetment.

In the most exposed area at the north-west corner of the Outer Camp, the footings of four-post buildings were found, each about 3 metres square, with internal hearths. At one point the huts had been renewed five times, leading the excavator, S. C. Stanford, to postulate that the site was occupied from at least 760 BC. The huts were finally destroyed by fire around 400 BC.

Almost immediately afterwards the Inner Camp was constructed with Cornovian guard rooms at the southern entrance. No huts have yet been found in this area. It seems likely that the hillfort was eventually abandoned following the burning of a corn-stack in the Outer Camp about AD 90.

At the south-west end of the earthworks is a low round mound, probably a bronze age round barrow.

SOMERSET
(Map on page 234)

1. Abbot's Way, Westhay
Neolithic
ST: 419425

On the Westhay to Burtle road, behind the Godwin Peat Works. Signposted.

A reconstruction of the neolithic trackway laid over a raised bog to form a dry route between the large sand island of Burtle and the rock island of Westhay, a distance of 3 km.

Details of the prehistoric trackways discovered in the district can be obtained at the Peat Moors Visitors Centre, situated at the Willows Garden Centre, Shapwick Road, Westhay (grid reference: 426415) (telephone: 01458 860697), where a number of archaeological exhibits and reconstructions related to the Somerset Levels have been assembled. It is open daily, April to October.

2. Alderman's Barrow, Exford
Bronze Age
SS: 837423

Just S of road going NW from Exford to Lucott Cross and Porlock Common.

A large heather-covered round barrow, 27.4 metres in diameter and 1.2 metres high, which has, probably since the thirteenth century, been used as one of the bounds of Exmoor Forest.

3. Ashen Hill barrows, Chewton Mendip
Bronze Age
ST: 539520

By footpath S of the B3135, W of the Miners' Arms restaurant.

A group of eight round barrows of considerable proportions. The second from the east was opened by the Reverend John Skinner early in the nineteenth century and yielded five amber beads, a small blue 'opaque glass bead' (possibly of faience), part of a bronze knife-dagger, and a pottery grape-cup (the last in Bristol City Museum). The group was known in Skinner's day as the Nine Barrows. The nearby hollows are the result of recent mining activities.

4. Bat's Castle, Dunster
Iron Age
SS: 988422

By road and very rough tracks from Carhampton to Aller Hill, or steep footpath from 980425. Best visited when the bracken is low.

On the crest of a hill overlooking Dunster deer park is a strongly defended oval hillfort enclosing 1.2 hectares. It is univallate, with a counterscarp bank that in places is higher than the main rampart. Tumbled stone rubble is visible in a number of places. There is a noticeable berm between the rampart and ditch, particularly on the south side. There are opposing entrances on the east and west, both slightly inturned. At the eastern entrance the high counterscarp bank turns outwards to form a broad barbican passageway some 40 metres long and 25 metres wide. It may have formed a pen for sheep or cattle. The ditch is unusual in being inside the bank at this point. 170 metres south-east of the fort is a massive cross-ridge dyke, with an unusual Z-shaped plan. It has been suggested that this and the fort's 'barbican' were added at the time of the Civil War siege of Dunster Castle, but they are both perfectly acceptable iron age features. There is a much lower cross-ridge dyke hidden in the bracken 100 metres to the north-west of the fort.

A footpath leads 1 km north-west from Bat's Castle to a small but strong univallate circular enclosure of 0.3 hectare on the slope of **Gallox Hill** – a name derived from a former gallows. It was probably a stock enclosure. There is a round barrow and probable hut circle near the entrance on the north-west side.

5. Beacon Hill barrows, Ashwick
Bronze Age
ST: 635462

Just S of the road over Beacon Hill N of Shepton Mallet.

A group of more than a dozen round barrows south of the ridgeway, starting in a grass field at the west, and extending through the wood to the east. The large circular enclosure about 180 metres in diameter is probably a tree-clump enclosure of the eighteenth century, but within it are three fine round barrows, one crowned by a boundary stone of perhaps the eighteenth century. The barrows in the fir plantation to the east are at present inaccessible. An urn probably from one of the barrows in this group is in Birmingham City Museum.

6. Brent Knoll Camp
Iron Age
ST: 341510

Approach from the A38(T) and by footpath from East Brent, past Lady Well. National Trust.

A notable univallate hillfort with external scarped terracing, enclosing about 1.6 hectares. The original entrance is probably in the middle of the east side. Roman pottery and coins have been found in the ploughed interior and provide evidence of a continuation or recurrence of occupation in that period. The site is a commanding position on an isolated hill surrounded by the Somerset Levels.

7. Cadbury Camp, Tickenham
Iron Age
ST: 454725

Approach from footpath leading S from road between Clevedon and Clapton-in-Gordano.

A bivallate hillfort enclosing just over 2.5 hectares. The ramparts are of the local Carboniferous limestone. On the north side is a well-preserved and elaborate entrance, with the north-east rampart turned outwards and the south-east rampart

There are a number of caves once occupied by early man in the Cheddar Gorge. The most famous, Gough's Cave, is open to the public. (J. E. Hancock)

The tumbled stone ramparts of Dolebury Camp near Churchill Gate, Somerset. (J. Dyer)

turned inwards. The site is in rough pasture. Trial excavation in 1922 produced evidence of iron age occupation with Roman continuation or recurrence. The few finds then made are in Taunton Museum. This site should not be confused with South Cadbury (no. 25) of 'Arthurian' fame.

8. Cheddar Caves (Gough's Cave) — Upper Palaeolithic and later
ST: 466539

By the B3135 through Cheddar. For opening times telephone: 01934 742343.

The outer portion of Gough's Cave was inhabited by man in late upper palaeolithic (Creswellian) times, 12,000–8000 BC. Recent excavations have shown evidence of extensive hunting and processing of horse and red deer. Disarticulated human bones from which the meat had been cut, and the bones broken for marrow extraction, might indicate cannibalism. More mundane evidence of occupation survives in the form of some seven thousand flint artefacts (mostly blades), a few objects of carved bone and antler including two perforated 'batons', one made from a human arm bone, and a lump of 'Baltic' amber, all now in the Cheddar Caves Museum, which also houses animal bones of the same and later periods, and a skeleton of 'Cheddar Man' dated by radiocarbon techniques very late in this period (about 7130 bc). Finds of later periods, from this and other caves at Cheddar, are shown in the same museum. Also in the Gorge are **Flint Jack's Cave** (463538), **Sun Hole** (467541) and **Soldier's Hole** (468539), all occupied during the late upper palaeolithic period between 12,000 and 9000 BC.

9. Cow Castle, Simonsbath — Iron Age
SS: 795374

Accessible from Simonsbath by a metalled byroad leading from Blue Gate (758377) via Wintershead Farm to the ford about 360 metres SE of the camp.

A fine and perfect univallate hillfort with well-preserved entrances at the north-east and south-east, on a little hill watered by the Barle and its tributary the White Water, and dominated by higher surrounding hills. There are added earthworks around the north-east entrance. An unusual feature is that in several places there is a ditch on the inner side of the rampart. The area enclosed is about 1.2 hectares. The site is very photogenic, especially from the north and east. The land usage is rough pasture.

10. Dolebury Camp, Churchill

Iron Age
ST: 4505

Approach by footpath 800 metres S of Churchill Gate crossroads, E of the A38.

This is the finest hillfort on Mendip. 9.1 hectares in extent, it is bivallate on all but the southern side, with ramparts of considerable proportions. The fortifications are of tumbled stone, and unexcavated. The main entrance is on the west and is inturned with additional outworks. The north-eastern gate is also likely to be original, though perhaps later in the fort's history. Two dykes run north–south across the hilltop, outside the fort to the east. The jingle 'If Dolebury digged were, of gold would be the share' was current in 1549 when it was recorded by John Leland.

In the seventeenth or eighteenth century the interior of Dolebury was used as an artificial rabbit warren. Eight pillow mounds (artificial warrens) were constructed, five still visible lying north–south, and three east–west. More than twenty vermin traps were constructed, some of which can be traced. In the north-eastern sector of the fort stood a warrener's house, surrounded by a circular garden wall. Most of these features are now very overgrown.

11. Dowsborough Castle, Holford

Iron Age
ST: 160392

Accessible by a footpath from the road between Nether Stowey and Crowcombe Park Gate on the Quantock Hills. Car park by Dead Woman's Ditch.

A small univallate hillfort enclosing about 3 hectares covered with scrub and trees. The original entrance is at the east, just south of where the trackway passes through. Within the enclosure at the western end is a circular mound, probably a bronze age round barrow. **Dead Woman's Ditch**, on the hill to the south (161381), may have been an outwork to Dowsborough. It consists of a rampart 1.7 metres high with a ditch on the west side. It is partly covered by forest.

12. Glastonbury and Meare lake villages

Iron Age
ST: 493407

Little remains of these two iron age lake villages excavated early in the twentieth century, except for a few humps and bumps in the flat fenland. The Glastonbury lake village site is owned by the Glastonbury Antiquarian Society and can be viewed at the above grid reference. The Meare village is on private land and can be seen from Meareway (a narrow public lane) between 44354225 and 44704210. Finds and descriptions can be found in the Taunton and Glastonbury museums. Two Glastonbury huts have been reconstructed at the Peat Moors Centre near Glastonbury and stand together with the original excavation hut used by Arthur Bulleid and Harold St George Gray at Meare (see Abbot's Way, no. 1).

13. Ham Hill, Stoke-sub-Hamdon

Iron Age and Roman
ST: 480168 (rough centre)

On hill immediately S of Stoke-sub-Hamdon. 2.4 km W of Montacute. Parking and picnic site near Prince of Wales public house.

A very large L-shaped hillfort of some 85 hectares, among the biggest in Britain. The ramparts are partly univallate and partly bivallate. The hilltop was intermittently used during the neolithic and bronze age, and the fort, which is unexcavated, seems to have been in occupation from at least the seventh century BC to the Roman period. It must have been an *oppidum* of the Durotriges. It has been badly mutilated by quarrying from the Roman period onwards for the celebrated honey-coloured Ham Hill limestone, which has been used for many purposes including Roman coffins and the main fabric of medieval and later churches. Many important iron age and Roman finds including chariot parts and currency bars are in Taunton Museum. This hillfort is almost unique in having an inn within it!

14. Hunters' Lodge Inn barrows

Bronze Age
ST: 559501 and 559498

Just N and S of the road between Priddy and the A39, nearly 1.6 km E of the inn.

North of the road is a finely formed bell-barrow with berm, ditch and outer bank, the overall diameter being about 40 metres and the mound about 1 metre high. The site is badly damaged by trial lead-mine shafts. It is normally in pasture.

South of the road is a circular earthwork with ditch and outer bank, 45 metres in overall diameter. This may be a 'henge' or, perhaps more likely, a disc-barrow with the central mound spread.

15. Joaney How and Robin How, Luccombe

Bronze Age
SS: 908426

Approachable by a walk of about 270 metres from the road going N to S over Dunkery Hill.

These are among the most conspicuous of a group of large circular cairns on the north-east spur of Dunkery Hill. Joaney How is about 24 metres in diameter and 1.5 metres high, and Robin How is about 22 metres in diameter and 3 metres high. The origin of their names is unknown; but a traditional connection with Robin Hood and Little John is possible. They are on National Trust property.

16. Maesbury Castle, Dinder and Croscombe

Iron Age
ST: 610472

Just N of road between Wells and Downhead via the crossroads S of Oakhill.

A fairly small bivallate hillfort, usually with water in its inner ditch. It encloses about 2.4 hectares. It is uncertain whether the present entrances at north-west and south-east are original.

17. Norton Fitzwarren hillfort

Bronze Age and Iron Age
ST: 196263

On N side of Norton Fitzwarren. A circular walk, with archaeology and natural history display panels, starts from the Blackdown View road car park, opposite the churchyard. Footpath signposted 'Norton Hillfort'.

The defences of this oval iron age hillfort are best preserved under the trees on the south-east. There is a probable entrance on the north-east. Three deep cuttings through the defences are probably post-medieval marl quarries. On the north-west side a bank runs under the hillfort defences, and excavations here in 1908 and 1971 showed that the bank lay on the outside of a ditch 2 to 3 metres deep, containing early to middle bronze age pottery. Ditch and outer bank were traced for 90 metres, and an entranceway was found. In the late bronze age, a palisade may have been sited along the ditch line, and the entrance defended by a timber gateway. A middle bronze age metalwork hoard of bracelets and axes (on display at Taunton Museum) was found outside the bank, and moulds for casting late bronze age swords were found in a gatepost pit. Pottery from the excavations suggested an unbroken sequence of occupation from the beginning of the bronze age through to the end of the iron age.

18. Ponter's Ball dyke, Glastonbury

Iron Age or Dark Age?
ST: 533377

Cut by the A361 between Glastonbury and Shepton Mallet.

A fine linear earthwork about 1.6 km long, with ditch on the east, considered by some to have been an outer defence for sites at Glastonbury some 3.2 km to the west. The site is on raised ground between two marshes.

19. Pool Farm stone cist, West Harptree
Bronze Age
ST: 537541

800 metres NW of the Castle of Comfort inn. Through gate N of the B3134, along footpath towards farm. The site is in the field to W before reaching the farm.

A remarkable stone cist, the south wall slab of which is decorated on its inner (north-facing) side with six foot-carvings and ten cup marks and a horned device. The original slab is now in Bristol City Museum but is replaced on the site by a copy in reinforced concrete. The cist was originally covered by a round barrow, removed in 1930.

20. Porlock stone circle
Bronze Age
SS: 845447

Just W of road between Porlock Common and Exford.

At present there are about ten standing stones and stumps, and eleven recumbent ones, arranged in a circle about 24 metres in diameter. The stones are quite small and difficult to see, as is usual with megalithic monuments on Exmoor.

21. Priddy circles, East Harptree
Bronze Age
ST: 540530 (rough centre)

The B3134 passes through them.

This site comprises four circles each about 180 metres in diameter with outer ditches. Excavation of the southernmost circle revealed a U-shaped ditch some 1.2 metres deep and 4 metres wide. The bank which was on the inner side of the ditch was composed of earth, turf and stones held in place by wooden posts and faced with drystone walling. The two southern circles have an entrance in their north-east sector. They are assumed to be ceremonial henge monuments. All except the southernmost circle have been damaged by lead-mining.

22. Priddy Nine Barrows
Bronze Age
ST: 538516 (rough centre)

By path W of the Miners' Arms restaurant, S from the B3135.

A group of seven conspicuous round barrows, with two more a little to the north, at about 304 metres altitude, on North Hill north-east of Priddy. They are under grass and average 45 metres in diameter and 3 metres high.

23. Robin Hood's Butts, Otterford
Bronze Age
North Group: ST: 230143
South Group: ST: 237128

W of the B3170 between Honiton and Taunton.

The North Group comprises five round barrows placed north–south, in a beech copse. They range between 18 and 27 metres in diameter and between 1.5 and 2 metres high. There are no known excavation records. The South Group is scattered and about four examples survive but one or two others are known to have been destroyed. One, opened in 1818 by 'a party of gentlemen from Chard', probably contained a primary cremation and was edged round with a retaining circle of stones.

24. Small Down, Evercreech
Bronze Age and Iron Age
ST: 666406

By a byroad from the A361 to S, via Chesterblade.

A univallate hillfort enclosing about 2 hectares. There is a counterscarp, and on the east side there is an extra rampart on both sides of the entrance. It is on the south-west extension of the oolite. Early iron age pottery has been found in its ditch.

Within the interior is a group of between ten and twelve rather ill-defined round barrows arranged in a line. They range from 3 to 4 metres in diameter and are up to 1 metre high. A bronze age urn from one of them is in Taunton Museum.

25. South Cadbury Castle
Neolithic to Saxon
ST: 628252

From the A303 by road from Chapel Cross to South Cadbury. Car park by church and then by steep lane to SW.

Excavations during 1966–70 revealed the sequence of occupations of this great multivallate hillfort of about 8 hectares. The earliest period of settlement is the neolithic, to which a bank and pottery and flints are attributed, and this occupation is provisionally dated before 3300 BC. There was late bronze age and unfortified iron age settlement on the hill between the eighth and sixth centuries BC.

The hill was more intensively occupied during the iron age between 500 and 200 BC, when the bold ramparts were added and rebuilt and combined with elaborate timberwork at least five times. Internal structures of this period include a smithy and possibly a temple, as well as many round and rectangular house foundations.

There is evidence of an attack and massacre at the time of the Roman conquest and Roman military equipment and foundations of a Roman military building have been found within the hillfort.

Much publicity has been given to the dark age or 'Arthurian' period of occupation around AD 470 when the innermost iron age rampart was refortified and a rectangular 'feasting hall' of timber was built, and in this were found sherds of eastern Mediterranean pottery.

Between about AD 1010 and 1020 the hill was the site of an emergency coin mint which had been moved from Bruton.

26. Stanton Drew
Iron Age
ST: 601634

From the B3130 by road S to Stanton Drew village. Closed on Sundays.

A group of megalithic monuments including three stone circles, two stone avenues, a cove (at 598631), and an originally standing (now recumbent) stone known as **Hautville's Quoit** (at 602638). The **Great Circle** is 113 metres in

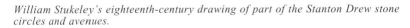

William Stukeley's eighteenth-century drawing of part of the Stanton Drew stone circles and avenues.

diameter and still has twenty-seven of a possibly original thirty stones. It is the second largest stone circle in western Europe (after Avebury). A stone avenue extends from it north-east towards the river Chew. The north-east circle is 30 metres in diameter and comprises eight stones, of which four are still standing. A stone avenue extends from it east towards the river Chew, meeting the avenue from the Great Circle. The south-west circle is 43 metres in diameter and has ten or eleven recumbent stones of a possibly original twelve. Hautville's Quoit and the centres of the Great and south-west circle are in a straight line.

The Cove, between the churchyard and the Druids' Arms inn, and well seen from the churchyard, comprises two upright stones of great size and a recumbent slab between them. It is in a straight line with the centres of the Great and north-east circles. The manner in which all these monuments are aligned strongly suggests that they were planned at the same time as a single entity.

A magnetic survey within the Great Circle in 1997 detected nine concentric rings of large post-holes, between 23 and 94 metres in diameter. Estimates suggest they contained at least four hundred posts, perhaps carved and painted like totem poles, or lintelled like Stonehenge. They almost certainly pre-date the stone settings. Outside the stone circle was a large ditch, 135 metres in diameter and about 7 metres wide. It was broken by an entrance gap, 40 metres wide, on the north-east. These features have yet to be tested by excavation.

The Great and north-east circles and their avenues are in a grass field and an entrance fee is payable at the adjoining farm. There is at present no admission on Sundays. The south-west circle is not accessible.

27. Stokeleigh Camp, Bristol

Iron Age
ST: 559733

A short distance W of Clifton Suspension Bridge, on hill just N of Nightingale valley.

A promontory fort, bivallate on the west, multivallate on the north-west, bounded by a cliff on the north-east. The area enclosed is about 2.4 hectares. There is an original entrance at the south-west. A small length of the rampart was excavated in 1898 for the Bristol Meeting of the British Association for the Advancement of Science and is still uncovered, revealing the stone-built core within the rampart. Excavations in 1966–7 produced evidence of occupation from c.200 BC to the Roman period. The site is in a beech wood and always accessible.

28. Stoney Littleton, Wellow

Neolithic
ST: 735572

By the A367 to Peasedown St John, then SE to Stoney Littleton Farm at 731567. A walk of 0.8 km along a field path from the farm to the barrow. A torch required. English Heritage; open at any reasonable time.

This is the most notable chambered long barrow in south-western England. It is about 30 metres in length, 15 metres broad at the south-east end, and 2.7 metres high. At the south-east end is a horned entrance and there is an ammonite cast on the western door-jamb. The entrance leads to a gallery with three pairs of side chambers and an end chamber. The gallery is 16 metres long but only about 1 metre high and adults have to stoop in the passage. The interior was partly explored by Reverend John Skinner in 1816 and two human crania which he found are in Bristol City Museum. Just inside the entrance is a tablet bearing the following inscription:

THIS TUMULUS - DECLARED BY COMPETENT JUDGES TO BE THE MOST PERFECT SPECIMEN OF CELTIC ANTIQUITY STILL EXISTING IN GREAT BRITAIN - HAVING BEEN MUCH INJURED BY THE LAPSE OF TIME - OR THE CARELESSNESS OF FORMER PROPRIE-TORS, WAS RESTORED IN 1858 BY MR T. R. JOLIFFE, THE LORD OF THE HUNDRED; THE DESIGN OF THE ORIGINAL STRUCTURE BEING PRESERVED, AS FAR AS POSSIBLE, WITH SCRUPULOUS EXACTNESS.

29. Sweet Track, Shapwick Heath

Neolithic
ST: 424408

The Sweet Track is the oldest wooden road in the world (about 4000 BC). It is buried and preserved in the National Nature Reserve, but a reconstruction has been built at the above grid reference. Access is only from the north end of the reserve along an abandoned drove, east of the Shapwick road. Entry is along the signposted path to the reconstruction. Access south of the reconstruction is not allowed without a written permit from the Nature Conservancy Council.

30. Trendle Ring, Bicknoller

Iron Age
ST: 118394

This site can be seen under suitable vegetation conditions from the lay-by on the A358 W of Bicknoller. It can be approached by walking from that road at either Bicknoller or Chilcombe.

A typical and well-preserved circular hillslope enclosure of just under 1 hectare on the south-west spur of Bicknoller Hill. An entrance is on the north-east side. There is an outwork some 400 metres up the hill to the north-east, not yet on the maps.

31. Wambarrows, Winsford Hill

Bronze Age
SS: 876343

On heath just N of the B3223 on National Trust property on Winsford Hill.

A group of three conspicuous round barrows near the National Trust pillar. There is a fourth and smaller example a short distance to the south-east. They have been dug into, but there is no record of their contents.

32. West Cranmore round barrows

Bronze Age
ST: 658427

By footpath from the A361 at 663433 W of the village.

The main group, in Old Down Field, comprises a superbly formed bell-barrow with bank outside the ditch, the overall diameter being about 48 metres and the height of the mound about 1.8 metres; another bell-barrow of similar dimensions to the west; and a bowl-barrow 18 metres in diameter and 1 metre high to the east. One of these barrows, opened in 1869, yielded a grooved bronze dagger, now in the collection of the Society of Antiquaries of London. In the field south of the old railway line are at least two other round barrows.

33. Withypool stone circle

Bronze Age
SS: 838343

Approach by footpath from the road between Withypool and Sandyway Cross (792332). On some OS maps the site is not quite correctly placed.

A well-preserved circle about 36 metres in diameter, at present comprising between thirty-seven and forty stones, none being more than 0.5 metre above ground. The site is difficult to find when the heather is at its height.

34. Wookey Hole caves

Palaeolithic to Roman
ST: 533478

Off the A371 W of Wells to N end of Wookey Hole village. For opening times telephone: 01749 672243. Entrance fee.

The outer portion of the show cave was occupied intermittently during the iron age and the Roman period, perhaps more particularly during the fourth century AD. Pottery and other finds from this occupation are in the Wookey Caves Museum.

The neighbouring **Hyena Den** (531480) and one or two other local caves were occupied alternately by hyenas and humans in middle and upper palaeolithic times, and the resulting finds of flint implements and animal bones (including mammoths, bison, woolly rhinoceros, cave lion, bear, elks and hyenas) are in Wells Museum and the university museums in Manchester and Oxford.

35. Worlebury Camp, Weston-super-Mare

Iron Age
ST: 315625

Approach by road from Weston or Worlebury. Car park in Weston Woods, east of the fort.

This is one of the most notable hillforts in Somerset. It is multivallate on the east, has a single rampart on the south and is defended by a natural scarp on the north and west. It encloses about 4 hectares. The buttressed drystone walls on the east, although collapsed, are amongst the most impressive of their kind in England and still stand 4.5 metres high in places. There is a main inturned entrance on the south, and others at the north-east and western end. The interior contains nearly a hundred storage pits, the pottery (including wares of Glastonbury types) and other finds from which are mostly in Woodspring Museum, Weston-super-Mare. The hillfort is believed to have been taken by assault, and the remains of at least eighteen human skeletons, more than half of which bore evidence of violent death, were found during the total excavation of the interior in 1851–2. It is uncertain whether this resulted from an attack by another iron age tribe or an early Roman attack.

It is accessible at all times, but visitors are warned of the rough scrambling necessitated by the ruined stone-built ramparts.

STAFFORDSHIRE
(Map on page 240)

1. Berry Ring, Bradley

Iron Age
SJ: 887212

Via path leading N from A518 at Billington.

An oval hillfort, partly tree-covered, with a rather flattened bank and ditch enclosing 2.8 hectares, with the suggestion of a second bank and ditch on the north side. A wide gap in the defences on the south side may have been the original entrance, widened in recent times.

2. Berth Hill, Maer

Iron Age
SJ: 788391

Immediately N of A51 800 metres N of Maer.

This irregularly shaped hillfort surrounds a steep-sided hill. It is at present obscured by trees and is 3.6 hectares in extent. A bank, ditch and counterscarp bank encircle the site and two complicated entrances lead in from the west and north-east, the former inturned and reached via a sunken trackway. An internal spring provides a water supply. Excavation has shown that the fort first had stone walls which were laced with timber, and later a dumped rampart. Aerial photographs show that it was connected by a trackway to a sub-rectangular fortified enclosure to the north at Maerfield Gate.

3. Bridestones, Rushton

Neolithic
SJ: 906622

In plantation on SW side of 'Bridestones', N of minor road from Dane in Shaw to Ryecroft Gate. Reached via gate in driveway alongside house.

This long cairn was once 90 metres long and 12 metres wide but the mound and two small lateral chambers were removed in the eighteenth century. The present remains consist of a parallel-sided burial chamber 5.6 metres long and divided into two sections by a now broken 'porthole' stone, a device more typical of Cotswold long barrows. To the east of the chamber is a semicircular forecourt, obscured by bushes, but it enclosed a cobbled area on which the remains of funeral pyres were found.

The Bridestones burial chamber, Staffordshire. (B. M. Marsden)

4. Bury Bank, Stone Rural
Iron Age
SJ: 883359

Immediately N of junction of A51 and A34 at Darlaston.

Sited to command the Trent, this small oval hillfort encloses 1.4 hectares. It is defended by a bank, ditch and counterscarp bank, but erosion has gradually rendered these features indistinct. A good inturned entrance is visible on the north-west.

5. Castle Ring, Cannock
Iron Age
SJ: 045128

Via a track running N from minor road at Cannock Wood.

A fine hillfort commanding views in all directions. It is a five-sided earthwork enclosing 3.4 hectares. On the north and west the defences consist of two banks and ditches and a counterscarp bank. On the rather more level south and south-east sides there are five banks and four ditches. The original entrance is on the east side where the innermost bank is inturned.

6. Devil's Ring and Finger, Mucklestone
Neolithic
SJ: 707379

In NE wall of Oakley Park 1.2 km SE of Norton in Hales via minor road leading W from B5415.

Two stones 1.8 metres by 1.2 metres now built into Oakley Park wall may have been part of a chambered tomb. One of them is D-shaped and contains a porthole 50 cm across.

7. Ilam Moor cairns
Neolithic and Bronze Age
(See below)

A collection of round cairns situated to the left and right of the minor road from Ilam to Stanshope. Driving N from Ilam, they can be seen in the following order.

Ilamtops Low (SK: 135526). Take the track to the right of the road at 134520, leading to old quarries. This imposing cairn is at the highest point of land on the left. It is 23 metres across and 2.1 metres high and is constructed of alternate layers of soil and stones. A rock-cut grave contained the remains of a bull resting on a layer of charcoal. Above this were adult bones, a child's skull, bell beaker fragments and a bronze awl.

Beechenhill cairns. Take track to Castern Hall on left of road at SK: 129529. Three cairns are on the right of this track. Two are together at 126528. The west one is 18 metres across and 1.5 metres high; no excavation record survives. The east one is 23 metres across and 2.1 metres high. Dug by Thomas Bateman (1845) and Samuel Carrington (1850), it was found to have been previously rifled. Further on to the east and closer to the road at 128529 is a cairn 12 metres across and 1.2 metres high. In 1852 Carrington found a crouched skeleton with a food-vessel on the south-east side.

Damgate. At SK: 124532 is a cairn best reached via the footpath to Castern which leads south-west off the road at 127537. The cairn lies to the right of the path 550 metres along. It is an oval mound 7.5 metres by 15 metres and 1.8 metres high. In 1845 Bateman found a crouched skeleton near the surface and a further skeleton in a rock-cut grave with a necked beaker.

Near Stanshope in two fields to the right of the road at 128537 are three low cairns each about 0.9 metre high. Carrington excavated them all in 1850 with little result.

Stanshope (Alstonefield parish). At Stanshope take the metalled track (Pasture Lane) to the right. At SK: 132542 on the left of the road is a large cairn, 30 metres across and 1.2 metres high, markedly dished in the centre as a result of past diggings. In 1849 Carrington found three rock-cut graves near the centre. Two held child skeletons with necked beakers and flints, a third an unaccompanied skeleton. On the east was a further rock-cut grave holding a crouched skeleton and a bronze round-heeled four-riveted dagger-blade. Two further skeletons and a cremation were also found in the mound.

Further down the slope at 135542, 300 metres east of the above, is a cairn 18 metres across and 2.1 metres high. Bateman (1846) and Carrington (1849) uncovered two skeletons in a cist, and three cremations, two in urns, one of them inverted.

8. Kinver   **Iron Age**
SO: 835832

6.4 km W of Stourbridge; 2.4 km W of A449, at N end of Kinver Edge. National Trust.

This promontory fort of 3.2 hectares has been cut off and fortified by the construction of a bank 3 to 4.5 metres high and a ditch facing south-west and south-east.

The other sides of the hill are protected by their natural slopes. It is uncertain where the entrance lies.

9. Long Low, Wetton   **Neolithic and Bronze Age**
SK: 122539

At end of metalled track (Stable Lane) running SE from Wetton. Visible to E of lane end and reached via stile in drystone wall on left.

A site unique in England, consisting of two round cairns connected by a bank (now surmounted by a field wall). The north mound, extensively cratered and damaged by past digging, is 23 metres across and still 2.4 metres high. This north cairn belongs to the 'Peak' series of chambered round cairns. Dug by Samuel Carrington in 1849, it contained a large megalithic burial chamber built of limestone slabs with a paved floor; thirteen skeletons and three leaf-arrowheads were deposited in this chamber, which had no exit passage. The south cairn is 15 metres across and 1.2 metres high and has suffered damage in the past. It covered traces of a cremation. Cremations were also found during the digging of the connecting bank, which was built of a double row of upright limestone slabs.

10. Musden Low, Waterhouses Bronze Age and Saxon
(See plan)

Eleven round cairns can be found between the villages of Calton and Blore, four of them grouped in a cemetery on Musden Low. The cemetery itself is centred on SK: 117501 and is reached via a cart-track leading north-east off the minor road from the A52 at Cottonmoor House to Calton. The cairns are well sited on the hill crest. They were all excavated by Samuel Carrington in 1849. From west to east they consist of (numbered according to the plan):

1. A cairn 21 metres across and 0.9 metre high. It contained a primary skeleton with a bronze round-heeled three-riveted dagger-blade and a flint scraper. There were five other skeletons, two with food-vessels, an urn cremation and two Anglian burials with a pair of seventh-century annular brooches.

2. A cairn 18 metres across and 1.5 metres high. It contained a cremation and a skeleton with two globular Anglian urns containing burnt bones.

3. A cairn 24 metres across and 1 metre high. It contained a skeleton and two cremations.

4. A cairn 17 metres across and 0.9 metre high. No discoveries were made in 1849.

Seven other cairns can be seen in the same general area:

5. At 113495 is a fine mound 24 metres across and 1.8 metres high. In a rock-grave was a crouched skeleton with a bronze round-heeled three-riveted dagger-blade. There was a further skeleton near the surface.

6. At 119494 is a tree-covered cairn called Dun Low, 23 metres across and 1.5 metres high. No discoveries have been made in the mound.

7. Hazelton Clump (125498) is a conspicuous landmark. It contains a cairn 17 metres across and 0.7 metres high. It contained a primary cremation in a rock-grave and three further cremations, one under an inverted food-vessel.

8. At 129491 is Top Low, an interesting oval mound 18 metres by 9 metres and now 0.9 metre high. No fewer than ten separate skeletons were found, one with a beaker, another with a bronze clasp, and three cremations, one with a collared urn.

9. East of the above is a cairn 12 metres across and 1 metre high (133491). On the south-west was an urn containing a miniature cup and a cremation. A secondary skeleton with an iron ring and fragments of kiln-baked pottery was also found.

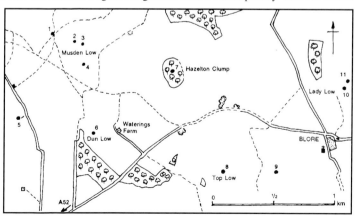

Musden Low cairns, Staffordshire. (After B. M. Marsden)

165

10. At 138497 is Lady Low, a mound 18 metres in diameter and 0.9 metre high. It contained a central cremation with a flint arrowhead and a bone pin.

11. A short distance to the north of 10 (139498) is a mound 17 metres across and 0.4 metre high. On the east side was a cremation with a small tanged bronze dagger.

11. Thor's Cave, Wetton
Iron Age
SK: 098549

Via track (at 101553) off minor road leading W from Wetton.

A spectacularly imposing cave with a huge main entrance in the hillside above the east bank of the river Manifold. A second entrance faces west and several small fissures branch off inside the cave. Although it was used sparsely in the upper palaeolithic period, the main domestic finds relate to the iron age and Roman period, showing that occupation lasted from about 200 BC till the third century AD.

SUFFOLK
(Map on page 238)

1. Brightwell Heath, Foxhall
Bronze Age
TM: 236442

With only one exception, all the barrows in this splendid cemetery have been destroyed in recent years by ploughing. The survivor can be seen beside the minor road across Foxhall Heath. Known as the Pole Hill barrow, it is 1.9 metres high and crowned with fir trees. The Devil's Ring, a large saucer-barrow which lay beyond the plantation, has been ploughed flat.

2. Burgh enclosure
Iron Age
TM: 224523

On the N side of the B1079 around St Botolph's church.

A large, roughly rectangular double-banked and ditched enclosure, with an area of 7 hectares. The earthwork has been much damaged by ploughing and the banks are now only about 0.5 metres high. They can best be seen on the north-east side, where they cross Drab's Lane. Excavations have shown that this was a rich late iron age site with close connections with *Camulodunum* (Colchester), and which continued in use as a Roman villa.

3. Clare Camp
Iron Age?
TL: 768458

A footpath from Bridewell Street, off the B1063 at N end of Clare.

A double-banked and ditched enclosure overlooking a tributary of the river Stour. It was formerly called Erbury, meaning 'earth fortification'. It is often claimed as of iron age date, but this remains unproven. It was used as a manorial compound in the fourteenth century. Internal features probably date to this period.

4. Martlesham Heath
Bronze Age
TM: 238468

In a small plot between houses on the N side of Portal Avenue, near the Suffolk Police Headquarters.

A large round barrow 30 metres in diameter and 2.4 metres high. Nothing is known of its contents. It is part of a once large, dispersed group of barrows on Martlesham, Brightwell and Foxhall heaths.

5. Seven Hills, Nacton and Bucklesham
Bronze Age
TM: 225413

Visible from the Ipswich to Felixstowe road (old A45).

Situated amongst trees on private land, this is the largest surviving group of bronze age barrows in Suffolk. There are fourteen altogether, some of which can be seen from the road.

SURREY
(Map on page 238)

1. Abinger mesolithic site
Mesolithic
TQ: 112458

1.6 km S of A25 and E of B2126 in the private grounds of Abinger Manor, W of the church. Visits by prior arrangement with Mr or Mrs R. S. Clarke. Telephone: 01306 730760. A minimum donation of £1 per head to a charity is expected.

This has been claimed to be the oldest humanly made and preserved dwelling in Britain. It was excavated by the late Dr L. S. B. Leakey, of Olduvai Gorge fame, in 1950. It consists of a pit 3 metres wide by 4.2 metres long and only about 0.9 metre deep, scooped into the natural greensand. A pile of stones with accompanying burnt bones could be a hearth area. There are two post holes at the west end, just outside the pit. They may have supported a primitive sloping roof of branches and skins. Along the east side of the pit there is a ledge, which it has been suggested was a sleeping bench.

Over seven thousand microlithic flint implements and flakes were found in the area, which would suggest that it was occupied for a considerable period. A natural spring rises at the foot of the nearby early Norman motte; this would have provided a ready water supply. The pit is preserved, the soil having been consolidated and the whole covered with a building which also contains a small museum of finds.

2. Anstiebury Camp, Capel
Iron Age
TQ: 153441

The camp is sited between two side roads, 5.6 km S of Dorking and 1.6 km NE of Leith Hill and W of A24.

This wooded hillfort is sited on a greensand promontory about 240 metres above sea level. It is roughly oval in plan and covers over 4.5 hectares, being one of the largest in Surrey. On the south side use is made of the very steep slope of the hill and there are no visible ramparts on that side. The north-east and north-west sides are, however, protected by triple banks with ditches between. The entrance was probably on the north-east side. Excavations suggest that the fort was occupied in the second to first centuries BC but never finished. It may have been attacked, as the inner rampart face had been destroyed and many slingstones were found. It was briefly re-occupied about the time of the Roman occupation in AD 43.

3. Crooksbury Common, Elstead
Bronze Age
SU: 893450

5.2 km SE of Farnham on Crooksbury Common N of B3001 in wooded area; 2 km NW of Elstead.

Three barrows are sited here; in line north to south they are surrounded by an oval ditch with traces of a bank. They cover an area of 76 metres by 37 metres. The barrows stand 1.8 metres to 2.7 metres high and vary from 9 metres to 18 metres in diameter and are randomly spaced within the ditch area. The bank is covered by a modern path on the west side of the group. The central barrow appears to have been excavated, but no reports exist. It is an unusual example of a triple barrow.

4. Frensham Common barrows
Bronze Age
SU: 854407

On Frensham Common W of A287. Footpath climbing up on to ridgeway 1.2 km S of Lane End passes through this group. In care of National Trust; always open.

A group of four badly eroded bowl-barrows. The largest, which has a pronounced ditch, is 23 metres in diameter and stands 2.1 metres high. These barrows are located at a point where they would have been conspicuous midway between Frensham Great and Little ponds. There is no record of finds from this group.

On the common, microlithic blades of the mesolithic period have been found and are in Haslemere Educational Museum.

5. Hascombe Hill

Iron Age
TQ: 004386

Located 6.4 km SE of Godalming and 1.2 km S of Hascombe village by footpath.

This tree-clad camp was noted by the antiquary Aubrey in 1668. Owing to the shape of the hill the fort tends to be square, and he therefore wrongly decided that it was of Roman origin. On three sides the single ditch is now used as a footpath which runs round the steep sides of the hill. The main ditch is on the north side, where a barbican-type entrance on the north-east has been made between two banks which go straight through the single rampart. It had front and rear timber gates. Here the ditch was 6.4 metres wide and 2.7 metres deep and the material thus obtained was used to provide an internal rampart 12 metres wide at its base. The camp was excavated in 1931 and 1975–7, the results suggesting an occupation date between 200 and 50 BC. The finds are in Guildford Museum.

6. Holmbury, Shere

Iron Age
TQ: 105430

The camp is sited 2.4 km SE of Holmbury St Mary and 3.2 km N of Ewhurst. Approach either by footpath from NW or by steep climb from SE of hill. The footpath passes across SW sector of camp.

The camp covers about 3.2 hectares and is sited at a fine commanding viewpoint 260 metres above sea level. Defences are slight on the steeply sloping south and east sides. On the west and north sides two banks and ditches can be seen. It was excavated in 1930, when the inner ditch was found to be 4 metres deep and over 9 metres across. No timber revetting was found in the construction. The original entrance was at the north-west. Occupation is dated between 200 and 50 BC. Finds include parts of beehive querns for corn-grinding and fragments of late iron age pottery. They are housed in Guildford Museum.

7. Horsell Common barrows

Bronze Age
TQ: 014598

There are two barrows here, one either side of minor road running S from junction of A320/B384. The W barrow is 400 metres from the road, and that on the E side is close to the road. Both lie N of the Basingstoke Canal.

The western bell-barrow is nearly 48 metres in diameter with a mound 30 metres across. It stands 1.5 metres high and has a separating berm of 6.4 metres; traces of an outer bank survive. The one east of the road also has a separating ditch and bank with a diameter of 40 metres. The berm is smaller, only 4.5 metres. Both show signs of having been excavated, but there are no available reports. They possibly date from 2000–1600 BC.

8. Reigate Heath barrows

Bronze Age
TQ: 238505

On E side of Reigate Heath, 1.2 km W of Reigate, S of A25. Four barrows stretch in line roughly N to S on the edge of a low ridge E of the windmill. They have been planted with fir trees.

This group of barrows was opened in 1809 when the trees were planted. A cinerary urn was found in one of them and a cremation pit in a second. A total of ten barrows has been noted on the heath but there are records of only four of them having been opened at that time.

9. St Ann's Hill, Chertsey

Iron Age?
TQ: 026676

Sited 1.6 km NW of Chertsey. Public footpath from St Ann's Hill S of B388 and of the hill gives access.

This hill stands in a commanding position on a bend of the river Bourne. On its south-west side a fragmentary ditch survives which is probably part of an iron age univallate fort. There are remains on the top of the hill of a medieval chapel associated with Chertsey Abbey.

10. St George's Hill, Walton-on-Thames

Iron Age
TQ: 085618

In a residential area 800 metres N of A245, off Camp End Road.

This badly damaged camp enclosed an area of 6 hectares, the ditches following the contour of the hill on its south side. Along the north-west and south-east, where the hillside is steeper, the defences are of clumped-bank and single-ditch type, but on the south-west, where the modern road goes through, there were double defences. It commands a good view of fords over the rivers Mole and Wey. On its north-east side there is an extra enclosure, possibly a cattle pound.

11. West End Common barrows, Lightwater

Bronze Age
SU: 931614

2.4 km NW of Bisley, W of A322. At roundabout N of West End, take minor road to Camberley. Barrows are on West End Common on S side of road.

These barrows have been excavated in the past, but there are no records of the results. They probably belong to the Wessex culture with a likely dating of about 2000 BC. They consist of four large bowl-barrows with two smaller ones between. They stand 1.6 metres high, the two largest being 30 metres in diameter with surrounding ditches.

SUSSEX: EAST
(Map on page 238)

1. The Caburn, Glynde

Iron Age
TQ: 444089

Footpath from the W of Glynde to Lewes over Mount Caburn passes just N of fort.

This small, circular hillfort of 1.4 hectares is magnificently placed to dominate the valley of the Ouse. It has a massive outer rampart and ditch, with a smaller inner set. These are broken at the north-east by an entrance with inturned ends. Excavations suggest that the hilltop was first protected by a light palisade about 500 BC. In the second century BC the fort was constructed, with a V-shaped ditch 1.5 metres deep and internal bank 1.5 metres high. Inside were about 150 grain storage pits, and numerous circular huts. The fortifications were strengthened at the time of the Roman invasion by constructing a hefty box-rampart and new ditch 2.5 metres deep and 9 metres wide. The gate at the north-east was remodelled and strengthened, but in vain. The fort was attacked, almost certainly by the II Augusta Legion, and the gate was burnt. As a result occupation came to an end. In the twelfth century AD an unauthorised castle was constructed on the hilltop.

2. Combe Hill, Jevington

Neolithic and Bronze Age
TQ: 574021

By footpath from Upper Willingdon at 585022.

This causewayed enclosure has two concentric rings of interrupted ditches. It is oval in shape and incomplete on the north owing to the steep scarp of the hill. The inner ditch, which is almost complete, encloses about 0.6 hectare. The site was excavated in 1949 when many pieces of local neolithic Ebbsfleet pottery were found. A radiocarbon date indicates that the site was occupied about 3200 BC.

To the west of the enclosure are bronze age barrows (576023), one of which produced four bronze flanged axes when excavated. There are also traces of bronze age fields on the slopes down towards Jevington.

3. Firle Beacon, West Firle

Neolithic
TQ: 486058

The South Downs Way passes amongst the barrows, from minor road at 468058.

There are about fifty barrows along the escarpment, including one capped by a triangulation pillar, once used as a beacon. The **Giant's Grave** long barrow measures 33 metres long, 20 metres broad and 2.5 metres high. A depression at the eastern end suggests a collapsed wooden burial chamber. The ditches are still visible at the sides and east end. The barrow is unexcavated.

4. High Rocks, Frant

Mesolithic, Neolithic and Iron Age
TQ: 559382 and 561383

2.4 km SW of Tunbridge Wells, S of A264 on by-road. The site is opposite the High Rocks Hotel; a small charge is made to view the rocks.

Excavations carried out in 1954–6 showed that this sandstone area was occupied from time to time in late mesolithic, neolithic and iron age times. The rocks were used as living shelters. An occupation layer with hearths was found 1.2 metres below the present level. More recently the iron age hillfort on top of the rocks has been examined. It covers 10 hectares and was constructed about 100 BC when the promontory was cut off by a dumped rampart and U-shaped ditch. At the time of the Roman invasion of AD 43 the rampart was increased in height, and a new bank and ditch were constructed inside it. At the same time an additional rampart was built to the north and east, with an elaborate entrance at the southern end. Steep cliffs protect the north-west side of the fort.

5. Hollingbury, Brighton

Iron Age
TQ: 322078

A choice of footpaths across the golf course: all equally dangerous!

This famous hillfort is roughly square in plan and encloses 3.6 hectares. It is defended by a single rampart and ditch with a counterscarp bank on the southern side. The rampart was constructed with two rows of posts 2 metres apart, running the length of the rampart, and tied together with cross-beams, forming a continuous box, which was filled with chalk rubble. The fort has given its name to this type of construction. The entrance on the west had inturned rampart ends, whilst that on the east was a simple straight-through example. Excavation showed the ditch to be flat-bottomed, 1.8 metres deep and 3 metres wide. Four mounds inside the fort are probably bowl-barrows.

6. Oxteddle Bottom, Glynde

Bronze Age
TQ: 444104 to 446093

A line of round barrows starting N of Mount Caburn and stretching over a distance of 1.2 km. The site can be visited at the same time as The Caburn hillfort (no. 1).

When dug in the mid nineteenth century, one of the barrows yielded an inhumation burial with two collared urns. Beads of shale, amber and a bronze finger ring were found together with faience beads and a faience annular pendant. The amber could have come from the east coast or Scotland. The shale beads could be from Kimmeridge (Dorset) or Whitby (Yorkshire) – examples of early trade, possibly dating from between 2000 and 1400 BC. The finds are in the British Museum.

7. Windover Hill, Arlington

Neolithic
TQ: 543033

Footpath from road between Wilmington and Litlington at 536037.

There are about nine flint mines on the escarpment, due south of the Long Man. They are unexcavated. There is a ditched bowl-barrow on the southern edge of the quarry. When it was opened in 1832 it was found to contain a cremation urn buried under a pile of flints. To the west of the quarry is a long barrow 55 metres in length and 15 metres wide. The chalk-cut figure of the Long Man of Wilmington probably dates from Saxon times. Most of these sites can be viewed at a distance with binoculars from Wilmington Priory, where there is an information board.

SUSSEX: WEST
(Map on page 238)

1. Bevis Thumb, Marden

Neolithic
SU: 787155

400 metres W of Fernbeds Farm, and beside road from Littlegreen.

This is a grass-covered neolithic long barrow, orientated east–west and standing today to a height of 1.8 metres at the east end. It is 64 metres long and 18 metres wide and the side ditches have been destroyed by the road and ploughing. Radiocarbon dates suggest that it was constructed around 3350 BC. It is also known as Baverse's or Solomon's Thumb.

2. Bow Hill, Stoughton

Bronze Age
SU: 820111

Sited on a downland ridgeway. Approach via trackway from S end of Stoughton village.

These barrows, known as the Devil's Humps, are well sited on an ancient trackway above Kingley Vale and comprise a small bronze age cemetery group. At the south-west of the area there are two bell-barrows close together with a small banked depression between them. To the north-east, and less obvious, is a pair of bowl-barrows. All four are in line and, despite having been dug into, still stand to a height of 3 to 4 metres. A cremation with a whetstone was found in one of the bowl-barrows. The group possibly has affinities with those of Wessex.

1.6 km south-east of this cemetery there is a twin bell-barrow, the only one in Sussex. There are traces of flint mines on the south-east spur of Bow Hill.

3. Chanctonbury Ring, Washington

Iron Age
TQ: 139120

Beside the South Downs Way from 119120.

Chanctonbury Ring is one of the best-known landmarks in Sussex. Beneath the beech trees lies a pear-shaped plateau fort of 1.4 hectares, dated to the end of the iron age. It is defended by a single bank and ditch, with entrances at its narrower south-west end and on the east. Only the latter is likely to be original. In the middle of the fort were two Romano-Celtic temples. One is 14 metres square, of the *cella* type, and was discovered during tree-planting in 1909. The footings, constructed of flint, and plastered on both faces, were uncovered. Its entrance appeared to face east towards the fort entrance. The second, smaller temple, also discovered in 1909, was polygonal in shape and excavated in 1991. The archaeologists found large quantities of pig bones, which led them to suggest that it may have formed the centre of a local pig cult.

The fort is unusually situated in the middle of a long narrow plateau. Its approaches are protected by cross-ridge dykes that lie some 200 metres to the east and west. The western dyke is much more pronounced than its eastern counterpart. There are three small round barrows outside the fort to the south-east. They were opened by Augustus Lane Fox (Pitt-Rivers) about 1869, who found nothing to date them.

4. Chichester Dykes

Iron Age
Various

In the century immediately preceding the Roman invasion the Atrebates of Gaul settled in southern England and established a capital somewhere between Chichester and Selsey. Although its site has yet to be discovered, its protective outer dykes can still be seen. Some still standing 3 metres high guard an enormous area between Bosham and Bognor, and stretching 3 km north of Chichester. Streams guard the east and west sides, and lines of dyke totalling 27 km run between. Amongst the better examples are the stretches at SU: 837080, 847080 and between 890085 and 913085.

5. Church Hill, Findon

Neolithic
TQ: 114083

Footpath from minor road off A24, south of Findon Place.

This site has been badly damaged by ploughing. It consists of about thirty-six flint mines. Excavation has revealed shafts 3 to 6 metres deep cutting through up to six seams of flint. The chalk is very soft here, and, instead of radiating galleries, the bottoms of the shafts bulge out into bell-shaped pits to uncover as much floor space as possible. Although few in number, the mines seem to have been in use a very long time. A radiocarbon date of 4250 BC has been obtained from an antler pick, whilst a cremation burial, accompanied by a beaker with 'barbed-wire' decoration and two flint axes, can be dated to around 2100 BC. This does not, of course, mean continuous mining, but rather a brief return perhaps in every generation.

The contour hillfort of Cissbury Ring in Sussex. The neolithic flint mines are clearly visible inside the rampart nearest the camera. (Cambridge University Collection)

6. Cissbury Ring, Worthing
Neolithic and Iron Age
TQ: 139080

1.6 km W of Findon village along second class road off A24. Leave car at end of track in parking area and climb to top of hill. National Trust; always open.

The hillfort is an elongated oval in plan and encloses 24 hectares. It is an imposing work with a commanding viewpoint and it has been calculated that 60,000 tonnes of chalk would have been moved in its construction. The original entrances are on the south and east; that at the north is modern. Sectioning of the bank showed four phases of occupation. The original bank was 9 metres wide and timber-revetted. A 3 metre berm separated it from the ditch, which was 7.5 metres wide and flat-bottomed. Late in the iron age it was under cultivation, and plough soil built up. There are traces of field lynchets in the south and east corner.

The flint mines are at the south-west end of the fort area. The large cluster of depressions in the soil, over a hundred in number, represent the only visible remains of neolithic quarrying for fresh and more easily workable flint. There is also a line of shafts outside and under the south entrance to the hillfort. Excavation has shown that the pits were about 12 metres deep and, like those at Harrow Hill (no. 9), had radiating galleries. Red deer antlers were used as picks and rakes, and shoulder blades of oxen, pigs and deer as shovels. A miner's lamp carved from a lump of chalk was found; it was much blackened and would have used a wick to burn fat. In 1867 and 1868 Colonel Lane Fox (later Pitt-Rivers) dug into some thirty pits and considered them to be broadly contemporary with the hillfort. It was not until he resumed work in 1875 and dug under the ramparts of the fort that he established the relative age of the flint mines and the hillfort and assigned the mines to the neolithic period. In 1875 he found six shafts with galleries and also a neolithic female skeleton who seems to have fallen head-first into the pit. Pottery was early neolithic, round-bottomed shouldered bowls. A carbon-14 date for three antler picks gives an average date of 3500 BC. A second burial was found of a young man about twenty-five years old and 1.5 metres tall, surrounded by a ring of chalk blocks.

Finds are in the British Museum, Lewes and Worthing museums.

7. Devil's Dyke, Poynings
Iron Age
TQ: 258111

On N side of the South Downs, 1.6 km SW of Poynings village. The road runs right into the hillfort area, now partly occupied by modern buildings.

In the construction of this fort use has been made of the steep natural features, particularly on the east side. Around the crest is a weak bank and ditch. There is a large rampart across the neck of the 16 hectare promontory of land on which it stands. Excavation suggests a period of use from 500 to 250 BC. Farming by late iron age people took place outside the fort area. Traces of a hut were found inside the enclosure.

8. Devil's Jumps, Treyford
Bronze Age
SU: 825173

On the top of Treyford Hill, 1.2 km SE of Treyford. Leave A286 at Cocking in westerly direction via Bepton. The site may be approached up track at S end of either Treyford or Didling villages.

In a line, roughly north-west to south-east, are five large bell-barrows which have been described as the finest barrow cemetery in Sussex. They vary from 26 to 34 metres in diameter and are up to 4.8 metres in height. They have been dug into, when cremations were found. There is a trace of a sixth barrow.

9. Harrow Hill, Angmering
Neolithic and Iron Age
TQ: 082100

Nearest approach from A283. From E end of Storrington minor road S climbs to top

The Devil's Humps bell-barrows on Bow Hill, West Sussex. (Cambridge University Collection)

Aerial photograph of the Harrow Hill flint mines and later iron age enclosure. (Owen Bedwin)

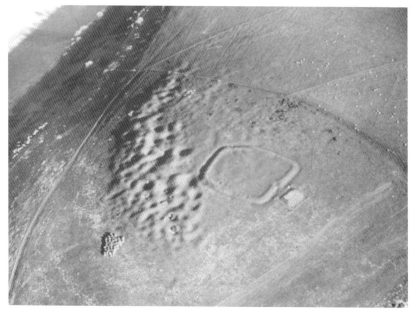

of Chantry Hill. From there about 2.4 km S.

About a hundred flint mines are visible as depressions in the downland. One was excavated in 1924–5 and three others in 1936. The first pit was 7 metres deep and 6 metres in diameter. At the bottom six galleries radiated outwards. A higher seam of flint has been worked on the way down. A series of criss-cross lines and scratches was found on detached chalk blocks and on the walls of the pit. In some galleries soot marks from miners' lamps were seen. Deer-antler wedges and picks were found together with shoulder blades used as primitive shovels. Flint axes and flakes were found but there was no evidence that any polishing of the axes was done on the site. Radiocarbon tests suggest a date around 3600 BC.

Here also on the south side of the mines is a small square earthwork covering about 1.2 hectares. In places it covers the mineshafts. It was excavated in 1936 when pottery sherds found indicated an iron age dating. Post holes for the surrounding timber palisades were found, also the gatepost sockets. Examination of a portion of the interior produced more than a hundred ox skulls, suggesting that it was used for the slaughter of cattle. The finds are in Worthing Museum.

10. Harting Beacon
Iron Age
SU: 806184

By track off road E of Turkey Island, either that signposted 'Crossdykes', or footpath few yards E of bus stop, leading through wood to W side of hill.

This magnificent hill is crowned by a large, but rather weak rectangular hillfort, defended by a single rampart and ditch. Excavations at the west gate produced two gold penannular rings, perhaps buried as a foundation deposit. The site was protected by a simple flat-bottomed ditch and timber-faced rampart. Four-post and six-post structures have been found in the south-east corner of the fort, together with grain storage pits. There are cross-dykes on the hill ridge to the east and west. A barrow, apparently overlying the latter (797186), may indicate that they are considerably earlier than the fort. There is a small bowl-barrow inside the camp, about 7.5 metres in diameter and 0.6 metre high.

11. Highdown Hill, Ferring
Iron Age
TQ: 093043

On Highdown Hill 5.6 km NW of Worthing. Approach by paths N of Ferring on A2032 or S from Clapham. In the care of the National Trust; always open.

This small univallate hillfort was excavated in 1939 when two sections were cut through the banks. The defences consisted of a steep-sided ditch 1.8 metres deep separated by a 1.8 metre berm from the bank. This latter was secured by two rows of timber posts.

Beneath the bank late bronze age pottery, spindle whorls and loom weights were found. These were associated with hearths and post holes in an earthen floor. It could have been a downland farm site. In the interior of the fort post holes of rectangular iron age and Romano-British huts were found. The fort was also re-occupied in the late third to fourth centuries. In 1901 an area of the interior revealed a Saxon cemetery; among the finds was a penannular gold ring of triangular section. The finds are in Worthing Museum.

12. Long Down, Eartham
Neolithic
SU: 932093

East of A285 on footpath across Long Down to Eartham.

About twenty flint mines were dug on the west side of the Down. Excavation has shown one large flint-working area. Radiocarbon dates around 3700 BC have been obtained. Environmental work suggests that the mines were surrounded by woodland at the time they were abandoned.

13. The Trundle, Singleton
Neolithic and Iron Age
SU: 877111

Turn E off A286 at Singleton. After about 1 km turn right just before Charlton. After 1.6 km stop where road forks and climb on top of St Roches Hill, 206 metres above sea level.

Causewayed enclosure. The interrupted ditches form two roughly concentric rings. The outer one tends to spiral partly on the summit and down the north-west slopes of the hill. The remains of a third series of interrupted ditches can be seen emerging from beneath the iron age hillfort ditch on the north side. A recent aerial survey suggests that the position could be even more complicated. A section of the bank behind a ditch section was excavated and found to consist of rubble, chalk and mud on a stripped land surface. The inner ditch was 1.5 metres deep and the outer one 2.7 metres. Finds included neolithic pottery and a bone phallus showing saw marks (these were more usually made of chalk in the neolithic period). Flint flakes, flint saws, bone awls and grain rubbers were found. The skeleton of a young woman was found in the outer ditch surrounded by chalk blocks. Radiocarbon dates suggest occupation between 4300 and 3600 BC.

Hillfort. This iron age feature was superimposed on top and follows the contour line of the hill. It is very approximately octagonal in shape and has two inturned entrances at the north-east and south-west. The north-east gate was found to have three phases of construction. The surrounding ditch has a stout bank on the inside with a lower counterscarp bank without. It was probably occupied from 500 BC, with additional defences around 320 BC. It was abandoned about 100 BC when the Atrebates reached Sussex. It is suggested that the inhabitants moved south to found Chichester. The finds are in Lewes Museum. A chapel dedicated to St Roche stood on the hilltop from the fifteenth century to the eighteenth. Whilst in the area one should visit the Weald and Downland Open Air Museum at Singleton.

WARWICKSHIRE
(Map on page 240)

1. Beausale Fort
Iron Age
SP: 246702

Immediately E of minor road from Beausale to A41.

The bank and ditch enclose an oval area of 2.2 hectares. The interior has been ploughed out and the defences reduced in height. No entrance is now identifiable.

2. Berry Mound, Solihull
Iron Age
SP: 095778

Via minor road E of A435, leading to Major's Green. 1.6 km SW of Shirley railway station.

A partly wooded hillfort with a single bank and ditch enclosing an oval area 4.4 hectares in extent. There were originally three banks and ditches on the south side. The east side of the earthworks has suffered plough damage; the original entrance possibly existed here.

3. Burrow Hill Camp, Corley
Iron Age
SP: 304850

On Burrow Hill, immediately E of Corley.

A still formidable bank and ditch surround a square-shaped area of 2.8 hectares. Ploughing has damaged the west side including an original entrance. Excavations on the bank have shown that it was timber-laced and revetted on the outside with a well-built drywall. The site has been dated between 50 BC and AD 50.

4. Meon Hill, Quinton

Iron Age
SP: 177454

Via track leading W off minor road from Lower Quinton to Mickleton.

The remains of a double bank and ditch and a counterscarp bank surround the contours of a hill 180 metres high, enclosing 9.6 hectares, although the steep slope on the west is protected by a single bank. Plough damage has obliterated the inner bank and ditch on the north, where a probably original drystone wall can be seen in the central bank. No entrances are now traceable. A hoard of 394 currency bars was found inside the earthworks in 1824.

5. Nadbury Camp, Ratley and Upton

Iron Age
SJ: 390482

Crossed by B4086 on N from Knowle End to Warmington.

Although large, the defences of this hillfort are badly denuded. A bank, ditch and counterscarp bank surround an oval area of 7 hectares on top of the steeply sloping hill. The main road runs along the north side, obscuring the sunken trackway approaching the entrance to the west. Minor excavations on the northern defences revealed a glacis rampart, with no evidence for a defensive ditch. The rampart was probably constructed around the sixth to fifth centuries BC. Pits were found which pre- and post-date this construction. There seems to have been considerable occupation inside the camp. A large annexe on the south-east has been destroyed by ploughing.

6. Oldbury Camp

Iron Age
SJ: 314947

Immediately N of Oldbury village.

A still considerable bank and ditch enclose a rectangular area 2.4 hectares in extent. The original entrance has not been identified.

WILTSHIRE
(Map on page 236)

1. Adam's Grave, Alton Priors

Neolithic
SU: 112634

On top of Walker's Hill, W of road N from Alton Barnes and Alton Priors. Nature Conservancy Council land: numerous footpaths.

This long barrow is about 60 metres long and 6 metres high. On either side are ditches still 6 metres wide and 0.9 metre deep. Traces of a sarsen stone burial chamber are visible at the south-east end. When this was opened by John Thurnam in 1860 it was found to contain parts of three or four skeletons and a leaf-shaped arrowhead. There seems originally to have been a retaining wall of sarsens and drystone around the barrow. There is an old quarry immediately north-east of the barrow. In AD 592 the barrow was known as *Wodnesbeorg* when Coel and Caewlin fought beside it.

2. Aldbourne Four Barrows (Sugar Hill)

Bronze Age
SU: 249773

2.4 km along track which runs N and NW from beside Aldbourne church.

These four barrows crown a hillspur north-east of the B4192. They consist of a bowl-barrow and three bell-barrows. The bowl-barrow at the southern end of the group is about 1.5 metres high and 18 metres in diameter. It contained a cremated adult burial covered by four sarsen stones and the bones of a young pig.

A few metres north is the first and largest of the bell-barrows, measuring 40 metres across, with a mound 3 metres high. Like all the barrows in the group, it was excavated in the 1870s by William Greenwell. In it he found a cremated adult and a bone pin with a perforated square head. There were pieces of beaker pottery in the covering mound. The second bell-barrow has a marked depression on its summit, the remains of Greenwell's shaft. It contained a skeleton with a grooved dagger and a tanged flint arrowhead. A second skeleton lay above this in the same grave. The most northerly bell-barrow contained an adult cremation with a small plain pottery vessel (an incense cup?), amber beads, a bone pin and a flint flake. Two secondary cremations and part of a beaker were found in the covering mound.

At the foot of the hill, beside the B4192, are two bowl-barrows. One has been almost levelled by ploughing. The other (247770), although ploughed, is still about 18 metres in diameter and 1.5 metres high. In its centre Greenwell found a cremation lying on a plank of wood. Beside it was a fine incense cup – the Aldbourne Cup (which gives its name to a series of similar vessels), parts of a bronze dagger, two bronze awls, beads of amber, faience, shale and encrinite, shale pendants and a V-bored button. To the north of this burial was a second cremation with an Aldbourne cup and a flint arrowhead.

Behind the wood on the hill 800 metres to the south lies another group of barrows, of which that on the southern end, **The Giant's Grave**, is the best known (245764). This is a bell-barrow about 36 metres in diameter with a mound 1.8 metres high. The central oval grave contained an adult cremation with bone pins. The bank surrounding the barrow may be original but is possibly the remains of a tree-clump enclosure.

3. Amesbury Down   Bronze Age
SU: 148394

Follow track SW from A345 at 157396. Barrows lie 400 metres W of spinneys.

This is the only known triple bell-barrow with an outer bank in Wiltshire. The mounds are all low, only 0.6 to 0.9 metre high, whilst the overall length from west to east is 57 metres. Nothing is known of their contents.

4. The Avebury triangle   Neolithic and Bronze Age
Centred on SU: 103700

National Trust. Stone circles on A361, 1.6 km N of the A4, and E of most of the present village of Avebury; open at all times. Main car and coach park signposted at 101697. Alexander Keiller Museum signposted behind St James's church, open daily, April to October 10–6, November to March 10–4, closed 24th to 26th December and 1st January; admission charge; guide books; telephone enquiries 01672 539250. National Trust shop. Refreshments and toilets in village.

'It does as much exceed in greatness the so renowned Stoneheng as a Cathedral doeth a parish Church': so wrote John Aubrey in 1649, and it was no exaggeration. Yet Avebury is a secret place. Its great stone circle is hidden behind high grass-covered banks and is revealed suddenly, dramatically and triumphantly as you pass through one of its four entrances, although visitors approaching along the line of the Kennet Avenue from the south-east will already have had a foretaste of things to come. Our delight is due to the philanthropic energies of Alexander Keiller, who bought, excavated and restored much of the site during the 1930s, clearing away many of the village buildings that had grown up within the monument in the process.

In the early middle ages the Avebury stones were viewed by the Christian church as the work of the Devil. As such they attracted all kinds of pagan superstitions and had to be destroyed. The local people were encouraged to dig pits and bury the stones from sight. During the 1938 excavations the skeleton of a man was found, trapped beneath a fallen stone that he was helping to demolish. With his remains were coins dated around 1320–5, iron scissors and a probe, suggesting that he was an itinerant barber-surgeon. By the middle of the sixteenth century stones were being destroyed to clear the land for ploughing or to provide building stone. John

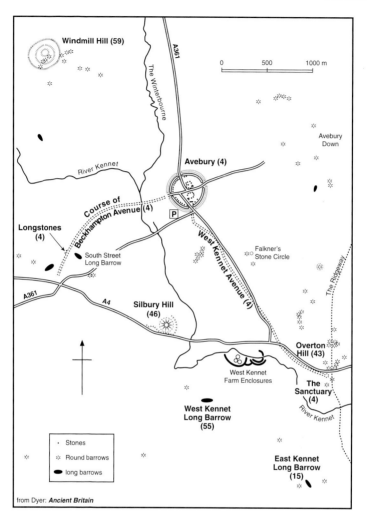

Earthworks in the Avebury area.

Aubrey recorded how the stones were smashed: 'make a fire on that line of stone, where you would have it crack; and then after the stone is well heated, draw over a line with cold water, & immediately give a knock with a Smyth's sledge, and it will break like the Collets at the Glass-House.' The demolition continued and was almost complete when William Stukeley first visited Avebury in 1719. Over the next ten years he recorded what remained, with numerous plans and drawings which are invaluable today in trying to form a picture of what the site had once been like. It is due to the persistence of Stukeley that many features no longer visible, like the Sanctuary and the Kennet Avenue, have been recovered by archaeologists, including Harold St George Gray, Maud Cunnington and Alexander Keiller.

At the apex of the Avebury triangle is a great earthwork, a henge monument

179

consisting of a ditch with external bank enclosing a roughly circular area of 10.5 hectares (inner ditch diameter 368 metres). On the inner edge of the ditch stood the Outer Circle of about ninety-eight great stones, and nearer the centre of the enclosure were at least two further inner circles of stones with internal settings.

From the southern entrance to the Avebury circle ran a double row of stones, the Kennet Avenue, for 2.4 km to the much smaller circle called the Sanctuary on Overton Hill. The destroyed Beckhampton Avenue left the western entrance of Avebury and ran for at least 1.4 km to the Longstones, and possibly beyond. These avenues form two sides of the Avebury triangle. Silbury Hill and the West Kennet long barrow mark the southern side, and have separate entries. There is nothing to be seen on the ground of the two massive timber-palisaded enclosures that stood next to each other beside the infant river Kennet near West Kennet Farm.

The Avebury circle. The great bank and ditch that surround Avebury are divided into four unequal arcs, each separated by a chalk entrance causeway, about 15 metres wide. At the top, the present ditch is about 21 metres wide, and its excavated depth varies between 7 and 10 metres. The bottom of the ditch was found to be flat and about 4 metres wide when dug in 1911 by Harold St George Gray. There were indications that it had been frequently cleaned out in prehistoric times. The chalk removed from the ditch was piled up to make the great bank, still 4.8 metres high and averaging 27 metres wide at the base, and 1353 metres in circumference. A wall of harder chalk blocks prevented the bank from slipping back into the ditch.

About 7 metres from the inner edge of the ditch stood the Outer Circle of great stones. Originally consisting of about ninety-eight, only twenty-seven stand today. Many were carefully re-erected by Alexander Keiller, who marked the excavated holes of missing stones in the western half of the site with small concrete plinths. The stones were all of the local sandstone, which is found lying on the Downs to the east, called sarsen stone (see Fyfield Down, no. 19); it is naturally shaped, not quarried. The name is possibly derived from 'saracen', a foreigner. Most of the stones still standing average 3.6 metres in height, although those at the north and south entrances reach 4.2 metres and weigh 40 tonnes. Much of the interior and eastern half of the site has not been excavated. It is believed that the earthworks and Outer Circle date from about 2600 BC.

Inside the earthwork were two smaller stone rings. The Southern one was 104 metres in diameter and almost all of its probable thirty stones have been destroyed. Excavation has found nine stones or stone holes to complete an arc on the western

An aerial view of Avebury henge circle from the south. (J. E. Hancock)

The Kennet Avenue of stones connecting Avebury and the Sanctuary on Overton Hill, Wiltshire. (J. Dyer)

side; the northern part lies under buildings. In the centre an enormous obelisk stone and a line of much smaller stones originally stood. It is recorded that the obelisk was 5.5 metres high and was destroyed in the eighteenth century. Its position is marked by a large and ugly concrete plinth with a cross-shaped base. The full extent of other stones inside this circle has not yet been established.

The Northern inner ring must have been about 98 metres in diameter. Only two of its stones are still standing, though two others are in fallen positions. In the centre were three very massive stones arranged to form a cove (or three sides of a box), the open side facing north-east. Only two of the stones survive today: one measuring 4.8 metres high and 2.4 metres wide; the other 4.2 metres high and 4.9 metres wide. In the nineteenth century they formed two walls of a barn!

There is reason to believe that these two inner circles predate the Outer stone circle and earthwork, perhaps by two hundred years. Recent geophysical survey work also suggests that there may have been a smaller concentric circle, possibly of wooden posts, 50 and 30 metres in diameter, in the north-eastern quadrant of the site. This remains to be tested by excavation.

Curving from the southern entrance to Avebury runs the **Kennet Avenue**, stretching for some 2300 metres to the Sanctuary on Overton Hill (SU: 103697 to 118680). It consists of a double row of standing stones, placed in pairs 15 metres apart across the avenue, and 24 metres apart along its length. The stones are smaller than those inside Avebury and seem to have been chosen for their shapes, which fall roughly into two types, either tall and narrow, or diamond-shaped. These shapes alternate along the avenue and it has long been thought that they might be male and female symbols expressing fertility. Only the northern part of the alignment has been excavated and restored. As the avenue approached the hamlet of West Kennet it curved south-east to run along the line of the A4 until it reached the top of Overton Hill, where it ended at the Sanctuary (119680).

Although it was totally destroyed by farmer Griffin in 1724 'to gain a little dirty profit', Maud Cunnington rediscovered the **Sanctuary** by careful field observation and excavation in 1930. It consisted of two concentric rings of small stones, the outer being 40 metres in diameter, the inner 14 metres. There were also six concentric rings of postholes that were once thought to have held timbers that formed a thatched wooden building. Re-excavation of part of the site in 1999 suggests that it was not so simple. Some of the rings may have consisted of free-standing posts, possibly carved or painted. Others held posts that were replaced many times and at very frequent intervals, with perhaps not all the holes being in use at one time. A human mandible, found in one of the inner stone ring holes, and the skeleton of an adolescent boy, buried with a 'barbed-wire' decorated beaker be-tween his legs and lying beside another stone, clearly indicate that the Sanctuary served a ritual rather than a domestic role. It is thought that the Sanctuary was broadly contemporary with the earthworks at Avebury, about 2600 BC, though the beaker burial may have been deposited some centuries later. The positions of the stones and posts have been unimaginatively marked on the site with concrete blocks.

North of the A4 roundabout at Beckhampton are the **Longstones** (or Devil's Quoits) (SU: 089693), where two stones known individually as Adam and Eve stand in a ploughed field. Eve is the only survivor of the north side of the Beckhampton Avenue. The larger (western) stone, Adam, formed the eastern wall of a four-sided cove. Although the other three stones had been removed, their deep holes were recovered during excavations in 2000, indicating that the destroyed sarsens had been massive. The cove had been partially open on its south-eastern side and faced towards the destroyed South Street long barrow 130 metres away (090693). The long barrow, which was excavated in 1964–5, seems to have formed some kind of cenotaph, since it covered no bodies but had been constructed around a series of wickerwork partitions that contained alternating layers of white chalk and black soil. Adam fell down in 1911 and was incorrectly re-erected (it should appear diamond-shaped but now leans too far south) by Maud Cunnington, who found the burial of a middle-aged man with a beaker at the foot of its inner face.

The excavations in 2000 also showed that the fourth stone on the south side of the cove had been destroyed by burning. 280 years before, Stukeley had recorded its destruction by Richard Fowler, landlord of the Hare and Hounds, who took away fifteen cartloads of pieces. This fourth stone seems to have stood in the centre of the **Beckhampton Avenue**, possibly forming a terminal. This avenue had all but disappeared in Stukeley's day, but sufficient stones remained for him to trace its course from Avebury's western entrance, through Avebury Trusloe and on towards Beckhampton. In 1999–2000 the excavators uncovered a 120 metre length of a double row of stone holes, placed in pairs 15 metres apart, exactly matching those in the Kennet Avenue. Some of the stones were buried, others had been burned and smashed, whilst the remainder were missing. Only the stone Eve remains standing. At the time of writing it is uncertain whether the avenue continues further west beyond the Longstones as Stukeley believed. The excavations also uncovered a small causewayed enclosure, some 140 metres by 100 metres, pre-dating the avenue

The excavation of the western stone hole of the cove beside the Longstone known as Adam, on the destroyed Beckhampton Avenue in 2000. (J. Dyer)

and lying immediately north-east of Adam. Revealed by aerial photography, it is quite invisible on the ground.

Most of the finds from the twentieth-century excavations have been placed in the Alexander Keiller Museum in Avebury or in the splendid museum at Devizes.

5. Barbury Castle, Wroughton
Iron Age
SU: 149763

Reached along the Ridgeway from Upper Herdwick or Hackpen Hill.

A remarkably strong hillfort enclosing 4.6 hectares, and surrounded by two ramparts with ditches. The fort is oval in shape with entrances at the west, and with outworks at the east. The interior has been extensively ploughed, and this has enabled aerial photographs to reveal huts and storage pits.

A boundary dyke cuts across the hill ridge from north-west to south-west to the east of the hillfort and may be contemporary. Further east along the Downs are extensive traces of field systems (centre 164762), which cover some 56 hectares. The fields are probably of iron age date, extending into the Roman period. A roughly rectangular enclosure (at 160765) overlies the fields and is likely to be of medieval date.

6. Battlesbury Camp, Warminster
Iron Age
ST: 898456

Approached from Sack Hill, 2.4 km NE of Warminster.

Sited on a spur facing south-east above the river Wylye, this irregular contour fort of 9.6 hectares has triple ramparts, except above the escarpment, where they are double. There are entrances with outworks on the east and north-west sides. Nine pits within the camp were excavated in 1922. They contained late iron age pottery and numerous examples of ironwork, including a key, saw and parts of a chariot wheel. Saddle and rotary quern stones indicated that corn was ground on the site.

Just outside the north-west entrance a pit was found containing a large number of burials, including a woman and child. This appears to have been a massacre, though whether by another tribe or the Roman legions is uncertain.

7. Bratton Castle
Neolithic and Iron Age
ST: 901516

Approached by metalled road SE from Bratton.

On a north-facing promontory above the Westbury White Horse, this fort encloses 10 hectares. It has a double bank and ditch on all sides, except the east where it is single. There is an entrance in the southern side with an outwork, and probably another on the east, through which the road passes. At this point the ramparts are widely spaced. There are traces of quarry scoops inside the southern rampart. The only finds recorded from the site are quern stones and a cartload of slingstones.

Inside the fort is a long barrow. It is 70 metres long and 3.6 metres high. It has been opened on a number of occasions. It is probable that the primary burials were those of two adults who had been partially cremated and were found lying on a platform at the eastern end of the barrow.

The oldest of the Wiltshire white horses, the **Westbury White Horse**, 'the charger of the Wiltshire wold', was re-cut close to the western rampart of the hillfort in 1778.

8. Bury Camp, Colerne
Iron Age
ST: 818740

Access from the SW and the Colerne to Marshfield road.

This is a promontory fort enclosing 8.8 hectares. The main rampart across the south-west side is bivallate and contains an entrance which was blocked at a later stage in the iron age. This earthwork may have been a cross-ridge dyke before it was incorporated into the hillfort. A single bank and ditch surmount the steep, wooded north and east sides. A funnel-shaped entrance in the north-east corner has been proved by excavation and had been destroyed by fire. There was another entrance on the north-west side. The small rectangular earthwork inside the fort, marked on some maps as a barrow, is also of iron age date. Mr D. Grant King, who excavated the fort for some years, was able to distinguish the general history of the site, beginning with its initial building perhaps about 350 BC. This was followed by a period of neglect with fires and damage to the ramparts. Later the north-east and north-west gates were repaired, as were the damaged ramparts. Some time in the second century BC the fort came to an end. How is not clear.

A cross-dyke 1600 metres to the east of the fort (832743), overlooking Ford and Slaughterford, is also likely to be of iron age date and may be connected with defining territory belonging to Bury Camp.

9. Casterley Camp, Upavon
Iron Age
SU: 115535

About 2 km along track SW of Upavon from A342.

Excavated by the Cunningtons between 1909 and 1912, this hillfort encloses 27 hectares and is roughly rectangular in plan. It bulges outwards at the north-east, leading to the suggestion that it is unfinished on this side. A single bank and ditch surround the enclosure, still 1.5 metres high at the south-east and shown to be V-shaped and 1.4 metres deep.

Three entrances can be seen at the south, west and north. In an oval enclosure at the centre of the camp was a pit in which a large post had stood. At its base four human burials and fourteen red deer antlers had been placed. It is believed that this was some form of sanctuary connected with Celtic worship.

Aerial photographs have also revealed a small Belgic farming settlement in the centre of the fort. Objects found can be seen in Devizes Museum.

10. Castle Ditches, Tisbury
Iron Age
ST: 963283

Approached by track off road between Tisbury and Swallowcliffe.

Crowning the top of a steep hill, this fort of 9.7 hectares is strongly fortified with double banks and ditches (triple on the south-east). There appear to be original entrances on the east and west. The fort is badly damaged by trees.

11. Chiseldon stone circle, Coate
Bronze Age
SU: 182824

Opposite Day House Farm, on minor road on SW of Swindon.

This probable stone circle was discovered by Richard Jefferies in the 1860s. Nine recumbent stones make an approximate circle about 70 metres in diameter. Sited close to a stream, it is almost insignificant compared with the other great circles of Wiltshire.

12. Cow Down, Collingbourne Ducis
Bronze Age
SU: 229516

On the N side of wood 800 metres SW of A338/A342 crossroads.

A group of twelve bowl-barrows and one disc-barrow. Nine of the barrows lie in a rough line from south-west to north-east, across the northern end of the wood, whilst the other bowl-barrows and the disc-barrow lie in a second line a little further north. The barrows may be described as follows, commencing with the southern line from west to east. Nos. 1–3 lie outside the wood to the west; nos. 4–7 lie in the wood.

1. Large ploughed mound overlapped by a smaller one. Now only 0.6 metre high. Pieces of pottery were found in the larger, ashes and charcoal in the smaller.
2. Badly ploughed, no record of its contents.
3. Only 0.3 metre high. Although its main burial has not been found, a secondary

cremation in an urn of Deverel-Rimbury type may belong to this period when the barrow was enlarged. Much later an old man with an iron knife was buried in the barrow.
4. This barrow contained a crouched skeleton that lacked an arm and both hands. In the middle bronze age thirteen cremations were added, three in urns.
5. A cremation with an antler macehead was buried in a tree-trunk coffin. The Deverel-Rimbury people added eight cremations (two in urns) to the barrow.
6. The primary burial was probably the skeleton of a child of three to four years, with a collared urn and food-vessel beside it. Later eighteen cremations and pieces of about forty-five urns of Deverel-Rimbury type were added to the barrow.
7. The first burial was a cremation. Above this, part of the skeleton of a man lay on a wooden plank. 0.6 metre above that was another cremation with shale and amber beads.
8. No record of contents.
9. A cremation burial.
   The second row of barrows are as follows, from west to east:
10. 15 metres in diameter but only 0.3 metre high. It contained an empty grave.
11. This disc-barrow measures about 45 metres from the outer banks. Its central mound is only 0.3 metre high. Opened by Cunnington in 1805 without record, and later by Lukis, it seems only to have produced an empty grave, although there is a tradition of it containing a 'small saucer' which could well have been an incense cup.
12. This barrow covered a central cremation burial and three later secondary cremations.
13. A child was buried in this barrow together with a shale bead and a handled cup 9 cm high.

13. Devil's Den, Preshute
Neolithic
SU: 152696

Footpath 800 metres N, 400 metres E of Fyfield village.

The mound of this long barrow has almost disappeared, but a burial chamber at its east end consisting of four upright sarsen stones and a capstone was re-erected in 1921. It has been suggested that it may have formed a false entrance of Cotswold type. The barrow remains unexcavated.

14. Durrington Walls
Neolithic
SU: 150437

The A345 from Netheravon to Amesbury runs through the site. Parking at Woodhenge to the SW.

Almost all that can be seen of this great henge monument today is a much ploughed bank encircling the upper end of a dry valley which runs down to the river Avon. It is best preserved on the north-eastern side. The interior is slightly oval in shape and measures 520 metres from north to south, and 450 metres from east to west. (The diameter of Avebury is 427 metres.) It encloses 12 hectares. Excavation has shown that the bank was originally 27 metres wide and was separated from the inner ditch by a berm or area of level ground, varying from 6 metres to 42 metres wide. The ditch was 6 metres deep with a flat bottom 7 metres wide. It is broken by two entrances, one at the north-west and the other at the south-east, 60 metres from the river Avon.

Excavations under the A345 in 1966–7 produced a number of features of interest. Most important of these was a complex circular structure of Woodhenge type, 38 metres in diameter, only 27 metres inside the earthwork on its southern side. It had been rebuilt or modified at least three times during its existence and consisted of five rings of posts, increasing in size from outside to the centre. Posts of the inner ring were about 0.6 metre in diameter. This was probably a large circular building.

A second smaller circular structure lay 120 metres north of the first. It consisted initially of two concentric posts 27 metres and 19 metres in diameter approached from the south by an avenue of posts. Later these circles were replaced by two more, smaller in diameter, but composed of larger posts, together with a new avenue on a different alignment. This is also seen as a round house. Geophysical surveys have shown that there are more, as yet unexcavated, round houses inside Durrington Walls. Outside the entrance to the south stood Woodhenge (no. 62).

Large quantities of grooved-ware pottery have been found at the site. This usually occurs at monuments believed to have been used for ceremonial purposes. However, it is not improbable that there was a domestic settlement for the people who performed the rituals; though whether these ceremonies were religious or secular remains unknown.

15. East Kennet long barrow
Neolithic
SU: 116669

In a field 800 metres S of East Kennet village.

This great tree-covered barrow measures some 105 metres long and stands 6 metres high. Although it has not been excavated in modern times, traces of sarsen stones at the south-east end probably indicate a burial chamber. The presence of side ditches has been shown by darker crop growth in the adjoining field.

16. Enford bowl-barrow
Bronze Age
SU: 129516

On the hillslope SW of Compton, W of the A342.

Although nothing is known of the contents of this barrow, it is of interest in that it is among the largest surviving bowl-barrows in England, being about 48 metres in diameter and 5 metres high. A cavity extends from the centre towards the east, indicating that it has been dug into at some time.

17. Everleigh barrows
Bronze Age
SU: 184561

Beside cart-track from Lower Everleigh to Pewsey Hill.

A group of five barrows, two bowls, a disc and two bell. One bowl is flattened, the other is very low. They were dug by Thurnam without result, as was the neighbouring disc-barrow, which is about 54 metres in diameter. Thurnam also dug the two bell-barrows, with more success. That on the east contained a primary cremation that may have been an adult male. The western barrow contained a similar cremation together with a flat bronze dagger.

A short distance north-east of the barrows is a square earthwork enclosure of possibly iron age date. 800 metres north-east of the barrows (187567) is the **Down Farm group** of eight barrows, including a badly damaged bell-barrow. Although these barrows were dug by Colt Hoare around 1800, there is some doubt as to which barrows contained what objects. Most seem to have contained cremation burials, one with a bronze awl, shale beads and perhaps an incense cup.

18. Figsbury Rings, Winterbourne
Iron Age
SU: 188338

Approached by a track from the A30. In the care of the National Trust.

This circular fort, enclosing about 6 hectares, is unusual in that its outer bank and ditch are separated by a wide flat space from an inner ditch which has no bank. This inner ditch, which varies in width from 13 metres to 16 metres and is 1.5 metres to 3.6 metres deep, may have provided a quarry for additional material for the outer bank. This seems rather odd in view of the distance that it was dug from the bank, and future excavations may have to reconsider an earlier idea that the ditch may have formed part of a ceremonial site, akin to the causewayed enclosures or henge monuments, or an earlier hillfort, as at Yarnbury (no. 63).

Excavations in 1924 by Maud and Ben Cunnington revealed very little occupation material. Most of the pottery was haematite-coated ware of the early iron age, but no metal was found. The outer bank had clearly been enlarged on two occasions. Two entrances cut through the bank, one on the west, the other on the east with traces of outworks which may once have formed a hornwork. Corresponding entrance gaps also occur in the inner ditch.

19. Fyfield Down and Overton Down

Iron Age
SU: 142710

A bridleway, 'The Herepath', runs from Avebury to Marlborough. The field systems lay on either side. The site is protected by the Nature Conservancy Council as a National Nature Reserve.

This is probably the finest example of a prehistoric 'landscape' in Wiltshire, consisting of many examples of rectangular 'Celtic' fields, some with banks between them standing 3 metres high. These grass-covered 'lynchets' originally had rows of boulders, stone walls, fences or ditches marking their edges, but a gradual creep of soil caused the characteristic banks of soil to pile up slowly against these obstructions. Between the fields were tracks which allowed access to them and to the nearby farmsteads. Excavation has shown that some of the Celtic fields were cross-ploughed with a simple ard. The fields, which may have begun as early as 700 BC, continued in use into the Roman period, although not always following the same shape.

Scattered over Fyfield Down and Overton Down are thousands of sarsen stones, the **Grey Wethers** used for building Stonehenge and Avebury. (The most accessible group lies at Piggle Dean further to the south, beside the A4 at 143688, and Lockeridge Dene at 145674.) On the north-west side of the downs a beaker settlement has been located, and beside it a large sarsen, its upper surface deeply grooved by the polishing of stone axes, around 128715.

Also on the downs is the Experimental Earthwork (129706) constructed by the British Association in 1960 and examined at specified intervals (the next in 2022), in order to investigate the way in which archaeological structures change with time, and the effect this has on objects buried within them.

20. Giant's Caves, Luckington

Neolithic
ST: 820830

At the SE corner of Badminton Park beside the road from Great Badminton to Luckington.

This trapezoidal long cairn was first excavated in 1932, and again in 1960–2. It measures 39 metres long and 2.4 metres high. It has a 'false entrance', between limestone horns at the eastern end. Four burial chambers have been found tucked into the sides of the cairn. It is possible that they were each originally free-standing and were later incorporated into the barrow. The north-west chamber contained burials of three men, two women and a child, whilst that on the north-east produced the partial remains of at least seven skeletons, with others in the approach passage. In the south-west chamber were the bones of a man, three women and three children, whilst the much disturbed south-eastern chamber held only a few fragments of a female skeleton. Many flint flakes and a few sherds of neolithic pottery were also found.

A second, poorly preserved, long barrow stands 225 metres to the south-east (821828).

21. Giant's Grave, Milton Lilbourne

Neolithic
SU: 189583

From the Pewsey to Everleigh road, take the farm road towards Milton Hill farm, turn left on to footpath after 1.2 km. Barrow lies 800 metres N.

This is one of the many Wiltshire long barrows excavated by John Thurnam. Built of chalk, it covered at its eastern end a pile of bones representing three or four people, one of whom had died from a blow which had cleft his skull. A leaf-shaped arrowhead lay nearby. The barrow has clearly defined quarry ditches on either side.

22. Gopher Wood barrows, Wilcot   Bronze Age
SU: 139639

In front of wood on hill-scarp, at end of track N from Draycot Fitz Payne.

On the steep slope of the hill is a disc-barrow about 25 metres in diameter. When excavated by William Cunnington it was found to contain an urn and incense cup, together with an awl and bone pin. There were two other cremations surrounded by flints. Extending north from the disc-barrow are seven bowl-barrows. Three of them are confluent and produced cremation burials, whilst two other contiguous barrows contained an urn and bone pins.

23. Grafton disc-barrows   Bronze Age
SU: 271563

Footpath due W for 1.6 km from Scot's Poor on Chute Causeway (286562), or E from road linking A346 to A338 over Fairmile Down.

Here are two unusual disc-barrows, each about 45 metres in diameter with central mounds about 1 metre high, overlapping one another. Nothing is recorded of their contents. A third disc-barrow can be found a short distance up the hill.

24. King Barrow, Warminster   Neolithic
ST: 897445

N of A36, behind Bishopstrow House (private) amongst trees.

This large round barrow, 60 metres long and 4.5 metres high, was already badly damaged when it was dug into twice by William Cunnington in 1800 and 1809. There seems to have been some sort of burial chamber cut into the chalk below the mound, containing the 'bones of birds and beasts' – mostly pigs, 'and the coarsest of pottery'. No primary burials seem to have been found, but three skeletons near the top, one with an iron sword, 'a man of very superior rank', were probably pagan Saxon.

25. Knap Hill, Alton Priors   Neolithic and Iron Age
SU: 121636

2.4 km NE of Alton Priors on E of road to Marlborough. Track from road at 116638. Footpath inside ploughed field on east (Nature Conservancy Council).

This was the first neolithic causewayed enclosure to be recognised in Britain. It lies on a steep-sided ridge, and an arc of six or seven ditch sections, broken by at least five causeways, forms the north and west side of an enclosure of about 1.6 hectares. There are indications that the ditch may have continued on the east and south sides, but this is uncertain and may even indicate that the site was never completed. The ditch seems to have been a chain of pits strung together, varying in depth between 1 and 3 metres but in width usually about 3.6 metres. A radiocarbon date of 3450 BC has been obtained for the initial silting of the ditches. Pottery from excavations in 1908 and 1961 was scarce but of Windmill Hill type. Later, when the ditches had almost silted up, a little beaker pottery was also dropped on the site. This was dated to 2200 BC.

Knap Hill is ideally sited for defensive purposes and, as more evidence emerges of attacks on causewayed enclosures, this may partly explain its siting. Until the interior is excavated we must continue to accept the more traditional views of mortuary enclosure and ceremonial gathering-ground.

On the north-eastern side of the neolithic earthwork is a roughly rectangular enclosure dated to the late iron age. Two round barrows, both very low, lie one inside the west end of the neolithic site (excavated by Thurnam; it contained a primary cremation) and one 15 metres outside the southernmost causewayed ditch

The causewayed enclosure rings the summit of Knap Hill, Wiltshire. (J. Dyer)

section (dug, without result). At the foot of the hill near the main road are two round barrows with a low mound between them.

26. Lake barrow cemetery, Wilsford

Bronze Age
SU: 109402

E of the green lane which runs SW from Stonehenge, across Normanton Down to Druid's Lodge on A360.

This is one of the large number of barrow groups around Stonehenge. Most of the barrows have been dug into on a number of occasions, and it is not clear what objects were found in which barrows. At least fifteen bowl-barrows, as well as four bell-barrows, two discs and a long barrow, lie in the plantation and on the southern side of it. Many of the barrows were opened by Cunnington and Duke in 1806. One of the bowl-barrows on the northern side was known as the Prophet Barrow. 18 metres in diameter and 1.8 metres high, it contained a cremation in a wooden box, buried in a chalk-cut grave, together with a grooved bronze dagger and a perforated slate pendant (in Devizes Museum). Under another bowl-barrow 3 metres high was the primary skeleton of a child with a beaker, and two secondary bronze age skeletons, together with an inverted urn containing burnt bones and a pin. One of the bell-barrows contained a primary cremation together with a bronze dagger, awl and some beads. Both the disc-barrows lie in thick vegetation and nothing is known of their contents. The wedge-shaped long barrow also lies in the plantation; it is 42 metres long and 2.4 metres high, with deep side ditches. It seems to be unopened.

27. Lake Down barrow cemetery, Wilsford

Bronze Age
SU: 117393

On S of track from Lake to Westfield Farm, and just E of farm.

Another of the great barrow cemeteries near Stonehenge, this contains at least sixteen burial mounds: ten bowl-barrows, one disc-barrow and five (an unusually high number) pond-barrows. Most of the barrows were opened by the Reverend E. Duke in 1806 and records of his finds are very scanty. The disc-barrow, which is 54 metres in diameter, with a very low central mound, contained a cremation in a small urn. One of the larger pond-barrows contained a cremation, whilst the others seem to have been opened without results. A linear earthwork appears to mark the western limit of the cemetery, separating it from ancient cultivated land.

28. Lanhill, Chippenham Without

Neolithic
ST: 877747

On the S side of the A420, 4 km W of Chippenham.

This long barrow has suffered intolerable disturbance and vandalism in the past four centuries. It originally measured about 56 metres in length and was over 3.6 metres high. At the east end stood a false entrance, removed in 1909, with a drystone horn-shaped wall on either side forming a funnel-shaped forecourt. The barrow contained three burial chambers, of which only one, on the south side, survives. This had a corbelled roof and is accessible. It measures 1.2 metres wide and 2.4 metres long and contained eleven or twelve burials. Of the two destroyed chambers of the north side, one, possibly opposite the south chamber, contained two burials, whilst another further north-west had a rough porthole entrance and held nine skeletons. These bones were examined by Dr A. J. E. Cave in 1938 and were shown to have marked family resemblances, suggesting that the tomb had formed a family vault.

29. Liddington Castle

Late Bronze Age, Early Iron Age
SU: 209797

Reached by a steep climb from the Ridgeway, 1 km S of Liddington.

This roughly oval hillfort, enclosing 3 hectares, is impressively situated on the escarpment at a height of 277 metres above OD. It is one of the earliest forts in Wiltshire and was defended by a single bank and ditch with a strong counterscarp bank. It appears to have originally had two opposing entrances. That on the west was blocked, leaving only the single causewayed entrance on the east, which may have been lined with sarsen stones. Access would have been along the ridge from the south-east. Excavation of the ramparts shows that there were at least two phases of construction. Initially they were of timber and turf, perhaps surmounted by a wooden palisade or platform, and with a small external ditch. Later the defences were heightened with a dump rampart of chalk obtained when the ditch was enlarged. The examination of a large surface hollow in the south-western quarter of the interior revealed the top of a possible 'ritual shaft' at least 1.5 metres in diameter and more than 2.4 metres deep. (It was too hazardous to dig deeper without proper equipment.) Similar shafts are known from Wapley Hill, Herefordshire, and Cadbury Castle, Devon.

Pottery of the late bronze age and very early iron age suggests that the fort was occupied between the seventh and fifth centuries BC.

Although there is a little evidence to suggest that the fort may have been casually occupied during the Roman period, there is none to support the theory that Liddington Castle was Mount Badon, the site of the elusive late-fifth-century AD battle between the British and Saxons, the *Mons Badonicus* of Gildas.

30. Lugbury long barrow, Nettleton

Neolithic
ST: 831786

W of the Fosse Way, beside a footpath from Nettleton Green to Horsedown on the B4039.

Although this barrow has been severely ploughed, it is still 60 metres long and 2 metres high. Three stones, forming a false entrance, stand at its eastern end. Four small stone chambers (not visible) have been excavated along its southern side, containing between them at least twenty-six skeletons, ten of them children. What may have been the original crouched primary burial was found by Colt Hoare in 1821 near the east end.

31. Manton long barrow, Preshute

Neolithic
SU: 152714

Near footpath running NW from Manton House.

This ruined long barrow is about 20 metres long and was badly damaged in recent times, after which it was excavated. An empty burial chamber at its east end opened on to a forecourt, in the centre of which a pit containing a poleaxed ox was uncovered. Pottery of Windmill Hill type was also found. Round the barrow was a peristalith wall of sarsen stones.

32. Manton round barrow, Preshute

Bronze Age
SU: 165691

90 metres N of the A4, about 2.4 km W of Marlborough.

This barrow is not very impressive. Two ditches enclose an area 18 metres in diameter and a mound 1.2 metres high. It is important because of its extremely rich contents excavated by B. H. Cunnington. He found that the corpse of an elderly woman had been wrapped in cloth, which had left its impression in the clayey soil. Buried with her were an incense cup and a grape cup, a bronze knife with an amber pommel, a necklace of 150 disc-shaped beads of shale graded in size from 2 mm to 5 mm, a large barrel-shaped shale bead encircled with five bands of gold, a gold-mounted amber disc identical with two from Wilsford, and a gold and bronze halberd-shaped pendant. There were also three bronze awls and numerous other beads and a clay stud.

South of the burial was a collared urn with a few bones beneath it. It may have been an offering to the old woman, or a secondary deposit. On the old ground surface under the barrow were a flint arrowhead and a piece of rock from the Penzance area of Cornwall. Most of the finds from the Manton barrow are in Devizes Museum.

33. Marden henge (Hatfield earthwork)

Neolithic
SU: 091584

The road from Marden to Woodborough passes through the site 400 metres NE of the river Avon. English Heritage; open at any time.

The site occupies an oval area of about 14 hectares on low-lying ground beside the headwaters of the river Avon. It is enclosed by a bank and internal ditch on the east, north and north-west sides, whilst the meandering river and its flood plain formed the south and west sides. Not only is Marden the largest henge monument so far identified in Britain, but it is also unique in having two entrances lying at right angles to one another on the north and east sides.

Excavations in 1969 at the northern entrance revealed that the ditch was more than 15 metres wide, but only 1.8 metres deep. On either side of the entrance causeway objects had been thrown into the ditch by prehistoric visitors, including antler picks, fragments of animal bone, flint tools and pieces of neolithic grooved-ware pottery. Just inside the entrance was a timber circle 10.5 metres in diameter, with three further posts set in a row near its centre. The surrounding bank is badly ploughed away, but it can still be seen for most of its course. The site is dated to about 2500 BC.

A great mound, the Hatfield barrow, once stood inside the earthwork, close to the original entrance. Originally claimed to have been 60 metres in diameter and 7 metres high, it was dug into in 1818 without any certain results. It has since been totally ploughed away.

South-west of Hatfield Farm in the southern part of Marden henge is a saucer-barrow, about 90 metres in diameter. Excavation by Sir Richard Colt Hoare produced pieces of 'old pottery and a little charred wood', but no burials.

34. Martinsell, Pewsey

Iron Age
SU: 177639

Approached by track from minor road running NW from Wootton Rivers to Clench Common.

Although occupying a commanding position, this hillfort is of no great strength.

Rectangular in shape, its single bank and ditch enclosed 13 hectares. Its entrance was probably at the north-east corner.

800 metres south-west on a spur of Martinsell Hill is a small promontory fort of 1 hectare called the **Giant's Grave**.

The neck of the fort is defined by a strong bank and ditch broken by an entrance; outside are two slighter defences.

35. Membury, Ramsbury Iron Age
SU: 302753

By minor road and footpath N from Whittonditch.

Straddling the county boundary, this fort is mainly in Wiltshire. It lies on level ground, is much overgrown by bushes and trees and encloses 14 hectares within strong single bank and ditch defences. There are traces of a counterscarp bank, and indications that the original entrances existed at the north-east and south-west.

36. Milston Down Neolithic
SU: 217463

Beside the military road from Bulford Camp to Tidworth Barracks.

Two long barrows lie side by side. Neither appears to have been excavated. One is 48 metres long and 2.1 metres high, the other 26 metres long and 1.2 metres high. The side ditches from which the material to build the barrows was quarried are still visible.

37. Normanton Down, Wilsford cum Lake Neolithic and Bronze Age
SU: 115413

Approached by green road off A303, SW of Stonehenge.

The Normanton barrow cemetery lies on the skyline to the south of Stonehenge, from where it is clearly visible. At least two dozen round barrows of almost every type lie in a broad band over an area some 1.2 km in length. These are the most celebrated group of barrows in England and are dealt with at some length. They are numbered according to the plan (page 193).

1. Bell-barrow north of the wood, 53 metres in diameter and 3.3 metres high. It contained the skeleton of a man placed on a plank of wood, together with a bronze dagger in a wooden scabbard and a beaker. Wooden poles around the burial may have been the remains of a hut over the corpse, covered over by the burial mound.

2. A disc-barrow beside the green lane, 60 metres in diameter with a very low central mound. It contained a cremation with beads of amber, shale and faience.

3. A second disc-barrow of similar size, probably excavated by William Stukeley in August 1723, contained a cremation burial.

4. **Bush Barrow**. A bowl-barrow 15 metres in diameter and 2.4 metres high. Probably the most famous barrow in England, owing to the rich contents excavated by Sir Richard Colt Hoare in 1808. On the floor of the barrow lay the skeleton of a 'stout and tall man', a Wessex chieftain. Near his head was a wooden shield with bronze decorations. An axe had been wrapped in cloth and placed by his shoulder. At his side lay two bronze daggers, one with a wooden hilt decorated with thousands of minute gold pins, each 1 mm long. There was a smaller bronze dagger by his right hand, and near his leg 'a very curious perforated stone'. This seems to have been a stone mace with a head made from a perforated fossil *tubularia* and a handle of wood decorated with bone rings. Although the man's clothes had not survived some of the objects sewn on to them were found. On his chest had been a lozenge-shaped plate of sheet gold measuring 18.3 cm; his belt had a hook of hammered gold with finely engraved ornament. These objects are in Devizes Museum.

5. A saucer-barrow, opened without result.

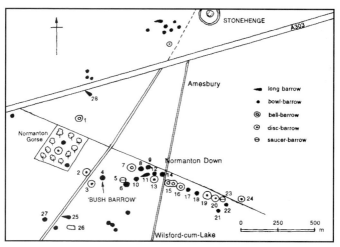

Normanton Down barrow cemetery, Wiltshire.

6. This bowl-barrow contained a skeleton, together with a grape cup, amber pendants and beads of gold, shale and fossils. At his feet stood a collared urn which may have contained a food offering.

7. A bell-barrow 41 metres in diameter and 3 metres high which contained a cremation burial with an incense cup, a shale button and two amber discs, each covered with gold, and a model halberd in amber and gold.

8, 9, 10. These bowl-barrows have all been disturbed, with no record of their contents.

11. This small long barrow is 20 metres in length and 2.7 metres high, with well-marked side ditches. Although it was examined by Colt Hoare, there is no record of the contents.

12. A bowl-barrow with an outer bank, opened without result.

13. A magnificent disc-barrow 67 metres in diameter, with a very low central mound. It was excavated in 1723 by Stukeley, who found a cremation.

14. Another small bowl-barrow.

15. A double bell-barrow consisting of two mounds enclosed by a single ditch. The overall measurements are 57 metres from west to east and 38 metres from north to south. Both mounds have been opened. That on the west produced a cremation with a bone belt-hook and pendant; the eastern contained a cremation with amber and shale beads and a small cup.

16. A bell-barrow 57 metres in diameter and 3.3 metres high. Although opened, there are no records of its contents.

17. Bowl-barrow. No records.

18. This bowl-barrow contained a crouched skeleton and a bronze dagger.

19, 20. Two fine disc-barrows, each 44 metres in diameter with low central mounds, but no record of their contents.

21. Bowl-barrow. No records.

22. This bowl-barrow held a cremation with two bronze daggers, a whetstone with hourglass perforation, a bronze crutch-headed pin and a perforated swan bone that might have been a flute.

23. A saucer-barrow 40 metres in diameter. No records.

24. A disc-barrow almost destroyed, about 36 metres in diameter, with no record of its contents.

25. The green road cuts the end of this long barrow south of the main cemetery. It is 38 metres long and 1.8 metres high. Cunnington found four skeletons at the eastern end 'strangely huddled together'. A secondary Saxon burial was also found.

26. Mention must be made of a site south-east of long barrow 25, now ploughed away. This was a mortuary enclosure excavated by Faith Vatcher in 1959. It consisted of an oval ditched enclosure broken by numerous causeways, measuring some 38 metres by 20 metres. At the eastern end were two roughly parallel trenches 4.8 metres apart. In each three posts had stood, all about 0.3 metre in diameter. Whether these formed some shrine linked by cross-timbers above ground or the entrance passage to a turf enclosure, we shall never know. At all events, they were probably part of a structure of neolithic date, c.3250 BC, which held corpses until a long barrow was built.

27. A low bowl-barrow containing a cremation together with a lignite ring and shale beads.

28. Long barrow 30 metres long and 1.8 metres high near the A303. Three primary burials, two with cleft skulls, were found by Thurnam. There were also two secondary burials.

38. Ogbury Camp, Durnford

Iron Age
SU: 143383

Minor road leads along S side of camp N of Durnford.

Although enclosing 25 hectares, this oval-shaped fort is of little natural strength. Its bank still stands 2.4 metres high, but its ditch is completely silted up. There are a number of gaps in the earthwork, although only that on the east, closest to the wood, is likely to be original. Sir Richard Colt Hoare, and subsequently aerial photography, found traces of internal enclosures, which may substantiate the reasonable claim that the camp was an agricultural enclosure rather than a defensive site.

39. Old and New King barrows, Amesbury

Bronze Age
New: S end SU: 135421
Old: SU: 134426

In woods N of the A303 1.4 km E of Stonehenge. Display panels on site.

The New King barrows consist of five bowl- and two bell-barrows running in a line south to north. After a gap through which runs the Stonehenge Avenue the woods continue. Here are the seven Old King barrows, all bowl-barrows. All these burial mounds were dug in the eighteenth century and seem to have been built of turf. No very clear records exist of what they contained. Reference by Stukeley to a 'very large Brass weapon of twenty pounds weight, like a pole-ax' and 'a bugle-horn tipt with silver at both ends' may indicate an all-bronze halberd of German type, and a musical horn, perhaps of Scandinavian origin.

40. Oldbury Castle, Calne

Iron Age
SU: 049693

Footpath up face of downs from A4 at Cherhill and Yatesbury by-road.

Roughly triangular, and enclosing 8 hectares, this fort has double banks and ditches to protect it. There is an inturned entrance on the east, and perhaps another original entrance at the south-east. Excavations in the nineteenth century produced early iron age pottery from storage pits. The interior has been damaged by recent flint-digging.

The **Cherhill White Horse** was cut in 1780 in the style of Stubbs by Dr Christopher Alsop of Calne, sometimes described as 'the mad doctor'.

41. Old Sarum, Stratford-sub-Castle

Iron Age, Roman, etc
SU: 137327

Beside the A345, 2.4 km N of Salisbury. English Heritage. Car park, guide books, etc.

Best seen from the Avon valley to the west, Old Sarum consists of an iron age hillfort, dominated by a Norman castle motte. Within the earthworks are the foundations of a castle, cathedral and bishop's palace (AD *c*.1068–78).

The hillfort is oval in shape, measuring some 360 metres from north to south and 405 metres from east to west, and consists of a single bank and ditch with an entrance on the eastern side. Excavations have been concentrated on the later occupation of the hill, and an iron age storage pit, together with pottery and brooches, was found only incidentally.

Old Sarum may have been the site of the Roman station of *Sorviodunum*. Certainly the remains of pottery and a small Roman building were found inside the fort in 1909, but it is more likely that the main station lay to the south or west.

42. Oliver's Castle, Bromham   Iron Age
SU: 001646

Footpath over the downs from Roundway village or Bromham.

A small promontory fort of 1.2 hectares commanding extensive views in all directions. Its single bank and ditch are broken on the east by an entrance which, when excavated, produced two holes for gateposts on either side. The ditch was 4 metres deep and of normal V-shape. Pits in the interior produced early iron age pottery.

Two round barrows south-west of the camp have been excavated. The southern contained an unusual handled urn, a bronze dagger and a cremation, whilst the northern also held a cremation together with part of an incense cup and a conical bone button.

43. Overton Hill barrows, West Overton   Bronze Age
SU: 119682

On the E side of the Ridgeway as it crosses the A4.

A small linear cemetery that was once considerably more extensive and formed part of the great groups around Avebury.

1. The southernmost barrow of the group lies south of the A4 and the Sanctuary (page 181). It is a bowl-barrow, some 18 metres in diameter and 3.7 metres high. Excavated by Colt Hoare, it contained a crouched skeleton in a tree-trunk coffin, together with a flat bronze dagger and axe and a crutch-headed pin of Germanic type.
2. The first barrow north of the A4 is a damaged bell-barrow whose berm can be seen only on the west. It contained a cremation and an incense cup – 'a very rude little cup, scratched over with the usual British pattern'.
3. The next bell-barrow is 41 metres in diameter and 3 metres high. It also contained a cremation.
4. A small bowl-barrow about 9 metres in diameter and 1 metre high lies between 3 and 5 and seems to overlap them. It contained a cremation and a bone pin.
5. The most northerly bell-barrow in the cemetery is about 38 metres in diameter with a mound 10 metres high. It contained a cremation with a bronze dagger and a bone belt-hook.
6. North-east of the last barrow is a bowl-barrow which covered a cremation.

The line of the Roman road from *Cunetio* (Mildenhall) to *Verlucio* (Sandy Lane) crosses the Ridgeway about 200 metres north of the A4. Just beyond it, and on the east of the Ridgeway were three low mounds, excavated in 1962 prior to cultivation. Originally they were Roman tombs of rather unusual design. Each consisted of a circle of closely placed wooden posts. Inside them were central pits, each containing a cremation and covered with small mounds of earth. They may have dated from early in the second century AD.

7. East of the Roman tombs is another ploughed bowl-barrow 0.9 metre high and 14 metres in diameter. It contained the burial of a man of about forty with a beaker and

leather-working tools. A baby and a child of about four were buried nearby, their graves being covered by a bank of flints and sarsens. Some time later three more child burials were added to the barrow, together with some cremations, two in urns. 8. A bowl-barrow lies 180 metres further north. It held a primary cremation and two other cremations, one in an inverted urn.

There are a number of other fine bell- and disc-barrows on Overton Hill and extending towards Avebury Down. Unfortunately most of them are on ploughed land. Amongst them, one of the best bell-barrows lies about 2.4 km north of the A4 at 117691, and a good disc-barrow close to a footpath towards Avebury (116689). There are no records of finds from either.

44. Pertwood Down, Brixton Deverill
Neolithic
ST: 872374

On the down about 1.6 km E of Monkton Deverill (on B3095). No direct track.

76 metres long and 2 metres high, this long barrow is unusual in having a berm to separate the mound from the side ditches. There are no indications that the barrow has been opened.

45. Scratchbury Camp, Norton Bavant
Iron Age
ST: 912443

Track from A36 to North Farm, steep climb at corner of wood.

Finely sited, this fort of 15 hectares has a single bank and ditch with counterscarp bank. Roughly four-sided, it has three entrances, two in the south-east side and one on the north-west. Inside is a smaller circular earthwork dated to about 350 BC, which may indicate an earlier enclosure as at Yarnbury (no. 63).

Low banks running from the south-west towards the northern gate in the south-eastern side may also be of iron age date. Two barrows lie inside the fort north of this gate, the nearest containing a cremation. Excavation of the large barrow in the south-west corner of the fort failed to produce a burial. There are some four other barrows in the camp, all much flattened. One opened by Cunnington in 1802 contained fifty amber beads and a large amber ring, a bronze dagger and a bronze pin. On the hill below the fort to the west are some strip lynchets.

46. Silbury Hill
Neolithic
SU: 100685

Beside the A4 midway between West Kennet and Beckhampton. Parking and viewing area, but no access to the monument.

Silbury is the largest prehistoric man-made mound in Europe. In shape a truncated cone, it is 40 metres high, its base covers 2 hectares, and its flat top is 30 metres in diameter. The chalk to build the hill was quarried from a ditch which is now largely silted up. The inner side of the ditch had been faced with chalk rubble and deliberately stepped with retaining timbers immediately after digging. This was probably done as a precautionary measure to stop the sides weathering and to prevent the mound above from slipping into the ditch.

A shaft was sunk into the centre of the mound by the Duke of Northumberland in 1776, which may well have destroyed any central burial or other deposit. In 2000 the shaft reappeared when its filling collapsed, offering a new opportunity to examine the hill's structure. In 1849 Dean Merewether drove a tunnel into the heart of the mound from the south side. Excavations by Richard Atkinson between 1968 and 1970 followed Merewether's tunnel and indicated that Silbury was built in four apparently continuous stages. The new tunnel has been sealed by English Heritage.

Silbury 1. A flat circular area about 20 metres in diameter was enclosed by a low wattle fence. In the centre of this a clay mound 4.9 metres in diameter and about 0.9 metre high was constructed. This was covered with turves and soil until it reached out to the fence. Over this were piled layers of gravel, chalk and topsoil until a

Silbury Hill is the largest prehistoric artificial mound in Europe. It may well cover a stone burial chamber. (J. E. Hancock)

primary mound 36 metres in diameter and 5 metres high was completed.

Silbury 2. Almost immediately the original mound was enlarged by capping it with chalk quarried from a surrounding ditch, creating a mound 73 metres in diameter. The ditch was some 21 metres wide, but it was not completed. A change of plan began.

Silbury 3. The mound was again extended to cover the Silbury 2 ditch, and to give a new diameter of about 158 metres. This new mound seems to have been built in a number of stages, producing the effect of a stepped cone. Each stage was constructed with a series of buttress-like dumps of chalk contained within retaining walls. Material came from a surrounding ditch 7 metres deep.

Silbury 4. Finally an extra quarry ditch was dug, west of the main ditch, perhaps to obtain material to fill in the steps of the cone and to give the hill its present-day smooth profile. Radiocarbon samples from the Silbury mound suggest a date around 2500 BC.

As to the purpose of Silbury Hill, there is no record of any burial having ever been found within it, although it has every appearance of being an enormous barrow. As stated above, such a burial might have been destroyed in 1776. If not, and Silbury was a burial mound, then the burial deposit must lie off centre, as in some of the great passage graves of Ireland and Orkney.

The top of Silbury is visible from many of the monuments in the vicinity including the Sanctuary, the East and West Kennet long barrows and the centre of Avebury circle, and it may be seen as the nodal point, linking them all together within a sacred prehistoric landscape. From its summit ceremonies linking earth-bound man and the heavens may well have taken place.

In the nineteenth century cricket matches were played on the flat summit!

47. Snail Down barrow cemetery

Bronze Age
SU: 218522

Approached by tracks leading S from A342. This is Ministry of Defence land, but is occasionally accessible when training (indicated by red flags) is not in progress.

This great semicircle of barrows contained some thirty burial mounds, a number of which were damaged by military activity during the Second World War. A large number of the barrows were examined in 1953–7. One, a disc-barrow, completely excavated in 1953, has been left open to view. The study of the cemetery shows five different types of barrow within the group. Its boundary is marked on the north, west and south by a long V-shaped ditch that separates it from the prehistoric field systems beyond.

48. Stonehenge, Amesbury

Neolithic and Bronze Age
SU: 122422

On the S side of the A344. Car park, toilets, souvenir shop and snack bar N of road. Site entered via subway. English Heritage; admission charge; daily opening times vary according to time of year, closed 24th to 26th December and 1st January. For information telephone: 01980 624715.

More than any other prehistoric site in western Europe, Stonehenge symbolises the skill and ingenuity of early man. A World Heritage Site and England's most famous archaeological monument, it is also its most enigmatic. Not a year passes without another book or television programme theorising about its origins. At the beginning of the twenty-first century we have a rough idea of the monument's development, but some aspects are still far from certain. Whilst this entry concentrates on Stonehenge, we must remember that it is only one component in the vast ritual landscape of Salisbury Plain.

If possible, the site is best approached early in the morning on foot across National Trust land from the north-east, so that it rises ahead on the horizon, grey and stark, or in the evening when the sun is setting in the west behind it. On entering the enclosure, first circle the monument and make for the Heel Stone, the isolated block of sarsen (hard sandstone) that rises 4.9 metres beside the road. This is the only unshaped sarsen at the monument. It was possibly the first stone erected about 2500 BC. It may have been set up to overlook the contemporary Stonehenge Cursus (no. 49), which lies 800 metres north, across the road. Excavation has shown that the Heel Stone originally had a partner standing some 5 metres to its north-west.

Turning your back to the Heel Stone, face the main group of stones. Notice the ditch, internal bank and slighter outer bank that run all round Stonehenge. This earthwork represents the earliest phase of development and dates from about 2950 BC. When half of the circumference of the ditch was excavated by William Hawley in the early 1920s it was found to be made up of very irregular linked segments, the inner edge describing a circle some 55 metres in diameter. The chalk quarried from it was piled up to make the inner bank, which originally stood about 1.8 metres high. It was broken by an 11 metre wide entrance gap on the north-east in front of the Heel Stone, and another 3 metre wide gap on the south. Deposits of already ancient animal bones were placed at the ditch ends.

It has been suggested that a large circular timber building about 30 metres in diameter was set up at the centre of the ditched enclosure. This is far from certain. Hawley, digging in 1924, described 'the ground honeycombed with postholes and craters of all sorts, sizes and depths, many of them having been cut into one another apparently in successive periods of digging'. The centre of the site was badly damaged when the great stones were set up, and by hundreds of years of burrowing animals and subsequent digging by would-be treasure hunters. Consequently any description of 'a building' is purely speculative. Study of the post-holes does seem to support the theory of a narrow avenue of posts leading towards the southern gap

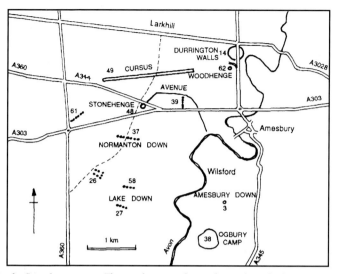

Sites in the Stonehenge area. The numbers are those of sites described in this guide.

through the bank. Finds of scattered human bones within the ditched area during the 1920s excavations might hint that it served as a mortuary enclosure and was used for the exposure of corpses (on posts or platforms) before they were transferred to one of the sixteen nearby neolithic long barrows.

Spread across the north-east entrance of the earthwork Hawley discovered fifty-six postholes arranged irregularly in six rows. These may have been used to mark the changing position of the northern moonrise. Elsewhere in the enclosure five or six larger postholes marked the main stages in an $18\frac{1}{2}$ year lunar cycle.

About 2900 BC a circle of fifty-six roughly spaced pits known as the Aubrey Holes was dug just inside the enclosure bank, their surfaces today marked with white chalk. These pits vary from 0.6 to 1.2 metres deep, and enigmatically they seem to have been refilled soon after they were dug, leaving no sign of what they originally contained. A century or two later small ritual deposits of cremated human bones, flints and one or two bone pins were inserted into the upper filling of most of the holes. Although some twenty-one Aubrey Holes have not yet been excavated it is possible that in total the holes could have contained the remains of more than two hundred people. It was at this stage in its history that Stonehenge can probably be seen as Britain's first cremation cemetery.

About 2600 BC, after a period of neglect, a number of important changes took place at Stonehenge. The width of the north-east entrance was enlarged by filling in part of the ditch. This resulted in a small change to the axis of the monument, aligning it approximately with midsummer sunrise when half the sun's disc was above the horizon, and with midwinter sunset. A small ditch was dug around the Heel Stone, and it was given a companion stone on its western side (later dismantled). A rectangular area was marked out, inside the earthwork bank, and a rough sarsen stone, called a Station Stone, was set up at each corner. The rectangle measured some 80 by 34 metres, with the long sides facing north-east and south-west. Its centre coincided exactly with the centre of Stonehenge. The short sides of the rectangle were approximately aligned on the midsummer sunrise, whilst the longer sides more or less lined up with the most northerly and southerly settings of the moon over its $18\frac{1}{2}$ year cycle.

Part of the outer circle of lintelled stones at Stonehenge. The smaller stones are part of the bluestone circle. (J. Dyer)

About eighty bluestones (spotted dolerite), each weighing about 4 tonnes, were assembled at Stonehenge around 2550 BC. These stones originated in the vicinity of the Preseli Mountains in Pembrokeshire (south-west Wales), but whether they were quarried and transported to the site by man or deposited in the vicinity of Salisbury Plain by glaciation and subsequently dragged to the monument is a subject of fierce debate. Human transportation of so many stones from Wales would have taken years and modern attempts to reconstruct a single journey have been less than successful. The bluestones were set up in pairs in the centre of the enclosure in a semicircle of holes known to archaeologists as the Q and R holes. This was a short-lived arrangement, and the stones were very soon dismantled. A 7 tonne pillar of sandstone, possibly from near Milford Haven, and known today as the Altar Stone, seems to have been left standing, west of the centre at that time.

About 2400 BC major changes took place with the arrival and erection of the great sarsen stone circle that survives today. Some eighty of these sarsen blocks, each weighing about 26 tonnes, were dragged on rollers for 32 km from the Marlborough Downs in north Wiltshire. Each stone, averaging 4 metres in height, was carefully shaped so that the thirty uprights appeared to be of the same size, each bulging slightly in the middle (entasis), perhaps to counteract the effect of perspective. The lintel stones across the top of the uprights are dovetailed into each other and 'mortised and tenoned' to the uprights. These have also been carefully curved on their long sides to make the whole ring of thirty stones into an almost perfect circle. This is the work of people more used to fashioning wood than stone, and yet employing refinements normally found only in classical architecture of the eastern Mediterranean. At the same time that the lintelled circle was being erected the five great trilithons (three stones) were set up inside it. On some of the trilithon and circle stones are carvings of native axeheads and a dagger, reminiscent of similar motifs more commonly found in Brittany during the early bronze age.

The so-called Slaughter Stone and its missing companion were set up on either side of the north-east entrance. Some time later a processional way, now called The

Avenue, was constructed. Marked by two low banks and ditches, and measuring 12.2 metres wide and 3.2 km long, it first ran north-east from Stonehenge, then east and finally south-east towards the river Avon near Amesbury. In 1978 the skeleton of a man, killed by half a dozen arrows tipped with barbed and tanged flint arrowheads about 2250 BC, was found in the ditch of Stonehenge, some 15 metres west of the entrance causeway.

Probably around 2000 BC the bluestones, which had lain idle for many years, were now reused to form an oval setting inside the five trilithons and capped with their own lintels. However, a century later, another change of plan necessitated the modification of this, and the oval became a horseshoe of bluestones without lintels, with a circle of similar stones between the trilithons and the outer sarsen circle. Two rings of pits dug outside the sarsen circle and known to archaeologists as the Y and Z holes seem to have been the final act in the prehistoric history of the site. Whatever they were dug for, they were never used to hold stones. Antler from one of the pits has been radiocarbon-dated to 1600 BC.

Altered and modified over fifteen centuries, there can never have been an overall long-term master plan for Stonehenge that had to be completed. The final monument was an accumulation of many different ideologies and changing beliefs that persisted until at least the middle of the second millennium BC. Since that time the ditches have silted up, and some of the less stable stones have fallen and been removed, perhaps with a little help from the Romans. This destruction process accelerated from the middle ages onwards when Stonehenge became a 'quarry' for local road builders.

Two legends connected with Stonehenge need to be aired. One is the association of the monument with the Druids. This did not begin until it was suggested by John Aubrey in the seventeenth century. As has been said already, Stonehenge developed between about 3000 and 1600 BC. The first Druids, a Celtic priesthood, did not appear in Britain until about 250 BC, well over a thousand years after Stonehenge was completed and by which time some of the stones had fallen down. Modern day 'Druidical rites' performed at Stonehenge are of an entirely spurious nature.

We have seen that the central axis of Stonehenge is aligned on the midsummer sunrise and midwinter sunset. There are indications that the site may have been used for some form of sun and moon observation, perhaps for fixing certain dates in the agricultural year. It should be noticed that the sun does not rise over the Heel Stone on 21st June and never has done. It has always risen some distance to the left and will not rise exactly over the stone until about the thirtieth century AD. It was only at the time when the Heel Stone had a partner that the midsummer sun rose between the two stones.

Objects found in excavations at Stonehenge and an explanatory display can be seen in the excellent Salisbury Museum, located in the Cathedral Close.

49. Stonehenge Cursus, Amesbury

Neolithic and Bronze Age
SU: 124430

Approached along track 800 metres N from Stonehenge car park. National Trust property, with information panels on all the sites.

This remarkable enclosure consists of two roughly parallel banks and ditches, approximately 100 metres apart, running for 2.8 km from east to west. The ditches were 1.8 metres wide and 0.9 metre deep. The western end was closed by bigger banks and ditches. At the eastern end, just beyond the cursus, was a long barrow, now badly damaged. The banks are low, although the ditches were 3 metres deep and 5 metres wide. Thurnam, digging in the nineteenth century, found only an ox skull and two secondary burials. A number of cursuses occur in Britain and are usually close to long barrows, suggesting that they played some part in the funeral ritual, perhaps as ceremonial paths for the spirits of the dead, and that they were built around 3000 BC.

Between the cursus and the A344 is a line of barrows (115428) which includes, from east to west, a bell-barrow, a double bell-barrow, three more bell-barrows and a bowl-barrow. Most of these contained cremation burials and beads of amber, faience, shale and bone. All the existing contents are displayed in Devizes Museum.

50. Thorny Down, Winterbourne
Middle Bronze Age
SU: 203338

About 230 metres N of A30, opposite the turning SE to Winterslow.

This small rectangular enclosure, slightly less than 0.2 hectare in extent, enclosed at least nine huts, which may have been circular or rectangular in plan. Storage pits, cooking holes and posts, perhaps for granaries or corn-drying frames, were contained together with the houses in a low bank, perhaps topped by a hedge, and external ditch. The domestic pottery was predominantly of globular vessels of Deverel-Rimbury type, dating to about 1200 BC.

51. Tidcombe long barrow
Neolithic
SU: 292576

Beside the road from Chute to Oxenwood.

This upstanding long barrow has been badly damaged in the past by the digging of a longitudinal trench through it. Four sarsens in a hollow at the southern end are the remains of a burial chamber which contained a skeleton when dug in 1750 by local folk searching for treasure. A ditch and bank a few metres to the east may represent an iron age cross-dyke.

2.4 km to the north in the wood on Botley Down is another fine long barrow about 64 metres long and 3 metres high with a rectangular robbers' pit at the southern end. Just outside the wood, and only a few metres from the long barrow, is a splendid disc-barrow (294599), with a later ditch cutting its northern side. This barrow, which is about 36 metres in diameter, was excavated by Peake and Crawford in 1910. They found a primary cremation together with a bronze awl and rivet, under the central tump, which had its own surrounding ditch. Also in the barrow was a Saxon skeleton accompanied by a socketed spearhead and a bronze buckle of sixth- or seventh-century date. These barrows are reached from the unmetalled track which runs north–south, west of the wood.

52. Tilshead Old Ditch
Neolithic
SU: 023468

On Ministry of Defence land, 800 metres S of Tilshead Lodge in belt of trees (access only at special times), but clearly visible from the Tilshead to Chitterne road at 021475.

This is probably the longest barrow in Britain, measuring 118 metres in length and 3.3 metres high. It lies roughly east to west along an old boundary ditch and is now being damaged by vehicle tracks over it. It was first excavated by William Cunnington (1802), and later by John Thurnam (1865), who found two burials, one of an adult that had been partially burnt, and the other of a small woman who probably died as the result of a blow which split her skull. The burnt burial lay on a mound of flints and ashes, suggesting some kind of funeral pyre, whilst a cairn of flints covered both burials and the pyre. Three more burials lay at the western end of the barrow: it is not certain whether they belonged to the original build of the barrow or if they were added later.

Another low long barrow lies beside the Tilshead to Chitterne road at 021475, **Tilshead Lodge**. This also contained two skeletons, one with a cleft skull, and the carcases of two slaughtered oxen.

53. Tilshead White Barrow

Neolithic
SU: 033468

Accessible along track from A360. National Trust.

This barrow is still 75 metres long and 2.1 metres high, with well-defined berms and side ditches. Although it was excavated by Sir Richard Colt Hoare and William Cunnington about 1800, only pieces of antler were found. The name *Whitebergh* is recorded as long ago as 1348.

54. Upton Great Barrow, Upton Lovell

Bronze Age
ST: 955423

E of track 1.6 km N of Upton Folly on A36, or 800 metres S from B390 on Ansty Hill.

This bell-barrow, measuring 53 metres in diameter and 3 metres high, is almost all that remains of a group of barrows which produced a number of famous objects when examined by William Cunnington and Richard Colt Hoare in 1801. At its centre was a cremation burial with necklace beads of amber, shale and faience.

30 metres east of the bell-barrow is the slight mound of a former bowl-barrow which contained a cremation with a grooved bronze dagger. The same barrow held a secondary cremation and an enormous urn.

530 metres north-east of the bell-barrow is another small bowl-barrow (958427), now only 0.3 metre high and 9 metres in diameter. It was unusual in containing the skeleton of a man in a chalk-cut grave who had been dressed in a long skin or fur garment, on the edges of which were sewn some sixty perforated bone points. On his chest lay a stone battleaxe, perhaps a symbol of his authority. Also in the grave were some stone rubbers, four marcasite cups and four flint axes.

The 'Golden Barrow', which lay south of Upton Lovell (944401), is now destroyed. The gold objects that it contained, together with the rest of the material from the Upton Lovell barrows, are in Devizes Museum.

55. West Kennet long barrow, Avebury

Neolithic
SU: 104677

Clearly signposted footpath S from A4, 400 metres E of Silbury Hill. Torch required.

This is one of the most impressive chambered long barrows in England. Its mound of chalk, over a core of sarsen boulders, is 100 metres long and 2.4 metres high. The chalk was quarried from two great flanking ditches that were originally 3 metres deep and 6 metres wide. Tucked into the eastern end of the barrow is an accessible burial chamber 12 metres long, with two pairs of transepts and an end chamber.

The first record of digging at West Kennet dates from about 1685, when Dr Toope of Marlborough seems to have come to the barrow to dig for human bones 'and stored myself with many bushells, of which I made a noble medicine that relieved many of my distressed neighbours'. In the autumn of 1859 John Thurnam cleared the west chamber and 4.5 metres of passage. In the chamber he found five adult male burials and that of an infant, as well as pieces of neolithic Peterborough ware and beaker pottery.

In 1955–6 Professors Stuart Piggott and Richard Atkinson began large-scale excavations, which produced four intact burial chambers that had been missed by the earlier diggers. They were also able to discover the original layout of the tomb's entrance. Subsequently the then Ministry of Public Building and Works was able to restore the barrow to something like its original appearance.

When first constructed the tomb had been entered from a semicircular forecourt of sarsen stones. This led into a roofed passage which ran down the centre of the barrow. On either side were the large north-east and south-east burial chambers. The gaps between the sarsen wall stones were filled in with panels of drystone. The roof of each chamber is roughly corbelled and then capped with massive roof stones, 2.3 metres above the floor. As well as a number of odd human bones, the north-east chamber

The interior of the West Kennet long barrow during restoration. (J. Dyer)

contained three more or less complete adult human burials, one with a flint arrowhead close to its throat. The south-east chamber also had a scatter of odd bones, which included single male and female adult burials and five children of between three and seven years, four babies under two years of age and a foetus of five or six months.

The south-west and north-west chambers were smaller, with lower capstones. All the bones contained in them were scattered and mixed with soil and pottery. The remains of about twelve adults were represented in the north-west chamber, and three men and two women in the south-west, as well as parts of other adults and children. Altogether it would seem that the whole tomb contained at least forty-six individuals. From these a number of skulls and long bones were missing.

It is interesting to consider why the burials became so disordered. There is evidence to show that the tomb remained open for something like a thousand years (compare the age of Westminster Abbey as a place of burial and worship). During this time new burials may have been made from time to time, the old ones being swept to one side. Perhaps, too, the tomb was sometimes raided for skulls or long bones for use as 'relics' or for some other ritual purpose. When burial finally ceased at the tomb, each chamber was filled to the roof with chalk rubble, mixed with charcoal, pieces of pottery, flint and beads. The pottery of Peterborough, grooved and beaker wares spans a period of some hundreds of years, and it has been suggested by the excavators that it originally lay in some kind of nearby mortuary temple to which it had been brought from time to time as offerings to the dead. From there it was collected up and deposited in the chambers and passages, filling them to the roof. The great blocking stones were then set across the entrance to the tomb and forecourt, sealing it off completely. Dating suggests that the tomb was built around 3600 BC but not finally sealed until about 2200 BC.

The visitor must remember that the present entrance to the tomb is one of convenience only. The great 3.6 metres high central blocking stone has been placed in its original position to give an indication of the final appearance of the tomb. It is worth noticing that on the entrance stone of the south-west chamber are two or three areas worn smooth by polishing stone axes, perhaps at a time during the construction of the tomb when timber would have been required as rollers to move the stones.

Visitors may find a torch helpful when visiting the tomb although it has modern roof lights. The objects from the 1859 and recent excavations, as well as models and photographs, are well displayed in Devizes Museum.

56. Whitesheet Castle, Stourton

Iron Age
ST: 804346

From Long Lane, 1.6 km W of the B3095, or by track 2.4 km N from here.

Roughly triangular, this fort of 6 hectares is surrounded by a single bank and ditch on the south and west, which become three banks and ditches facing the plateau on the north and east. A number of gaps break this triple defence, but which of them are original is uncertain.

57. White Sheet Hill, Kilmington

Neolithic and Bronze Age
ST: 802352

Access via Long Lane from either the B3092 near Stourton, or the B3095 1.6 km N of Mere. Situated at bend of lane on W spur of hill. Not to be confused with neighbouring hillfort (no. 56).

This neolithic camp was first recognised by L. V. Grinsell in 1950. It consists of an oval-shaped earthwork of about 1.6 hectares, whose bank is interrupted at irregular intervals by twenty-one causeways of undug chalk. Excavation in 1951 showed that the ditch was about 3 metres wide with a depth that varied from 0.3 to 1.3 metres. On the bottom were pieces of Windmill Hill pottery and the skull of a small ox.

A bronze age bowl-barrow overlies the ditch of the camp on the south-east side. Although it has been opened on a number of occasions there is no clear information about it.

58. Wilsford barrow cemetery

Bronze Age
SU: 118398

In a wood to the W of the green road from Stonehenge which leads S to Springbottom Farm and Lake Bottom.

This group of eighteen barrows has been badly damaged by farm activities. All except one of the disc-barrows have been almost flattened. Only that on the south side of the group survives, and that is so overgrown that it is impossible to see if it has one or two central mounds. There is no record of its contents. The plough has similarly obliterated the only saucer-barrow. The bell-barrow at the western end of the group survives. It is 45 metres in diameter with a central mound 3.5 metres high. In it was found the skeleton of a man lying on his right side holding a greenstone battleaxe. Beside him were a bronze axe and a bone musical instrument, as well as a metal handle (or possibly part of a ceremonial bronze standard).

To the east of the bell-barrow are four bowl-barrows in a row. There is no record of the contents of the first (western). The second contained a primary skeleton burial and a cremation buried with two whetstones. The third bowl-barrow also produced no result. In the fourth, still 1.8 metres high, lay a skeleton with a long-necked beaker. Next in line was a pond-barrow 28 metres in diameter. We do not know what it contained. The adjoining bowl-barrow is 1 metre high and 12 metres in diameter. A cremation accompanied by a small flanged axe, a bone pin and a ring was covered by a large cairn of flints, on top of which was the skeleton of a dog. The last bowl-barrow in the row (and the most easterly) held two cremations in one grave pit, one in an urn, the other with a burnt bronze dagger.

59. Windmill Hill, Winterbourne Monkton

Neolithic
SU: 087714

2.4 km due N of Beckhampton crossroads, via minor road from Avebury Trusloe. Cars can approach to within 1.2 km.

Three approximately concentric rings of causewayed ditches ring a low hilltop, a little less than 2.4 km north-west of Avebury. This is the largest causewayed enclosure yet recognised in England. It has an area of 8.5 hectares, and its outer ditch has a diameter of some 360 metres. The mean diameter of the middle ditch is 200 metres, whilst the inner measures about 85 metres. The ditches do not lie round the summit of the hill but tend to hang lop-sidedly down the steeper northern slope.

All the sections of the ditch are very irregular. Apart from having flattish bottoms, there are no other similarities. Depth and width vary from area to area and it gives every appearance of having been the work of many separate groups of workmen. The causeway gaps between ditch sections can vary from a few centimetres to 7 metres. It has been generally observed that the outer ditch sections are largest and deepest, whilst the inner ring is made up of smaller, shallower sections.

The material from the ditches was piled up to form inner banks. Only on the eastern side of the outer circle can this now be seen. For the rest it has been ploughed away or can be deduced only from the ditch silting.

Windmill Hill was the first of the causewayed enclosures to be systematically excavated between the world wars, by Alexander Keiller, and to be interpreted and published by Dr Isobel Smith in 1965. More recent work took place in 1988. Almost all the material found is in the Avebury museum.

The site has given its name to some of the earliest round-based, baggy pottery to be found in southern Britain. The enclosure was constructed about 3300 BC, but it is known that an open settlement existed from at least 3700 BC. The purpose of the site is obscure. Apart from domestic settlement, it may also have acted as a trading centre, where pottery and axes were exchanged. Many bones of farm animals suggest herding and slaughtering for ceremonial purposes, and human cadavers may have been exposed as at Hambledon Hill, Dorset, prior to burial in a long barrow.

In the middle ditch enclosure on Windmill Hill is a fine bell-barrow known as **Picket Barrow** (086713). It is 24 metres in diameter and stands 2.4 metres high. When the ditch was cleaned out in 1939 it was found to contain a number of stone axes. On its summit a secondary bronze age urn of about 1800 BC was brought to light by a rabbit, though nothing is known of the other material from the barrow. There is also a bowl-barrow within the enclosure, some 9 metres in diameter and 1.8 metres high. Outside and to the east are two further bowl-barrows and, a little further down the hillslope, two ploughed-down saucer-barrows, one of which seems to have contained a crouched skeleton, and the secondary burial of a child's unburnt bones in a bronze age urn.

60. Winklebury Camp, Berwick St John
Iron Age
ST: 952218

Above Berwick St John, tracks climb the hill on the E and W.
An unfinished promontory fort of 5 hectares was protected by two lines of rampart and ditch, separated from each other by a wide entrance gap. Later, perhaps about 250 BC, a new rampart and ditch were begun around the edge of the spur. These were never completed, and it is still possible to see dumps of unused material. Much later, around 50 BC, the fort was reduced considerably in size by isolating the northern tip of the spur with a curved rampart and ditch. There is an entrance near the eastern end of this rampart, and also at the northern extremity of the spur.
Excavations by Pitt-Rivers in 1881–2 found storage pits of both the early iron age and the first century BC.

61. Winterbourne Stoke crossroads
Neolithic and Bronze Age
SU: 101417

Lay-by E of the roundabout at the junction of the A303 and A360; barrows ranged along NW side of wood. Nos. 2 to 10 are National Trust property.

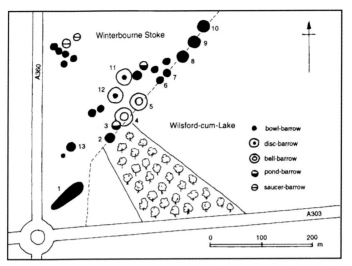

Winterbourne Stoke crossroads barrow group. Entry is through the plantation beside the A303.

Round barrows stretch north-east in two lines from the neolithic long barrow closest to the crossroads.

1. The long barrow is 74 metres long and 3 metres high; it is well preserved with deep side ditches. Thurnam found a primary male skeleton and an unusual flint implement near the north-eastern end in 1863. There were six crouched secondary burials of a man, a woman and four children together with a food-vessel.

North-east from the long barrow, along the edge of the wood, are:

2. A low bowl-barrow which contained a cremation.

3. A pond-barrow which overlaps, and is therefore later than, an adjacent bell-barrow. It does not appear to have been opened. (There is a modern pond south of the pond-barrow, with which it should not be confused.)

4. A fine bell-barrow, 54 metres in diameter and 4 metres high. A wooden box contained a cremation with two daggers, a bone pin and tweezers.

5. A second bell-barrow follows, slightly smaller than no. 4. It contained a skeleton in an elm-trunk coffin, with an urn of Breton type, two bronze daggers and a bronze awl with a wooden handle.

6. The first of five bowl-barrows stands 1.8 metres high and held a central cremation buried under a pile of flints.

7. A small bowl-barrow whose contents are not recorded.

8. 24 metres in diameter and 1.5 metres high, this bowl-barrow was built for a primary burial which was disturbed when a later cremation was added to the mound. A grape cup and incense cup, two whetstones and a bronze awl were amongst the grave goods. The bones of a dog and a deer were found in the covering mound.

9. This bowl-barrow held a skeleton in a boat-shaped wooden coffin, shale and amber beads, a bronze dagger and small pottery cup.

10. The last bowl-barrow in the immediate group held two primary inhumations and a long-necked beaker.

There are more barrows further along the field boundary, but space does not permit description. Returning to the two bell-barrows already described (nos. 4 and 5) and using them as an observation point, one can see to the north-west two fine disc-barrows.

11. The northern disc-barrow is 53 metres in diameter and has three small tumps or

grave mounds in it. The central one covered a cremation burial with amber beads and a small cup. The others also covered cremations, one with beads.

12. The southern disc-barrow is similar in size and covered a cremation.

13. The bowl-barrow to the south, near the road, held a cremation and a small pottery vessel.

62. Woodhenge, Amesbury

Neolithic
SU: 150434

On slip road to Larkhill, to W of A345, 1.6 km N of Amesbury.

This was one of the first major cropmark sites to be discovered by aerial photography in Britain. It was photographed by Squadron Leader Insall in June 1926 and excavated later that year by Maud and Ben Cunnington of Devizes Museum.

The site consisted of six ovals of concentric posts surrounded by a ditch with an outer bank. It has been suggested that the structure was roofed to form a large circular building, but it is more probable that it was open to the sky like a wooden 'Stonehenge' – as the name given to the site by the Cunningtons implies.

The enclosing ditch, which was dug around 2200 BC, was irregular in shape, but averaged 2 metres deep and 3.5 to 6 metres wide. Its internal diameter was about 52 metres. It was broken by an entrance causeway in the north-eastern side, about 10 metres wide, and approximately facing midsummer sunrise. A male skeleton lay on the ditch bottom on the eastern side. The material from the ditch had been piled outside to form a bank.

Inside the enclosure were six concentric rings of posts (their positions marked today by concrete pillars), all of which need not have been contemporary. Within the inner ring of posts was the grave of a child of about three years who may have died from a blow to the skull. The skeleton, which was stored in London, was lost during the Second World War, and the cause of death cannot now be checked. The position of the grave is marked by a cairn of stones.

The site has produced neolithic grooved-ware pottery and later beaker pottery, suggesting an occupation of at least two hundred years from 2200 to 2000 BC. The material excavated is now in Devizes Museum.

Woodhenge must be seen in relation to the neighbouring Durrington Walls henge (no. 14) with its internal timber circles, which were interpreted as buildings.

63. Yarnbury Castle, Steeple Langford

Iron Age
SU: 035404

N of the A303, 3.2 km W of Winterbourne Stoke. Modern farm track runs into site on S.

An upstanding circular earthwork on level ground enclosing some 10.5 hectares. This splendid fort is surrounded by two banks 7.5 metres high and deep ditches, with traces of a third, slighter outer defence. The inside of the inner bank is pitted with what appear to be quarry scoops. There is a strong inturned entrance on the east, 9 metres wide, with elaborate outworks including a kidney-shaped enclosure which forces the entrance passage south and east. The entrance on the south side is modern. Inside the fort are traces of an earlier 3.6 hectare enclosure which has been shown by excavation to have a V-shaped ditch 2.7 metres deep and an entrance on its western side that had been closed by a wooden gate. A small triangular enclosure of Roman date was added to the outside of the fort on the west.

From the eighteenth century until 1916 an annual sheep fair was held inside the fort. The sheep-pens have left rectangular ridge-traces on the eastern side of the central enclosure.

WORCESTERSHIRE
(Map on page 236)

1. Bredon Hill, Bredon's Norton
Iron Age
SO: 957401

Footpaths from Bredon's Norton or Elmley Castle, both 3 km.

A promontory fort with superb views to the Vale of Evesham. Two separate lines of ramparts and ditches defend the northern spur of the hill enclosing 9 hectares. Elsewhere sheer slopes afford natural protection. The excavations of Mrs T. C. Hencken in 1935–7 have been reinterpreted by A. H. A. Hogg. He suggests that the outer defences, consisting of a drystone wall with a rock-cut V-shaped ditch outside, were probably built first, around 300 BC. Long inturned entrances existed at either end of this wall, though they are now largely missing, owing to landslides. The inner rampart, perhaps built about 150 BC, is made of dumped clay in a glacis style. It also had a V-shaped ditch. At the centre of the inner rampart is an entrance which showed three periods of construction. In its final state it formed an inturned passage 30 metres long and 7.5 metres wide, with a strong gateway at the inner end, and a bridge halfway along carrying a rampart walk. Early in the first century AD the fort was attacked, perhaps by a Belgic war party, and the inner gateway was burned down, carrying with it, as it fell, a number of skulls – probably trophies – set on poles above it. Around the gate more than fifty skeletons were found hacked to pieces. Mainly young men, they suggest a last desperate stand by the inhabitants.

2. Conderton Camp
Iron Age
SO: 972384

Via minor road and trackway (at 967377) leading NE from Conderton.

A small 1.2 hectare hillfort set on a spur with steep slopes on all sides but the north and commanding wide views of the Cotswolds to the south-east. Excavations suggest a two-phase construction. Around 300 BC a roughly oval bank and ditch with entrances at the north and south were built as a cattle enclosure. In the first

Reconstruction of one of the iron age huts from Conderton Camp at the Avoncroft Museum, Stoke Prior, near Bromsgrove. (Peter Reynolds)

century BC a bank was thrown across the spur inside the original earthwork, isolating 0.8 hectare to the north. The bank was drywalled on the south and had no ditch. It was provided with an inturned entrance. The south area probably still served as a cattle enclosure. The north area became the site of a village consisting of a group of circular huts with associated storage pits. The north inturned entrance was reconstructed, its inturns lined with drywalling. Later it was blocked off with another drystone wall. Finds from the site indicate that it was abandoned before the Roman occupation. A reconstruction of one of the Conderton Camp huts can be seen at the Avoncroft Museum of Buildings at Stoke Prior, near Bromsgrove.

3. Gadbury Bank, Eldersfield

Iron Age
SJ: 793316

Immediately S of B4208 800 metres NW of Eldersfield.
   A single bank and ditch defend a level area, partly tree-covered, 4 hectares in extent, on top of an isolated knoll. An original inturned entrance exists at the north-east.

4. Garmsley Camp, Stoke Bliss

Iron Age
SO: 620618

On a footpath from the B4214 at Bank Street, W to Sallings Common.
   An oval hillfort of 3.6 hectares, defended by a single rampart, ditch and counterscarp. The rampart is specially strong on the west where the ground slopes uphill. An inturned entrance follows a hollow on the western side, and there was another, also inturned, at the north-east.

5. Woodbury Hill, Great Witley

Iron Age
SO: 749645

Immediately W of B4197, 1.6 km S of Great Witley.
   An impressive bank, ditch and counterscarp bank protect a figure-of-eight-shaped area enclosing 10 hectares. A possible inturned entrance can be seen at the north-west.

6. Wychbury Hill Camp, Hagley

Iron Age
SO: 920818

Approached from a track N from A456 at 925813.
   This triangular fort of 9.2 hectares is situated on a west-facing spur of the Clent Hills. The natural steepness of the hill adds to the strength afforded by the three banks and two ditches on the south and the single rather slight bank on the even steeper north side. There are strongly inturned entrances at the east and west corners. On the south side of the fort is an annexe which may have been a cattle pound.

YORKSHIRE: EAST RIDING
(Map on page 243)

1. Arras barrow cemetery, Market Weighton

Iron Age
SE: 930413

Group is bisected by A1079(T) from Market Weighton to Beverley SE of Arras.
   This once large barrow cemetery opened in 1815, and formerly containing over a hundred round barrows, has now been almost totally destroyed: only three mounds can still be seen. All were small – up to 9 metres across and 1 metre high – and all excavated examples contained single inhumations with a few personal ornaments, usually crouched in pits with heads to the north or south. A number of the barrows were in square enclosures 9 to 12 metres across formed by ditches about 2 metres wide and 1 metre deep.
   Four graves in the cemetery were particularly noteworthy. One called the Lady's Barrow contained a female skeleton with an iron mirror and the dismantled remains of a cart and trappings. The King's Barrow also contained a cart and two horses laid

around the extended skeleton of an old man. A third mound, the Charioteer's Barrow, held a skeleton, cart and a bronze shield boss. A female skeleton in the fourth, Queen's Barrow, wore a necklace of almost a hundred blue and white glass beads, an amber ring, two bronze armlets, a bronze pin, a gold finger ring, a bronze brooch and pendant both decorated with white coral, and a pair of bronze tweezers.

Since the 1970s a number of other cart burials have been found in the East Riding of Yorkshire, as well as hundreds of square-ditched barrows, revealed by aerial photography. They seem to define the territory of a particular tribe, perhaps the Parisi, who adopted a burial rite found in north-east France.

2. Callis Wold barrow cemetery
Bronze Age
SE: 830555 (centre)
To the E and W of the minor road from Millington to its junction with the A166.

A rather scattered barrow group, originally consisting of eighteen mounds all now damaged by the plough. They were opened between 1860 and 1892 by J. R. Mortimer. At 829556 a barrow covered a crouched inhumation with a food-vessel and stone battleaxe. The mound had been built over the remains of two concentric rings of wooden stakes 6.5 and 8.5 metres across; the surrounding ditch was 30 metres in diameter.

The mound at 825569 contained two collared urns, side by side, containing cremations and jet and faience beads.

Other mounds in this gradually accumulated group covered beakers, food-vessels, collared urns, a fine jet necklace and inhumation and cremation burials.

3. Dane's Dyke, Flamborough
Iron Age
SE: 216694 (S)
The Dyke begins on Bempton Cliffs on the N at 214730. It crosses the B1229 and B1259 and finishes above Sewerby Rocks at 126694.

This pre-Roman defensive earthwork is 4 km long. Running north to south, it cuts off the peninsula, 8 sq km in extent, from coast to coast. It consists of a massive bank, 6 metres high in places, and a west-facing ditch 18 metres across, with a counterscarp bank.

Reconsideration of an excavation by Augustus Lane Fox (Pitt-Rivers) in October 1879 suggests that the rampart was originally revetted with turves. The site may have protected a large iron age *oppidum* or defended a beach-head. Herman Ramm suggested that it could even have been a beach-head for the sixth-century AD landing of Ida, the first Anglian king of Bernicia, at Flamborough before he moved north to Bamburgh.

4. Dane's Graves, Kilham and Nafferton
Iron Age
SE: 018633
Via minor road from Kilham leading E to junction with B1249. Take track S at 015643. The barrows are in a group on the W of the track, many in a plantation. They are very overgrown.

Once consisting of perhaps four hundred barrows, this cemetery has been reduced to about two hundred by extensive farming operations. The mounds average 3 to 9 metres in diameter and up to 1 metre high; some have surrounding ditches. As at Arras, the burials were crouched inhumations in pit-graves, some with jewellery and food offerings (usually of pork), brooches, pins, armlets and beads. One grave contained a dismantled cart and its trappings and the skeletons of two men.

5. Kilham long barrow
Neolithic
TA: 056673
Immediately W of the minor road from Kilham to Thwing.

This much denuded mound, orientated north-east to south-west, was dug in the nineteenth century and in 1965–9. The more recent excavations revealed two parallel ditches 36 metres and 42 metres long and 7 metres apart. These were half-filled with silt, when a trapezoidal mortuary enclosure of upright timbers was set up, some 58 metres long, 8.5 metres wide at the south-western end, and 11 metres wide at the north-eastern end. There were entrances at either end of this enclosure, and an avenue of posts led north-east for at least 18 metres. Inside the north-eastern end of the enclosure was a burial chamber constructed of earth and timber in which Canon Greenwell seems to have found the remains of two burials in 1868. Outside the enclosure, quarry ditches were dug on either side, at first only at the south-western end. The chalk derived from the ditches was piled into the western end of the enclosure. The timber walls of the enclosure then appear to have been burnt, after which the remainder of the barrow mound was constructed at the eastern end. All this seems to have happened by about 3470 BC.

Some time later, in the bronze age, two crouched burials accompanied by food-vessels were added to the barrow, one under a circular mound that had been added to the south-western end of the long barrow. A ring ditch was also dug 18 metres east of the long barrow, over the avenue of posts. It probably surrounded a round barrow, long since destroyed. At its centre were pits containing a collared urn and food-vessel.

6. Rudston cult centre   Neolithic
                                                                    TA: 099658

Although little is visible on the ground today, in neolithic times Rudston was clearly a cult centre of great importance. Around the village are at least three cursuses, only visible as cropmarks, except at 099658 where there remains the clearly seen squared-off end of one of the sites, its bank still 1 metre high from the outside. Canon Greenwell found the remains of half a dozen adults and children in the bank when he dug into it in 1869, believing it to be a long barrow.

In the nineteenth century two earthen long barrows were also recorded, but they have since been destroyed. The most impressive feature is the monolith in the churchyard at Rudston (097677): a massive block of gritstone from Cayton Bay,

Willie Howe, a huge tree-covered neolithic round barrow at Thwing in East Yorkshire. (S. W. Feather)

some 16 km to the north. This is the tallest single standing stone in Britain, being 7.7 metres high, 1.8 metres wide and 0.8 metre thick. It was probably slightly taller when first set up, but the top appears to have been broken, perhaps by weathering or lightning. There is a second, smaller gritstone monolith on the north-east side of the churchyard. Close by, two cists constructed of sandstone slabs were moved to the churchyard, after they were excavated by Greenwell in a barrow on Rudston Wold, 2.4 km south of the church, in 1869.

7. Towthorpe Plantation, Fimber

Bronze Age

SE: 879629 (centre)

A green track leads E from B1248 at 879638. The line of barrows follows this track.

This cemetery is staggered along the green track from Aldro to Sledmere, suggesting the existence of a former prehistoric trackway here. At 879638, alongside the B1248, is a barrow about 40 metres across and 3.6 metres high when opened by J. R. Mortimer in 1870. A central grave contained an extended adult skeleton with a fine 'Wessex' type bronze dagger-blade, a perforated stone battleaxe and a flint knife. The mound also contained the cremation of a child, originally in a wooden box. The barrow at 885641, originally 2.4 metres high, seems to have contained a wooden burial chamber. The primary burial was a crouched skeleton with a bronze dagger-blade, also of Wessex type. Further barrows opened by Mortimer in this linear group have revealed inhumations with beakers, food-vessels and flint tools.

8. Willie Howe, Thwing

Neolithic

TA: 063724

Via minor road from Burton Fleming to Wold Newton. A track at 064725 leads to the barrow S of the road.

This round barrow measures 37 metres in diameter and is 7.5 metres high. It is covered with trees. It was opened by Lord Londesborough in 1857 and Canon Greenwell thirty years later. It contained a central pit, rectangular in shape and 3.7 metres deep. Filled with successive layers of earth and chalk, fragments of animal bone and chippings of flint, it failed to produce any burials. In all probability these still remain to be discovered.

YORKSHIRE: NORTH

(Map on page 243)

1. Acklam Wold cemetery

Bronze Age

SE: 796620 (centre)

NW and SE of minor road leading E from Acklam.

This group of plough-damaged round barrows originally numbered seventeen or more, but many have been sadly denuded by intensive farming. The most interesting ones included one at 802620 where a crouched skeleton had two pairs of jet buttons at its feet, perhaps originally securing leggings. The barrow at 795622 covered six or more inhumations, one with a fine flat bronze dagger-blade 12.7 cm long. The barrow at 794624 contained four skeletons: two men, a woman and child. One of the men was accompanied by a beautiful white flint dagger 18.5 cm long, a jet ring and an amber button.

The other mounds also contained burials by inhumation and cremation.

2. Blakey Topping, Allerston

Bronze Age

SE: 873934

Via bridlepath to Newgate Foot E of A169 at 853939.

The remains of this stone circle are on the south-west side of Blakey Topping and consist of three stones and depressions showing where others once stood. The surviving stones are 2 metres high, and the circle was once about 15 metres in diameter.

3. Boltby Scar Camp
Iron Age
SE: 506857

1 km W of minor road leading N from Dialstone House, N of the A170.

This promontory fort is defended on the west side by a steep cliff. On the east are the badly damaged remains of a rampart some 2 metres wide and 1 metre high, with a rough-cut outer ditch. These earthworks enclose about 1 hectare. No entrance has been identified. A pair of beaker-period gold basket earrings were found beneath the ramparts but need not be contemporary with the fort, since two round barrows stood inside the defences. One of these barrows, which contained a cremation in a collared urn, still survives, together with a small rectangular enclosure of uncertain date.

4. Bradley long cairn, Bradleys Both
Neolithic
SE: 009476

Take minor road N from Kildwick to Low Bradley. Park by plantation on left and follow line of field wall up hillside to summit. Cairn is on left-hand side of wall.

This damaged long cairn is 70 metres long, 15 metres wide at its eastern end, and almost 2.4 metres high at this point. In plan it resembles a long parallel bank or 'tail' leading from a circular eastern cairn. At 18 metres from the east end is a large megalithic cist, originally containing a few burnt bones. Under the paving stones on the cist floor were a few unburnt human remains. Upright stones in the mass of the cairn suggested traces of a vestigial passage or façade. 30 metres to the south is a round cairn 30 metres across and 1.8 metres high.

5. Bransdale long cairn
Neolithic
SE: 607967

Take unfenced road S from Cockayne to footpath at 613966. A further path leading N off the first passes the cairn.

This long cairn has a north to south orientation. It is 16 metres long, and 7.5 metres wide at its southern end where it still stands 1.2 metres high. It is composed of large boulders and has suffered considerable disturbance in the past.

6. Castle Steads, Gayles
Iron Age
NZ: 112075

Take minor road SW from Dalton. A track leads SW off this to the hillfort at 109079.

This strongly protected Brigantian hillfort combines powerful natural and artificial defences. It lies on a steep-sided spur between two streams. Its defences comprise a stone-built rampart, ditch and counterscarp bank enclosing about 1.6 hectares but now badly preserved.

7. Castleton Rigg, Westerdale
Bronze Age
NZ: 682041

Immediately W of the unfenced road from Hutton-le-Hole to Castleton.

Two earthworks cut across a long narrow spur; the southern one, High Stone Dyke, has the remains of a close-set wall running along the top of the bank. Both banks were originally stone-faced. Within the spur defended by the banks are traces of huts, fields and cairns.

8. Cleave Dyke system
Iron Age
Various (see below)

A series of linear banks and ditches stretches intermittently from north to south for 9 km parallel to the western scarp of the Hambledon Hills, from Sutton Bank almost to Steeple Cross. Several other dykes lie at right angles to the main system. They all seem to be of broadly iron age date and delimit territorial areas, probably related to the efficient management of agricultural land. Boltby Scar Camp (no. 3) occupies a central position in the system, though it is not directly connected to it. Much of the dyke system is no longer visible on the ground, but good sections can still be seen between the following grid references:

Cleave Dyke – SE: 502896 to 506887; SE: 513840 to 520827; Kepwick Dyke – SE: 489905 to 501911; Steeple Cross Dyke – SE: 494901 to 511902.

9. Danby Rigg

mostly Bronze Age
around NZ: 707060

Spread over the N slopes of Danby Rigg, approached by footpath, the 'Old Wife's Stone Road', S of minor road from Ainthorpe at 707074.

Danby Rigg is a steep-sided moorland spur rising to a plateau 100 metres above the surrounding agricultural land. On the northern slopes of the hill are more than 850 diminutive stone cairns, each about 3 to 5 metres in diameter, together with traces of low, badly damaged ancient field boundaries, all partially covered by peat deposits.

Also in this area, and difficult to find, are at least four (and possibly seven) ring-cairns, including one adjacent to the path across the rigg at about 708065 that contains a standing stone some 1.8 metres high in its western sector. Excavations by Anthony Harding in 1986–9 found no evidence to show that it was once part of a stone circle. Canon J. C. Atkinson dug in the centre of this cairn in 1863 and found two inverted collared urns and cremated bones. Two other ring-cairns lie in a line 120 metres and a further 136 metres south of this cairn.

Running east to west along a break of slope on the moor is a cross-ridge dyke or boundary bank, with a large gap in the centre. Although badly damaged, the dyke still stands 1 metre high in places, and between 2 and 4 metres wide. There are traces of a ditch on the south side. The eastern section runs for 157 metres, whilst that on the west is 100 metres long. The gap in between is 75 metres wide, possibly left by the dyke builders in respect for an earlier oval barrow that stands at its centre. The dyke is probably of early bronze age date.

A single prominent round barrow mound (at about 712063) was excavated in 1955 and found to have been previously disturbed. It still contained a cremation burial together with pieces of two food-vessels, a collared urn, a pygmy cup, part of a copper alloy knife and a flint fabricator. Another large mound 250 metres north-east of the barrow is a slag heap.

Some 600 metres south of the cross-ridge dyke the end of the plateau is marked by the Triple Dykes. Between them are noticeably fewer cairns. The cairns on the rigg seem to have been stone clearance heaps on marginal agricultural land, in use some time during the middle bronze age. Amongst the cairns are badly eroded stretches of field banks that form no obvious pattern but were probably part of the same agricultural system.

About half way across this area is a circular 'earthwork', possibly a settlement enclosure or very large ring-cairn, about 20 metres in diameter. This may be the ring-cairn opened by Canon Atkinson in 1863, in which he found a central pit '6 feet in diameter and 4 in depth, partly quarried out of the rock. This was filled with loose stones of no great size, but which had been disturbed at some former period and the deposit – for no doubt there had been one – had been removed, and the stones thrown back into the rifled cavity.' Elsewhere Atkinson refers to finding burnt human bones in the bottom of the pit. Re-excavation in 1956 failed to find any trace of the pit, or any conclusive evidence to suggest a settlement. Since such settlement enclosures of Danby type are exceedingly rare on the North York Moors, a ring-cairn is perhaps the better option!

The Triple Dykes mark the southern end of the archaeological sites on the spur,

One of the three megaliths, the Devil's Arrows, at Boroughbridge. (S. W. Feather)

and lie at a point where the ground begins to rise markedly once more. They run in two lengths from north-west to south-east. The north-western section consists of three banks and two ditches and is about 200 metres long. That at the south-east has two banks and one ditch and runs for 120 metres. The banks still stand about a metre high. Both stretches were built at right angles to the escarpment and converge on each other at an angle marked by a gap some 20 metres wide. A date in the late bronze age might seem logical for these dykes, but radiocarbon dates obtained during Harding's excavations in 1986 suggested that they were constructed in the eleventh century AD, perhaps by Viking settlers.

Visitors should note that bracken tends to obscure many of the smaller features on Danby Rigg, particularly in high summer.

10. Devil's Arrows, Boroughbridge   Bronze Age
SE: 391666

Best approached from the village. The monoliths are situated between Boroughbridge and the A1(T). They can be clearly seen from the latter.

Three large naturally shaped standing stones, almost in a straight line north to south, 60 and 112 metres apart. They have heights of 5.5 metres (north), 6.4 metres and 6.9 metres (south) and are of millstone grit quarried from Knaresborough 10 km to the south-west. Grooves at the top of the stones have been caused by weathering. They are probably related to the Thornborough–Cana–Hutton Moor henge complex (nos. 23 and 33). The sixteenth-century antiquaries Leland and Camden recorded the existence of further stones here at the time they wrote.

11. Duggleby Howe, Kirby Grindalythe   Neolithic
SE: 880669

Immediately E of the B1253 Duggleby to Sledmere road, S of Duggleby.

One of the biggest prehistoric round barrows in Britain, this spectacular example is 38 metres across and 6 metres high, although the original height was over 9 metres. Excavated by J. R. Mortimer in 1890, the barrow consisted of a chalk mound covered by a layer of clay and an outer chalk capping. In and above a deep grave pit were ten skeletons of adults and children with long bone pins, a flint knife with ground edges and other flints, an antler macehead, a flint axe, a Towthorpe ware bowl and a dozen boar tusks. In the upper part of the mound were twenty-two cremations, three with bone skewer pins. Other cremations found in the mound make a total of fifty-three, although not all the barrow was excavated and more probably exist. The mound was enlarged at an unknown date to take a post-mill.

Aerial photography has revealed that Duggleby Howe stands at the centre of a cropmarked circular enclosure of 10.5 hectares and about 370 metres in diameter. It consists of a wide inner ditch broken by causeways and a narrow outer ditch. Assuming it to be neolithic in date, it is exceeded in size only by the largest Wessex

The massive mound of Duggleby Howe neolithic cairn, Kirby Grindalythe, North Yorkshire. (S. W. Feather)

henges and may well be related to that type of monument.

12. East Ayton long barrow   **Neolithic**
TA: 000864
E of the cart-track from East Ayton N to Irton Moor, alongside plantation.
   This long barrow is 25 metres long and orientated north to south. At the north it is 1 metre high. Within the mound was a cairn surrounded by a kerb of large stones. The rubble on top of the cairn showed signs of burning. Beneath the cairn were two heaps of human bones, each with a flint arrowhead. 20 cm below the barrow surface near the centre was a flat stone, partially covering a few human bones accompanied by five lozenge-shaped flint arrowheads, three flint axes and an adze, two polished-edge knives, two boar's tusks and an antler macehead – a rare example of votive grave goods from this type of site, which is usually sparse in associations.

13. Elbolton Cave, Thorpe   **Neolithic and Bronze Age**
SE: 008616
On E slope of hill 400 metres W of Thorpe.
   This cave provided a temporary shelter for family groups in the later neolithic and early bronze ages. Sherds of Mortlake, food-vessel and collared urn pottery suggest extended occupation; later on, the site was used for burials, and several skeletons have been found.

14. Eston Nab Camp   **Iron Age**
NZ: 567183
Footpath leads E from Eston at 560186, up the hillside. The fort is to the N at the top of the slope.
   This magnificent D-shaped scarp-edge fort, situated at the northern extremity of the Eston Hills, stands 242 metres above sea level. The main defence consists of a damaged stone bank between 0.75 and 1 metre high, fronted by a silted ditch and discontinuous counterscarp bank. There are a number of gaps through these defences, but the most likely entrance was probably on the eastern side, close to the Napoleonic beacon tower. Excavations have established that the site was first occupied by two successive palisaded enclosures, probably of late bronze age date, with entrances on the east. The enclosures were used for permanent settlement. They occupied only the centre of the later fort. Perhaps as early as the seventh century BC a boulder wall was constructed, some 5 metres wide, enclosing about 1 hectare. The outer face of the wall had been carefully built to display a smooth surface and is still standing some 1.5 metres high. About a hundred years later a clay

The entrance to Elbolton Cave, which has produced burials and domestic remains of the neolithic and bronze ages. (S. W. Feather)

bank, ditch and counterscarp bank were constructed at the front of the boulder wall to form the defences visible today. Post holes found inside the fort and pottery suggest that occupation lasted from the eighth to fifth centuries BC. A small semicircular stone enclosure wall inside the south-eastern side of the main rampart is undated, but likely to be later than the boulder wall. Burnt human bone found during excavations of the fort almost certainly came from a badly damaged bronze age round barrow that once stood on the scarp edge. There are two fine bronze age round barrows 200 metres south of the Nab.

15. Flat Howe and High Bridestones, Eskdale cum Ugglebarnby

Bronze Age
NZ: 855046

Via unfenced minor road leading W from A169 to Grosmont. Flat Howe is to the E of the road, High Bridestones circle to the W.

The Flat Howe round cairn is encircled by a revetment kerb of stones. To the west are two possible stone circles known as the High Bridestones. Both were originally 9 to 12 metres across, but only three stones stand erect in each circle; a few fallen ones also survive. The tallest stone is 2.1 metres high. The circles have outliers, one to the south, and three to the north. It is not impossible that the stones once formed rows rather than circles.

16. Folkton round barrow

Bronze Age
TA: 059778

Track to Folkton Wold Farm off Flixton to Wold Newton minor road at 047776. Path leads S from farm; the barrow is on top of a rise to the E (see Sharp Howes, no. 30).

This small but important mound, some 16 metres in diameter, covered two concentric ditches. Between them was a grave containing the bones of a child, together with a bone pin and three drum-shaped chalk objects, carved with geometric patterns and 10–14 cm in diameter. It has been suggested that they were either solid copies of the miniature incense cups of the period, or chalk idols. Their decoration of chevrons, triangles and lozenges, together with eyebrow, nose and eye motifs, is reminiscent of megalithic art, found in many parts of western Europe. The drums are now in the British Museum, London. Within the inner ditch were the skeletons of four adults and a child on the old ground surface. At the barrow centre a pile of flints covered the bones of a man and woman and a bell beaker, the bones apparently reburied after the removal of the skulls.

17. Gilling long cairn, Gilling East
Neolithic
SE: 603742

In plantation immediately left of minor road leading W from the B1363 from Gilling at 604741.

This long cairn is best seen in winter or spring when bracken growth is low. It is 45 metres long, 12 metres wide and 2.4 metres high at its south-eastern end. It has been damaged by a series of excavation pits along its length, perhaps when it was dug in the nineteenth century. It is constructed of sand, with a stone kerb. An area of stone paving on the old ground surface, suggesting a mortuary enclosure, probably marked the site of the burials, perhaps destroyed by the acid soil. A later cist burial with a food-vessel and flints was inserted into the mound.

18. Grassington
Iron Age
SD: 995655 to SE: 004655

Footpaths lead N from Grassington to the settlement areas.

These sites include the remains of iron age and Roman huts, enclosures and fields. On the highest ground, High Close and Sweetside, are regular rectangular fields 100 to 120 metres long and 22 metres wide with lynchets 1 metre wide separating them. Several associated hut circles can be seen. Elsewhere the fields are smaller and less regular, several enclosing circular and rectangular hut enclosures.

On Lea Green the fields are large and form broad rectangles 60 to 90 metres wide and 150 metres long. Among them are oval and circular hut enclosures 15 to 30 metres across. At the north end of Lea Green is a well-defined 'village' of stone hut circles clustered together inside a rough stone wall. Objects dug up here include iron knives, bronze tweezers and pins, bone pins and a bone spoon, as well as pottery and spindle whorls.

19. Great Ayton cairns
Neolithic, Bronze Age and Iron Age
NZ: 595115 (centre)

Via minor road leading E past Great Ayton station. Footpath leads N at 593110.

This group of cairns and associated hut circles includes an interesting group of monuments at its south-western edge. This consists of a bank 75 metres long and 3 metres wide running north-west from a cairn 15 metres across and 1.5 metres high, similar to the 'tailed' neolithic round cairn at Bradley (West Yorkshire). Beneath this cairn was a stone chamber, the slabs leaning inwards to form a gable. This was empty, but the body of the cairn produced collared urns and a miniature cup. Linked by the cairn on the north is an oval embanked enclosure 27 by 42 metres. South-east of the cairn are two ring cairns, each 6 metres across. One of them produced three cremations grouped round a central pit. The easternmost structure of this group (598114) is a rectangular embanked enclosure with rounded corners and a ditch inside the bank. An entrance exists on the east side. Excavation produced pottery of iron age type in the central area and the footings of a circular stone-walled hut.

20. Hanging Grimston, Thixendale
Neolithic and Bronze Age
SE: 810608 (centre)

To the E and W of the minor road from Leavening to Uncleby Wold.

This barrow group consists of a long barrow and a group of now almost obliterated round barrows. The long barrow (810608) is orientated east to west and was originally 24 metres long and 15 metres wide. Though ploughed over, it is still almost 1 metre high and has flanking ditches 8 metres wide and 1.8 metres deep. Excavation showed that the eastern end had a timber façade. Inside was a burned and collapsed mortuary house dated to *c*.3450 BC. Many animal bones, chiefly pig, and four Grimston-ware bowls were found, but no burials.

Most of the now nearly levelled round barrows produced burials, pottery and artefacts of the early bronze age. At 806613 the central mound of three contiguous barrows covered an internal stone ring 6 metres across, enclosing eleven burials, one cremated, and one with a beaker. One of the four most southerly mounds produced a funeral pyre *in situ*.

21. Hedon Howe, Burythorpe   Neolithic
SE: 784665

Take the minor road W from Langton. Turn left at crossroads (787668). To the right a path leads to the barrow.

When excavated by J. R. Mortimer in 1893, this late neolithic barrow was 15 metres across and 2.4 metres high. It contained five stone cists holding human remains, one central, the others placed round it in cruciform plan. The central one contained three skeletons and a cremation. Pottery from the cists and in the mound included a Grimston-ware bowl, a beaker and a food-vessel together with joints of meat and flint tools. The pottery suggests that the mound was constructed in the transitional late neolithic/early bronze age period and used over a considerable period of time.

22. Helperthorpe long barrow   Neolithic
SE: 963679

Take minor road N from B1253 at 978674. 400 metres along, a narrow road leads left at 975677. The barrow is to the right of this road.

This almost destroyed long barrow lies on an east to west axis. It was 30 metres long and 14 metres across. Side ditches have been identified. Five pits were found by Mortimer in 1868; all were empty, except one near the centre which contained a cremation. Much wood ash was found on the old ground surface, sealed by the mound.

23. Hutton Moor and Cana henges, Hutton Conyers and Marton-le-Moor
Neolithic
SE: 353735 (Hutton)
SE: 361718 (Cana)

Hutton henge reached by access road to Moor House off A61 at 347744. Site is to E of house. For Cana, turn W off A1(T) at 369728 on to minor road. Turn S off this road opposite Marrow Flat. Henge is in the field to the W.

These henges are part of the complex of ritual sites between the Ure and Swale, which include the three Thornborough henges (no. 33) and the ploughed Nunwick (323748) close by. All exist in a corridor only 11 km long. Both Hutton Moor and Cana are similar in dimensions, each measuring about 170 metres across. Both have suffered heavy plough damage. Hutton consists of a circular bank with internal and external ditches and entrances at the north-west and south-east. Cana is similar but its ditches have been ploughed out.

24. Ingleborough Camp, Ingleton   Iron Age
SD: 742745

Take track N from B6255 at 702731. A gradually ascending and steepening footpath leads to the hillfort 4 km from the road. Definitely a trip for enthusiasts!

The tumbled stone ramparts of Ingleborough Camp, the highest hillfort in England. (J. Dyer)

This Brigantian hillfort is the highest in England. It is situated on a level plateau at the top of Ingleborough at 723 metres OD and commands extensive views of the surrounding limestone countryside. The natural crags protecting the summit were reinforced by thousands of blocks of millstone grit, often backed on the inside by similar orthostatic blocks. The rampart is 900 metres long but has been robbed to build a huge and pointless modern cairn. Two possible entrances exist, on the east and at the north-east corner. The latter is more probable. Inside the camp, about twenty circular huts, a few with south-east-facing entrances, are still visible.

25. Ingleby Greenhowe cairns
Bronze Age
NZ: 607033

Above Greenhowe Bank, via track E from Ingleby leading along W edge of Ingleby Moor.

There are four round cairns in this small cemetery. The northern cairn is 14 metres across and 1 metre high. The turf mound may have contained an inhumation destroyed by the acid soil. The next cairn to the south, 11 metres across and 0.6 metre high, covered a ring of stones surrounding a rough cist with a cremation and sherds of a collared urn. The third cairn covered a cremation with urn sherds. The most southerly mound, 15 metres across and 2.4 metres high, is revetted by a stone kerb. A robbed central cist contained burnt bones and urn sherds and was probably covered by some form of wooden canopy represented by four post holes. There was a further cremation in the south-eastern area of the cairn. At 573036, the bulldozing of a mound of naturally bedded shale revealed a skeleton with a beaker in a stone cist, and seven cremations, one with a miniature cup and one with collared-urn sherds.

26. Kepwick long barrow, Over Silton
Neolithic
SE: 492904

Reached via minor road from Hawnby. Turn right at 509877. Barrow is to N of plantation bordering road on left.

This long barrow is situated at over 360 metres OD. It is orientated north-west to south-east and measures 31 metres long, 9 metres wide and 1.2 metres high. Excavations by Greenwell and Rolleston in 1868 uncovered the disarticulated remains of at least two adults and three children, scattered along the axis of the barrow and covered by stones.

27. Loose Howe, Ugthorpe — Bronze Age
NZ: 703008

Via the unfenced moorland road leading N from Rosedale Abbey. It is clearly visible on the right to visitors heading N.

This imposing cairn stands at 430 metres. It is 18 metres across and 2 metres high and was dug by the Elgees in 1937. It had an earth core covered by stones held in by a revetment wall. The primary burial was in an oak-trunk coffin, preserved as at Gristhorpe (in Scarborough Museum), by waterlogging. The corpse was not preserved but had been fully dressed in linen, with leather shoes. It had lain extended on a layer of reeds, rushes and straw, with a straw headrest. Hazel branches and nut husks suggested an autumn burial. A flat bronze dagger-blade lay by the burial, and alongside the coffin in the gravepit was a 2.7 metres long dug-out canoe with a beak-shaped prow and a stern slot for a stabilising board. Both the coffin and its lid had also been designed as canoes. This is surprising, as the nearest navigable water is 5 km away.

East of centre was a cremation in a collared urn with a miniature cup, stone battleaxe, bronze dagger-blade and a crutch-headed pin.

28. Roulston Scar Camp, Hood Grange — Iron Age
SE: 514816

Trackways lead along the spur S from the A170 at 515826 or off the minor road leading N from Kilburn at 514812.

One of the largest and strongest of the north-east Yorkshire promontory forts, the site encloses 21 hectares. Its rampart, which cuts off the south-west spur, is still 3 metres high in places. A ditch exists on the north-east side. A terrace running south-east along the valley is a continuation of the eastern end of the rampart.

29. Scamridge long barrow, Allerston — Neolithic
SE: 892861

Take track from Ebberston N at 891832 along Kirk Dale to Pheasant Hill. The barrow is 800 metres further N, right of plantation.

This long barrow is orientated east to west. It is 50 metres long and about 3 metres high at the eastern end, where it is 16 metres across. Excavations in the nineteenth century revealed the disordered bones of fourteen people lying on a bed of yellow clay in a trench 12 metres long and 1 metre wide down the mound centre. They had been partly burnt by a large fire 12 metres from the eastern end, covered by rubble and limestone boulders. The bones had probably been stored for some time and the skulls seem to have been battered, perhaps prior to burial.

30. Sharp Howes, Folkton — Bronze Age
TA: 049777

Straddling the track to Folkton Wold Farm (see Folkton barrow, no. 16).

Of the six round barrows originally existing in this ragged linear cemetery, one at the east, which contained the skeleton of an old man and a food-vessel, has been destroyed. All were excavated by Canon Greenwell in the nineteenth century. The most southerly is 24 metres across and 2.4 metres high. It was evidently built on a platform of chalk and revetted with chalk slabs covered by earth and a capping of chalk rubble. A central grave contained a female skeleton with a food-vessel. A small mound north-west of the above contained a male skeleton with a flint knife.

There were three other graves, one with a food-vessel, and one also containing a cremation. North-east of this a mound of earth was capped by one of chalk, and held in position by a wall of chalk blocks with an entrance on the south side. Inside were a male skeleton with a food-vessel and an empty grave. Nothing is known of the contents of the barrow to the north-west of this. The most northerly mound of the series contained two cremations: one in a pit with a food-vessel, flint knife and bone pin. A further pit contained a cremation.

31. Stanwick hillfort, Stanwick St John   Iron Age and Roman
Around NZ: 180115

To the E and W of the B6274 and on either side of the Forcett to Aldbrough road. See map on page 224.

This is the largest and most complex iron age monument in northern England. 6.4 km of earthworks enclose some 290 hectares. As a result of his excavations in 1951-2 Mortimer Wheeler suggested a four-phase development of the site, which he attempted to link with the historical stand of Venutius against the Roman invasion between AD 71 and 74. It is now certain from more recent excavations that this was an oversimplification of the evidence. It is clear that the Tofts area, south of St John's church, Stanwick, was occupied as an undefended settlement of stone and timber houses for many years prior to the construction of the major earthworks. These must all have been built within a relatively short time around the middle of the first century AD. Until the full results of the new excavations are published we cannot be more precise.

Much of the earthwork circuit at Stanwick can be easily followed, but in view of the enormous extent of the earthworks, it is perhaps best to concentrate on the defences immediately east of Forcett village at 178123. In Cat Wood, north of the road, English Heritage displays a section excavated by Wheeler across the flat-bottomed ditch, cut into solid rock, 5 metres deep and 12 metres wide, with a reconstructed earth and rubble bank faced by a drystone wall. On the south side of the road, at the same grid point, one rampart can be seen heading towards Forcett church, whilst another runs south-east for 130 metres before stopping at the original north-west entrance gap in the earthwork known as Maiden Gill. An iron age roadway had existed here before the earthworks were constructed. Later an imposing

Mortimer Wheeler's excavation of part of the Stanwick defences is permanently open for inspection. The rampart has been reconstructed. (S. W. Feather)

223

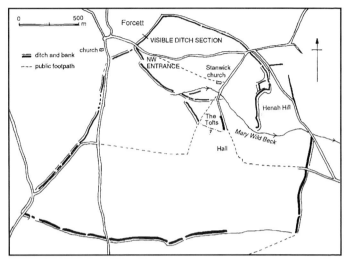

The Stanwick earthworks, North Yorkshire.

entrance of drystone was erected, probably intended as much for display as defence. In the waterlogged ditch-end, close by, Wheeler found a fine sword with wooden scabbard, a wooden bowl, basketwork and even a puff-ball!

32. Staple Howe, Scampston
Iron Age
SE: 898749

Via footpath leading S off the A64(T) at 896757.

The flat-topped hill called Staple Howe forms a natural platform 54 metres long and 12 metres wide, providing an excellent defensive site for one of at least two possible farmsteads built along the edge of the Wolds in the iron age. The original structure was an oval hut 9 metres by 6 metres, with stone walls and a gabled roof, surrounded by a wooden palisade.

The hut was later replaced by two round huts and a granary. Excavations showed that these huts had timber walls and conical roofs and south-east-facing porches. Hearths and ovens and the remains of an upright loom were uncovered. The granary, at the farm centre on one of the highest points, was a small hut set on a platform supported by five stout posts.

Domestic and wild animal remains and carbonised grain were found, the latter dated by radiocarbon to 440±150 BC. Large amounts of pottery and bone, antler and jet objects were also recovered. Bronze objects, including a razor, were numerous, but only two small iron fragments, part of a pin and a ring, turned up.

The sites of the two huts and granary have been marked with concrete posts.

33. Thornborough henges, East and West Tanfield
Neolithic
SE: 285795

The N henge lies in a wood alongside minor road leading S from Nosterfield. The central one is N of the minor road leading W from Thornborough. The S henge is S of the above road, just N of the disused railway line.

The sites consist of three henges set in a line north-east to south-west 800 metres apart. The northern circle, covered by a clump of trees, is the best-preserved. The central circle is oval in shape, with a bank 3 metres high and 18 metres across, separated by a berm 12 metres wide from its inner ditch, which is 19.5 metres wide and was originally 3 metres deep. A second ditch, exists outside the bank, but surface traces have been obliterated by cultivation. The bank is broken by entrances on the north-west and south-east, the latter 12 metres wide. Excavation in 1952

The entrance to the Victoria Cave near Settle, which has been occupied during palaeolithic, mesolithic and Roman times. (J. Dyer)

suggests that the bank of this and the other henges was coated with gypsum crystals to whiten them, perhaps in imitation of the chalk earthworks of the south.

All three henges have similar dimensions. The southernmost is the most damaged, and its ditches and south-eastern entrance are no longer visible. Beneath the central henge is a ceremonial avenue or cursus. It is 1.6 km long and runs in a straight line from north-east to south-west into a modern gravel pit, south-west of the circle. It is only visible from the air and its ditches, 44 metres apart and lined with an inner bank, were silted up and overgrown before the henge was built.

A group of round barrows, some plough-damaged, exist around the henge. North-west of the southern henge is the **Centre Hill barrow**, a mound 27 metres across and 1 metre high. A nineteenth-century dig produced a skeleton in a tree-trunk coffin with a food-vessel, flint knife and scraper. A second barrow, 30 metres across and 1.2 metres high, is east-southeast of this circle. East of the northern henge are the **Three Hills**, three round barrows dug into in the nineteenth century by W. C. Lukis, who found cremation burials (286801).

34. Three Howes, Cockayne
Bronze Age
SE: 633983

E of Cockayne. Follow the footpath leading NE uphill from minor road at 626984. The cairns lie to the S along the summit.

There are four cairns in this group, spread out in a semicircle. They range from 10 to 24 metres across and from 1 to 3 metres high. All were dug in the nineteenth century, the largest, south cairn producing two cremations in collared urns.

35. Victoria Cave, Langcliffe
Palaeolithic and Mesolithic
SE: 838650

Follow minor road leading NE from Langcliffe, to track at 829653. The track leads to the N edge of Langcliffe Scar. The cave is 400 metres S along the Scar.

Victoria Cave contains three chambers. During the last phases of the final ice age it was a hyena den. Buried deepest in the cave were the remains of hippopotamus, woolly rhinoceros, hyena and elephant. Higher up were bear, fox and red deer bones. Above these deposits were the remains of tools of late palaeolithic and mesolithic hunters; two antler points date to the former period and a barbed red deer antler harpoon head to the latter. The cave was re-occupied during the Roman period and has produced pottery, coins, bronze brooches, bone combs and spindle whorls.

36. Western Howes, Westerdale   Bronze Age
NZ: 682023

N of the moorland road leading N from Rosedale Abbey, at its junction with the Castleton road at 677018.

Three round barrows exist here. The largest is 10 metres across and contained a central core of stones 4 metres in diameter, among which two collared urns were found in the 1860s. One contained a cremation, miniature cup, bone pins and a stone battleaxe. The smallest mound contained a cremation. The third mound, 8.5 metres across and 1.2 metres high, has not yet yielded a burial.

37. Wharram Percy barrows, Wharram   Bronze Age
SE: 837636

Take minor road E from Aldro to 837633. The line of barrows is to the N.

This cemetery includes nine barrows, six in an east to west line, perhaps following the route of a former ancient track. All the barrows were opened by J. R. Mortimer in 1866. Of the six in line, the two eastern mounds contained cremations, the third a skeleton and cremation together in a grave with a food-vessel, a ring-headed bone pin, a flint knife and punch. The fourth had a cremation and a later collared urn. The primary burial in the fifth barrow was marked by an upright stake. It contained the skeleton of a youth with two jet ear-plugs. A pit in the most westerly barrow contained a cremation in a collared urn; a second collared urn, near the mound top at the centre, also contained a cremation.

38. Willerby Wold House   Bronze Age
TA: 015763

Immediately S of the Ganton to Fordon minor road, almost opposite the house.

This circular mound is 13.5 metres across but now less than 0.6 metre high. The primary burials consisted of two skeletons in a pit. Later a second pit was dug through this, containing a skeleton and a beaker. The central area was surrounded by a shallow ditch, and a great fire had been lit inside it before the depositing of the first burials. Lying on the old ground surface near the edge of the mound were four beautifully decorated bronze flat axes of Irish type, almost certainly contemporary with the primary burials.

39. Willerby Wold long barrow   Neolithic
TA: 029761

Immediately to the right of the Ganton to Fordon minor road where the road bends sharp right 2 km to the E of Willerby Wold House.

Dug in the nineteenth century and in the 1960s, this long barrow is 40 metres long and 1.2 metres high at the east end. It was originally trapezoidal in shape, 36 metres long and 10.5 metres wide at the east, with flanking ditches. It had been built over the site of a trapezoidal mortuary enclosure, marked out with a narrow ditch and a concave palisade of wooden posts at the east end, set in a bedding trench, and deliberately burnt down before the construction of the mound.

The bodies stored in the enclosure were placed between the walls of a crematorium built at the east end of the enclosure, and heaped over with chalk rubble and timber. A radiocarbon date for the palisade timbers was about 3000 BC.

East of the long barrow is a round barrow 20 metres across and over 1.8 metres high. It contained a primary skeleton with a food-vessel.

40. Windypits, Scawton

Neolithic and Bronze Age
(see below)

Four fissures in the Upper Ryedale valley contained important remains of beaker date. Only experienced potholers should attempt to explore them. The sites include:
Buckland's windypit (SE: 588827). *In the north-east slope of Duncombe Park.*

First explored by the Reverend W. Buckland in 1821, the blocked site was opened in 1955. Fissures in the windypit contained hearths, with assorted animal bones around them. To the north of one fissure six human skulls and bones were found in a mass of stone and clay which had slid down a 9 metre deep shaft sealed by a mass of stone and blocked in antiquity.

Near one hearth were two sherds of corded beaker ware and further human bones.
Slip Gill windypit (SE: 577836). *Take track leading along heights above W bank of river Rye. This track runs SE from the minor road at 570844. The fissure is by the path.*

A dangerous vertical shaft 18 metres deep produced most of a handled beaker on a ledge 9 metres from the surface. In a mass of stones blocked by a large boulder 34 metres deep were pottery sherds, two human skulls, further bones and a bone pin.
Antofts windypit (SE: 582829). *Alongside footpath across Duncombe Park, W of 'Antofts', the old keeper's lodge, formerly a farm.*

Blocked by tons of rubbish, Antofts was penetrated in 1955, revealing a complicated series of horizontal and vertical fissures. On the chockstone floor of one fissure was the part-skeleton of a female. Further along was a hearth in a small chamber, with animal bones, charcoal, flint tools and sherds of a corded beaker. Radiocarbon tests on the charcoal gave a date of about 2100 BC. Nearby were further human skulls and bones representing six or seven persons, a footed bell beaker and a carinated bowl, together with further animal bones.
Ashberry windypit (SE: 571849). *On the N side of Ashberry hill, SW of Rievaulx.*

A large cave-like opening leads to a series of small chambers. In one chamber, approached by a 25 cm 'squeeze', were part of a skeleton, a flint knife, a bone pin and beaker sherds representing six pots including a fine large corded beaker, evidently a domestic vessel, a further corded beaker and a rusticated beaker, together with a flint scraper and saw and animal bones. A further chamber produced Romano-British remains, including a bronze trumpet brooch, bangle, chain, strapends, scale armour, two bone spoons and iron objects.

41. Yockenthwaite circle, Buckden

Bronze Age
SD: 899794

Take minor road NW from Buckden. Cross river Wharfe at Yockenthwaite Farm. Park and follow footpath to left of farm along riverbank to circle.

The site consists of twenty limestone boulders set edge to edge forming a circle 7.5 metres across with a south-eastern gap, probably recent. On the north-west are four further stones forming an arc concentric to the main circle. The site may represent the revetment kerb of a destroyed round cairn.

YORKSHIRE: SOUTH
(Map on page 240)

1. Carl Wark, Hathersage

Iron Age
SK: 260815

Prominently situated 800 metres N of the A625.

Standing in a very prominent position and commanding extensive views, Carl Wark is a rectangular hillfort 0.9 hectare in extent. It is protected on all sides but the west by steep slopes. Fortifications are visible on the west and south and once probably existed all round. They consist of a turf and earth rampart faced on the exterior by a masonry wall, still 3 metres high on the west. This was originally vertical but now inclines inwards. A fine inturned entrance exists at the south-western corner, 5.5 metres long and 1.5 metres wide at its inner end. The excavator, Mrs C. M. Piggott, suggested a post-Roman date for the site, but most experts now consider it to be late iron age.

2. Roman Rigg, Brampton, Rawmarsh, Rotherham, Sheffield, Swinton, Wath, Wentworth

Iron Age
(see below)

These defensive earthworks, from Sheffield to Mexborough, are possibly part of a system dug by the Brigantes against enemies from the south-east, though excavation has failed to confirm this. They follow fairly low ground, never far from the river Don. They begin about SK: 358880, run as a single earthwork north-east through Grimesthorpe, east of the Wincobank hillfort to Hill Top (397927). Here they fork, the western branch running 800 metres east of Scholes Wood hillslope fort to Wentworth Park at 403957, where it is well preserved, with two banks and a medial ditch. Bending east at 420985, it can be seen in the south part of Wath Wood and east of the A633. It is also visible across Bow Broom and ends west of Mexborough Hospital. The eastern branch crosses Greasbrough and runs through the east end of Wentworth Park, where it is visible to Upper Haugh. It bends here towards Piccadilly and disappears at 448981.

3. Scholes Wood, Rotherham

Iron Age
SK: 395952

In Scholes Coppice. A path leads NW off minor road from Greasbrough to A629 at 400950.

Lying in a hollow on the north-eastern slope of a sandstone ridge, this oval earthwork encloses 0.4 hectare. A bank, ditch and counterscarp bank protect the site, with an entrance to the north-east. The main bank is still about 1 metre high. The site is overlooked at the north-east, south and west by higher ground.

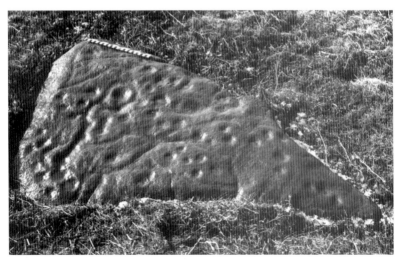

A carved stone on Baildon Moor, West Yorkshire. (S. W. Feather)

4. Wincobank, Sheffield

Iron Age
SK: 378910

800 metres W of B6082 at Wincobank, on top of hill.

Surrounded on all sides by industrial Sheffield, Wincobank, an oval hillfort, covers 1 hectare, defended by a continuous bank, ditch and counterscarp bank, except on the north. The bank stands 1 metre high, and there is an entrance on the north-east side where one end of the bank runs outside the other, thickened bank end for 9 metres to form an out-turn.

A trench through the rampart in 1899 showed a stone-faced wall 5.5 metres thick, with rubble core. It seems to have been timber-laced and to have been extensively burnt, causing the stones to fuse together and vitrify.

YORKSHIRE: WEST
(Map on page 240)

1. Baildon Moor

Bronze and Iron Age
(See below)

Take road from Baildon to Eldwick. Car park is shown on map, and the moor is accessible via tracks leading S from road. For Shipley Glen take road signposted 'Glen Road' at SE: 135407.

The flat platform to the north of Dobrudden Farm caravan park contains some two dozen cup-and-ring marked rocks, the best of which are shown on the map. One fine

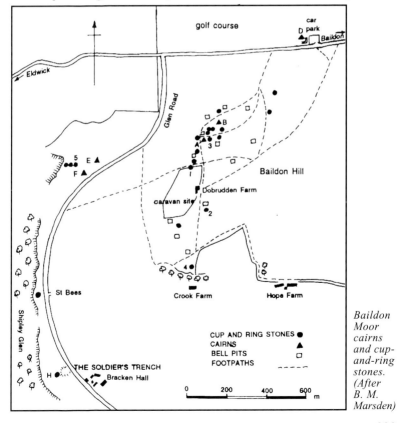

Baildon Moor cairns and cup-and-ring stones. (After B. M. Marsden)

229

example (no. 1) has been cemented against the north wall of the caravan site at 137401. The others are scattered across the moor, and include several good specimens, including one (no. 2) at the edge of a bell-pit (a former coal working) south-east of the farm at 138399. No. 3 is north-east of the farm on the edge of the remains of cairn A at 137402, whilst no. 4 is well south of the farm at 137396. The area north and north-east of Dobrudden was the site of an extensive bronze age field system (now destroyed) and the two ring cairns sited at A and B. Traces of A are still visible, and B survives as a low circular spread some 15 metres across. J. M. Colls examined both ring cairns in 1845, finding a bucket urn and cremation in B.

At 142407, at D on the map, are the slight traces of 'Coll's Burial Mound', immediately west of the car park. The arc of this ring cairn is some 18 metres across. It is surrounded by a double reversed L-shaped bank, with a central ditch still 1 metre deep. This is possibly of iron age date. The ring cairn was opened several times and produced two urns and cremations, a food-vessel and flint arrowhead.

West of Glen Road are three cup-marked stones, east of the large quarry, at no. 5 on the map. Two flattened cairns can be discerned nearby at E and F. At H on the plan is the Soldier's Trench or Soldier's Ring, a restored circular stock enclosure of uncertain date, comprising a double ring of large upright stones, the gaps perhaps originally packed with rubble.

2. Bradup, Keighley

Bronze Age
SE: 090440

Take minor road from East Morton to Silsden. Turn off right to Upwood. The circle is on the left of this road.

This badly damaged circle contains twelve stones, less than half its original number. Most of the stones are small in size and form a ring 9 metres across. No finds are recorded from the site.

3. Burley Moor, Burley in Wharfedale

Neolithic and Bronze Age
SE: 126451, etc

On the east side of Rombald's Moor is a series of dispersed burial sites and ritual monuments. They follow the gradual down-slope of the moor from 400 to 350 metres, with one outlier to the north and one to the south. The rest of the sites, six in number, are all south of the east to west line of reservoirs which cross Burley Moor. There are a number of tracks for visitors to follow, but perhaps the best route is along the path leading north from Dick Hudson's public house at 124420. From here a walk of some 2.4 km leads to the Twelve Apostles embanked stone circle at 126451. This monument has twelve upright stones set into an earth bank 16 metres across, but the site has been vandalised more than once, and some of the original stones have disappeared. Most of the survivors are recumbent or leaning. Just over 800 metres south-east is the Grubstones circle at 136447, either a ring cairn or the kerb of a vanished round cairn. The circle is 10 metres across and has twenty stones set edge to edge in a low bank. One third of the circle on the south side has been destroyed by shooting butts. Burnt bones and a flint spearhead were unearthed at the centre in the 1840s.

400 metres south-east at 140455 is the Skirtful of Stones, a huge ruined cairn 26 metres across and 1.5 metres high, despite stone-robbing and illicit digging which has left a large central hole. Just south of this mound at 141455 is a ring cairn 28 metres across with a bank still 0.8 metre high and entrances on the east and west. 800 metres north-west of this pair, at 138451, is another round cairn, the Little Skirtful of Stones, 18 metres across, and less disturbed than its namesake. At 144442, further south-east of the great Skirtful, is another ring cairn 24 metres across and again with entrances on the east and west. Just above the 300 metres contour and near the old rifle range at 145441 is a small cairn from which no discoveries have been recorded. Finally, 800 metres south-west of the latter is another stone circle at Horncliffe

(133435). This ring is again probably the kerb of a destroyed round cairn. It is oval in plan, 13 metres across, and contains forty-three stones, each 1 to 1.5 metres high, set close together. J. M. Colls recorded a central circle here consisting of seven uprights, and traces of this are still visible.

4. Castle Hill, Almondbury
Iron Age
SE: 153141
1.6 km south-east of Huddersfield town centre, via numerous minor roads.

The motte and bailey castle built for the De Laci family in the twelfth century AD has largely obliterated the earlier occupation of this prominent hilltop. It was originally settled in neolithic times. The first iron age enclosure, built before 700 BC on the south-west half of the hill, was surrounded by a drystone wall with clay core, and no ditch. It was entered through a simple entrance with a possible guardroom or house on the north-east. After many years this site fell into decay and a number of stone-walled huts up to 8 metres in diameter were built both inside and out of the earlier enclosure. Later, a second stone rampart with a wooden fence on top was built, almost following the line of the earlier one and enclosing 2.2 hectares. This was accompanied by a surrounding ditch and counterscarp bank. The earlier entrance seems to have been reinstated.

Half a century later the stone rampart was extended to enclose the whole of the 3.7 hectare hilltop, and a new outer rampart and ditch were constructed. A new entrance was built at the north-eastern end, approached by a hollow-way. This defence was in turn strengthened by enlarging the ramparts and ditches, and adding extra banks and ditches on the north-east side. A rectangular annexe was also added at this end, containing a small two-roomed hut. Finally an outer bank enclosing 13 hectares was built round the foot of the hill, which was removed by the medieval work, which also destroyed most traces of interior iron age occupation. The fort came to an end around 500 BC after a catastrophic fire which destroyed substantial parts of the ramparts. It was not re-occupied until the twelfth century AD. As a consequence, Castle Hill is not likely to have been a stronghold of the Brigantes at the time of Venutius in AD 69 as has often been claimed. The ditch which separates the Victoria Tower (1897) from the rest of the fort is medieval.

5. Ilkley Moor
Bronze Age
(See below)

An important group of mainly bronze age remains is concentrated on Ilkley (or more properly Rombald's) Moor. They include cup-and-ring marked rocks, burial and ritual sites and settlements. For convenience this section has been divided into two localities, shown on the plans overleaf. (See also Burley Moor, no. 3.)

The visitor should set aside plenty of time for an expedition and wear suitable clothing and carry a reliable map: some of the monuments are remotely sited and far from the nearest road. More detailed information will be found in *The Carved Rocks on Rombalds Moor* (Ilkley Archaeology Group and West Yorkshire Archaeology Service, 1986).

Barmishaw. Most cup-and-ring rocks are sited around the 320 metres contour, following the edges of the steep slopes around the moor. The most interesting ones are plotted on the plan. Site no. 1 is in the public gardens in Ilkley. In an enclosure opposite St Margaret's church are three large boulders which once stood on Panorama Rocks (SE 105470). They were transferred to their present site in 1890, but the largest block, the Panorama Stone, had to be cut into four parts for transportation. All three stones are carved and the largest bears a series of concentrically ringed cups circled with up to five outer rings, many with ladder markings leading from the cups. Periodical vandalism and erosion explain their present condition.

Near the Silver Well Cottage turn are two carved stones (nos. 3 and 4). Between the main road and the house, south of the cottage, at the angle of the boundary wall,

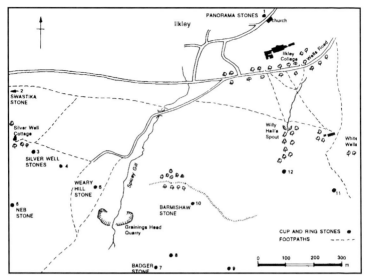

Barmishaw Moor, Ilkley, West Yorkshire. (After B. M. Marsden)

is another cup-marked rock known as the Neb Stone (no. 5). Opposite the turn a path leads north up Weary Hill and alongside this is a small boulder (no. 6) carved with a series of ringed-and-tailed cups. At the highest point of the road and due east across the moor are several carved stones (nos. 7–9), including the superb landmark rock known as the Badger Stone, which carries multiple cups and rings and grooves in a tree-like configuration on its west face, whilst on the south-west corner are an unfinished swastika and a ringed-and-tailed cup. North down the moor towards a conifer plantation is another isolated boulder, the Barmishaw Stone (no. 10). Here the decoration includes concentrically ringed cups, some with ladders and comet-like tails. North-east of this rock is a plantation called Willy Hall's Wood, and at the south end of the trees is a large boulder, no. 12, inscribed with eroded cups and channels. A final cup-stone, no. 11, stands south-east of 12.

Green Crag Slack. This locality, between Cow Close Gill and Coldstone Beck, contains the main bronze age settlement area, some 2 km long and 360 metres across, with carved stones and traces of cairns, ancient walls and settlements. In Hangingstone Quarries are the Hanging Stones, a diverse series of carvings on a horizontal rockface. There are several examples along Pancake Ridge, including the Pancake Stone and the Haystack Rock, visible for a considerable distance across the moor and carrying some forty to fifty cups on its sloping top, some ringed and tailed.

A short distance south-east and south-west of the covered Gill Head Reservoir is a pair of stones, both beside pathways, with cups and grooved channels. The east stone is located inside the Backstone Beck walled enclosure, which measures 160 by 72 metres and lies north to south along a natural ridge. This earthwork, under excavation since 1985, has produced pottery, flints, hearths and the foundations of two circular huts, one with a west entrance, and built into the wall which surrounds most of the site and has an entrance to the south-east. Sections of the wall have been neatly restored. The site, one of a number in the area, some obscured by heather and bracken, can best be interpreted as a small agricultural settlement, which existed by growing crops and herding animals.

South of Backstone Beck is another similar unexcavated enclosure. At its east end is a large flat stone with a few cup-marks. Further east are two excellent carved stones, including the Idol Rock with its four lines of cups, including seven at the centre, ringed by a long oval channel, but now much eroded. Nearby is a large boulder lavishly adorned with cups. (For adjoining area, see Burley Moor, no. 3.)

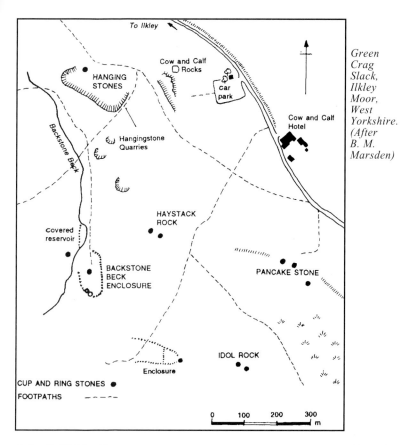

Green Crag Slack, Ilkley Moor, West Yorkshire. (After B. M. Marsden)

CUP AND RING STONES ●
FOOTPATHS - - - - -

6. South Kirkby Camp

Iron Age
SE: 435105

Take minor road to South Kirkby, E from B6273 at Brierley Gap. Bear left at fork; the fort is immediately to the right of the road 400 metres further on.

This hillfort encloses 1.8 hectares on rather low ground between two streams. Roughly oval in plan, it is defended by a bank and ditch, the former well preserved at the south-west and north-east, where it stands 2.5 to 3 metres high. The original entrance may be the break near the centre on the north side.

The carved Hanging Stones rock on Green Crag Slack, Ilkley Moor, West Yorkshire. (S. W. Feather)

233

MAP 1 (opposite): key.

Cornwall: 1, Advent triple barrow; 2, Bodrifty; 3, Boleigh fogou; 4, Boscawen-un stone ring; 5, Brane or Chapel Euny round barrow; 6, Carn Brea; 7, Carn Euny village and fogou; 8, Carn Gluze (Ballowal); 9, Castilly henge monument; 10, Castle-an-Dinas; 11, Castle Dore; 12, Chun Castle; 13, Chun Quoit; 14, Chysauster; 15, Duloe stone ring; 16, Four Barrows; 17, The Hurlers; 18, Lanyon Quoit; 19, Men-an-Tol; 20, Merry Maidens stone circle; 21, Mulfra Quoit; 22, Nine Maidens; 23, Pelynt round barrows; 24, Rillaton barrow; 25, Rocky Valley labyrinth carvings; 26, Rough Tor area; 27, The Rumps; 28, Stripple Stones; 29, Treen (Treryn) Dinas; 30, Tregeare Rounds; 31, Tregiffian; 32, Trencrom; 33, Trethevy Quoit; 34, Trevelgue Head; 35, Trippet Stones; 36, Zennor Quoit.

Isles of Scilly: 37, Bant's Carn and Halangy Down; 38, Cruther's Hill; 39, Giant's Castle; 40, Innisidgen entrance graves; 41, Porth Hellick Down entrance grave.

Devon: 1, Berry Down; 2, Blackbury Castle; 3, Blackdown Rings; 4, Black Hill; 5, Bolt Tail promontory fort; 6, Brisworthy stone circle; 7, Broad Down; 8, Burridge Camp; 9, Butterdon Hill; 10, Cadbury Castle; 11, Chapman barrows; 12 Clovelly Dykes; 13, Corringdon Ball; 14, Cranbrook Castle; 15, Denbury; 16, Dumpdon Great Camp; 17, Farway Hill and Gittisham Hill; 18, Fernworthy stone circle; 19, Five Barrows; 20, Foales Arrishes; 21, Grey Wethers; 22, Grimspound; 23, Halwell Camps; 24, Hameldown; 25, Hembury

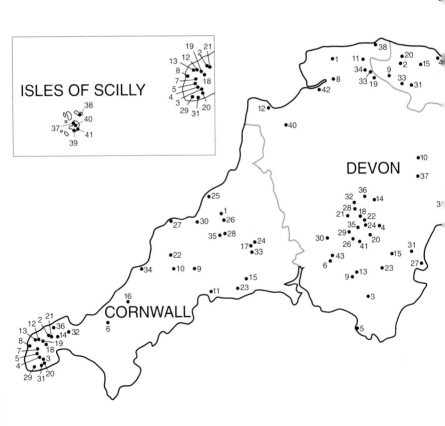

fort; 26, Huccaby Rings; 27, Kent's Cavern; 28, Kestor settlement; 29, Lakehead Hill; 30, Merrivale; 31, Milber Down Camp; 32, Scorhill stone circle; 33, Setta Barrow; 34, Shoulsbury Castle; 35, Soussons Plantation; 36, Spinsters' Rock; 37, Three Barrows; 38, Wind Hill promontory fort; 39, Woodbury Castle; 40, Wrangworthy Cross; 41, Yar Tor stone rows and round barrow; 42, Yelland stone rows; 43, Yellowmead Down.

Dorset: see map 2, page 236.

Somerset: 1, Abbot's Way; 2, Alderman's Barrow; 3, Ashen Hill barrows; 4, Bat's Castle; 5, Beacon Hill barrows; 6, Brent Knoll Camp; 7, Cadbury Camp; 8, Cheddar Caves (Gough's Cave); 9, Cow Castle; 10, Dolebury Camp; 11, Dowsborough Castle; 12, Glastonbury and Meare lake villages; 13, Ham Hill; 14, Hunter's Lodge Inn barrows; 15, Joaney How and Robin How; 16, Maesbury Castle; 17, Norton Fitzwarren hillfort; 18, Ponter's Ball dyke; 19, Pool Farm stone cist; 20, Porlock stone circle; 21, Priddy circles; 22, Priddy Nine Barrows; 23, Robin Hood's Butts; 24, Small Down; 25, South Cadbury Castle; 26, Stanton Drew; 27, Stokeleigh Camp; 28, Stoney Littleton; 29, Sweet Track; 30, Trendle Ring; 31, Wambarrows; 32, West Cranmore round barrows; 33, Withypool stone circle; 34, Wookey Hole caves; 35, Worlebury Camp.

Wiltshire: see map 2, page 236.

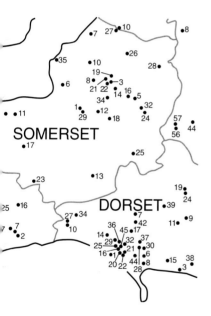

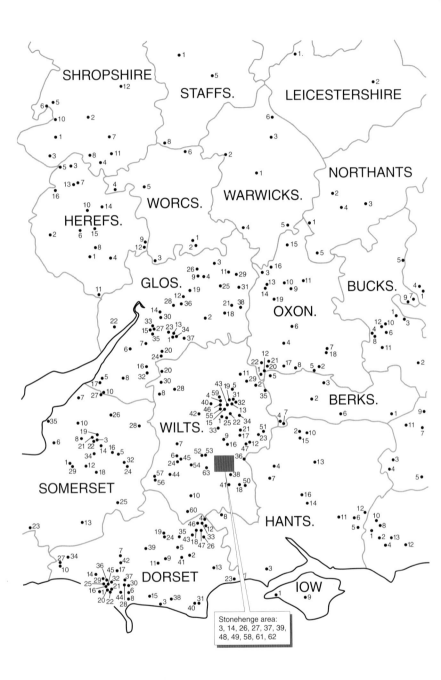

SHROPSHIRE

STAFFS.

LEICESTERSHIRE

NORTHANTS

WORCS.

WARWICKS.

HEREFS.

GLOS.

OXON.

BUCKS.

BERKS.

WILTS.

SOMERSET

HANTS.

DORSET

IOW

Stonehenge area:
3, 14, 26, 27, 37, 39,
48, 49, 58, 61, 62

MAP 2 (opposite): key.
Bedfordshire: see map 3, page 238.
Berkshire: see map 3, page 238.
Buckinghamshire: see map 3, page 238.
Dorset: 1, Abbotsbury Castle; 2, Badbury Rings; 3, Bindon Hill; 4, Bokerley Dyke; 5, Buzbury Rings; 6, Came Wood; 7, Cerne Giant; 8, Chalbury; 9, Coneybury's Castle; 10, Coney's Castle; 11, Deverel Barrow; 12, Dorset Cursus; 13, Dudsbury; 14, Eggardon Camp; 15, Five Marys; 16, Grey Mare and Her Colts; 17, Grimstone Down; 18, Gussage Hill; 19, Hambledon Hill; 20, Hampton stone circle; 21, Hardy Monument round barrows; 22, Hell Stone long barrow; 23, Hengistbury Head; 24, Hod Hill; 25, Kingston Russell stone circle; 26, Knowlton circles; 27, Lambert's Castle; 28, Maiden Castle; 29, Martin's Down; 30, Maumbury Rings; 31, Nine Barrows; 32, Nine Stones; 33, Oakley Down; 34, Pilsdon Pen; 35, Pimperne long barrow; 36, Poor Lot; 37, Poundbury; 38, Povington Heath; 39, Rawlsbury Camp; 40, Rempstone stone circle; 41, Shapwick; 42, Smacam Down; 43, Thickthorn long barrows; 44, Upwey Ridgeway; 45, Valley of Stones; 46, Wor Barrow; 47, Wyke Down henge.
Gloucestershire: 1, Avening burial chambers; 2, Bagendon; 3, Beckbury Camp; 4, Belas Knap long barrow; 5, Blaise Castle; 6, Bloody Acre Camp; 7, Brackenbury Ditches; 8, Bury Hill Camp; 9, Cleeve Hill; 10, Clifton Down Camp; 11, Cow Common barrow cemetery; 12, Crickley Hill; 13, Gatcombe Lodge barrow; 14, Haresfield Beacon and Ring Hill; 15, Hetty Peggler's Tump long barrow; 16, Horton Camp; 17, King's Weston Hill; 18, Lamborough Banks chambered long barrow; 19, Leckhampton Hill; 20, Leighterton long barrow; 21, Lodge Park long barrow; 22, Lydney hillfort, temple, etc.; 23, Minchinhampton Common earthworks; 24, Nan Tow's Tump; 25, Notgrove long barrow; 26, Nottingham Hill; 27, Nympsfield long barrow; 28, Painswick Beacon; 29, Pole's Wood South; 30, Randwick long barrow; 31, Salmonsbury Camp; 32, Sodbury Camp; 33, Soldier's Grave; 34, Tinglestone barrow; 35, Uley Bury hillfort; 36, West Tump; 37, Windmill Tump; 38, Windrush Camp.
Hampshire and Isle of Wight: 1, Afton Down; 2, Beacon Hill; 3, Buckland Rings; 4, Bury Hill; 5, Butser Ancient Farm; 6, Butser Hill cross-dykes; 7, Danebury; 8, Duck's Nest, Grans and Knap barrows; 9, Five Barrows; 10, Ladle Hill; 11, Old Winchester Hill; 12, Petersfield Heath barrow group; 13, Popham Beacon round barrows; 14, St Catherine's Hill; 15, Seven Barrows; 16, Winchester.
Herefordshire: 1, Aconbury Hill; 2, Arthur's Stone; 3, Brandon Camp; 4, Capler Camp; 5, Coxall Knoll; 6, Credenhill Camp; 7, Croft Ambrey; 8, Dinedor Camp; 9, Herefordshire Beacon; 10, Ivington Camp; 11, King Arthur's Cave; 12, Midsummer Hill; 13, Pyon Wood; 14, Risbury Camp; 15, Sutton Walls; 16, Wapley Camp.
Leicestershire: see map 3, page 238.
Northamptonshire: see map 3, page 238.
Oxfordshire: 1, Alfred's Castle; 2, Blewburton Hill; 3, Chastleton Camp; 4, Cherbury Camp; 5, Churn Farm; 6, Devil's Quoits; 7, Dyke Hills; 8, Grim's Ditch, East and West Hendred to Blewbury; 9, Grim's Ditch, North Oxfordshire; 10, Hoar Stone, Enstone; 11, Hoar Stone, Steeple Barton; 12, Knighton Bushes; 13, Lyneham Camp; 14, Lyneham long barrow; 15, Madmarston hillfort; 16, Rollright Stones; 17, Segsbury Camp or Letcombe Castle; 18, Sinodun Camp; 19, Slatepits Copse; 20, Uffington Castle; 21, Uffington White Horse; 22, Wayland's Smithy.
Shropshire: see map 4, page 240.
Somerset: see map 1, page 234.
Staffordshire: see map 4, page 240.
Surrey: see map 3, page 238.
Sussex, West: see map 3, page 238.
Warwickshire: 1, Beausale Fort; 2, Berry Mound; 3, Burrow Hill Camp; 4, Meon Hill; 5, Nadbury Camp; 6, Oldbury Camp.
Wiltshire: 1, Adam's Grave; 2, Aldbourne Four Barrows; 3, Amesbury Down; 4, Avebury triangle; 5, Barbury Castle; 6, Battlesbury Camp; 7, Bratton Castle; 8, Bury Camp; 9, Casterley Camp; 10, Castle Ditches; 11, Chisledon stone circle; 12, Cow Down; 13, Devil's Den; 14, Durrington Walls; 15, East Kennet long barrow; 16, Enford bowl-barrow; 17, Everleigh barrows; 18, Figsbury Rings; 19, Fyfield Down and Overton Down; 20, Giant's Caves; 21, Giant's Grave; 22, Gopher Wood barrows; 23, Grafton disc-barrows; 24, King Barrow; 25, Knap Hill; 26, Lake barrow cemetery; 27, Lake Down barrow cemetery; 28, Lanhill; 29, Liddington Castle; 30, Lugbury long barrow; 31, Manton long barrow; 32, Manton round barrow; 33, Marden henge; 34, Martinsell; 35, Membury; 36, Milston Down; 37, Normanton Down; 38, Ogbury Camp; 39, Old and New King barrows; 40, Oldbury Castle; 41, Old Sarum; 42, Oliver's Castle; 43, Overton Hill barrows; 44, Pertwood Down; 45, Scratchbury Camp; 46, Silbury Hill; 47, Snail Down barrow cemetery; 48, Stonehenge; 49, Stonehenge Cursus; 50, Thorny Down; 51, Tidcombe long barrow; 52, Tilshead Old Ditch; 53, Tilshead White Barrow; 54, Upton Great Barrow; 55, West Kennet long barrow; 56, Whitesheet Castle; 57, White Sheet Hill; 58, Wilsford barrow cemetery; 59, Windmill Hill; 60, Winklebury Camp; 61, Winterbourne Stoke crossroads; 62, Woodhenge; 63, Yarnbury Castle.
Worcestershire: 1, Bredon Hill; 2, Conderton Camp; 3, Gadbury Bank; 4, Garmsley Camp; 5, Woodbury Hill; 6, Wychbury Hill Camp.

MAP 3 (opposite): key.

Bedfordshire: 1, Five Knolls; 2, Galley Hill; 3, Houghton Conquest long barrow; 4, Maiden Bower; 5, Sandy hillforts; 6, Sharpenhoe Clappers hillfort; 7, Waulud's Bank.

Berkshire: 1, Caesar's Camp; 2, Grimsbury Castle; 3, Grim's Ditch; 4, Inkpen long barrow; 5, Lambourn Seven Barrows and long barrow; 6, Mortimer Common barrow cemetery; 7, Walbury hillfort.

Buckinghamshire: 1, Boddington Camp; 2, Bulstrode Camp; 3, Cholesbury Camp; 4, The Cop Barrow; 5, Danesborough hillfort; 6, Grim's Ditch; 7, Ivinghoe Beacon; 8, Lodge Hill; 9, Pitstone Hill and Grim's Ditch; 10, Pulpit Hill; 11, West Wycombe Camp; 12, Whiteleaf Barrows.

Cambridgeshire: 1, Flag Fen; 2, Stonea Camp; 3, Thornhaugh Henge; 4, Wandlebury hillfort.

Derbyshire: see map 4, page 240.

Essex: 1, Ambresbury Banks; 2, Colchester (*Camulodunum*); 3, Colchester, Lexden Tumulus; 4, Danbury hillfort; 5, Loughton Camp; 6, Pitchbury Ramparts; 7, Ring Hill; 8, Wallbury Camp.

Greater London: 1, Caesar's Camp, Wimbledon; 2, Grim's Ditch; 3, Hampstead Heath barrow; 4, Keston, Caesar's Camp hillfort.

Hampshire: see map 2, page 236.

Hertfordshire: 1, Arbury Banks; 2, The Aubreys; 3, Beech Bottom Dyke and Devil's Ditch; 4, Ravensburgh Castle; 5, Therfield Heath; 6, Wheathampstead, Devil's Dyke.

Isle of Wight: see Hampshire, map 2, page 236.

Kent: 1, Addington and Chestnuts long barrows; 2, Bigbury Camp hillfort; 3, Coldrum long barrow; 4, Julliberrie's Grave; 5, Kit's Coty House and Countless Stones; 6, Oldbury hillfort; 7, Oldbury rock shelters; 8, Ringwould barrows; 9, Squerryes Park hillfort; 10, Swanscombe, Barnfield Pit.

Leicestershire: 1, The Bulwarks; 2, Burrough-on-the-Hill.

Lincolnshire: 1, Ash Hill long barrow; 2, Ash Holt long barrow; 3, Bully Hills; 4, Burgh on Bain long barrow; 5, Butterbumps barrow cemetery; 6, Careby Camp; 7, Deadmen's Graves long barrows; 8, Fordington barrows; 9, Hoe Hill long barrow; 10, Honington Camp; 11, Revesby Barrows; 12, Round Hills fort; 13, Spellows Hills; 14, Tathwell long barrow.

Norfolk: 1, Arminghall henge monument; 2, Bircham Common barrows; 3, Broome Heath long barrow; 4, Grimes Graves flint mines; 5, Harpley Common barrow cemetery; 6, Holkham Camp; 7, Little Cressingham barrow cemetery; 8, Salthouse Heath; 9, Seven Hills barrow cemetery; 10, South Creake hillfort; 11, Thetford Castle; 12, Warham Camp; 13, Weasenham Plantation; 14, West Rudham long barrows.

Northamptonshire: 1, Arbury Camp; 2, Borough Hill; 3, Hunsbury; 4, The Larches; 5, Rainsborough Camp.

Nottinghamshire: 1, Oldox Camp.

Oxfordshire: see map 2, page 236.

Suffolk: 1, Brightwell Heath; 2, Burgh enclosure; 3, Clare Camp; 4, Martlesham Heath; 5, Seven Hills.

Surrey: 1, Abinger mesolithic site; 2, Anstiebury Camp; 3, Crooksbury Common; 4, Frensham Common barrows; 5, Hascombe Hill; 6, Holmbury; 7, Horsell Common barrows; 8, Reigate Heath barrows; 9, St Ann's Hill; 10, St George's Hill; 11, West End Common barrows.

Sussex, East: 1, The Caburn; 2, Combe Hill; 3, Firle Beacon; 4, High Rocks; 5, Hollingbury; 6, Oxteddle Bottom; 7, Windover Hill.

Sussex, West: 1, Bevis Thumb; 2, Bow Hill; 3, Chanctonbury Ring; 4, Chichester Dykes; 5, Church Hill; 6, Cissbury Ring; 7, Devil's Dyke; 8, Devil's Jumps; 9, Harrow Hill; 10, Harting Beacon; 11, Highdown Hill; 12, Long Down; 13, The Trundle.

Warwickshire: see map 2, page 236.

Yorkshire, South: see map 4, page 240.

Yorkshire, West: see map 4, page 240.

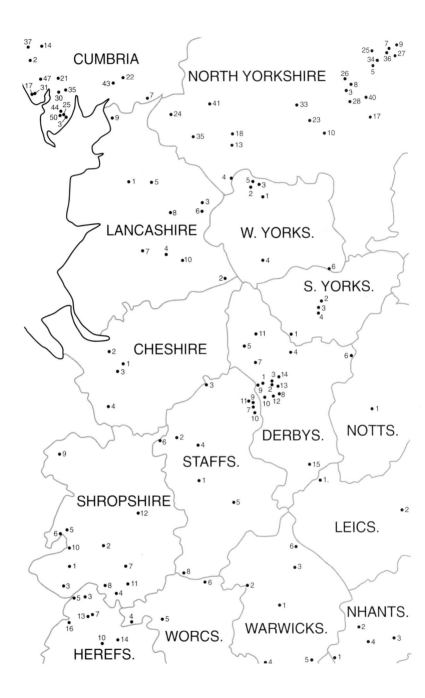

CUMBRIA

NORTH YORKSHIRE

LANCASHIRE

W. YORKS.

S. YORKS.

CHESHIRE

DERBYS.

NOTTS.

STAFFS.

SHROPSHIRE

LEICS.

WORCS.

WARWICKS.

NHANTS.

HEREFS.

MAP 4 (opposite): key.

Cheshire: 1, Castle Hill; 2, Helsby hillfort; 3, Kelsborrow Castle; 4, Maiden Castle.

Cumbria: see map 5, page 242.

Derbyshire: 1, Arbor Low and Gib Hill; 2, Bateman's Tomb; 3, Bee Low; 4, Big Moor and Ramsley Moor; 5, Bull Ring; 6, Creswell Crags; 7, Fivewells; 8, Green Low; 9, Hartington Cairns; 10, Liffs Low; 11, Mam Tor; 12, Minning Low; 13, Nine Stone Close; 14, Stanton Moor cairn cemetery; 15, Swarkestone Lows.

Herefordshire: see map 2, page 236.

Lancashire: 1, Bleasdale circle; 2, Buckton Castle; 3, Castercliffe Camp; 4, Chapel Town (Cheetham Close); 5, Fairy Holes; 6, Mosley Height; 7, Pikestones; 8, Portfield Camp; 9, Warton Crag hillfort; 10, Whitelow.

Leicestershire: see map 3, page 238.

Northamptonshire: see map 3, page 238.

Nottinghamshire: see map 3, page 238.

Shropshire: 1, Bury Ditches; 2, Caer Caradoc, Church Stretton; 3, Caer Caradoc, Clun; 4, Caynham Camp; 5, Hoarstone circle; 6, Mitchell's Fold; 7, Nordy Bank; 8, Oldfield barrows; 9, Old Oswestry; 10, The Roveries; 11, Titterstone Clee Camp; 12, The Wrekin.

Staffordshire: 1, Berry Ring; 2, Berth Hill; 3, Bridestones; 4, Bury Bank; 5, Castle Ring; 6, Devil's Ring and Finger; 7, Ilam Moor cairns; 8, Kinver; 9, Long Low; 10, Musden Low; 11, Thor's Cave.

Warwickshire: see map 2, page 236.

Worcestershire: see map 2, page 236.

Yorkshire, North: see map 5, page 243.

Yorkshire, South: 1, Carl Wark; 2, Roman Rigg; 3, Scholes Wood; 4, Wincobank.

Yorkshire, West: 1, Baildon Moor; 2, Bradup; 3, Burley Moor; 4, Castle Hill; 5, Ilkley Moor; 6, South Kirkby Camp.

MAP 5: key.

Cumbria: 1, Asby Common; 2, Barnscar; 3, Birkrigg Common; 4, Blakeley Raise; 5, Broomrigg circles; 6, Burwens; 7, Casterton circle; 8, Castle How; 9, Castlerigg circle; 10, Castlesteads; 11, Crosby Garrett settlement; 12, Dunmallard hillfort; 13, Elva stone circle; 14, Eskdale Moor circles; 15, Ewe Close; 16, Gamelands stone circle; 17, Giant's Grave; 18, Gretigate stone circles; 19, Grey Croft circle; 20, Gunnerkeld circle; 21, Heathwaite Fell settlement; 22, Helm Hill; 23, Holborn Hill; 24, Hollin Stump cairn; 25, Holme Bank enclosure; 26, Howarcles; 27, Hugill; 28, Kemp Howe; 29, King Arthur's Round Table; 30, Kirkby Moor; 31, Lacra stone circles; 32, Leacet circle; 33, Little Meg and Glassonby cairn circles; 34, Long Meg and Her Daughters; 35, Lowick ring cairn; 36, Mayburgh henge; 37, Mecklin Park cairn; 38, Moor Divock; 39, Mungrisdale cairns; 40, Raiset Pike long cairn; 41, Reecastle Crag; 42, Shoulthwaite hillfort; 43, Sizergh settlement; 44, Skelmore Heads; 45, Skirsgill Hill; 46, Studfold Gate stone circle; 47, Swinside stone circle; 48, Threlkeld Knott; 49, Towtop Kirk; 50, Urswick Stone Walls; 51, Yanwath Wood.

Durham: 1, Batter Law; 2, Copt Hill; 3, Hasting Hill barrow; 4, Low Hills; 5, Maiden Castle.

Lancashire: see map 4, page 240.

Lincolnshire: see map 3, page 238.

Northumberland: 1, Bellshiel Law; 2, Clinch Castle; 3, Coupland henge; 4, Dod Law; 5, Duddo stone circle; 6, Five Barrows and Five Kings; 7, Fordwood Camp; 8, Goatstones Circle; 9, Great Hetha Camp; 10, Harehaugh Camp; 11, Hethpool stone circle; 12, Lordenshaw hillfort, cairns and carved stones; 13, Old Bewick hillfort; 14, Roughting Linn; 15, Roughting Linn hillfort; 16, Swinburn Castle standing stone; 17, Tosson Burgh; 18, Weetwood Manor; 19, West Hill Camp; 20, Wooler hillfort; 21, Yeavering Bell.

Yorkshire, East Riding: 1, Arras barrow cemetery; 2, Callis Wold barrow cemetery; 3, Dane's Dyke; 4, Dane's Graves; 5, Kilham long barrow; 6, Rudston cult centre; 7, Towthorpe Plantation; 8, Willie Howe.

Yorkshire, North: 1, Acklam Wold cemetery; 2, Blakey Topping; 3, Boltby Scar Camp; 4, Bradley long cairn; 5, Bransdale long cairn; 6, Castle Steads; 7, Castleton Rigg; 8, Cleave Dyke system; 9, Danby Rigg; 10, Devil's Arrows; 11, Duggleby Howe; 12, East Ayton long barrow; 13, Elbolton Cave; 14, Eston Nab Camp; 15, Flat Howe and High Bridestones; 16, Folkton round barrow; 17, Gilling long cairn; 18, Grassington; 19, Great Ayton cairns; 20, Hanging Grimston; 21, Hedon Howe; 22, Helperthorpe long barrow; 23, Hutton Moor and Cana henges; 24, Ingleborough Camp; 25, Ingleby Greenhowe cairns; 26, Kepwick long barrow; 27, Loose Howe; 28, Roulston Scar Camp; 29, Scamridge long barrow; 30, Sharp Howes; 31, Stanwick hillfort; 32, Staple Howe; 33, Thornborough henges; 34,Three Howes; 35, Victoria Cave; 36, Western Howes; 37, Wharram Percy barrows; 38, Willerby Wold House; 39, Willerby Wold long barrow; 40, Windypits; 41, Yockenthwaite circle.

Yorkshire, South: see map 4, page 240.

Yorkshire, West: see map 4, page 240.

CUMBRIA

LANCASHIRE

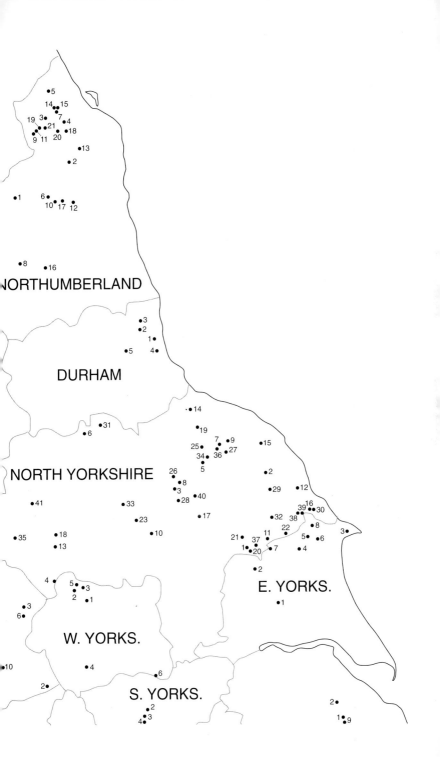

NORTHUMBERLAND

DURHAM

NORTH YORKSHIRE

E. YORKS.

W. YORKS.

S. YORKS.

Further reading

General background

Burl, A. *The Stone Circles of Britain, Ireland and Brittany.* Yale, second edition 2000.
Darvil, T.C. *Prehistoric Britain.* Routledge, 1987.
Dyer, J. *Discovering Archaeology in England and Wales.* Shire, sixth edition 1997.
Dyer, J. *Ancient Britain.* Routledge, 1997.
Muir, R. *The New Reading the Landscape: Fieldwork in Landscape History.* University of Exeter Press, 2000.
Parker Pearson, M. *Bronze Age Britain.* Routledge, 1993.
Pitts, M. *Hengeworld.* Century, 2000.
Pollard, J. *Neolithic Britain.* Shire, 1997.
Wymer, J. *Mesolithic Britain.* Shire, 1991.

Types of sites: Shire Archaeology series

Beckensall, S. *Rock Carvings of Northern Britain.* Shire, 1986.
Burl, A. *Prehistoric Astronomy and Ritual.* Shire, 1983; reprinted 1991.
Burl, A. *Prehistoric Stone Circles.* Shire, fourth edition 1997; reprinted 2001.
Burl, A. *Prehistoric Henges.* Shire, 1991.
Dyer, J. *Hillforts of England and Wales.* Shire, second edition 1992; revised 1999.
Holgate, R. *Prehistoric Flint Mines.* Shire, 1991.
Lynch, F. *Megalithic Tombs and Long Barrows.* Shire, 1997.
Mercer, R.J. *Causewayed Enclosures.* Shire, 1990.
Reid, M.L. *Prehistoric Houses in Britain.* Shire, 1993.

Some further guide books

Adkins, L. and R. *Field Guide to Somerset Archaeology.* Dovecote Press, 1992.
Aston, M., and Iles, R. *The Archaeology of Avon.* Avon County Council, 1989.
Aston, M., and Burrow, I. *The Archaeology of Somerset.* Somerset County Council, 1982.
Barber, M., *et al. The Neolithic Flint Mines of England.* English Heritage, 1999.
Barnatt, J. *The Henges, Stone Circles and Ringcairns of the Peak District.* University of Sheffield, 1990.
Barnatt, J., and Smith, K. *The Peak District, Landscapes through Time.* Batsford, 1997.
Beckensall, S. *British Prehistoric Rock Art.* Tempus, 1999.
Bowen, H.C. *The Archaeology of Bokerley Dyke.* Royal Commission on Historical Monuments, 1990. (Cranborne Chase sites.)
Burl, A. *A Guide to the Stone Circles of Britain, Ireland and Brittany.* Yale, 1995.
Butler, J. *Dartmoor: Atlas of Antiquities* (five volumes). Devon Books, Kingskerswell, 1991.
Children, G., and Nash, G. *Prehistoric Sites of Herefordshire.* Logaston Press, 1994.
Clare, T. *Archaeological Sites of the Lake District.* Moorland Publishing, 1981.
Clare, T. *Archaeological Sites of Devon and Cornwall.* Moorland Publishing,

1982.

Darvill, T. *Prehistoric Gloucestershire.* Gloucestershire County Library and Alan Sutton, 1987.

Dyer, J. *Penguin Guide to Prehistoric England and Wales.* Allen Lane/Penguin, 1982.

Fox, A. *Prehistoric Hillforts in Devon.* Devon Books, 1996.

Green, M. *A Landscape Revealed.* (Cranborne Chase.) Tempus, 2000.

Hart, C.R. *The North Derbyshire Archaeological Survey.* Derbyshire Archaeological Society, 1984.

Jobey, G. *A Field-guide to Prehistoric Northumberland.* Frank Graham, 1974.

Johnson, N., and Rose, P. *Cornwall's Archaeological Heritage.* Cornwall Archaeological Unit, 1997.

Ratcliffe, J. *Scilly's Archaeological Heritage.* Cornwall Archaeological Unit, 1995.

Taylor, A. *Archaeology of Cambridgeshire.* Cambridgeshire County Council, first two volumes 1997, 1998.

Thomas, N. *Guide to Prehistoric England.* Batsford, 1976.

Vyner, B. (editor). *Moorland Monuments. The Archaeology of North-east Yorkshire.* Council for British Archaeology, 1995.

Weatherhill, C. *Belerion: Ancient Sites of Land's End.* Alison Hodge, 1981.

Index of sites

Page numbers in italic refer to illustrations

246